T0181870

Communications in Computer and Information Science 1325

More information about this series at http://www.springer.com/series/7899

Joao Gama · Sepideh Pashami ·
Albert Bifet · Moamar Sayed-Mouchawe ·
Holger Fröning · Franz Pernkopf ·
Gregor Schiele · Michaela Blott (Eds.)

IoT Streams for Data-Driven Predictive Maintenance and IoT, Edge, and Mobile for Embedded Machine Learning

Second International Workshop, IoT Streams 2020
and First International Workshop, ITEM 2020
Co-located with ECML/PKDD 2020
Ghent, Belgium, September 14–18, 2020
Revised Selected Papers

 Springer

Editors
Joao Gama (ID)
University of Porto
Porto, Portugal

Albert Bifet (ID)
Waikato University
Hamilton, New Zealand

Holger Fröning (ID)
Heidelberg University
Heidelberg, Germany

Gregor Schiele (ID)
University of Duisburg-Essen
Essen, Germany

Sepideh Pashami (ID)
Halmstad University
Halmstad, Sweden

Moamar Sayed-Mouchawe (ID)
University of Lille
Lille, France

Franz Pernkopf (ID)
Graz University of Technology
Graz, Austria

Michaela Blott (ID)
XILINX Research
Dublin, Ireland

ISSN 1865-0929   ISSN 1865-0937 (electronic)
Communications in Computer and Information Science
ISBN 978-3-030-66769-6   ISBN 978-3-030-66770-2 (eBook)
https://doi.org/10.1007/978-3-030-66770-2

This Springer imprint is published by the registered company Springer Nature Switzerland AG
The registered company address is: Gewerbestrasse 11, 6330 Cham, Switzerland

IoT Streams 2020 Preface

Maintenance is a critical issue in the industrial context for preventing high costs and injuries. Various industries are moving more and more toward digitization and collecting "big data" to enable or improve the accuracy of their predictions. At the same time, the emerging technologies of Industry 4.0 empower data production and exchange, which leads to new concepts and methodologies for the exploitation of large datasets in maintenance. The intensive research effort in data-driven Predictive Maintenance (PdM) is producing encouraging results. Therefore, the main objective of this workshop is to raise awareness of research trends and promote interdisciplinary discussion in this field.

Data-driven predictive maintenance must deal with big streaming data and handle concept drift due to both changing external conditions and also normal wear of the equipment. It requires combining multiple data sources, and the resulting datasets are often highly imbalanced. The knowledge about the systems is detailed, but in many scenarios there is a large diversity in both model configurations as well as their usage, additionally complicated by low data quality and high uncertainty in the labels. Many recent advancements in supervised and unsupervised machine learning, representation learning, anomaly detection, visual analytics and similar areas can be showcased in this domain. Therefore, the overlap in research between machine learning and predictive maintenance has continued to increase in recent years.

This event was an opportunity to bring together researchers and engineers to discuss emerging topics and key trends. Both the previous edition of the workshop at ECML 2019 and the latest edition at ECML 2020 have been very popular.

Aims and Scope

This workshop welcomed research papers using Data Mining and Machine Learning (Artificial Intelligence in general) to address the challenges and answer questions related to the problem of predictive maintenance. For example, when to perform maintenance actions, how to estimate components' current and future status, which data should be used, what decision support tools should be developed for prognostic use, how to improve the estimation accuracy of remaining useful life, and similar. It solicited original work, already completed or in progress. Position papers were also considered. The scope of the workshop covered, but was not limited to, the following:

- Predictive and Prescriptive Maintenance
- Fault Detection and Diagnosis (FDD)
- Fault Isolation and Identification
- Anomaly Detection (AD)
- Estimation of Remaining Useful Life of Components, Machines, etc.
- Forecasting of Product and Process Quality
- Early Failure and Anomaly Detection and Analysis
- Automatic Process Optimization

- Self-healing and Self-correction
- Incremental and evolving (data-driven and hybrid) models for FDD and AD
- Self-adaptive time-series-based models for prognostics and forecasting
- Adaptive signal processing techniques for FDD and forecasting
- Concept Drift issues in dynamic predictive maintenance systems
- Active learning and Design of Experiment (DoE) in dynamic predictive maintenance
- Industrial process monitoring and modelling
- Maintenance scheduling and on-demand maintenance planning
- Visual analytics and interactive Machine Learning
- Analysis of usage patterns
- Explainable AI for predictive maintenance

It covered real-world applications such as:

- Manufacturing systems
- Transport systems (including roads, railways, aerospace and more)
- Energy and power systems and networks (wind turbines, solar plants and more)
- Smart management of energy demand/response
- Production Processes and Factories of the Future (FoF)
- Power generation and distribution systems
- Intrusion detection and cybersecurity
- Internet of Things
- Smart cities

We received a total of 19 papers and 13 of those were accepted. Each paper was reviewed by three PC members and camera ready papers were prepared based on the reviewers' comments.

Many people contributed to making this workshop a successful event. We would like to thank the Program Committee members and additional reviewers for their detailed and constructive reviews, the authors for their well-prepared presentations, and all workshop attendees for their engagement and participation.

IoT Streams 2020 Organization

Program Committee Members

Bruno Veloso	LIAAD - INESC TEC, Portugal
Maria Pedroto	University of Porto, Portugal
Sofia Fernandes	University of Aveiro, Portugal
Vinícius Souza	University of New Mexico, USA
Paula Branco	University of Ottawa, Canada
Hadi Fanaee T	Halmstad University, Sweden
Jonathan De Andrade Silva	University of São Paulo, Brazil
Rita P. Ribeiro	University of Porto, Portugal
Shazia Tabassum	University of Porto, Portugal
João Vinagre	INESC TEC, Portugal
Mario Cordeiro	ProDEI, Portugal
Nuno Moniz	INESC TEC/University of Porto, Portugal
Chetak Kandaswamy	FEUP, Portugal
Jacob Montiel	University of Waikato, New Zealand
Gustavo Batista	UNSW Sydney, Australia
Douglas Castilho	Federal University of Minas Gerais, Brazil
Raquel Sebastião	IEETA, Portugal
Heitor Murilo Gomes	University of Waikato, New Zealand
Carlos Ferreira	LIAAD INESC Porto LA, Portugal
Paulo Paraíso	INESCTEC, Portugal
Florent Masseglia	Inria, France
Indre Zliobaite	University of Helsinki, Finland
Brais Cancela	Universidade da Coruña, Spain
Thiago Andrade	INESC TEC, Portugal
Richard Hugh Moulton	Queen's University, Canada
Andre de Carvalho	University of São Paulo, Brazil
Anders Holst	RISE, Sweden
Elaine Faria	Federal University of Uberlândia, Brazil
Ana Nogueira	LIAAD - INESC TEC, Portugal
Herna Viktor	University of Ottawa, Canada

Workshop Organizers

Joao Gama	University of Porto, Portugal
Albert Bifet	Télécom Paris, France
Moamar Sayed Mouchaweh	IMT Lille Douai, France
Grzegorz J. Nalepa	Jagiellonian University, Poland
Sepideh Pashami	Halmstad University, Sweden

ITEM 2020 Preface

Background

There is an increasing need for real-time intelligent data analytics, driven by a world of Big Data and society's need for pervasive intelligent devices. Application examples include wearables for health and recreational purposes, infrastructure such as smart cities, transportation and smart power grids, e-commerce and Industry 4.0, and autonomous robots including self-driving cars. Most applications share facts like large data volumes, real-time requirements and limited resources including processor, memory and network. Often, battery life is a concern, data might be large but possibly incomplete, and probably most important, data can be uncertain. Notably, often powerful cloud services are unavailable, or not an option due to latency or privacy constraints.

For these tasks, Machine Learning (ML) is among the most promising approaches to address learning and reasoning under uncertainty. In particular deep learning methods in general are well-established supervised or unsupervised ML methods, and well understood with regard to compute/data requirements, accuracy and (partly) generalization. Today's deep learning algorithms dramatically advance state-of-the-art performance in terms of accuracy of the vast majority of AI tasks. Examples include image and speech processing such as image recognition, segmentation, object localization, multi channel speech enhancement and speech recognition, and signal processing such as radar signal denoising, with applications as broad as robotics, medicine, autonomous navigation, recommender systems, etc.

As a result, ML is embedded in various compute devices, ranging from power cloud systems over fog and edge computing to smart devices. Due to the demanding nature of this workload, which is heavily compute- and memory-intensive, virtually all deployments are limited by resources, this being particularly true for edge, mobile and IoT. Among the results of these constraints are various specialized processor architectures, which are tailored for particular ML tasks. While this is helpful for a particular task, ML is advancing fast and new methods are introduced frequently. Notably, one can observe that very often the requirements of such tasks advance faster than the performance of new compute hardware, increasing the gap between application and compute hardware. This observation is emphasized by the slowing down of Moore's law, which used to deliver constant performance scaling over decades.

Furthermore, to address uncertainty and limited data, and to improve in general the robustness of ML, new methods are required, with examples including Bayesian approaches, sum-product networks, capsule networks, graph-based neural networks and many more. One can observe that, compared with deep convolutional neural networks, computations can be fundamentally different, compute requirements can substantially increase, and underlying properties like structure in computation are often lost.

As a result, we observe a strong need for new ML methods to address the requirements of emerging workloads deployed in the real world, such as uncertainty, robustness and limited data. In order to not hinder the deployment of such methods on various computing devices, and to address the gap between application and compute hardware, we furthermore need a variety of tools. As such, this workshop aimed to gather new ideas and concepts on ML methods for real-world deployment, methods for compression and related complexity reduction tools, dedicated hardware for emerging ML tasks, and associated tooling like compilers and mappers. Similarly, the workshop also aimed to serve as a platform to gather experts from ML and systems to jointly tackle these problems, creating an atmosphere of open discussions and other interactions.

Workshop Summary

In September 2020, the first edition of ITEM took place, collocated with ECML-PKDD as the premier European machine learning and data mining conference. Even though the workshop had to take place virtually, there was a lively discussion and interaction, also due to inspiring keynote presentations by Luca Benini from ETH Zürich ("From Near-Sensor to In-Sensor AI") and Song Han from MIT ("MCUNet: TinyNAS and TinyEngine on Microcontrollers"). Those keynotes created the right environment for a couple of contributed talks in the areas of hardware, methods and quantization, coming from institutions including Universidade da Coruña, Heidelberg University, Bosch Research, University of Duisburg-Essen, Technical University of Munich, KU Leuven, Università di Bologna and Graz University of Technology, among others.

Early take-aways include on the hardware side observations on open-source digital hardware (PULP) as well as analog hardware (BrainScaleS-2) as promising emerging alternatives to established architectures, that code generation for specialized hardware can be challenging, and that designing processor arrays is more difficult than one might think. From a methodological point of view, 8bit seems to be a natural constant when it comes to quantization, and time-multiplexing as well as on-device learning can be viable options. On the compression side, observations include that predictive confidence can help dynamic approaches to switching among models, heterogeneous uniform quantization as well as application-specific (radar) quantization.

Outlook

It is planned to continue ITEM for the next couple of years, so any interested researcher or scientist is invited to contribute to future editions. Also, while ITEM's main focus is to be an academic platform with peer-reviewed contributions, there is also a more informal counterpart called the Workshop on Embedded Machine Learning (WEML), which is held annually at Heidelberg University. WEML is distinguished from ITEM by being a platform that only includes invited presentations from the community for mutual updates on recent insights and trends, but without the rigorous demands of scientific peer review. For more information about these two workshops, please refer to:
ITEM: https://www.item-workshop.org
WEML: https://www.deepchip.org

Finally, the co-organizers of ITEM would like to acknowledge the comprehensive commitment of the Workshop Co-Chairs at ECML-PKDD (Myra Spiliopoulou and Willem Waegeman), who had to face a mandatory shift to online events due to the pandemic, which they handled very swiftly and with excellent communication and organization. Similar acknowledgements go to the time and effort spent by our program committee, and last but not least the strong commitment of our program chair (Benjamin Klenk). Ultimate acknowledgement goes to Springer for publishing the workshop's proceedings.

Holger Fröning
Franz Pernkopf
Gregor Schiele
Michaela Blott

ITEM 2020 Organization

Co-organizers

Holger Fröning	Heidelberg University, Germany (holger.froening@ziti.uni-heidelberg.de)
Franz Pernkopf	Graz University of Technology, Austria (pernkopf@tugraz.at)
Gregor Schiele	University of Duisburg-Essen (gregor.schiele@uni-due.de)
Michaela Blott	XILINX Research, Ireland (michaela.blott@xilinx.com)

Program Chair

Benjamin Klenk	NVIDIA Research, USA

Technical Program Committee

Costas Bekas	Citadel Securities, Switzerland
Herman Engelbrecht	Stellenbosch University, South Africa
Giulio Gambardella	XILINX, Ireland
Tobias Golling	University of Geneva, Switzerland
Domenik Helms	OFFIS e.V. - Institut für Informatik, Germany
Eduardo Rocha Rodrigues	IBM, Brazil
David King	Air Force Institute of Technology, USA
Manfred Mücke	Materials Center Leoben Forschung GmbH, Austria
Dimitrios S. Nikolopoulos	Virginia Tech, USA
Robert Peharz	Eindhoven University of Technology, The Netherlands
Marco Platzner	Paderborn University, Germany
Thomas B. Preußer	ETH Zürich, Switzerland
Johannes Schemmel	Heidelberg University, Germany
Wei Shao	Royal Melbourne Institute of Technology (RMIT), Australia
David Sidler	Microsoft, USA
Jürgen Teich	Friedrich-Alexander-Universität Erlangen-Nürnberg (FAU), Germany
Sebastian Tschiatschek	University of Vienna, Austria
Nicolas Weber	NEC Labs Europe, Germany
Matthias Zöhrer	Evolve.tech, Austria

Contents

ITEM 2020: Methods

ITEM 2020: Quantization

IoT Streams 2020: Stream Learning

Self Hyper-parameter Tuning for Stream Classification Algorithms

Bruno Veloso[2,3]([✉]) [iD] and João Gama[1,2] [iD]

[1] FEP, University of Porto, Porto, Portugal
jgama@fep.up.pt
[2] INESC TEC, Porto, Portugal
bruno.m.veloso@inesctec.pt
[3] Universidade Portucalense, Porto, Portugal

Abstract. The new 5G mobile communication system era brings a new set of communication devices that will appear on the market. These devices will generate data streams that require proper handling by machine algorithms. The processing of these data streams requires the design, development, and adaptation of appropriate machine learning algorithms. While stream processing algorithms include hyper-parameters for performance refinement, their tuning process is time-consuming and typically requires an expert to do the task.

In this paper, we present an extension of the Self Parameter Tuning (SPT) optimization algorithm for data streams. We apply the Nelder-Mead algorithm to dynamically sized samples that converge to optimal settings in a double pass over data (during the exploration phase), using a relatively small number of data points. Additionally, the SPT automatically readjusts hyper-parameters when concept drift occurs.

We did a set of experiments with well-known classification data sets and the results show that the proposed algorithm can outperform the results of previous hyper-parameter tuning efforts by human experts. The statistical results show that this extension is faster in terms of convergence and presents at least similar accuracy results when compared with the standard optimization techniques.

Keywords: Self-parameter tuning · Double pass · Classification · Data streams

1 Introduction

The emergence of 5G mobile communication technology will support the appearance of smart devices that generate high rate data streams. With this exponential growth of data generation, businesses need to apply machine learning algorithms to extract meaningful knowledge. However, the application of these algorithms to data streams is not an easy task, and it requires the expertise of data scientists to maximize the performance of the models. Based on this necessity of

© Springer Nature Switzerland AG 2020
J. Gama et al. (Eds.): ITEM 2020/IoT Streams 2020, CCIS 1325, pp. 3–13, 2020.
https://doi.org/10.1007/978-3-030-66770-2_1

obtaining knowledge from data scientists, a new trend is emerging: the progressive automation of machine learning (AutoML). AutoML algorithms aim to solve complex problems that arise from the application of standard machine learning algorithms such as hyper-parameter optimization or model selection.

Hyper-parameter optimisation is studied since the 80s with the help of algorithms such as grid-search [10], random-search [1] and gradient descent [11]. Hyper-parameter optimisation algorithms can be parameter-free, *e.g.*, Nelder-Mead [13], and parameter-based, *e.g.*, gradient descent. All these approaches require train and validation stages, making them not applicable to the data stream scenario.

The exception is the case of the Hyper-Parameter Self-Tuning Algorithm for Data Streams (SPT) that we proposed in [17,18]. SPT performs a double pass direct-search to find optimal solutions on a search space for the regression and recommendation tasks. Specifically, it applies the Nelder-Mead algorithm to dynamic size data stream samples, continuously searching for optimal hyper-parameters, and can react to concept drifts in the case of the regression task.

The main contribution of this work is the application of the SPT algorithm for the classification task. This extension not only processes recommendation, regression, and classification problems successfully but is, to the best of our knowledge, the single one that effectively works with data streams and reacts to concept drifts. We used four different data sets to assess the applicability of the SPT on the classification task.

The paper has five sections, Sect. 2 describes a systematic literature review on automatic machine learning. Section 3 presents the extended SPT version for the classification task. Section 4 details the experiments and discusses the results. Finally, Sect. 5 concludes and suggests future developments.

2   Related Work

The first work-related with AutoML to select models appears in the year 2003 by Brazdil et al. [3], but there is a small set of works regarding AutoML for hyper-parameter selection. There are two recent surveys on the topic regarding actual solutions and open challenges [4,5]. We focused our literature search on hyperparameter optimization algorithms and Nelder-Mead-based optimization algorithms.

In terms of hyper-parameter optimization algorithms, we identified the following contributions [6,9,14]. Kohavi and John [9] describe a method to select a hyper-parameter automatically. This method relies on the minimization of the estimated error and applies a grid search algorithm to find local minima. The problem of this solution is that the number of required function assessments grows exponentially. Finn *et al.* [6] propose a fine-tuning mechanism for the gradient descent algorithm, which is applied periodically to fixed-size data samples. The problem with this proposal is that the solution can fall in a valley (local minimum). Nichol *et al.* [14] propose a scalable meta-learning algorithm which learns a parameter initialisation for future tasks. The proposed algorithm tunes the parameter by repeatedly using Stochastic Gradient Descent (SGD) on the training task. The problem with this proposal is that the solution can fall in a valley (local minimum). All these three solutions are computationally expensive and require manual parameter tuning.

Several works rely on the Nelder-Mead algorithm for optimization [7, 8, 15, 16]. Koenigstein *et al.* [8] adopt the Nelder-Mead direct search to optimize multiple meta-parameters of an incremental algorithm applied to data with multiple biases. The optimization occurs in a batch process with training data for learning and test data for validation. Kar *et al.* [7] apply an exponentially decay centrifugal force to all vertices of the Nelder-Mead algorithm to obtain better objective values. However, this batch process requires more iterations to converge to a local minimum. Fernandes *et al.* [16] proposes a batch method to estimate the parameters and the initialization of a CANDECOMP/PARAFAC tensor decomposition for link prediction. The authors adopt Nelder-Mead to identify the optimal hyper-parameter initialization. Pfaffe *et al.* [15] present an on-line auto-tuning algorithm for string matching algorithms. It uses the e-greedy policy, a well-known reinforcement learning technique, to select the algorithm to be used in each iteration and adopts Nelder-Mead to tune the parameters, during some tuning iterations.

These optimization solutions show the applicability of Nelder-Mead to different Machine Learning Tasks. However, they all adopt batch processing, and our approach transforms the Nelder-Mead heuristic optimization algorithm into a stream-based optimization algorithm. This new implementation only requires a double pass over the data during the exploration phase to optimize the set of parameters, making it more versatile and less computationally expensive.

3 Self Parameter Tuning Method

This paper presents an extension of the SPT algorithm[1] which optimizes a set of hyper-parameters in vast search spaces. To make our proposal robust and easier to use, we adopt a direct-search algorithm, using heuristics to avoid algorithms that rely on hyper-parameters. Specifically, we adapt the Nelder-Mead method [13] to work with data streams.

Figure 1 represents the application of the proposed algorithm. In particular, to find a solution for n hyper-parameters, it requires $n + 1$ input models, *e.g.*, to optimise two hyper-parameters, the algorithm needs three alternative input models. The Nelder-Mead algorithm processes each data stream sample dynamically, using a previously saved copy of the models until the input models converge. Each model represents a vertex of the Nelder-Mead algorithm and is computed in parallel to reduce the time response. The initial model vertexes are randomly selected, and the Nelder-Mead operators are applied at dynamic intervals. The following subsections describe the implemented Nelder-Mead algorithm, including the dynamic sample size selection.

---

[1] The source code is available on https://github.com/BrunoMVeloso/SPT/blob/ master/IoTStream2020.zip – The password of the source file is "SPT".

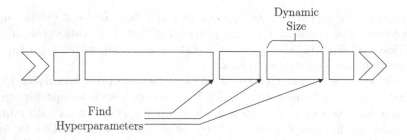

Fig. 1. Application of the proposed algorithm to the data stream [17]

3.1 Nelder-Mead Optimization Algorithm

This algorithm is a simplex search algorithm for multidimensional unconstrained optimization without derivatives. The vertexes of the simplex, which define a convex hull shape, are iteratively updated in order to sequentially discard the vertex associated with the most significant cost function value.

The Nelder-Mead algorithm relies on four simple operations: *reflection, shrinkage, contraction* and *expansion*. Figure 2 illustrates the four correspond-

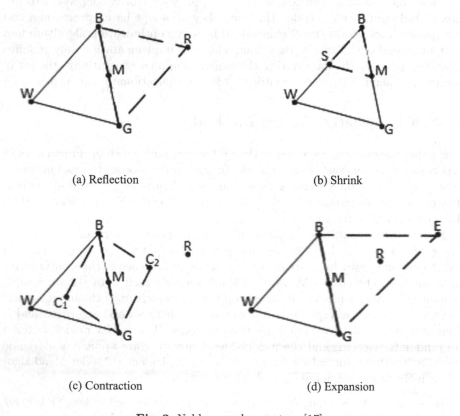

(a) Reflection   (b) Shrink

(c) Contraction   (d) Expansion

Fig. 2. Nelder mead operators [17]

ing Nelder-Mead operators R, S, C and E. Each black bullet represents a model containing a set of hyper-parameters. The vertexes (models under optimization) are ordered and named according to the root mean square error (RMSE) value: best (B), good (G), which is the closest to the best vertex, and worst (W). M is a mid vertex (auxiliary model).

The following Algorithm 1 presents the reflection and extension of a vertex. For each Nelder-Mead operation, it is necessary to compute an additional set of vertexes (midpoint M, reflection R, expansion E, contraction C, and shrinkage S) and verify if the calculated vertexes belong to the search space. First, the algorithm computes the midpoint (M) of the best face of the shape as well as the reflection point (R). After this initial step, it determines whether to reflect or expand based on the set of predetermined heuristics (lines 3, 4, and 8).

Algorithm 1. Nelder-Mead - reflect (a) or expand operators (d).

1: $M = (B + G)/2$
2: $R = 2M - W$
3: **if** $f(R) < f(G)$ **then**
4:     **if** $f(B) < f(R)$ **then**
5:         $W = R$
6:     **else**
7:         $E = 2R - M$
8:         **if** $f(E) < f(B)$ **then**
9:             $W = E$
10:         **else**
11:             $W = R$
12:         **end if**
13:     **end if**
14: **end if**

The following Algorithm 2 calculates the contraction point (C) of the worst face of the shape – the midpoint between the worst vertex (W) and the midpoint M – and shrinkage point (S) – the midpoint between the best (B) and the worst (W) vertexes. Then, it determines whether to contract or shrink based on the set of predetermined heuristics (lines 3, 4, 8, 12, and 15). The goal, in the case of data stream regression, is to optimize the learning rate, the learning rate decay, and the split confidence hyper-parameters. These hyper-parameters are constrained to values between 0 and 1. The violation of this constraint results in the adoption of the nearest lower or upper bound.

3.2 Dynamic Sample Size

The dynamic sample size, which is based on the RMSE metric, attempts to identify significant changes in the streamed data. Whenever such a change is detected, the Nelder-Mead compares the performance of the $n + 1$ models under analysis to choose the most promising model. The sample size S_{size} is given by

---

Algorithm 2. Nelder-Mead - contract (c) or shrink (b) operators.

1: $M = (B + G)/2$
2: $R = 2M - W$
3: **if** $f(R) \geq f(G)$ **then**
4:      **if** $f(R) < f(W)$ **then**
5:          $W = R$
6:      **else**
7:          $C = (W + M)/2$
8:          **if** $f(C) < f(W)$ **then**
9:              $W = C$
10:         **else**
11:             $S = (B + W)/2$
12:             **if** $f(S) < f(W)$ **then**
13:                 $W = S$
14:             **end if**
15:             **if** $f(M) < f(G)$ **then**
16:                 $G = M$
17:             **end if**
18:         **end if**
19:     **end if**
20: **end if**

Eq. 1 where σ represents the standard deviation of the RMSE and M the desired error margin. We use $M = 95\,\%$.

$$S_{size} = \frac{4\sigma^2}{M^2} \tag{1}$$

However, to avoid using small samples, that imply error estimations with large variance, we defined a lower bound of 30 samples.

3.3   Stream-Based Implementation

The adaptation of the Nelder-Mead algorithm to on-line scenarios relies extensively on parallel processing. The main thread launches the $n + 1$ model threads and starts a continuous event processing loop. This loop dispatches the incoming events to the model threads and, whenever it reaches the sample size interval, assesses the running models and calculates the new sample size. The model assessment involves the ordering of the $n + 1$ models by RMSE value and the application of the Nelder-Mead algorithm to substitute the worst model. The SPT algorithm has two phases: the exploration phase tries to find an optimal solution on the search space, which requires a double pass over data to apply the Nelder Mead operators; and (ii) the exploitation phases reuses the solution found on the machine learning task, and it requires only a single pass over data.

4   Experimental Evaluation

The goal of the classification experiments is to optimize the grace period and tie-threshold hyper-parameters. The experiments consist of the defining new classification tasks in the Massive On-line Analysis (MOA) framework [2]. The created tasks use the Extremely Fast Decision Trees (EFDT) classification algorithm [12] together with the different parameter initialization approaches (default, grid search, and our extended version of the double-pass SPT). At the start-up, each task initializes three identical classification models. The SPT tasks start with random hyper-parameter values.

Table 1 presents the data sets used for the classification experiments: Electricity, Postures, Sea and Bank Marketing. The Electricity[2] contains 45 312 instances and 8 attributes; the Avila[3] contains 20 867 instances and 10 attributes, the Sea[4] contains 60 000 instances, 3 attributes and four concept drifts separated by 15 000 examples; and Credit[5] holds 30 000 instances and 24 attributes.

Table 1. Classification Data Sets

Data set	Instances	Attributes
Electricity	45 312	8
Avila	20 867	10
Sea	60 000	3
Credit	30 000	24

The first set of experiments compares the extended double pass version of SPT for classification algorithms, the grid search, and the default initialization, considering accuracy and time. Figure 3 displays the critical distance accuracy plots for the four data sets and the different optimization techniques. The results show that, for all data sets and with a confidence level of 95%, the proposed double pass SPT is not significantly different from the default initialization on all data sets. In terms of accuracy ranking, the double pass SPT present worst results when compared with the grid search optimization and similar results when compared with the default initialization. The great advantage of the double pass SPT is that it converges faster than the analyzed optimization methods for all data sets – see Table 2.

---

[2] https://datahub.io/machine-learning/electricity#resource-electricity_arff.
[3] https://archive.ics.uci.edu/ml/datasets/Avila.
[4] http://www.liaad.up.pt/kdus/products/datasets-for-concept-drift.
[5] https://archive.ics.uci.edu/ml/datasets/default+of+credit+card+clients.

Table 2. Algorithms – Average Run time (ms)

Data set	Double Pass	Grid Search	Default Parameters
Avila	5636.07 (1.00x)	38 378.40 (6.80x)	389.07 (0.07x)
Credit	10 991.7 (1.00x)	72 698.10 (6.61x)	585.10 (0.05x)
Electricity	14 931.67 (1.00x)	52 702.60 (3.53x)	491.00 (0.03x)
SEA	7377.90 (1.00x)	25 806.57 (3.50x)	314.43 (0.04x)

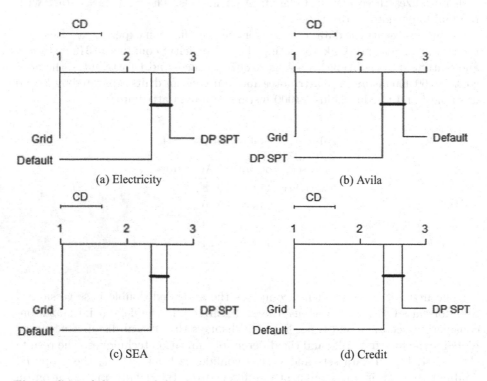

Fig. 3. Critical distance of the three optimisation methods in terms of accuracy. DP - Double Pass SPT; Grid - Grid Search; Default - Default Parameters.

In the exploration phase and for all data sets, the double pass SPT is faster. The exploration time of the double pass SPT for the Avila, Credit, Electricity and SEA data sets is, respectively, 46.08%, 55.67%, 43.80% and 63.97% of the total time presented on Table 2. From Table 3, we can observe that the SPT presents a better accuracy when compared with the default parameters, and almost a similar result when compared with the grid search. Taking both the time to converge to an optimal local solution and the accuracy, the results show that the double pass SPT is the better solution. With the lack of comparable stream-based optimization solutions, we used the grid search to have some baseline results. The grid search is more accurate but requires more time for exploration when compared with the SPT.

Table 3. Algorithms – Accuracy (%)

Data set	Double Pass	Grid Search	Default Parameters
Avila	60.9 (1.00x)	60.8 (0.99x)	56.1 (0.92x)
Credit	80.4 (1.00x)	80.9 (1.01x)	80.0 (0.99x)
Electricity	89.8 (1.00x)	91.9 (1.02x)	82.2 (0.92x)
SEA	88.2 (1.00x)	88.1 (0.99x)	86.6 (0.98x)

5   Conclusion

The goal of this research is to explore and present a solution for a new research topic called AutoML, which embraces several problems like automated hyper-parameter optimization.

The main contribution of this paper is an extension of the SPT algorithm which is, to the best of our knowledge, the single one that effectively works with data streams and reacts to the data variability. The SPT algorithm was modified to work with classification algorithms. The SPT algorithm is, in terms of existing hyper-parameter optimization algorithms, less computationally expensive than Bayesian optimizers, stochastic gradients, or even grid search algorithms. SPT explores the adoption of a simplex search mechanism combined with dynamic data samples and concept drift detection to tune and find proper parameter configuration that minimizes the objective function.

We adapted SPT to work with the Extremely Fast Decision Trees (EFDT) proposed by [12]. We conducted experiments with four classification data sets and concluded that the selection of the hyper-parameters has a substantial impact in terms of accuracy. The performance of our algorithm with classification problems was affected by the data variability and, consequently, we used the SPT concept drift detection functionality.

Our algorithm can operate over data streams, adjusting hyper-parameters based on the variability of the data, and does not require an iterative approach to converge to an acceptable minimum. We test our approach extensively on classifications problems against baseline methods that do not perform automatic adjustments of hyper-parameters and found that our approach consistently and significantly outperforms them in terms of time and obtains good accuracy scores. The statistical tests show that the grid search approach obtains better accuracy results but loses on execution time. The double pass SPT obtains at least better or comparable results that the default parameters.

Future work will include two key points: enrich the algorithm with the ability to select not only hyper-parameters but also models and change the exploration phase of the SPT to requires only one single-pass over the data.

Acknowledgments. This research was Funded from national funds through FCT - Science and Technology Foundation, I.P in the context of the project FailStopper (DSAIPA/DS/0086/2018).

This work is financed by National Funds through the Portuguese funding agency, FCT - Fundação para a Ciência e a Tecnologia, within project UIDB/50014/2020.

References

1. Bergstra, J., Bengio, Y.: Random search for hyper-parameter optimization. J. Mach. Learn. Res. **13**(1), 281–305 (2012). https://doi.org/10.5555/2188385. 2188395
2. Bifet, A., Holmes, G., Kirkby, R., Pfahringer, B.: Moa: massive online analysis. J. Mach. Learn. Res. **11**, 1601–1604 (2010). https://doi.org/10.5555/1756006. 1859903
3. Brazdil, P.B., Soares, C., da Costa, J.P.: Ranking learning algorithms: Using IBL and meta-learning on accuracy and time results. Mach. Learn. **50**(3), 251–277 (2003). https://doi.org/10.1023/A:1021713901879
4. Elshawi, R., Maher, M., Sakr, S.: Automated machine learning: state-of-the-art and open challenges (2019)
5. Feurer, M., Hutter, F.: Hyperparameter Optimization, pp. 3–33. Springer, Cham (2019). https://doi.org/10.1007/978-3-030-05318-5_1
6. Finn, C., Abbeel, P., Levine, S.: Model-agnostic meta-learning for fast adaptation of deep networks. In: Precup, D., Teh, Y.W. (eds.) Proceedings of the 34th International Conference on Machine Learning. Proceedings of Machine Learning Research, vol. 70, pp. 1126–1135. PMLR, International Convention Centre, Sydney, Australia, 06–11 August 2017. https://doi.org/10.5555/3305381.3305498
7. Kar, R., Konar, A., Chakraborty, A., Ralescu, A.L., Nagar, A.K.: Extending the nelder-mead algorithm for feature selection from brain networks. In: 2016 IEEE Congress on Evolutionary Computation (CEC), pp. 4528–4534, July 2016. https://doi.org/10.1109/CEC.2016.7744366
8. Koenigstein, N., Dror, G., Koren, Y.: Yahoo! music recommendations: modeling music ratings with temporal dynamics and item taxonomy. In: Proceedings of the Fifth ACM Conference on Recommender Systems, RecSys 2011, pp. 165–172. ACM, New York (2011). https://doi.org/10.1145/2043932.2043964
9. Kohavi, R., John, G.H.: Automatic parameter selection by minimizing estimated error. In: Prieditis, A., Russell, S. (eds.) Machine Learning Proceedings 1995, pp. 304–312. Morgan Kaufmann, San Francisco (CA) (1995). https://doi.org/10.1016/B978-1-55860-377-6.50045-1
10. Lerman, P.M.: Fitting segmented regression models by grid search. J. Royal Stat. Soc.: Ser. C (Appl. Stat.) **29**(1), 77–84 (1980). https://doi.org/10.2307/2346413
11. Maclaurin, D., Duvenaud, D., Adams, R.P.: Gradient-based hyperparameter optimization through reversible learning. In: Proceedings of the 32nd International Conference on International Conference on Machine Learning, ICML2015, vol. 37, pp. 2113–2122. JMLR.org (2015). https://doi.org/10.5555/3045118.3045343
12. Manapragada, C., Webb, G.I., Salehi, M.: Extremely fast decision tree. In: Proceedings of the 24th ACM SIGKDD International Conference on Knowledge Discovery & Data Mining, pp. 1953–1962 (2018)
13. Nelder, J.A., Mead, R.: A simplex method for function minimization. Comput. J. **7**(4), 308–313 (1965). https://doi.org/10.1093/comjnl/7.4.308
14. Nichol, A., Achiam, J., Schulman, J.: On first-order meta-learning algorithms. CoRR abs/1803.02999 (2018)

15. Pfaffe, P., Tillmann, M., Walter, S., Tichy, W.F.: Online-autotuning in the presence of algorithmic choice. In: 2017 IEEE International Parallel and Distributed Processing Symposium Workshops (IPDPSW), pp. 1379–1388, May 2017. https:// doi.org/10.1109/IPDPSW.2017.28
16. da Silva Fernandes, S., Tork, H.F., da Gama, J.M.P.: The initialization and parameter setting problem in tensor decomposition-based link prediction. In: 2017 IEEE International Conference on Data Science and Advanced Analytics (DSAA), pp. 99–108, October 2017. https://doi.org/10.1109/DSAA.2017.83
17. Veloso, B., Gama, J., Malheiro, B.: Self hyper-parameter tuning for data streams. In: Soldatova, L., Vanschoren, J., Papadopoulos, G., Ceci, M. (eds.) Discovery Science, pp. 241–255. Springer, Cham (2018). https://doi.org/10.1007/978-3-030-01771-2_16
18. Veloso, B., Gama, J., Malheiro, B., Vinagre, J.: Self hyper-parameter tuning for stream recommendation algorithms. In: Monreale, A., et al. (eds.) ECML PKDD 2018 Workshops, pp. 91–102. Springer, Cham (2019). https://doi.org/10.1007/978-3-030-14880-5_8

Challenges of Stream Learning for Predictive Maintenance in the Railway Sector

Minh Huong Le Nguyen[1,2]([⊠]), Fabien Turgis[1]([⊠]),
Pierre-Emmanuel Fayemi[1]([⊠]), and Albert Bifet[2]([⊠])

[1] IKOS Consulting, 92300 Levallois-Perret, France
{mhlenguyen,fturgis,pefayemi}@ikosconsulting.com
[2] Telecom Paris, 91120 Palaiseau, France
albert.bifet@telecom-paris.fr

Abstract. Smart trains nowadays are equipped with sensors that generate an abundance of data during operation. Such data may, directly or indirectly, reflect the health state of the trains. Thus, it is of interest to analyze these data in a timely manner, preferably on-the-fly as they are being generated, to make maintenance operations more proactive and efficient. This paper provides a brief overview of predictive maintenance and stream learning, with the primary goal of leveraging stream learning in order to enhance maintenance operations in the railway sector. We justify the applicability and promising benefits of stream learning via the example of a real-world railway dataset of the train doors.

Keywords: Predictive maintenance · Stream learning · Railway

1 Introduction

The rapid evolution of smart machines in the era of Industry 4.0 has led to an abundant amount of data that need to be analyzed accurately, efficiently, and in a timely manner. Maintenance 4.0, also known as Predictive Maintenance (PdM), is an application of Industry 4.0. It is characterized by smart systems that are capable to diagnose faults, predict failures, and suggest the optimized courses of maintenance actions. Combined with the available equipment data, data-driven PdM has a great potential to automate the diagnostic and prognostic process, correctly predict the remaining useful life (RUL) of equipment, minimize maintenance costs, and maximize service availability. With the advent of IoT devices, equipment data are generated on-the-fly, thus making stream learning a promising methodology for learning from an unbounded flux of data.

This paper provides a brief overview of PdM and stream learning, with the primary goal of leveraging stream learning on the abundance of data in order to enhance maintenance operations in the railway sector. First, we establish the state-of-the-art in PdM and in stream learning with a broad overview (Sect. 2

© Springer Nature Switzerland AG 2020
J. Gama et al. (Eds.): ITEM 2020/IoT Streams 2020, CCIS 1325, pp. 14–29, 2020.
https://doi.org/10.1007/978-3-030-66770-2_2

and 3, respectively). Then, we discuss the benefits of data-driven PdM and stream learning in the railway sector (Sect. 4). Finally, we conclude the paper in Sect. 5. This study is part of an ongoing research on the application of stream learning for PdM in the railway system at IKOS Consulting.

2 An Overview of Predictive Maintenance

This section broadly reviews the approaches for solving PdM. They can be classified into two groups: **knowledge-based** approach that relies on knowledge solicited from domain experts, and **data-driven** approach that leverages the data to extract insightful information without domain specifications (Fig. 1).

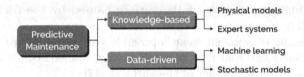

Fig. 1. Taxonomy of PdM approaches

2.1 Knowledge-Based Approach

The knowledge-based approach resorts to the help of domain experts to build PdM models. This approach can be further divided into two subclasses that are **physical models** and **expert systems**. Physical models consist of mathematical equations that describe the underlying behavior of a degradation mode, whereas expert systems formalize expert knowledge and infer solutions to a query given the provided knowledge.

Physical Models. A physical model is a set of mathematical equations that describe explicitly the physics of the degradation mechanism in an equipment, combining extensive mechanical knowledge and domain expertise. The three most common degradation mechanisms are *creep*, *fatigue*, and *wear* [37].

Creep is the slow, permanent deformation in a material under high temperature for a long duration of time. Once initiated, a creep starts growing in the equipment and eventually leads to a rupture of operation (Fig. 2). In [10], the Norton creep law is used to model the creep growth and is combined with a Kalman filter to estimate the RUL of turbine blades. Fatigue occurs in components subject to high cyclic loading, such as repeating rotations or vibrations. Models for fatigue modeling include the S-N curve, Basquin law, Manson-Coffin law, or cumulative damage rule [32]. *Crack* is a common consequence of long-term fatigue damage. After initiation, a crack is propagated at a constant rate then grows rapidly until a fracture occurs (Fig. 2). In [28], the Paris law is used

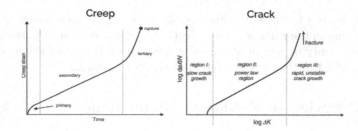

Fig. 2. The creep and crack curves in three regions [37] (ΔK is the stress intensity factor range, $\frac{da}{dN}$ is the increased crack length a per load cycle N)

to calculate the crack growth in rotor shafts for diagnostics and prognostics. Wear is a gradual degradation at the surface caused by the friction between two parts in sliding motions, resulting in a loss of material of at least one of the parts. Modeling component wear is possible with the Archard law, but it is challenging because external factors, such as environment conditions, have an important impact on the contact of the surfaces [17].

Physical models tackle lifetime prediction via explicit equations to describe the degradation mechanisms with the help of domain expertise and mechanical knowledge. An adequately chosen model will reflect accurately the physical behavior of the degradation, providing reliable insights into the equipment health state and its long-term behavior. However, such approach is not always practical. The complexity of real-life systems hinders correct modeling. A model tailored to one specific system cannot be adapted to another. In place of data, physical tests are carried out to validate the parameters of the equations, but these tests interrupt the operation of the equipment.

Expert System. An expert system (ES) is a knowledge base of formalized facts and rules solicited from human experts and uses an automated inference engine for reasoning and answering queries [30]. ES are particularly useful for fault diagnostics. In [15], an ES is combined with a Markovian model to perform fault anticipation and fault recovery in a host system. Tang et al. [36] implemented an ES-based online fault diagnosis and prevention for dredgers. ES can be flexible in its implementation. For example, Turgis et al. [38] proposed a mixed signaling system in train fleet. Health indicators are extracted from the data by a hard-coded set of rules. The system issues alerts and schedules maintenance operations when the indicators exceed a predefined preventive threshold, or when a failure is deemed imminent.

ES profit from the power of hardware computation and from reasoning algorithms to generate solutions faster than human experts. ES are one of the first successful forms of Artificial Intelligence, being capable to deduce new knowledge for reasoning and solving problems on their own. Nonetheless, converting human expertise to machine rules demands an immense effort. Some relationships between system variables cannot be expressed by a simple IF-ELSE rule

[36]; therefore, more complicated modeling is required to properly formulate such relationships. Once built, an ES cannot handle unexpected situations not covered by the rules. A complex equipment may result in a large set of rules, consequently causing the "combinatorial explosion" phenomenon in computation [31].

2.2 Data-Driven Approach

To compensate the lack of domain expertise, data-driven approach learns from the available data, such as log files, maintenance history, or sensor measurements, to discover the failure patterns and to predict future faults. Data-driven approach can be further categorized to **machine learning** and **stochastic models**.

Machine Learning. With its versatility and ability to learn without domain specifications, machine learning has become a major player in PdM applications [14]. Overall, machine learning can be supervised or unsupervised, depending on the availability of labeled data.

Supervised learning extracts a function $f : \mathbb{X} \to \mathbb{Y}$ to map an input space $\mathbb{X}$ to an output space $\mathbb{Y}$ from a dataset $S = \{x_i, y_i\}_{1 \leq i \leq N}$ with $x_i \in \mathbb{X} \subseteq \mathbb{R}^{N \times D}$ and $y_i \in \mathbb{Y}$, where N is the dataset size and D the dimension. The task is classification if y_i is discrete, and regression otherwise. Classification for PdM seeks the discrete health states of the equipment. Robust models, such as Decision Trees, Support Vector Machines, Random Forests, and Neural Networks, have seen their applications in PdM [1, 23, 35, 39]. However, it is difficult to classify future health indicators, as future data cannot be obtained at current time. Moreover, rare failure events in critical systems lead to class imbalance. Regression is generally more complicated than classification, but it returns more intuitive result for PdM, such as the RUL [9, 20] or the probability of future failures [22].

Unsupervised learning attempts to discover patterns from the data without knowing the desired output, that is, when the dataset only has $S = \{x_i\}_{1 \leq i \leq N}$ without y_i. In PdM, unsupervised learning is useful to identify clusters of dominant health states [7], to detect anomalies [41], or to reduce the data dimension.

Machine learning models have seen remarkable improvement throughout the years, but the quality and amount of data remain essential for an accurate machine learning model. A moderate or long training time is expected, and the model must be retrained as new data become available. Although supervised learning has proven its effectiveness, labeled data are not always available or must be obtained through tedious manual annotation, as it is the case in the railway sector.

Stochastic Models. A failure can be the consequence of a gradual degradation that slowly decreases the equipment performance until it becomes nonfunctional. We distinguish two types of failures: *hard failure* when random errors interrupt the system abruptly and can only be remedied by corrective maintenance, and *soft failure* when a gradual deterioration occurs in the equipment until the outcome is unsatisfactory [25]. The latter can be effectively studied with stochastic modeling. The deterioration process is stochastic because it contains random small increments of changes over time. This process is formulated as $\{X(t) : t \geq 0\}$, where $X(t)$ quantifies the amount of degradation. When $X(t)$ crosses a threshold, the equipment service is considered unsatisfactory (Fig. 3). Markov-based models are used when the degradation is studied in a finite state space [24]. Otherwise, Lévy processes, such as the Wiener processes [40] and Gamma processes [27], are commonly used for continuous stochastic processes.

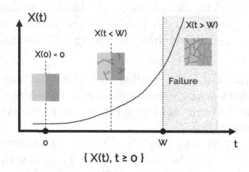

Fig. 3. Degradation as a stochastic process

In some cases, it is more realistic to consider the health evolution of the equipment as a gradual degradation process, which can be effectively modeled using stochastic tools. The suitable modeling tool must be chosen based on the degradation physics of the targeted equipment. The available data aid parameter tuning, making the model more accurate and robust. However, stochastic modeling is more complicated than machine learning. Furthermore, stochastic modeling requires a strong mathematical background to fully understand and to correctly apply the models.

3   An Overview of Stream Learning

In this section, we discuss the methodology for learning from a stream that possibly exhibits dynamic changes known as concept drifts. We define "learning" as the process of extracting knowledge from the data using statistical techniques from machine learning, deep learning, and data mining.

3.1   Algorithms

Generally, the methods for traditional offline learning are adapted to an incremental fashion to address the requirements of stream learning. We will now look at two primary learning paradigms on data streams.

Supervised Stream Learning. Similar to offline machine learning, supervised stream learning consists of classification and regression.

The Hoeffding Tree (HT) [18] is a popular stream classification algorithm. It is a tree-based method that leverages the Hoeffding's bound to handle extremely large datasets with a constant learning time per instance. The resulting tree is guaranteed to be nearly identical to that produced by a traditional decision tree algorithm, if given enough training examples. The classic Naïve Bayes is easily adapted to an online streaming fashion by simply updating the priors, i.e., the occurrences of the attribute values, incrementally.

Stream regression can be tree-based or rule-based. The Fast Incremental Model Trees with Drift Detection is a representative tree-based algorithm for data streams [21]. It shares the same principle with the HT for growing the tree and for splitting attribute selection. Each leaf now has a linear model that is updated every time it receives a new data instance. This model then performs regression for an unlabeled instance in the leaf. The Adaptive Model Rules from High Speed Data Streams is a rule-based regression algorithm [5]. It starts with an empty set of rules and expands or removes rules as new data arrive. Each rule contains a linear model that is incrementally trained on the data covered by this rule. The predicted value of an unseen instance is averaged from the individual regressions given by rules that cover this instance.

Unsupervised Stream Learning. It is unlikely that data from a fast stream are fully labeled. Unsupervised learning attempts to discover structures in the data, using common tasks, such as clustering and anomaly detection.

CluStream [2] is the most representative example of two-phase clustering methods. The online phase efficiently collects and updates summary statistics from the incoming data in form of *micro-clusters*. The offline phase treats these clusters as pseudo-points and runs K-Means to produce the clustering result within a requested time horizon. Other stream clustering methods that adopt the two-phase approach are DenStream [13] and D-Stream [16]. HPStream [3] addresses the problem of high-dimensional data streams by deploying a projection technique to select the best attribute set for each cluster.

Anomaly detection finds abnormal points with respect to the dominant data distribution in the data streams. Ahmad et al. [4] used Hierarchical Temporal Memory algorithm to detect outliers from data streams that exhibit noises and dynamic changes. xStream [26] performs density-based anomaly detection in a feature-evolving data stream, where an instance does not arrive with its full set of attributes, but the attributes arrive piece by piece over time.

3.2   Concept Drifts

Concept drifts occur in non-stationary environments where the relation between the data and the target variable changes over time. This variability is encountered in real-world applications, such as recommendation systems where users change their preferences over time. Concept drifts manifest in four forms (Fig. 4):

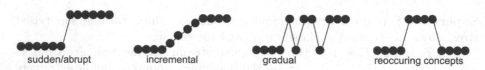

Fig. 4. The four forms of concept drifts [19]

sudden drift (abrupt changes), incremental drift (slow transition), gradual drift (alternating concepts), and recurrent drift (temporary changes) [19]. An incremental algorithm, by nature, can adapt to incremental drifts by continuously incorporating new data. However, the other forms are challenging: a sudden drift affects the model accuracy until it receives enough data to adapt to the new concept; the same thing happens with recurrent drifts until the previous concept returns; gradual drifts are most difficult to deal with - in the worst case, the model never adapts to such changes.

Learning and Forgetting. Learning new instances is the default behavior of online algorithms. Such algorithms learn from a single or multiple instances at a time. The latter requires the windowing technique: a number of instances is accumulated in a window of fixed or variable size, and the model is kept up to date with the data stored in the latest window. Old instances are removed from the window to leave space for recent ones. The window size is therefore a crucial parameter: a small window makes the model sensitive to changes but prone to constant updates; a large window implies slower adaptation to drifts, but the model is more stable in stationary phases of streams.

Within a limited memory space, incorporating new knowledge implies discarding the old one. The windowing technique already entails the forgetting mechanism: an instance removed from the window is forgotten. However, such abrupt forgetting is not ideal in the case of gradual or recurrent drifts. To maintain a more consistent memory of past data without storing them, past examples are weighted according to their age. Suppose that the data until a time t is summarized into a statistics S_t and that there exists a function G that updates S given an instance X, the new statistics at $t + 1$ is $S_{t+1} = G(\alpha S_t, X)$ where $\alpha \in (0, 1)$ is the fading factor. A high value of α signals a high relevance assigned to past data.

Change Detectors. Adaptation to concept drift can be implicit via the learning and forgetting mechanism. Nevertheless, using an explicit change detector to identify where a drift occurs may bring forth insightful discoveries.

CUSUM is a simple, memoryless test that measures the changes accumulated over time: $g_t = \max(0, g_{t-1} + (x_t - \delta))$, where g_t measures the cumulative changes, x_t is the new data instance, and δ represents the allowed magnitude of change. $(x_t - \delta)$ expresses how much the new instance deviates from the acceptable value. If x_t is constantly superior to δ, g_t are increased until g_t exceeds the user-defined threshold λ. A change detection alarm is then triggered, after which g_t is reset to 0.

Algorithm 1: ADWIN

1 Initialize W
2 **foreach** x_t *from the stream* **do**
3 $\quad$ $W \leftarrow W \cup \{x_t\}$ # add x_t to the head of W
4 $\quad$ **repeat**
5 $\quad$ $\quad$ | drop elements from W
6 $\quad$ **until** $|\hat{\mu}_{W_0} - \hat{\mu}_{W_1}| < \epsilon_{cut}$;

ADWIN is a more sophisticated window-based change detector [11], described in Algorithm 1. ADWIN slides a window W over the last n instances from the stream and splits this window into two subsequent windows W_0 of size n_0 and W_1 of size n_1 such that $n_0 + n_1 = n$. ADWIN signals a change when the difference between the averages $\hat{\mu}_{W_0}$ of W_0 and $\hat{\mu}_{W_1}$ of W_1 is superior than the threshold $\epsilon_{cut} = \sqrt{\frac{1}{2m} \times \log \frac{4}{\delta'}}$, where $m = \frac{1}{\frac{1}{n_0} + \frac{1}{n_1}}$ is the harmonic mean of n_0 and n_1 and $\delta' = \frac{\delta}{n}$ (δ is a confidence value $\in (0, 1)$). If a change is detected, the old subwindow in W is dropped, thus shrinking the size of W. Otherwise, W grows increasingly as it incorporates new data. Consequently, ADWIN can dynamically adapt the window size: W shrinks when changes are detected to discard outdated data, but it can grow infinitely when the stream is static.

4 Application in the Railway Sector

4.1 The Need of Maintenance for the Railway

As one of the most popular forms of mass transit, the railway transportation system has gone through a long history, from the appearance of steam locomotives to the development of modern high-speed trains. The railway system consists of many sub-systems that interact between them via sophisticated communication protocols to ensure a smooth operation of the entire system as a whole. Sub-systems of the railway include, but not limited to, the rolling stocks (passenger and freight cars), the infrastructure (ballast, tracks, sleepers, switches), the energy supply source (catenary, electric rails), the signaling system, the operation and maintenance module, the RAMS, as illustrated in Fig. 5.

Since the railway is designed for passenger use, reliability is crucial to guarantee the safety of workers and passengers. Reliability can be delivered with effective maintenance operations.

Maintenance aims to preserve an equipment in a state that allows it to correctly perform its functions, thus ensuring the system reliability. There exists two

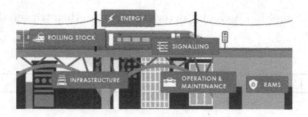

Fig. 5. Typical components of the railway system (*Source: IKOS Consulting*)

primary maintenance strategies: corrective maintenance and preventive maintenance (Fig. 6). Corrective maintenance, also called reactive maintenance, only
interferes when a problem has occurred in the system. Preventive maintenance
avoids undesired problems by scheduling maintenance operations in advance,
either by fixed intervals of time (time-based maintenance) or based on the current or projected health of the system (condition-based/predictive maintenance).

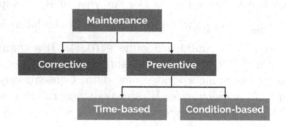

Fig. 6. Taxonomy of maintenance strategies

With the advent of IoT devices, modern railway equipment can generate a
large volume of data that enable insightful analytics on the health state of the
equipment, thus favoring PdM. Nevertheless, the other maintenance strategies
are still commonly used. Corrective maintenance remains necessary because some
failures cannot be modeled and predicted. Preventive time-based maintenance
allows systematic scheduling of maintenance operations in a large-scale railway
network; it also handles the failures that do not generate analyzable data: it may
not be possible to acquire such data, or the installation of the data acquisition
equipment is too costly (for example, camera systems to examine whether the
paint color of a train has faded away). Therefore, maintenance of equipment
cannot be entirely predictive. The purpose is not to replace one strategy by
another. Instead, the scope of maintenance should be clearly defined in order to
determine which strategy is most suitable for a specific scenario. The final goal is
to harmoniously combine diverse maintenance strategies together for maximized
reliability, availability, and safety of the railway system.

4.2   Predictive Maintenance for the Railway

In this section, we connect the PdM approaches in Sect. 2 to the railway sector. Specifically, we analyze the strengths and weaknesses of the knowledge-based and data-driven approaches when applied to railway maintenance.

Knowledge-Based Approach. A railway company may have the needed expertise to undertake knowledge-based approach, but it does not make modeling of complex systems easier. A physical model or an expert system built for one specific railway component cannot be easily adapted to another, because each component is susceptible to different degradation modes. For instance, the train wheels are subject to wear due to its contact with the rail tracks and to fatigue because of intensive rotations. The brakes are prone to creep and wear. Wear often occurs in the pantographs. Therefore, we need one model for each degradation mode of a component. Additionally, maintaining and expanding an existing knowledge-based PdM model may require extensive training effort.

Data-Driven Approach. For this approach, data are the essence. Fortunately, modern railway equipment can supply a large amount of data regularly. However, this causes the following issues. First, the data volume increases rapidly. A railway network, especially one on a national scale, comprises multiple systems and sub-systems that generate their own data. Timely and efficient data processing algorithms are therefore essential to deploy PdM applications on a large-scale network. Second, railway components are intertwined. That is, the performance of one system may largely affect that of another, thus during data analysis, cross-system correlations must be taken into account. Third, the lack of labels in most railway datasets impedes the use of robust machine learning models, making practitioners resort to unsupervised methods. Fourth, in critical systems, such as the passenger doors or the brakes, it would be preferable to have a human expert occasionally verifying the output, instead of entirely delegating the maintenance decision process to automated predictive models.

4.3   Benefits of Stream Learning in Railway Maintenance

An Example of Railway Data. This research focuses on the application of stream learning for real-time data analysis in order to improve the maintenance of the railway sector. For a case study, we are supplied with a dataset that consists of raw signals collected from the passenger door systems in operation. The scenario is illustrated in Fig. 7 and is described as follows.

The targeted equipment are smart trains with sensors installed on the doors. When entering a station, the train opens its doors to welcome passengers, then closes them when preparing for departure. If a closing operation is not successful (e.g. the path is blocked by an obstacle), the door reopens and attempts to close again. A cycle of opening or closing generates physical signals, such as the current or tension needed to manipulate the doors, which are recorded by the sensors.

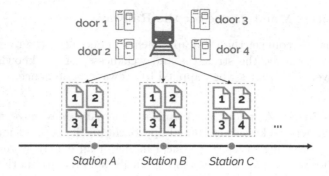

Fig. 7. The dataset of interest

Once all the doors are closed and the train leaves the station, the signals of a door are stored in one file. If a train has four doors, it will generate four files every time it enters and leaves a station. These files are temporarily stored in-place and are later sent in bulk to a server for analysis. In this scenario, we deem stream learning a promising approach for the following reasons.

Unbounded Volume. The amount of data is unbounded as long the trains continue to operate, thus it can be considered a *stream of data*. How do the knowledge-based and data-driven approach handle this type of data? Knowledge-based models are generally not affected. Because the knowledge is already incorporated in the models and the outputs are dictated by a set of hard-coded rules, knowledge-based models do not need to learn new patterns from the data. Nonetheless, the decision process of these models must be optimized to deal with such volume of input. As for data-driven models, especially machine learning algorithms, that are designed to work with static datasets, they do not comply with the unboundedness of data streams. Although it is possible to re-train a model when new chunks of data arrive, model training per se is a costly and time-consuming process. It would be more economic to maintain one model that continuously incorporates new data and learn incrementally over time, which justifies the benefits of stream learning.

Adaptivity. Stream learning algorithms are designed to be highly adaptive. Because a stream algorithm incorporates new data examples to incrementally update its "understanding" about the data, it can detect changes and adapt to the novelty in the data. These changes include the altered relationship between the classes and the independent variables, or the emergence of new classes. In either cases, machine learning models cannot handle the data that are not included in the learning process and perform poorly when the new data bear little resemblance to the training set. For stochastic models, the parameters that were fine-tuned based on the training set may not fit to the new data. The same issue also happens to physical models. An expert system yields unreliable inference result when it encounters a scenario that is not covered by the rules, except when the rules can grow dynamically.

Readiness. Stream learning, after all, is adapted from traditional machine learning to work in an online fashion. Given its incremental nature, a stream learning model is ready for use from day 1, i.e., when the equipment and the model are first initialized, then it receives new instances of data for learning when they are made available on the stream. On the contrary, traditional offline learning necessitates a certain amount of data and time for training. Knowledge-based models do not require training data but need to be constructed in advance. However, it should be noted that the performance of the stream model will fluctuate significantly at the beginning until it has seen enough data examples to achieve a stable performance. Indeed, given a stream learning and an offline learning algorithm that share the same nature (e.g. both are tree-based), the convergence point above which both algorithms achieve the same accuracy is an interesting subject to reflect on.

Strengths and Limitations of Stream Learning. Having explained a railway dataset and justified the choice of stream learning in this scenario, we will now discuss the strengths and limitations of stream learning.

Strengths. Stream learning is attractive for its incremental characteristics, its adaptivity to dynamic changes, and its readiness in a no-data scenario. In contrast, traditional learning models, once trained, cannot adapt to new data that were not included in the training set. The amount and the speed at which the data are generated make stream learning a better fit for online learning. The ability to update as new data arrive and to make prediction when required increase the reactivity of stream learning models. Moreover, as modern monitoring systems tend to become more reactive and real-time, a transition from offline learning to online learning should be anticipated in the near future. Therefore, stream learning is potential for PdM where the data are produced ceaselessly and must be analyzed in a timely manner.

Limitations. However, stream learning does not outperform offline learning in all aspects. To update the model on new data quickly, stream learning prefer simple calculations[1] and subsequently lowers the model complexity. The size of the stream makes iterations over the data infeasible, thus the constraint of one-pass learning. Powerful tools, such as Deep learning, cannot (yet) be learned incrementally on a data stream. Parameters tuning is also difficult, as traditional techniques, such as cross-validation or grid search, cannot be applied efficiently on an infinite stream.

Especially in the railway sector, stream learning must deal with two relevant challenges. The first challenge involves the volume of data. Given the complexity

---

[1] Heavy calculations can be tolerated if we have powerful machines. This weakness concerns the limitation of the technology rather than the limitation of the algorithm.

and the number of equipment used in a railway system, a huge volume of data is created daily and must be handled efficiently. The second challenge resides in labeling the data. Data labeling itself is a tedious process, and is more difficult on data streams than on static datasets because the labeling process may not keep up with the speed of the streams. The small amount of labels, or the total lack of it, greatly limits the choice of learning algorithms, leading to the use of less robust algorithms that can miss out the precursors of failures. Unanticipated problems in the railway may lead to serious, even fatal consequences, thus anomalies must be assessed fast and accurately.

Prospects. Stream learning is a relatively new research domain and, to the best of our knowledge, there have not been any applications of stream learning algorithms in maintenance. The study in [29] examines the accuracy of the Hoeffding Tree for vibration condition monitoring of compressed ignition engines; however, their data are not simulated as a real-time stream and the study does not yield a conclusive result on the potential of stream learning over offline learning. Sahal et al. [33] provides a mapping of PdM requirements to a range of existing stream processing solutions, but overlooks the learning aspect. Currently, works that implemented real-time PdM systems do not use proper stream learning algorithms. Instead, a model is trained using a robust offline learning algorithm (e.g., Random Forest) and is deployed online for real-time prediction [6,8,12,34]. Hence, the potentials of stream learning are to be explored, in order to assess its usefulness to the development of a full-fledged real-time PdM model.

5   Conclusion

In this paper, we present a brief overview of predictive maintenance and of stream learning, and reflect on the merits of stream learning applied to data-driven predictive maintenance in the railway sector. Given the amount of railway data and the speed at which they are being generated, we deem stream learning a promising solution for an efficient analysis of these data. Even so, we are open to the possibility of using offline learning in combination with stream learning, because it would be beneficial to balance the weaknesses of one with the strengths of the other. Future works will focus on the application of stream learning models in railway maintenance.

Additionally, the convergence point of offline learning and stream learning is an interesting study subject. Given an offline learning and a stream learning algorithm that share the same nature (for instance, the Decision Tree and the Hoeffding Tree) and work on the same dataset, is there a convergence point, e.g., the number of examples, above which both algorithms are equally good? The answer to this question will further explain the applicability of stream learning models over traditional learning models.

References

1. Accorsi, R., Manzini, R., Pascarella, P., Patella, M., Sassi, S.: Data mining and machine learning for condition-based maintenance. Procedia Manuf. **11**, 1153–1161 (2017)
2. Aggarwal, C.C., Han, J., Wang, J., Yu, P.S.: A framework for clustering evolving data streams. In: Proceedings of the 29th International Conference on Very Large Data Bases, vol. 29, pp. 81–92. VLDB Endowment, Berlin, Germany (2003)
3. Aggarwal, C.C., Han, J., Wang, J., Yu, P.S.: A framework for projected clustering of high dimensional data streams. In: Proceedings of the 30th International Conference on Very Large Data Bases, vol. 30, pp. 852–863. VLDB Endowment (2004)
4. Ahmad, S., Lavin, A., Purdy, S., Agha, Z.: Unsupervised real-time anomaly detection for streaming data. Neurocomputing **262**, 134–147 (2017)
5. Almeida, E., Ferreira, C., Gama, J.: Adaptive model rules from data streams. In: Blockeel, H., Kersting, K., Nijssen, S., Železný, F. (eds.) Machine Learning and Knowledge Discovery in Databases, pp. 480–492. Springer, Heidelberg (2013). https://doi.org/10.1007/978-3-642-40988-2_31
6. Amaya, E.J., Alvares, A.J.: SIMPREBAL: an expert system for real-time fault diagnosis of hydrogenerators machinery. In: 2010 IEEE 15th Conference on Emerging Technologies Factory Automation (ETFA 2010), pp. 1–8 (2010)
7. Amruthnath, N., Gupta, T.: Fault class prediction in unsupervised learning using model-based clustering approach. In: 2018 International Conference on Information and Computer Technologies (ICICT), pp. 5–12 (2018)
8. Bansal, D., Evans, D.J., Jones, B.: A real-time predictive maintenance system for machine systems. Int. J. Mach. Tools Manuf. **44**, 759–766 (2004)
9. Baptista, M., Sankararaman, S., de Medeiros, I.P., Nascimento, C., Prendinger, H., Henriques, E.M.: Forecasting fault events for predictive maintenance using data-driven techniques and arma modeling. Comput. Ind. Eng. **115**, 41–53 (2018)
10. Baraldi, P., Mangili, F., Zio, E.: A kalman filter-based ensemble approach with application to turbine creep prognostics. IEEE Trans. Reliab. **61**, 966–977 (2012)
11. Bifet, A., Gavaldà, R.: Learning from time-changing data with adaptive windowing. In: Proceedings of the 7th SIAM International Conference on Data Mining (2007)
12. Canizo, M., Onieva, E., Conde, A., Charramendieta, S., Trujillo, S.: Real-time predictive maintenance for wind turbines using Big Data frameworks. In: 2017 IEEE International Conference on Prognostics and Health Management (ICPHM), pp. 70–77 (2017)
13. Cao, F., Ester, M., Qian, W., Zhou, A.: Density-based clustering over an evolving data stream with noise. In: Proceedings of the Sixth SIAM International Conference on Data Mining, April 20–22, 2006, Bethesda, MD, USA, vol. 2006 (2006)
14. Carvalho, T.P., Soares, F.A.A.M.N., Vita, R., Francisco, R.d.P., Basto, J.P., Alcalá, S.G.S.: A systematic literature review of machine learning methods applied to predictive maintenance. Comput. Ind. Eng. **137** (2019)
15. Chande, P., Tokekar, S.: Expert-based maintenance: a study of its effectiveness. IEEE Trans. Reliab. **47**, 53–58 (1998)
16. Chen, Y., Tu, L.: Density-based clustering for real-time stream data. In: Proceedings of the 13th ACM SIGKDD International Conference on Knowledge Discovery and Data Mining, pp. 133–142. Association for Computing Machinery, San Jose (2007)

17. Cubillo, A., Perinpanayagam, S., Esperon-Miguez, M.: A review of physics-based models in prognostics: application to gears and bearings of rotating machinery. Adv. Mech. Eng. **8**(8) (2016)

18. Domingos, P., Hulten, G.: Mining high-speed data streams. In: Proceedings of the 6th ACM SIGKDD International Conference on Knowledge Discovery and Data Mining. Association for Computing Machinery, Boston, Massachusetts (2000)

19. Gama, J., Žliobaitė, I., Bifet, A., Pechenizkiy, M., Bouchachia, A.: A survey on concept drift adaptation. ACM Comput. Surv. **46**, 44:1–44:37 (2014)

20. Heimes, F.O.: Recurrent neural networks for remaining useful life estimation. In: International Conference on Prognostics and Health Management, pp. 1–6 (2008)

21. Ikonomovska, E., Gama, J., Džeroski, S.: Learning model trees from evolving data streams. Data Mining Knowl. Discov. **23**, 128–168 (2011)

22. Korvesis, P., Besseau, S., Vazirgiannis, M.: Predictive maintenance in aviation: failure prediction from post-flight reports. In: 2018 IEEE 34th International Conference on Data Engineering (ICDE), pp. 1414–1422 (2018)

23. Li, H., Parikh, D., He, Q., Qian, B., Li, Z., Fang, D., Hampapur, A.: Improving rail network velocity: a machine learning approach to predictive maintenance. Transp. Res. Part C: Emerg. Technol. **45**, 17–26 (2014)

24. Liang, Z., Parlikad, A.: A Markovian model for power transformer maintenance. Int. J. Electr. Power Energy Syst. **99**, 175–182 (2018)

25. Liao, H., Elsayed, E.A., Chan, L.Y.: Maintenance of continuously monitored degrading systems. Eur. J. Oper. Res. **175**, 821–835 (2006)

26. Manzoor, E., Lamba, H., Akoglu, L.: xStream: outlier detection in feature-evolving data streams. In: Proceedings of the 24th ACM SIGKDD International Conference on Knowledge Discovery & Data Mining, pp. 1963–1972. Association for Computing Machinery, London, United Kingdom (2018)

27. van Noortwijk, J.M.: A survey of the application of gamma processes in maintenance. Reliab. Eng. Syst. Safety **94**, 2–21 (2009)

28. Oppenheimer, C.H., Loparo, K.A.: Physically based diagnosis and prognosis of cracked rotor shafts. In: Willett, P.K., Kirubarajan, T. (eds.) Component and Systems Diagnostics, Prognostics, and Health Management II, vol. 4733, pp. 122–132. International Society for Optics and Photonics, SPIE (2002)

29. Naveen Kumar, P., Sakthivel, G., Jegadeeshwaran, R., Sivakumar, R., Saravana Kumar, D.: Vibration based IC engine fault diagnosis using tree family classifiers - a machine learning approach. In: 2019 IEEE International Symposium on Smart Electronic Systems (iSES), pp. 225–228 (2019)

30. Pau, L.F.: Survey of expert systems for fault detection, test generation and maintenance. Expert Syst. **3**, 100–110 (2007)

31. Peng, Y., Dong, M., Zuo, M.J.: Current status of machine prognostics in condition-based maintenance: a review. Int. J. Adv. Manuf. Technol. **50**(1), 297–313 (2010)

32. Qiu, J., Seth, B.B., Liang, S.Y., Chang, C.: Damage mechanics approach for bearing lifetime prognostics. Mech. Syst. Sig. Process. **16**, 817–829 (2002)

33. Sahal, R., Breslin, J.G., Ali, M.I.: Big data and stream processing platforms for Industry 4.0 requirements mapping for a predictive maintenance use case. J. Manuf. Syst. **54**, 138–151 (2020)

34. Su, C.J., Huang, S.F.: Real-time big data analytics for hard disk drive predictive maintenance. Comput. Electr. Eng. **71**, 93–101 (2018)

35. Susto, G.A., Schirru, A., Pampuri, S., McLoone, S., Beghi, A.: Machine learning for predictive maintenance: a multiple classifier approach. IEEE Trans. Ind. Inform. **11**(3), 812–820 (2015)

36. Tang, J.Z., Wang, Q.F.: Online fault diagnosis and prevention expert system for dredgers. Expert Syst. Appl. **34**, 511–521 (2008)
37. Tinga, T.: Principles of Loads and Failure Mechanisms. Applications in Maintenance, Reliability and Design. Springer Series in Reliability Engineering, Springer, Heidelberg (2013). https://doi.org/10.1007/978-1-4471-4917-0
38. Turgis, F., Auder, P., Coutadeur, Q., Verdun, C.: Industrialization of condition based maintenance for complex systems in a complex maintenance environment, example of NAT. In: 12th World Congress on Railway Research (2019)
39. Yang, C., Létourneau, S.: Learning to predict train wheel failures. In: Proceedings of the Eleventh ACM SIGKDD International Conference on Knowledge Discovery in Data Mining, pp. 516–525. Association for Computing Machinery (2005)
40. Zhang, Z., Si, X., Hu, C., Lei, Y.: Degradation data analysis and remaining useful life estimation: a review on Wiener-process-based methods. Eur. J. Oper. Res. **271**, 775–796 (2018)
41. Zhao, P., Kurihara, M., Tanaka, J., Noda, T., Chikuma, S., Suzuki, T.: Advanced correlation-based anomaly detection method for predictive maintenance. In: IEEE International Conference on Prognostics and Health Management, pp. 78–83 (2017)

CycleFootprint: A Fully Automated Method for Extracting Operation Cycles from Historical Raw Data of Multiple Sensors

Hadi Fanaee-T[1(✉)], Mohamed-Rafik Bouguelia[1], Mahmoud Rahat[1],
Jonathan Blixt[2], and Harpal Singh[2]

[1] Center for Applied Intelligent Systems Research, Halmstad University,
Halmstad, Sweden
{hadi.fanaee,mohamed-rafik.bouguelia,mahmoud.rahat}@hh.se
[2] Alfa Laval Tumba AB, Tumba, Sweden
{jonathan.blixt,harpal.singh}@alfalaval.com

Abstract. Extracting operation cycles from the historical reading of sensors is an essential step in IoT data analytics. For instance, we can exploit the obtained cycles for learning the normal states to feed into semi-supervised models or dictionaries for efficient real-time anomaly detection on the sensors. However, this is a difficult problem due to this fact that we may have different types of cycles, each of which with varying lengths. Current approaches are highly dependent on manual efforts by the aid of visualization and knowledge of domain experts, which is not feasible on a large scale. We propose a fully automated method called CycleFootprint that can: 1) identify the most relevant signal that has the most obvious recurring patterns among multiple signals; and 2) automatically find the cycles from the selected signal. The main idea behind CycleFootprint is mining footprints in the cycles. We assume that there should be a unique pattern in each cycle that shows up repeatedly in each cycle. By mining those footprints, we can identify cycles. We evaluate our method with existing labeled ground truth data of a real separator in marine application equipped with multiple health monitoring sensors. 86% of cycles extracted by our method match fully or with at least 99% overlap with true cycles, which sounds promising given its unsupervised and fully automated nature.

Keywords: Cycle detection · Sensors · IoT

1 Introduction

Health monitoring of machines plays a significant role in improving their safety, reliability, and their effective lifetime. The cost of machines' failures is usually high and potentially fatal [3]. Anomaly detection is a central component

© Springer Nature Switzerland AG 2020
J. Gama et al. (Eds.): ITEM 2020/IoT Streams 2020, CCIS 1325, pp. 30–44, 2020.
https://doi.org/10.1007/978-3-030-66770-2_3

of self-maintenance systems, and it provides failure warnings in advance, which ultimately prevents emergency shutdown and catastrophic consequences.

Based on the availability of labeled data, the methods for anomaly detection can be divided into unsupervised, semi-supervised, and supervised methods. Unsupervised methods such as statistical process control (SPC) methods are typically applied when there is no prior information about data. The central assumption of these methods is that the significant part of operation goes normal so that they look for those instants that fit least to the rest of the data. When data is partially labeled, for instance, regular operation, we can use semi-supervised methods. These methods construct a model representing normal behavior and then compute the deviation of a test instant from the learnt model. The third group of approaches is supervised learning that assumes that we have the labeled data for both "normal" and "abnormal" states. The general rule is that supervised methods outperform the other two methods, and the semi-supervised methods outperform unsupervised methods [3, 4, 6].

In the industrial setting, labeling of normal states is much easier and cheaper than acquiring the abnormal states. The reason is that the machines are healthy in the majority of times, while faults occur on rare occasions. This setting is more relevant for semi-supervised models, where labeled is required for only normal states.

However, in practice, collecting a high-quality dataset of regular operation is not that straightforward. For instance, the clients of our industrial partner have some machines that produce a huge volume of data provided by various sensors. The majority of devices are in operation for a long time. Now our partner is interested in using this raw historical data for real-time anomaly detection. The main issue is that the raw data includes a mixture of normal and abnormal states and neutral states where the machine has been shut down due to some reasons. The more challenging issue is that the length of cycles in each operation is not constant and spans from 2 min to 2 h. Besides, we may have different shapes of regular periods.

The current in-use approach for annotating regular cycles relies on some parameters that machines have collected during the operation. A domain expert then goes through the visualization plot of the time series of different sensors in combination with those parameters to annotate regular cycles. This is a very time-consuming task, and it is infeasible for more massive data sets, which is the case for the majority of machines. The second issue is that those parameters used for the identification of cycles sometimes do not match appropriately with the right periods and are not reliable for automation of this process.

To automate the process of regular cycle identification, we propose a fully automated approach that makes no assumption about the distribution of data and does not require any expert knowledge about sensors and their utility. The user can feed into the algorithm as many as sensors she wants. Our algorithm will first find the right sensor that exhibits more recurring behavior, and then it segments the data into some initial cycles. Finally, it prunes the irrelevant sequences by applying the cycle validation condition set by the user.

Besides the main contribution, for the first time, we propose a novel data discretization for transferring time series into a sequence of discrete states.

So, our contributions are as follows.

– We propose a fully automatic approach for the identification of operation cycles. Our method is conservative, in the sense that it is strict in small deviations. Thus is an ideal approach for producing normal labeled data required by semi-supervised methods.
– We propose a new method for converting time series into discrete sequences, which is an alternative to Symbolic Aggregate approximation (SAX) [7]. Although SAX is a state-of-the-art method for time series discretization, our initial investigation showed poor performance in this application. We explain this in detail later.

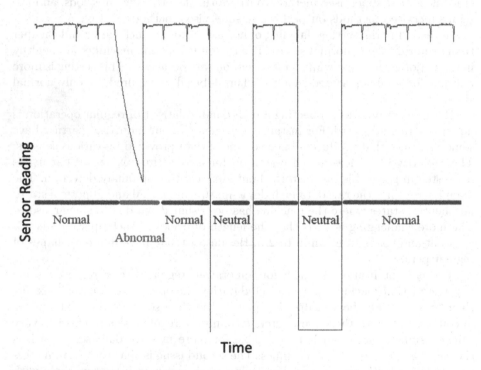

Fig. 1. Historical Raw signals include mixture of cycles: Normal operation (Green), failures (red) and missing values/ inactivity (blue) (Color figure online)

2   Problem Definition

Figure 1 illustrates a simplified time series of a sensor in a particular machine. The historical time series of sensors include a mixture of cycles: regular operation, failures, and neutral states (where the device has been inactive due to shutdown

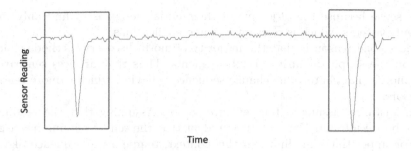

Fig. 2. An example of cycle footprint

or repair). In the example figure, we can see twelve regular cycles with different lengths, one abnormal cycle, and two neutral cycles (one with missing values and one with a fixed amount over a period). All sequences, though appear differently, typically share a sub-segment with a unique pattern. For instance, in the time of discharge, the measurements show a sudden change, and then goes back to normal. However, abnormal cycles might have different causes. Thus the shape and measurements during an irregular period can be completely different from another unusual situation.

We are interested in identifying cycles that share a unique repeating pattern. An example of a simple cycle footprint is illustrated in Fig. 2. However, footprints can be more complicated than this, sometimes not identifiable by eye. The advantage of extracting cycles is that we can then use clustering to separate normal cycles from abnormal cycles and construct an abstract model or dictionary from normal cycles and exploit these in semi-supervised anomaly detection. But this is a challenging problem because footprints are not necessarily the same length. For instance, in one cycle, footprint might appear during one minute, while in the next cycle, we may observe it during a longer or shorter period.

3 Related Work

Perhaps the most relevant solutions can be motif discovery methods from time series [2,8]. However, for various reasons, these types of solutions are not an ideal fit for our problem.

The first reason is that motif discovery methods look for most similar frequent motifs, and not all similar patterns. For instance, the design of state-of-the-art techniques such as Matrix Profile [9,10] allows us to detect only the top-k motifs with the time complexity of $O(N^2)$. A modification to enable these methods to obtain all frequent patterns not only elevate the time complexity but also is complicated to implement. Because, for instance, in matrix profile, k most similar segments are assumed to be motifs. But since our target is to identify all motifs of different types, then we cannot merely pick the closest sections. Because, for instance, among those top-k, we may have different motif types. The separation of multiple kinds of motifs is not trivial with these methods. It makes sense because the objective of their initial design is to find only top-k frequent patterns, which is relevant in some applications.

The second reason is that the majority of motif discovery methods concentrate on the shape similarity of sub-segments. Thus they are less sensitive to those motifs that share value change sequence behavior, which is more relevant in sensors.

For instance, assume a temperature sensor. Assuming that the reading is always between 0 and 100, we are confident that the sensor reading never goes lower or upper than this limit. In this context, temperature sequence like [20, 30, 20] is different from [80, 90, 80]. However, motif discovery methods identify these two patterns as motifs, because they appear in U-shape in a sliding window. However, they refer to completely different machine states (one normal and one abnormal).

To understand the problem better, let's look at another example. Suppose a machine that, at the end of cycles, enters into a discharge phase. So if we look at the pressure sensor, we would see a U-shape pattern in the last part of each cycle. By further investigation, we see that in one cycle, the pressure stays in 2 for 30 s, goes down to 1 for 5 s, and then return to 2 and remain at that level for 9 s. In the next cycle, we see that it stays at 2 for 70 s, goes down to 1 and stays there for 7 s, and then return to 1 and stays at that level for 7 s. Now, suppose that in the third operation cycle, at the last part of the cycle the pressure stays at 6 for 30 s, goes down to 5 and stays there for 5 s, and returns to 6, and it remains at that level for 9 s. The third pattern is an anomaly if repeated only a few times. However, motif discovery methods return all these tree patterns as motifs since they appear in the same shape in the sliding window.

4   Proposed Solution

Our solution is based on mining footprints in the cycles. An ideal method should be able to track unique patterns with different lengths and should have some tolerance in the small variations in the patterns. For instance, in the example provided in the last paragraph of the previous section, the range of values is different, but the difference is at the tolerance level.

Finding such footprints in each cycle from a sizeable raw signal is an NP-hard problem. The exhaustive solution is to move windows of varying lengths over the whole signal and make pairwise comparisons between all varying-length windows. If we could assume that footprints appear in the same size, then the solution could be solved with $O(N^2)$ comparisons. However, this is not the case, and footprints can be in different lengths.

Given the above arguments, we have no choice to seek an approximation solution for the problem. We propose to discretize the time series and then reformulate the problem into mining frequent patterns. SAX is perhaps state-of-the-art for this problem, but due to previously-mentioned reasons, SAX is not appropriate for this problem since it focuses on the shape similarity without being able to check the range of values within the shape.

To solve this problem, we propose CycleFootprint, a new algorithm for the detection of operation cycles. CycleFootprint is composed of two main parts: state transformation and mining footprints. For the first part, we propose a new method for converting signals into a sequence of states. Then we mine the discrete space of states to find footprints. After finding the positions of footprints, it is straightforward to detect cycles, since cycles are expected to be found between the two consecutive footprints.

In the following section, we describe our algorithm CycleFootprint in more detail.

5   Algorithm CycleFootprint

CycleFootprint algorithm is presented in Algorithm 1. It is composed of two modules: Timeseries2States and FootprintMiner. The input of algorithm are: x_n: time series of multiple sensors; w_{min} and w_{max}: minimum and maximum of the length of sliding window; ϵ: The minimum number of members for one state be considered valid; δ: The minimum number of cycles for being considered a valid output. a and b: The minimum and maximum length of cycle to be identified as valid.

The module Timeseries2States transforms the time series of each sensor to state sequences. Then state sequences is fed into module FootprintMiner for identification of primary cycles. The algorithm tests different sliding window sizes and various sensors. We omit those outputs where the number of cycles is lower than the threshold δ. After that, we check the correctness ratio (P) of cycles obtained for different window sizes and various sensors. The final output corresponds to the maximum P obtained within different window sizes and sensors.

In the next subsections, we describe the modules Timeseries2States and FootprintMiner.

Algorithm 1. CycleFootprint

    Input x_n, w_{min}, w_{max}, ϵ, δ, a, b
    Output: *Cycles*
1: **for** each sensor x_n **do**
2:    $s \leftarrow Timeseries2States(x_n, \epsilon)$
3:    $C_n, P_n \leftarrow FootprintMiner(s, w_{min}, w_{max}, a, b)$
4:    **for** $L = w_{min}$ to w_{max} **do**
5:        **if** $|C_n^L| < \delta$ **then**
6:            $P_n^L \leftarrow 0$
7:        **end if**
8:    **end for**
9: **end for**
10: $L', n' \leftarrow max(P)$
11: $Cycles \leftarrow C_{n'}^{L'}$

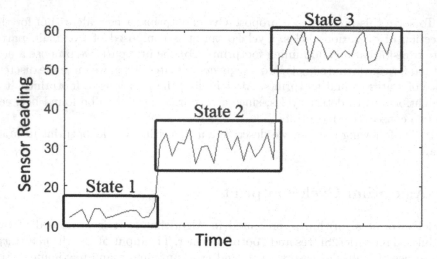

Fig. 3. A principle idea behind our discretization approach. Our method applies to whole signal and we do not assume any specific distribution, contrary to methods such as PAA.

5.1 Transformation of Signal to State Sequences

Due to previously mentioned reasons, we cannot use popular time-series discretization methods such as Piecewise Aggregate Approximation (PAA) [5]. Besides, we want to keep our approach non-parametric. Any assumption about the distribution of data can lead to poor performance if it is not met for some reason.

The architecture of our method is not window-based like SAX. We believe that since the measurements are in a finite range, a global approach should work better.

We use this principle that in a time series that measurements vary in a finite range, the values normally stay within a particular group of ranges. If we somehow manage to identify those meaningful ranges, then we can allocate each range group a number representing that state. Then the transformation of time series is just to read elements and put their corresponding state at each instant. Figure 3 illustrates the idea. The time series in the figure has 55 instants, but it turns out that the values are with three principal ranges of (10–15), (25–35), and (50–60). So our state transformation method converts this time series to [1, 2, 3], each number representing one state. In the following, we introduce algorithm Timeseries2State, and describe how it finds meaningful range groups and subsequently transform time series to state sequences.

Algoritm Timeseries2States. Algorithm Timeseries2States (Algorithm 2) transforms any time series x into state sequences s. The algorithm has one input in addition to x, and that is ϵ, which is a parameter that allows the user to control the minimum number of required members belonging to one state. For instance, if we find a specific range that has matching members lower than ϵ that would not be considered as a basis for forming a state, and the corresponding elements simply will be ignored.

We first start by re-scaling the time series (line 4) using floor operator over min-max normalization with a range of (1, 3). So, any value in time series is converted to either 1, 2, or 3. The rationale behind this choice is that one reserves the places for low measurements, two for median quantities, and 3 for large values.

After [1, 2, 3] transformation we count the number of elements whose corresponding transformed value is either 1, 2 or 3 (line 5). Afterward, we select two minority counts. For instance, assuming the number of 1, 2, 3 are respectively repeated 100, 50, and 20 times, we operate only on those elements in x that their corresponding projection is either 2 or 3. Then, if the count was upper than a pre-defined threshold ϵ we create a state and allocate those elements to that state. Otherwise, we simply ignore those elements. Then we replace elements corresponding to minority groups (in above example 2 and 3) with NaN.

We repeat this procedure iteratively until all elements of x become NaN. $y \in [1, .., d]$ keeps the state sequences. The final step (line18) accounts for converting y to s by keeping only non-repeating elements. For instance, state sequence such as 122233334 is transformed to 1234 at this step. This is a crucial part that allows us to find semantic footprints, i.e., footprints like the example that are similar but appear in different lengths.

Algorithm 2. TimeSeries2States

    Input x, ϵ
    Output s
1:   $d \leftarrow 0$
2:   $y \leftarrow zeros(size(x))$
3:   **while** x is not empty **do**
4:      $z = 1 + floor(\frac{2(x - min(x))}{max(x) - min(x)})$
5:      $c \leftarrow sort(count(unique(z)))$
6:      $r_1 \leftarrow$ corresponding elements to $c(1)$
7:      $r_2 \leftarrow$ corresponding elements to $c(2)$
8:      **if** $|r_1| \geq \epsilon$ **then**
9:          $d \leftarrow d + 1$
10:        $y(r_1) = d$
11:     **end if**
12:     **if** $|r_2| \geq \epsilon$ **then**
13:        $d \leftarrow d + 1$
14:        $y(r_2) = d$
15:     **end if**
16:     Replace elements in x with NaN for elements r_1 and r_2
17: **end while**
18: **for** each element y_i in y **do**
19:     **if** $y_i \neq y_{i+1}$ **then**
20:        Append y_i to s
21:     **end if**
22: **end for**

5.2   Mining Footprints

Converting time series to state sequences allows us to work in discrete space and develop efficient methods for mining footprints. For this purpose, we use a sliding window approach over state sequences and test windows of different sizes to find our footprints of interest.

We form a word from the observed states in each window (e.g., ABCDE or ABABA for window length of 5). Among all words obtained from sliding windows, we look for words that contain more information. For instance, ABCDE is preferred over ABABA because it includes five unique states, while ABABA contains two unique states. Patterns such as ABABA usually cannot be footprints. Instead, they are non-interesting parts of signals (like a fixed line with some little deviations). Good footprints usually are sub-segments of the signal that have more variance.

After removing less informative words (like the ABABA in the above examples), we convert each word to an order-blind pattern. For instance, ABCDE and BCDEA both will be converted to ABCDE. Similarly, CDEFH and DEFHC are converted to CDEFH (unique letters, without considering the order of states). This step is designed to merge similar patterns that have some shifts. For instance, ABCDE and BCDEA probably refer to the same concept, only with one shift.

Afterward, we count the number of the appearance of the order-blind patterns and pick the most repeated one. For instance, if ABCDE is repeated 150 times and CDEFH is repeated 80 times, we pick ABCDE. This is the point that we realize that our footprints should contain letters of A, B, C, D, and E.

In the next step, we revisit the sliding windows and look for words that contain A, B, C, D, and E. For instance, ABCDE, BEACD both match the condition. So we count the number of occurrences of these two candidates and pick the most frequent one. For example, if ABCDE is repeated 200 times and BEACD occurs 190 times, ABCDE is our footprint. This step is designed to pick the best ordering among similar patterns that differ only in order.

After we found our footprints, we find their positions in the original signal. Then the initial list of cycles is assumed to be those periods between two consecutive footprints. However, from domain knowledge, we might know that a valid cycle should have a specific length. If we apply this condition, we can estimate how many cycles fail to pass this condition. Then, we can obtain the ratio of valid cycles (hereafter we call it cycle correctness ratio) to initial cycles, which is an excellent criterion to verify the correctness of our cycle mining process.

The rationale behind the usefulness of correction ratio is that in the ideal cycle detection scenario, all cycles (accuracy of 100%) should match the length criterion (e.g., in our application context cycles should be greater than 2 min and lower than 2 h). This is against a random cycle detector, which probably generates lots of cycles that are out of length condition. Hence, the ratio of valid cycles is an excellent factor to look at when choosing the right signal or window size.

To find the final cycles, we test different window sizes and signals and compute the cycle correctness factor to pick the one that gives the most accurate cycles.

In the following, we describe the algorithm in more detail.

FootprintMiner Algorithm. FootprintMiner Algorithm is presented in Algorithm 3. The algorithm receives four inputs: s: state sequence vector obtained from Timeseries2States process; w_{min} and w_{max}: Minimum and maximum length of sliding windows; a, and b: minimum and maximum length of a valid cycle.

At line 2 we begin by moving a sliding window of varying length L (from w_{min} to w_{max}) over state sequences s. At line 4 we a create a word of length L from states observed at window w. At the next line we obtain the unique characters from S_w^L.

At lines 6–11 we check if there is more informative word comparing already observed ones. If the new observed word has more unique characters than previously observed words so far, we forget all words and start recording from the current window.

At lines 14–17 we first obtain the most frequent order-blind patterns and then look for words containing letters of that pattern. Among the matched words, we pick up the most frequent word.

Algorithm 3. FootprintMiner

Input s, w_{min}, w_{max}, a, b
Output: C, P

1: $mx^L \leftarrow 0, L \in \{w_{min}, .., w_{max}\}$
2: **for** each sliding window w over s **do**
3:     **for** $L = w_{min}$ to w_{max} **do**
4:         $S_w^L \leftarrow s(w . w + L - 1)$
5:         $M_w^L \leftarrow \text{Unique}(S_w^L)$
6:         **if** $count(M_w^L) > mx^L$ **then**
7:             $mx^L \leftarrow count(M_w^L)$
8:             Empty S_w^L, M_w^L
9:             $S_w^L \leftarrow s(w : w + L - 1)$
10:            $M_w^L \leftarrow \text{Unique}(S_w^L)$
11:         **end if**
12:     **end for**
13: **end for**
14: **for** $L = w_{min}$ to w_{max} **do**
15:     $T^L \leftarrow$ words in S^L that contain unique states corresponding to most frequent M^L
16:     $F^L \leftarrow$ Search positions in s that correspond to most frequent T^L
17: **end for**
18: **for** $L = w_{min}$ to w_{max} **do**
19:     **for** each element F_i^L in F^L **do**
20:         $Ri^L \leftarrow x(F_i^L : F_{i+1}^L)$
21:         **if** $a < |Ri^L| < b$ **then**
22:             Append R_i^L to C^L
23:         **end if**
24:         $P^L = |C^L|/|R^L|$
25:     **end for**
26: **end for**

Finally, at lines 14–25, we first obtain the initial cycles and then compute the correctness ratio by applying the expected length condition.

The algorithm ends with returning the obtained cycles (C) and cycle correctness ratio (P) for all window sizes.

6   Experimental Evaluation

6.1   Dataset

The dataset includes historical data of multiple health monitoring sensors installed on a fuel separator in operation on a ship. Fuel separators remove oil and unwanted particles using centrifugal process. The sensors measure parameters such as water transducer, various temperatures, outlet/inlet/drain pressures, bowl speed, etc. The studied data corresponds to almost two months between Feb 2020 to April 2020, sampled at a frequency of 1 s, which makes 17 signals of length 5,324,858.

6.2   Configuration

We set the following parameters for CycleFootprint algorithm. $\epsilon = 5$, $\delta = 100$, $w_{min} = 4$, $w_{min} = 20$, $a = 120$, $b = 8000$.

6.3   Results

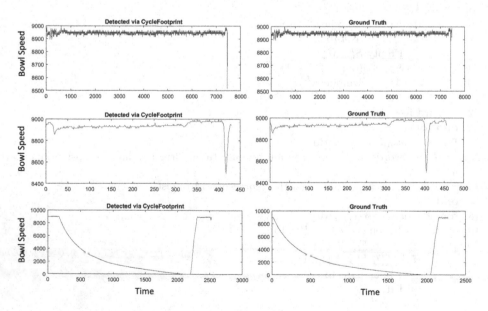

Fig. 4. Examples of detected cycle via Cyclefootprint (left) vs. ground truth (right)

Table 1 shows the output of CycleFootprint algorithm for different sensors on the separator dataset. The first column refers to the extracted footprints. Each state is represented with a number with three digits with leading zeros for lower quantities than 100 and 10. For instance, 013014015017 should be read as [13, 14, 15, 17]. The second column of the table contains the number of total found cycles. The third column presents the number of valid cycles after applying the length condition. L is the size of the window. The fifth column also shows the unique states in the footprint. Finally, P represents the cycle correctness ratio.

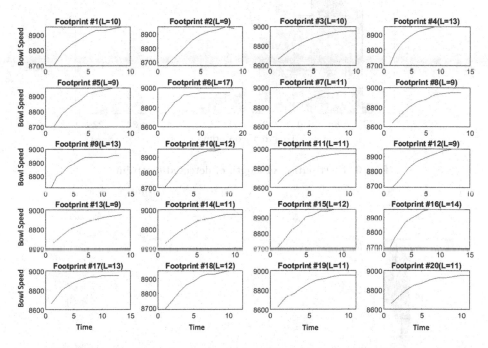

Fig. 5. Example of semantic footprints detected by pattern [8, 10] on bowl speed sensor via CycleFootprint algorithm.

The interesting observation is that the algorithm has been able to find relevant signals, which was identified by the domain expert, the most relevant signals for cycle identification. Out of $340 = 17 \times 20$ tested scenarios (17 sensors by 20 window sizes), we find 24 unique footprints. Among them, "Bowl Speed" with a window length of 6 has produced 236 valid cycles, out of 303 total cycles, which makes the correction ratio of 77.88%. Therefore, the states' segment [8, 10] on bowl speed sensor is the selected footprint. Figure 5 illustrates some footprints discovered by this pattern. As we can see, our method can detect semantic footprints, in the sense that they can be in different length (See the range of lengths in Fig. 6). If we rely only on same-length footprints, then probably we will lose lots of true cycles.

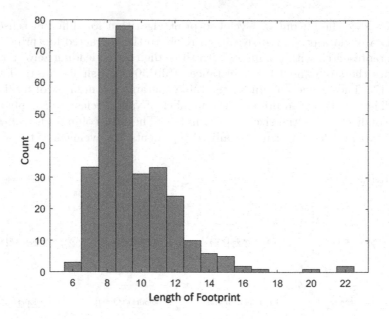

Fig. 6. Distribution of length of detected footprints

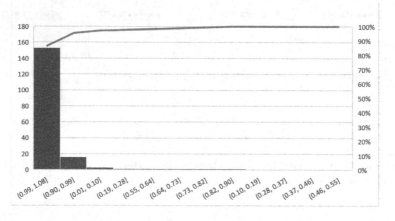

Fig. 7. Accuracy of cycle detection according to ground truth

Comparing the cycles obtained by this footprint with ground truth, we find that the majority of cycles match with the true cycles. Figure 7 shows the recovery ratio of extracted cycles comparing ground truth. Almost 86% of cycles have a full or at least 99% match with ground truth. 9% of cycles reconstruct the cycles in ground truth with coverage of 90–99%, and the rest 5% partially cover some cycles in the ground truth. Figure 4 illustrates some examples from extracted cycles versus their corresponding ones in the ground truth.

Table 1. Output of CycleFootprint Algorithm on Separator dataset

Footprint	TotalCycles	ValidCycles	L	Unique	P
Outlet Pressure					
013014015017	12854	792	4	4	0.061615061
010013014015017	3864	1033	5	5	0.267339545
010013014015017018	1400	688	6	6	0.491428571
010013014015017018019	278	167	7	7	0.600719424
010013014015017018019020	35	7	8	8	0.2
Inlet Pressure					
017018019020	1491	310	4	4	0.207914152
017018019020021	16	5	5	5	0.3125
012013014016017018019020021	2	1	13	9	0.5
012013014016017018019020021	3	1	14	9	0.333333333
012013014016017018019020021	4	1	15	9	0.25
012013014016017018019020021	5	1	16	9	0.2
012013014016017018019020021	6	1	17	9	0.166666667
012013014016017018019020021	7	1	18	9	0.142857143
012013014016017018019020021	8	1	19	9	0.125
012013014016017018019020021	9	1	20	9	0.111111111
Drain Pressure					
013014016019	3396	601	4	4	0.176972909
013014016019020	406	32	5	5	0.078817734
005007009011013015	42	17	6	6	0.404761905
003005007009011013015	37	16	7	7	0.432432432
Water Transducer					
012014015018	6567	1183	4	4	0.18014314
012014015017018	398	283	5	5	0.711055276
012014015017018020	23	13	6	6	0.565217391
Bowl Speed					
013014015016	2407	1796	4	4	0.746157042
011013014015016	593	387	5	5	0.652613828
008010012014015016	303	236	6	6	**0.778877888**
008010012013014015016	226	127	7	7	0.561946903
008010011012013014015016	133	49	8	8	0.368421053
008009010011012013014015016	16	2	9	9	0.125
001003005006008010012013014015	10	1	10	10	0.1
003005006008009010011012013014015	9	1	12	12	0.111111111
Temperature					
007008009010011012013014015	3	1	11	9	0.333333333

7   Conclusion

We introduce a new approximation method based on mining footprints for the detection of operation cycles from the historical time series of multiple sensors. Our experimental evaluation on a real separator in marine shows that our method can detect the majority of right cycles with good coverage, i.e., in 86% of cycles full or at least 99% recovery.

Our method is a general solution that can be used for any kind of machine operation that is composed of a time series with a finite range. The time series of interest can be discrete (e.g., count), continues, and with any distribution. Our method, however, does not apply to time-series that the range of values is infinite or time series with weak periodic behavior.

This is an under development study. We still need to evaluate the proposed method on larger scales, as well as other settings and machines. The next step is to separate regular cycles from abnormal and neutral states using spectral models (e.g., [1]). Our ultimate goal is to learn the normal state of all machines, making a semi-supervised model, and transfer the summarized models/dictionaries to sensor devices for real-time anomaly detection.

References

1. Fanaee-T, H., Oliveira, M.D., Gama, J., Malinowski, S., Morla, R.: Event and anomaly detection using tucker3 decomposition. arXiv preprint arXiv:1406.3266 (2014)
2. Fu, T.C.: A review on time series data mining. Eng. Appl. Artif. Intell. **24**(1), 164–181 (2011)
3. Jin, X., Wang, Y., Chow, T.W., Sun, Y.: MD-based approaches for system health monitoring: a review. IET Sci. Measur. Technol. **11**(4), 371–379 (2017)
4. Jin, X., Zhao, M., Chow, T.W., Pecht, M.: Motor bearing fault diagnosis using trace ratio linear discriminant analysis. IEEE Trans. Ind. Electron. **61**(5), 2441–2451 (2013)
5. Keogh, E., Chakrabarti, K., Pazzani, M., Mehrotra, S.: Dimensionality reduction for fast similarity search in large time series databases. Knowl. Inf. Syst. **3**(3), 263–286 (2001)
6. Laskov, P., Düssel, P., Schäfer, C., Rieck, K.: Learning intrusion detection: supervised or unsupervised? In: Roli, F., Vitulano, S. (eds.) ICIAP 2005. LNCS, vol. 3617, pp. 50–57. Springer, Heidelberg (2005). https://doi.org/10.1007/11553595_6
7. Lin, J.: Finding motifs in time series. In: Proceedings of Workshop on Temporal Data Mining, pp. 53–68 (2002)
8. Torkamani, S., Lohweg, V.: Survey on time series motif discovery. Wiley Interdisc. Rev.: Data Mining Knowl. Discov. **7**(2), e1199 (2017)
9. Yeh, C.C.M., et al.: Matrix profile i: all pairs similarity joins for time series: a unifying view that includes motifs, discords and shapelets. In: 2016 IEEE 16th International Conference on Data Mining (ICDM), pp. 1317–1322. IEEE (2016)
10. Yeh, C.-C.M., et al.: Time series joins, motifs, discords and shapelets: a unifying view that exploits the matrix profile. Data Mining Knowl. Discov. **32**(1), 83–123 (2017). https://doi.org/10.1007/s10618-017-0519-9

Valve Health Identification Using Sensors and Machine Learning Methods

M. Atif Qureshi[1,2] , Luis Miralles-Pechuán[1,2](✉) , Jason Payne[3],
Ronan O'Malley[3], and Brian Mac Namee[1]

[1] Ireland's Centre for Applied AI (CeADAR), University College Dublin,
Dublin, Ireland
{luis.miralles,brian.macnamee}@ucd.ie
[2] Technological University Dublin, Dublin, Ireland
muhammadatif.qureshi@tudublin.ie
[3] Wood, Galway Technology Park, Parkmore, Galway, Ireland
{jason.payne,ronan.omalley}@woodplc.com

Abstract. Predictive maintenance models attempt to identify developing issues with industrial equipment before they become critical. In this paper, we describe both supervised and unsupervised approaches to predictive maintenance for subsea valves in the oil and gas industry. The supervised approach is appropriate for valves for which a long history of operation along with manual assessments of the state of the valves exists, while the unsupervised approach is suitable to address the cold start problem when new valves, for which we do not have an operational history, come online.

For the supervised prediction problem, we attempt to distinguish between healthy and unhealthy valve actuators using sensor data measuring hydraulic pressures and flows during valve opening and closing events. Unlike previous approaches that solely rely on raw sensor data, we derive frequency and time domain features, and experiment with a range of classification algorithms and different feature subsets. The performing models for the supervised approach were discovered to be Adaboost and Random Forest ensembles.

In the unsupervised approach, the goal is to detect sudden abrupt changes in valve behaviour by comparing the sensor readings from consecutive opening or closing events. Our novel methodology doing this essentially works by comparing the sequences of sensor readings captured during these events using both raw sensor readings, as well as normalised and first derivative versions of the sequences. We evaluate the effectiveness of a number of well-known time series similarity measures and find that using discrete Frechet distance or dynamic time warping leads to the best results, with the Bray-Curtis similarity measure leading to only marginally poorer change detection but requiring considerably less computational effort.

Keywords: Time-series · Classification · Anomaly detection · Predictive maintenance models · Sensor data

M. Atif Qureshi and L. Miralles-Pechuán equally contributed to this work.

© Springer Nature Switzerland AG 2020
J. Gama et al. (Eds.): ITEM 2020/IoT Streams 2020, CCIS 1325, pp. 45–60, 2020.
https://doi.org/10.1007/978-3-030-66770-2_4

1   Introduction

Predictive maintenance models attempt to identify developing issues with industrial equipment before they become critical [1]. In this paper, we explore predictive maintenance tasks for subsea valves in the oil and gas industry. A valve is a key component in any industrial piping system. Valves are used to regulate the flow of fluids in one direction by opening and closing passageways. To monitor the status of valves each time they are opened or closed a suite of sensors measure volumes and pressures within the valve during the event. These measurements generate a multivariate time series that describes the behaviour of the valve during the opening or closing event.

In this paper, we present strategies to identify the state of a valve following an opening or closing event, using both supervised and unsupervised machine learning methods. In the supervised scenario, we classify valves as *healthy* or *unhealthy* following an opening or closing event based on the sensor data generated during the event. We are concerned with benchmarking the performance of different supervised machine learning algorithms and data representations for this classification task. In particular, our proposed data representation methods are able to extract frequency and time domain features from raw sensor data, increasing the accuracy, which is critical in this scenario.

In the unsupervised scenario, we propose a strategy for anomaly detection by capturing sudden or abrupt changes in valve behaviour. To achieve this, we contrast consecutive readings from a sensor for the same event (open or close), by calculating the distance between the readings. We make use of a number of popular time-series similarity measures, such as dynamic time warping, symbolic aggregate approximation and discrete Frechet distance, and evaluate their suitability for this task. The novelty of our investigation stems from the various signal transformations, such as normalisation and derivative calculations, prior to calculating distances.

The rest of the paper is organised as follows. In Sect. 2, we review the current state of the art in predictive maintenance, examining classification techniques, time series similarity measures, and anomaly detection. In Sect. 3, we discuss the dataset and derived features sets used in this paper. In Sect. 4 and Sect. 5, we present the supervised and unsupervised approaches, respectively, along with the results of experiments that were conducted to evaluate these approaches. Finally, in Sect. 6, conclusions and directions for future work are discussed.

2   Related Work

In an environment of lower oil prices, companies in the international energy sector are exploring new ways to reduce the cost of condition-based monitoring services for operating equipment such as subsea valves and actuators. This is being done through the development of models that can simulate the thought processes of experienced hardware engineers and automate or semi-automate the condition-based monitoring process.

Maintenance and intervention for energy assets, typically require costly down-time, deferred energy production and very expensive resources [2]. Tracking the health of equipment from design and installation through to early indicators of functional degradation is important as it enables cost-effective planning of maintenance and intervention programs. Hence, there is a pressing need to build predictive models that identify the state of equipment, determining its health and predicting possible failures as early as possible (or even before that happens).

Various techniques have been proposed for predictive maintenance tasks in the oil and gas industry, despite it being a relatively new concept [3]. A broad categorisation of methods reveals two categories: model-based methods and pattern recognition methods [4]. Model-based methods utilise mathematical calculations and involve a manual analysis of the parameter values measured during the monitoring time and their comparison with the nominal power curve of every oil pump [5]. The more modern pattern recognition methods typically involve the use of sensor data and their working principle is based on the intuition that different system faults initiate different patterns of evolution of the interested variables [6]. These are the patterns that data-driven machine learning methods aim to capture. The model-based methods are, unfortunately, still based on the approximated statistical distribution model, and significant uncertainty is involved in the interpretation of the results [3]. This led the community to investigate artificial intelligence approaches for signal-based fault detection with commonly used techniques, including Artificial Neural Networks, regression models, and Bayesian models [7].

At the same time, a different class of fault detection utilises techniques from the domain of anomaly detection whereby patterns that do not conform to expected behaviour are detected, and extracted [8]. Anomaly detection approaches are particularly suited in scenarios where there is a lack of labelled datasets from the sensor signals, such as ongoing oil and gas operations. Among unsupervised methods, estimates on remaining useful life are also modelled as gradual change detection strategies for predictive maintenance [9].

Our paper particularly concerns benchmarking the performance of different supervised machine learning algorithms with a special focus on the extraction of derived features. Additionally, we also focus on unsupervised learning and especially anomaly detection based fault identification of valve failures. Since our data is essentially time-series data, we essentially capture the anomalies by calculating the distance between signals through the application of time-series similarity metrics. The distance metrics we investigated include dynamic time warping (DTW) [10], symbolic aggregate approximation (SAX) [11], Bray-Curtis [12] and Frechet distance [13].

3   Data

In this section, we first describe the dataset used throughout this paper and how it was labelled. We then discuss the derived feature sets that were created from this original dataset.

3.1   Dataset Description

The dataset used in this paper is based on monitoring 583 subsea valves over multiple years. The valves are owned by BP (www.bp.com), one of the world's leading integrated oil and gas companies, and the monitoring is supported by Wood (www.woodplc.com), an international energy services company. During the time that the valves were monitored, there was a total of 6,658 open (48.87%) and close (51.12%) events. Each time an event (a valve being opened or closed) takes place, the state of the valve is captured by three different sensors. Sensors 1 and 3 measure pressure, and sensor 2 cumulative volume. During the event, each sensor records 120 readings at regular intervals. This results in three time series (one for each sensor) for each event. Figure 1 (a) shows two examples of the sensor readings for two different closing events.

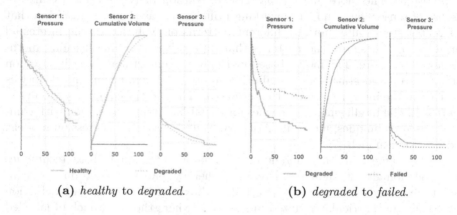

(a) *healthy* to *degraded*.   (b) *degraded* to *failed*.

Fig. 1. Usage of distance metric as an anomaly detector.

As part of the on-going monitoring of these valves engineers review visualisations similar to Fig. 1 (a) and label the current state of the valve as one of the three possible classes: *healthy*, *degraded*, or *failed*. The *healthy* class represents that the valve is performing within the optimal condition, the *degraded* class represents that the valve's performance has declined from the optimal condition but is still functioning, and the *failed* class represents that the valve has failed to perform the basic function and should be replaced. In Fig. 1 (a), one set of readings represents a *healthy* valve and the other represents a *degraded* valve. The difference is most apparent from the sensor 2 readings because the abrupt change of the slope on the top of the healthy signal is transformed into a gradual curvature with smooth transitions in the degraded signal.

The total number of instances in the dataset is 6,658, where 6,232 (93.6%) are *healthy*, 122 (1.83%) are *degraded*, and 304 (4.56%) are *failed*. And each instance represents 120 captured points for sensor 1, sensor 2, and sensor 3, and the category of the output (*healthy, degraded, or failed*). Due to the fact that degraded and failed valves were quickly replaced the number of instances belonging to these categories is very low compared to the number of healthy valves. This results in a highly imbalanced dataset, which is common in predictive maintenance scenarios where *healthy* instances tend to dominate.

3.2   Time and Frequency Domain Features

To make the classification task more accurate, we extracted a set of time and frequency domain derived features from the raw sensor signals. Feature extraction techniques have been shown repeatedly to make classification tasks easier [14,15]. Table 1 shows the time domain features which were extracted. Table 2 shows the frequency domain features which were calculated after applying a fast Fourier transform (FFT) [14,15] on the raw data generated from each of the three sensors. Derived features were calculated independently for the time series arising from each of the three sensors.

Table 1. Time domain features applied over the 120 data points generated by each sensor.

Features	Description
$\sigma(X)$	The standard deviation of the signal
$\overline{X}$	The mean of the signal
$\|X\|$	The mean of the absolute of the signal
$\|\tilde{X}\|$	The absolute value of the median of the signal
$\|Var(X)\|$	The variance of the absolute of the signal
$\|max(X)/min(X)\|$	The absolute value of the ratio of the maximum to the minimum of the signal
$max(X)$	The maximum value of the signal
$min(X)$	The minimum value of the signal
$maxInd(X)$	The index of maximum value of the signal
$minInd$	The index of the minimum value of the signal
$rms(X)$	The root mean square value of the signal
$zcr(X)$	The zero-crossing rate of the signal
$skew(X)s$	The skewness of the signal
$kurtosis(X)$	The kurtosis of the signal
$P_1(X)$	The first percentile of the signal
$P_3(X)$	The third percentile of the signal
$IQR(X)$	The interquartile range of the signal
$acf(X)$	The autocorrelation of the signal.

3.3   Signal Transformations

As well as calculating derived features, which are primarily used with the supervised approaches in our experiments, we also performed a set of transformations of the signals. The transformations were used to normalise the signals and take their first derivative. The first derivative is calculated by taking the first-order discrete difference across the sequential 120 points in a signal. This captures the rate of change that takes place across the signals (one for each sensor). We normalise the original signals by applying range normalisation [16], where each signal is linearly scaled to the range $(0, 1)$.

Table 2. Frequency domain features applied over the fast Fourier transform on the 120 data points generated by each sensor.

Features	Description
$\lVert FFT(X) \rVert$	The mean of the absolute of the FFT is calculated
$\lVert FF\tilde{T}(X) \rVert$	The absolute of the media of the FFT is calculated
$rms(FFT(X))$	The root mean square value of the FFT is calculated
$S(FFT(X))$	The entropy of the FFT is calculated
$\eta(FFT(X))$	The Shannon Entropy of the FFT is calculated
$flatness(FFT(X))$	The spectral flatness of the FFT is calculated
$\circ(FFT(X))$	The mode of the FFT is calculated
$\omega_p(FFT(X))$	The peak frequency of the FFT is calculated

4   Classifying Valve States

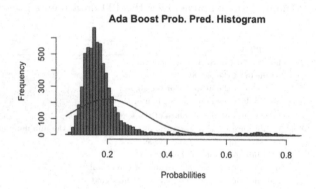

Fig. 2. The distribution of classification scores across the cross-validation experiment for the AdaBoost classifier using the 'Derived' features.

In this section, we present a supervised prediction approach to distinguish between healthy and unhealthy valves using sensor data. In this experiment we reduced the set of target values in the dataset to binary classes by combining the *degraded* and *failed* classes into a new class called *unhealthy*. This is done to addresses the issue of class imbalance within the dataset (see Sect. 3.1).

In a benchmark experiment we seek to find the best performing classification model and data representation for this task. We consider nine different classification algorithms: support vector machines (SVM) [17], decision trees (C5.0) [18], k-nearest neighbour algorithms (kNN) [19], random forest ensembles (RF) [20], boosted ensembles (AdaBoost) [21], a deep learning gradient boosting machines (GBM) which is a H2O's implementation of GBM using distributed trees [22,23], gradient boosting (Xgb) [24], multi-layer perceptrons (NNet) [25], and a deep feed-forward networks (DL) [26]. We explored three different data representations: '*Raw*' representing the original raw data from three sensors, '*Derived*' representing the set of features explained in Tables 1 and 2, and '*Combined*' which is a combination of both 'Raw' and 'Derived'.

Table 3. Full benchmark with leaving-15-out strategy. The *, **, and *** show the top one, two, and three ranked in each column, respectively.

Features	Model	Spec	Precision	F1$_{score}$	AUC	Time(Sec)
Derived	AdaBoost	***0.9974	***0.9420	***0.8112	*0.9900	86.63
Derived	RF	0.9973	0.9397	*0.8191	**0.9887	7.64
Derived	DL Gbm	0.9974	0.9396	0.7905	***0.9881	81.24
Derived	C5	0.9965	0.9160	0.7655	0.9841	17.31
Combined	RF	0.9968	0.9145	0.7145	0.9823	73.54
Combined	C5	0.9968	0.9228	0.7660	0.9819	236.08
Combined	DL Gbm	0.9974	0.9396	0.7905	0.9806	474.31
Combined	AdaBoost	0.9971	0.9348	0.8050	0.9805	940.63
Raw	RF	0.9961	0.8966	0.6969	0.9779	58.67
Raw	DL Gbm	0.9947	0.8850	0.7791	0.9770	516.40
Raw	C5	0.9960	0.8884	0.6757	0.9763	234.20
Raw	AdaBoost	0.9961	0.8961	0.6946	0.9687	882.33
Raw	NNet	0.9918	0.7583	0.5556	0.9466	21.79
Combined	NNet	0.9937	0.8274	0.6328	0.9451	26.13
Raw	Gbm	0.9871	0.7173	0.6266	0.9228	5.33
Derived	NNet	0.9957	0.9069	0.8030	0.9165	25.85
Derived	Gbm	0.9919	0.6324	0.3433	0.9158	0.85
Combined	Gbm	0.9913	0.6516	0.3884	0.9034	6.00
Derived	kNN	0.9969	0.9333	**0.8185	0.8757	3.22
Raw	kNN	0.9953	0.8953	0.7726	0.8675	17.53
Combined	kNN	0.9942	0.8800	0.7940	0.8525	8.76
Combined	Xgb	**0.9976	**0.9436	0.7956	0.8426	3.64
Derived	Xgb	*0.9981	*0.9537	0.7917	0.8374	0.53
Raw	SVM	0.0047	0.0527	0.0998	0.8142	356.01
Combined	SVM	0.0127	0.0495	0.0937	0.7732	286.40
Raw	Xgb	0.9965	0.9009	0.6814	0.7722	3.40
Raw	DL	0.9775	0.8941	0.5276	0.6759	541.61
Derived	DL	0.9742	0.9258	0.5219	0.6688	459.35
Derived	SVM	0.0023	0.0507	0.0960	0.6247	478.72
Combined	DL	0.9566	0.7565	0.3459	0.5904	43.37

The parameter values were selected after performing grid-search to tune the hyper-parameters over the 10-fold cross-validation [24]. After this process, the models were implemented in R Studio with the following configurations: SVM (method = "C-classification", kernel = "linear"), C5.0 (trials = 100, winnow = TRUE, model = "tree"), kNN (k = 3, probability = TRUE, algorithm = "cover tree"), RF (ntree = 450, norm.votes = FALSE), AdaBoost (mfinal = 300, maxdepth = 5, coeflearn = "Zhu"), NNet (size = 21, rang = 0.01, decay = 5e-4, maxit = 500), DL Gbm (ntrees = 2500, learn rate = 0.001, sample rate = 0.7, max depth = 15, col sample rate = 0.8), DL NN (activation = "Tanh", balance classes = TRUE, hidden = c(100, 100, 100), epochs = 3, rate = 0.1, rate annealing = 0.01), Xgb (booster = "gbtree", eval metric = "auc", eta = 0.02, max depth = 15, subsample = .8, colsample bytree = .87, min child weight = 1, scale pos weight = 1).

The signals represent independent events when a valve was opened or closed. Therefore there are no dependencies between the instances. Additionally, there are only 120 points, which is a very small number for applying a time window. To evaluate the performance of each algorithm-data representation combination, we performed a leave-n-subjects-out cross-validation experiment [27]. We chose this evaluation strategy as each of the 583 valves represented in our dataset appears multiple times in the 6,648 events. This means that in a standard k-fold cross-validation experiment events from the same valve would be likely to appear in both the train and test sets which could lead to an overly optimistic assessment of model performance. Specifically, we use all events from 15 valves as the test set in each fold of the cross-validation which leads to 39 folds. We measure the performance of models using macro-averaged F1 score [28] and area under the ROC curve (AUC) [29]. Table 3 shows the results of the complete benchmark ordered by AUC scores. We also show the time taken to perform the leave-n-subjects-out cross-validation experiment in each case.

As can be seen from Table 3, the Adaboost and Random Forest ensembles using the 'Derived' features outperform the other models in terms of AUC. In the operational context, in which these models are likely to be deployed, the goal is to ensure the detection of more true *unhealthy* valves even if some *healthy* valves are incorrectly predicted as *unhealthy*. There are scenarios in which reducing the errors of one class is more important than doing so in the other classes. For example, it is better to diagnose a patient with cancer when he or she is healthy than the opposite case. Likewise, for our problem, we want to avoid predicting valves as healthy if they are not. And as some authors suggest [30], a class can be prioritised by applying a threshold. In other words, we can tune the classification threshold to reduce the number of false negatives while still predicting a reasonable number of true negatives.

Table 4. Best cut-off parameter for AdaBoost leaving 15 valves out. SUM represents the summation of sensitivity and specificity. According to the established criteria to minimise the errors in both classes, we select the threshold where SUM gets the higher value.

Cut-off	AUC	Acc	Sens	Spec	Prec	F1$_\text{score}$	TP	FP	FN	TN	SUM
0.300	0.9879	0.9675	0.9351	0.9697	0.6730	0.7827	389	189	27	6040	1.9048
0.295	0.9879	0.9657	0.9351	0.9677	0.6593	0.7733	389	201	27	6031	1.9028
0.290	0.9879	0.9636	0.9447	0.9649	0.6422	0.7646	393	219	23	6013	1.9096
0.285	**0.9879**	**0.9607**	**0.9519**	**0.9613**	**0.6217**	**0.7522**	**396**	**241**	**20**	**5991**	**1.9132**
0.280	0.9879	0.9571	0.9519	0.9575	0.5991	0.7354	396	265	20	5967	1.9094
0.275	0.9879	0.9528	0.9567	0.9525	0.5735	0.7171	398	296	18	5936	1.9092
0.270	0.9879	0.9495	0.9591	0.9488	0.5557	0.7037	399	319	17	5913	1.9079

This issue is illustrated in Fig. 2, which shows the distribution of classification scores across the cross-validation experiment for the AdaBoost classifier. Most classification scores are close to 0.2, the default classification threshold is 0.5, but better performance can probably be achieved with a different value. We use a criterion to select the best classification threshold value by maximising the sum of specificity and sensitivity as described in [31]. Table 4 shows the results of setting different cut-off values for AdaBoost, where the area-under-the-curve, accuracy, sensitivity, specificity, precision, F1-score, true positives, false positives, false negatives, and true negatives are shown. As can be seen from the results, we are able to tune the classification threshold value while minimising false positives and yet maximising true negatives. According to the established criteria to minimise the errors in both classes, we select the threshold where *SUM* gets the higher value.

The overall results of this experiment show that it is possible to classify valve states to a high level of accuracy and balance false alarms with detecting actual defects. This approach should work well in operational contexts in which valves in operation are of a similar model and operate under similar conditions to those in the labelled training set. This is the case in many scenarios. There is, however, a *cold start* problem in other scenarios in which valves that are new or that will operate under unique conditions are deployed. The supervised learning approach will not work in these scenarios. The next section describes an unsupervised anomaly detection approach that addresses this scenario.

5 Detecting Anomalous Valve Behaviour

If new valve types come online or valves are put into operation in contexts very different from what has been seen before, the supervised approach to recognising valve health will not work as the data generated by these new valves will be so different to what has been seen before. This is what we refer to as the *cold start problem*. Instead, an unsupervised approach is more appropriate. To detect anomalous behaviour in valves we calculate the distance between signals over consecutive events from the same valve and flag an anomaly when this distance is sufficiently large. Performing this anomaly detection, therefore, requires selecting an appropriate distance metric to compare consecutive signals, and then thresholding this signal to flag anomalies. Figure 3(a) shows an example with the distance between readings R_3 and R_2 highlighted by the bi-directional arrows. Figure 3(b) shows a typical plot of distances between consecutive signals over time.

In this section, we present two sets of experiments. First, we conduct an experiment to select the top-performing distance metrics for the anomaly detection task. Then we use the winning distance metrics from the first experiment to evaluate the feasibility of using it to perform anomaly detection. We refer to this as a feasibility study, as we currently do not implement an approach to set the threshold algorithmically but rather choose the best possible threshold for a given test dataset.

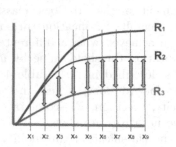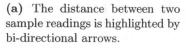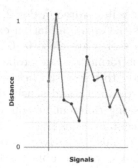

(a) The distance between two sample readings is highlighted by bi-directional arrows.

(b) The distance between consecutive signals can be used to detect anomalies.

Fig. 3. Usage of distance metric as an anomaly detector.

5.1 Effectiveness of Distance Metrics

To evaluate the suitability of different distance metrics to the kind of data we are studying, we performed a classification experiment using a 1-nearest-neighbour-classifier [19], which is known to be a robust approach for time series problems [32]. To conduct this experiment, we selected a subset of the valves in the dataset described in Sect. 3 for which at least 7 events labelled as *healthy* and one event labelled either *degraded* or *failed* existed. 11 valves matched this criterion and for these 11 valves, 389 events were present in the dataset. We randomly choose 201 of these as training examples (128 *healthy*, 61 is *degraded*, and 12 *failed*) and 188 as test examples (107 *healthy*, 68 *degraded*, and 13 *failed*). We then performed a simple experiment in which we trained 1-nn classifiers based on different distance measures on the training set and evaluated them on the test set. We measured classifier performance using F1 score. We perform these experiments independently for the time series that come from the three different sensors.

We experiment with twelve well-known distance measures that are used with time series data: Euclidean, Minkowski, Manhattan, Chebyshev, discrete Frechet [13], Bray-Curtis [12], dynamic time warping (DTW) [10], Hausdorff, Levenshtein, Canberra, SAX [11], and SAX+DTW (better explanations on these measures can be found in [16,32]). Table 5 shows the performance of different distance measures for all sensors, an average of the performance of all sensors, and the running time.

Table 5. The performance of distance metrics using raw sensor data along with running time. The *, **, and *** show the top one, two, and three ranked $F1scores$ in the column, respectively.

No.	Metric	F1$_{score}$ S.1	F1$_{score}$ S.2	F1$_{score}$ S.3	Avg-F1$_{score}$	Time(Sec)
1	DTW	*0.8677	*0.9101	*0.8307	*0.8695	4795.43
2	Hausdorff	0.7884	***0.9048	0.8148	**0.836	173.31
3	Manhattan	0.8095	0.873	**0.8254	**0.836	51.87
4	Bray-Curtis	0.8095	0.873	***0.8148	0.8324	55.96
5	Frechet-DISC	**0.8148	0.8466	***0.8148	0.8254	4310.39
6	Euclidean	0.7831	***0.9048	0.7725	0.8201	54.38
7	Minkowski	0.7831	***0.9048	0.7725	0.8201	53.31
8	SAX	0.7302	*0.9101	0.7196	0.7866	196.13
9	Canberra	0.7249	0.8783	0.7566	0.7866	53.31
10	Chebyshev	0.7778	0.8466	0.7249	0.7831	50.71
11	SAX+DTW	0.7725	0.8201	0.6402	0.7443	1172.69
12	Levenshtein	**0.8148	0.7143	0.6825	0.7372	1169.29

We can see that DTW outperforms all other distance metrics, however, this is at the expense of significant running time. For use as the basis of an anomaly detector, for each sensor and the average we selected the 3 best performing distance measures. These are: DTW, Frechet-DISC, Levenshtein, SAX, Hausdorff, Euclidean, Minkowski, Manhattan, and Bray-Curtis.

5.2   Anomaly Detection Using Distance Metrics

In this experiment, we evaluate the suitability of the distance measures, selected from the previous experiment, as the basis for an anomaly detector that captures an abrupt change in the state of a valve. For this experiment, we use the same subset of 11 valves used in the previous section. We attempt to classify each opening or closing event by each valve as *anomalous* or *normal*. To use as a gold standard for measuring performance in our experiments we mark the transitions between event labels as *anomalous* and all other events as *normal*. So, for example, when an event labelled as *degraded* follows an event labelled as *healthy* we mark that event as *anomalous*. If, however, subsequent events by the same valve are also labelled as *degraded* then they are labelled in this experiment as *normal* as the approach is designed to recognise abrupt changes in behaviour. This means that for each valve we have a series of distance measures similar to that shown in Fig. 3(b) with each point marked as *anomalous* or *normal* and measure how well this signal allows anomalous events to be separated from normal ones when it is based on different distance measures. We also experiment with applying the distance measures to the original raw sensor signals, the first derivative of the sensor signals, and range normalised versions of the sensors signals (see Sect. 3.3). In all cases, we measure the ability of an approach to detect anomalies using F1 score.

In addition to measuring the ability of our approach to capturing anomalies using just one of the three sensors we also investigate an approach that allows voting among sensors with following strategies: *(i)* If the signal from any sensor identifies an event as anomalous, it is flagged as an anomaly. *(ii)* If the signals from the majority of sensors identify an event as an anomaly, it is flagged as an anomaly. *(iii)* If the signals from all of the sensors identify an event as anomalous, it is flagged as an anomaly.

In this experiment, we do not attempt to determine thresholds algorithmically. Instead, for the signal arising from each valve, we examine all possible thresholds and report the one that leads to the highest F1 score. This indicates the best possible performance that could be achieved using a particular data representation and distance measure and is sufficient to compare the feasibility of using this approach for anomaly detection. We leave the algorithmic selection of thresholds for future work.

Table 6. The performance of anomaly detectors based on different distance metrics for valve opening and closing events when comparing the distance between the last two signals. (s), (δs), and $(norm)$ indicate that the named measure was applied to the original signal, the derivative of the original signal, or the normalised signal, respectively. The subscripts All, Maj, and S.x indicate that the anomaly detection decisions were made using all sensor agreement voting, majority voting, or only with sensor x, respectively.

Opening Events		Closing Events	
Metric	$F1_{score}$	Metric	$F1_{score}$
Bray-Curtis$(s)_{All}$	0.7745	Frechet-DISC$(norm)_{All}$	0.8847
Euclidean$(s)_{Maj}$	0.7603	DTW$(\delta s)_{All}$	0.8762
Minkowski$(s)_{Maj}$	0.7603	Bray-Curtis$(\delta s)_{All}$	0.8578
Manhattan$(s)_{Maj}$	0.7571	Euclidean$(norm)_{All}$	0.8451
Hausdorff$(s)_{Maj}$	0.7521	Hausdorff$(norm)_{All}$	0.8451
Frechet-DISC$(s)_{Maj}$	0.7285	Minkowski$(norm)_{All}$	0.8451
DTW$(s)_{All}$	0.7213	SAX$((\delta s)_{S.2}$	0.8335
SAX$(\delta s)_{All}$	0.6654	Manhattan$(\delta s)_{All}$	0.8249
Levenshtein$(\delta s)_{All}$	0.6516	Levenshtein$(s)_{All}$	0.7555

Table 6 shows the best combination of signal and sensor voting strategy for each distance measure. From this table, we can see a reasonably good ability to recognise anomalies using several distance measures.

Rather than basing the anomaly detection signal on the distance between just a pair of signals we also experiment with comparing the current signal to the average of the preceding three signals, as this could help with smoothing noise from the signal. We refer to this approach as avg_{step-3} to distinguish it from the previous approach, referred to as abs_{step-1}. Table 7 shows the performance of the anomaly detectors based on the avg_{step-3} approach. This addition, however, did not improve the performance of the anomaly detectors.

Table 8 shows a summary of the results from Tables 6 and 7 (average F1-scores are based on micro averaging). Based on the average scores Frechet-DISC performs the overall best, with DTW close behind. Both Frechet-DISC

Table 7. The performance of distance metrics as an anomaly detector for the open and close event of the valve when comparing distance between the average of last three signal and the most recent signal. Where, (s), $(norm)$, show the original signal and normalised signal, respectively. Furthermore, $_{All}$ and $_{Maj}$ show all sensor agreement and majority agreement, respectively.

Open Event		Close Event	
Metric	$F1_{score}$	Metric	$F1_{score}$
Frechet-DISC$(s)_{All}$	0.6667	Manhattan$(s)_{Maj}$	0.8710
Bray-Curtis$(s)_{All}$	0.6269	DTW$(norm)_{Maj}$	0.8684
DTW$(s)_{All}$	0.6269	Bray-Curtis$(s)_{Maj}$	0.8436
Manhattan$(s)_{All}$	0.6269	Euclidean$(norm)_{All}$	0.8344
Euclidean$(s)_{All}$	0.6197	Hausdorff$(norm)_{All}$	0.8344
Hausdorff$(s)_{All}$	0.6197	Minkowski$(norm)_{All}$	0.8344
Minkowski$(s)_{All}$	0.6197	Frechet-DISC$(s)_{All}$	0.8318
SAX$(s)_{All}$	0.4823	SAX$(s)_{Maj}$	0.7105
Levenshtein$(s)_{All}$	0.3169	Levenshtein$(\delta s)_{All}$	0.4086

and DTW are computationally very expensive (see Table 5), however, so the third-best measure, Bray-Curtis, is interesting as it is at least 77 times faster than the other two and only marginally more poorly performing. Therefore, if computational speed is a consideration (as may be the case in real-time field deployments), our findings demonstrate Bray-Curtis as a good choice, and if computational speed is a not a crucial requirement then Frechet-DISC or DTW are good choices.

Table 8. Shows the overall best performing metric using micro averaging of $F1_{score}$. There are 115 and 189 open and close events respectively, for abs_{step-1}, and 77 and 154 open and close events respectively for avg_{step-3}. These instances report those valves where at least an anomalous behaviour was once observed. The top ranked ones for in each column is represented in bold with the (*).

Metric	abs_{step-1}			avg_{step-3}			Overall
	Open	Close	Avg.	Open	Close	Avg.	Avg.
Frechet-DISC	0.7285	*0.8847	0.8256	*0.6667	0.8319	0.7694	0.8013
DTW	0.7213	0.8762	0.8176	0.6269	0.8685	0.7771	0.8001
Bray-Curtis	*0.7745	0.8578	*0.8263	0.6269	0.8437	0.7617	0.7984
Manhattan	0.7571	0.8249	0.7993	0.6269	*0.871	*0.7787	0.7904
Euclidean	0.7603	0.8451	0.813	0.6197	0.8344	0.7532	0.7872
Minkowski	0.7603	0.8451	0.813	0.6197	0.8344	0.7532	0.7872
Hausdorff	0.7521	0.8451	0.8099	0.6197	0.8344	0.7532	0.7854
SAX	0.6654	0.8335	0.7699	0.4823	0.7105	0.6242	0.707
Levenshtein	0.6516	0.7555	0.7162	0.3169	0.4087	0.374	0.5685

6   Conclusion and Future Directions

In this contribution, we presented predictive maintenance models for the identification of developing issues in the subsea valves. We discussed supervised and unsupervised approaches to aid in the assessment of the health of the valve using the sensor data. For the supervised approach, we modelled the problem as a binary classification problem between healthy and unhealthy valves due to operational needs. AdaBoost was discovered to be the best performing model and was able to gain 1.21% in terms of AUC using derived frequency and time domain features (0.99 with derived features) compared to original raw data features from sensors (0.9725 with raw features). Random Forest performed comparable to the AdaBoost but required considerably less computational effort (11.33 times faster than AdaBoost). Furthermore, in order to address an acceptable trade-off between the number of true negatives (TN) and the number of false negatives (FN), we adjusted the cut-off parameter to maximise TN (predicting *healthy* as *healthy*) while minimising FN (predicting unhealthy as healthy). We use a criterion to justify the trade-off and reported 0.961 of accuracy, with as little as 20 FN and yet a high value of 5991 TN. For the unsupervised approach, we found discrete Frechet and dynamic time warping as the best performing distance metric for anomaly detection and Bray-Curtis under-performed the best by a small fraction of 0.03 F1-score, but performed 77 times faster.

As a future direction for the supervised approach, we intend to investigate the application of two cut-off parameters instead of one to predict three classes: *healthy* (higher than the first cut-off), *unhealthy* (lower than the second cut-off) and *warning* (between the first and second cut-off parameters). This will aid in the reduction of the FN along with the FP and can be used to notify the maintenance team of the valves which are likely to fail. Consequently, this idea can be transformed into a regression approach informing the maintenance team about the number of days after which the valve is likely to fail. For the unsupervised anomaly detection approach, we intend to investigate strategies to establish the optimal threshold, and also, we intend to investigate the performance of derived frequency and time domain features as a metric for anomaly detection.

Acknowledgements. This publication has emanated from research conducted with the support of Enterprise Ireland (EI), under Grant Number IP20160496 and TC20130013. The data was kindly supplied by BP, supported by Wood.

References

1. Delmas, A., Sallak, M., Schön, W., Zhao, L.: Remaining useful life estimation methods for predictive maintenance models: defining intervals and strategies for incomplete data. In: Industrial Maintenance and Reliability Manchester, UK, 12–15 June 2018, p. 48 (2018)
2. Fernandes, M., et al.: Data analysis and feature selection for predictive maintenance: a case-study in the metallurgic industry. Int. J. Inf. Manag. **46**, 252–262 (2019)

3. Wu, S., Gebraeel, N., Lawley, M.A., Yih, Y.: A neural network integrated decision support system for condition-based optimal predictive maintenance policy. IEEE Trans. Syst. Man Cybern.-Part A: Syst. Hum. **37**(2), 226–236 (2007)
4. Di Maio, F., Hu, J., Tse, P., Pecht, M., Tsui, K., Zio, E.: Ensemble-approaches for clustering health status of oil sand pumps. Expert Syst. Appl. **39**(5), 4847–4859 (2012)
5. Tian, J., Gao, M., Li, K., Zhou, H.: Fault detection of oil pump based on classify support vector machine. In: IEEE International Conference on Control and Automation, ICCA 2007, pp. 549–553. IEEE (2007)
6. Wang, H.Q., Chen, P.: Fault diagnosis of centrifugal pump using symptom parameters in frequency domain. CIGR J. Agric. Eng. Int. (2007)
7. Animah, I., Shafiee, M.: Condition assessment, remaining useful life prediction and life extension decision making for offshore oil and gas assets. J. Loss Prevention Process Ind. (2017)
8. Martí, L., Sanchez-Pi, N., Manuel Molina, J., Garcia, A.C.B.: Anomaly detection based on sensor data in petroleum industry applications. Sensors **15**(2), 2774–2797 (2015)
9. Wang, Q., Zheng, S., Farahat, A., Serita, S., Gupta, C.: Remaining useful life estimation using functional data analysis. In: 2019 IEEE International Conference on Prognostics and Health Management (ICPHM), pp. 1–8. IEEE (2019)
10. Keogh, E., Ratanamahatana, C.A.: Exact indexing of dynamic time warping. Knowl. Inf. Syst. **7**(3), 358–386 (2004). https://doi.org/10.1007/s10115-004-0154-9
11. Lin, J., Keogh, E., Wei, L., Lonardi, S.: Experiencing SAX: a novel symbolic representation of time series. Data Mining Knowl. Discov. **15**(2), 107–144 (2007)
12. Bray, J.R., Curtis, J.T.: An ordination of the upland forest communities of Southern Wisconsin. Ecol. Monographs **27**(4), 325–349 (1957)
13. Eiter, T., Mannila, H.: Computing discrete fréchet distance. Technical report, Citeseer (1994)
14. Ponce, H., Miralles-Pechuán, L., de Lourdes Martínez-Villaseñor, M.: A flexible approach for human activity recognition using artificial hydrocarbon networks. Sensors **16**(11), 1715 (2016)
15. Sayakkara, A., Miralles-Pechuán, L., Le-Khac, N.-A., Scanlon, M.: Cutting through the emissions: feature selection from electromagnetic side-channel data for activity detection. Forensic Sci. Int.: Digit. Invest. **32**, 300927 (2020)
16. Kelleher, J.D., Namee, B.M., D'Arcy, A.: Fundamentals of Machine Learning for Predictive Data Analytics: Algorithms, Worked Examples, and Case Studies. MIT Press, Cambridge (2015)
17. Suykens, J.A.K., Vandewalle, J.: Least squares support vector machine classifiers. Neural Process. Lett. **9**(3), 293–300 (1999)
18. Quinlan, J.R.: C4. 5: programs for machine learning. Elsevier (2014)
19. Cover, T., Hart, P.: Nearest neighbor pattern classification. IEEE Trans. Inf. Theory **13**(1), 21–27 (1967)
20. Breiman, L.: Random forests. Mach. Learn. **45**(1), 5–32 (2001)
21. Dietterich, T.G.: Ensemble methods in machine learning. In: Kittler, J., Roli, F. (eds.) MCS 2000. LNCS, vol. 1857, pp. 1–15. Springer, Heidelberg (2000). https://doi.org/10.1007/3-540-45014-9_1
22. Click, C.: Gradient boosted machines with H2O (2015)
23. Friedman, J.H.: Greedy function approximation: a gradient boosting machine. Ann. Stat. 1189–1232 (2001)
24. Chen, T., He, T., Benesty, M., et al.: Xgboost: extreme gradient boosting. R package version 0.4-2, pp. 1–4 (2015)

25. Haykin, S., Network, N.: A comprehensive foundation. Neural Netw. **2**(2004), 41 (2004)
26. Bengio, Y., et al.: Learning deep architectures for AI. Found. Trends® Mach. Learn. **2**(1), 1–127 (2009)
27. Xu, G., Huang, J.Z., et al.: Asymptotic optimality and efficient computation of the leave-subject-out cross-validation. Ann. Stat. **40**(6), 3003–3030 (2012)
28. Goutte, C., Gaussier, E.: A probabilistic interpretation of precision, recall and F-score, with implication for evaluation. In: Losada, D.E., Fernández-Luna, J.M. (eds.) ECIR 2005. LNCS, vol. 3408, pp. 345–359. Springer, Heidelberg (2005). https://doi.org/10.1007/978-3-540-31865-1_25
29. Sokolova, M., Lapalme, G.: A systematic analysis of performance measures for classification tasks. Inf. Process. Manag. **45**(4), 427–437 (2009)
30. Branco, P., Torgo, L., Ribeiro, R.P.: A survey of predictive modeling on imbalanced domains. ACM Comput. Surv. (CSUR) **49**(2), 1–50 (2016)
31. Habibzadeh, F., Habibzadeh, P., Yadollahie, M.: On determining the most appropriate test cut-off value: the case of tests with continuous results. Biochemia medica: Biochemia medica **26**(3), 297–307 (2016)
32. Giusti, R., Batista, G.E.A.P.A.: An empirical comparison of dissimilarity measures for time series classification. In: 2013 Brazilian Conference on Intelligent Systems (BRACIS), pp. 82–88. IEEE (2013)

Failure Detection of an Air Production Unit in Operational Context

Mariana Barros[1]($\boxtimes$), Bruno Veloso[4,5], Pedro M. Pereira[4],
Rita P. Ribeiro[2,3,4], and João Gama[1,3,4]

[1] Faculdade de Economia, Porto, Portugal
{up201801860,jgama}@fep.up.pt
[2] Faculdade de Ciências, Porto, Portugal
rpribeiro@fc.up.pt
[3] University of Porto, Porto, Portugal
[4] INESC TEC, Porto, Portugal
bruno.miguel.veloso@gmail.com, pm.pereira.mail@gmail.com
[5] University Portucalense, Porto, Portugal

Abstract. The transformation of industrial manufacturing with computers and automation with smart systems leads us to monitor and log of industrial equipment events. It is possible to apply analytic approaches, and to find interpretive results for strategic decision making, providing advantages such as failure detection and predictive maintenance.

Over the last years, many researchers have been studying the application of machine learning techniques to improve such tasks. In this context, we develop a system capable of detect anomalies on an Air Production Unit (APU), taking into consideration the peak frequency of each sensor. The study started with the analysis of the sensors installed on the APU, defining its normal behavior and its failure mode. Using that information, we define rules, to monitor the APU, to detect anomalies on its components, and to predict possible failures. The definition of rules was based on the peak frequency analysis, which allowed the setting of boundaries of normality for the APU working modes and, thus, the identification of anomalies.

Keywords: Predictive maintenance · Anomaly detection · Frequency analysis keyword

1 Introduction

This work describes a data-driven predictive maintenance system to detect anomalies on an Air Production Unit (APU). The goal is to notify the maintenance team of an anomaly (undetectable with traditional maintenance criteria), avoiding its occurrence during the equipment operation. A set of sensors in the APU system collects data at regular time intervals. The learning process extracts information in (almost) real-time to build an early failure detection model. Ideally, this model should trigger an alarm to allow the intervention in an embryonic

© Springer Nature Switzerland AG 2020
J. Gama et al. (Eds.): ITEM 2020/IoT Streams 2020, CCIS 1325, pp. 61–74, 2020.
https://doi.org/10.1007/978-3-030-66770-2_5

phase of the fault, avoiding the failure on one of the components that will affect the whole unit. The analysis of the peak frequency allows to define rules for anomaly detection. When one of those rules is displayed, the maintenance team will be notified. It provides the opportunity to replace a component from the APU, prevents the failure of the compressor, and the equipment operation interruption.

The paper contains five sections: Sect. 2 consists of the problem definition, explaining the context and challenges of the developed work, Sect. 3 describes other studies carried in the context of predictive maintenance. In Sect. 4, we present our proposal for identifying anomalies and prevent the failure of the components of our system. Section 5 shows the analysis of the results obtained with the peak frequency approach and, finally, in Sect. 6, we explain the contributions of our work to the described problem and what can be done in the future to achieve better results.

2   Problem Definition

The Air Production Unit (APU) is part of a compressed air system, that converts the power from an electric motor into kinetic energy by compressing and pressurizing air. When this system fails, the equipment that is receiving its energy will consequently fail. Apply predictive maintenance here is essential to predict the equipment failure before it happens, decreasing costs and optimizing the service, by lowering the number of equipment taken out of service for inspection and maintenance.

Reliability Centered Maintenance (RCM) method, Failure Mode and Effect Analysis (FMEA) and Failure Mode, Effects & Critically Analysis (FMCA) table to determine the failures that most affect the system. This approach was used to report the failure history and find the most common failures on the compressor system: (i) electrical valve; (ii) pressure valve; (iii) oil leaks; (iv) electrical motor; (v) pressure switches; and (vi) drying towers. The sensors and places to install them were strategically defined, taking into consideration the most common failures of the system. Eight analogical sensors and eight digital sensors were defined.

The considered analogical sensors were the following.

1. TP2 - Measures the pressure on the compressor.
2. TP3 - Measures the pressure generated at the pneumatic panel.
3. H1 - This valve is activated when the pressure read by the pressure switch of the command is above the operating pressure of 10.2 bar.
4. DV pressure - Measures the pressure exerted due to pressure drop generated when towers are discharged air dryers, and when it is equal to zero, it means that the compressor is working under load.

5. Motor Current - Measure the current of one phase of the three-phase motor, that should present values close 0 A when the compressor turns off, close 4 A when the compressor is working off loaded and close 7 A when the compressor is working under load. When the compressor starts to work, the motor current presents values close to 9 A.
6. Oil Temperature - Measure the temperature of the oil present on the compressor.

The digital sensors only assume two different values: zero when they are inactive or one, when a certain event activates them. The considered digital sensors were the following.

1. COMP - The electrical signal of air intake valve on the compressor. It is active when there is no admission of air on the compressor, meaning that the compressor turns off or working off loaded.
2. DV electric - electrical signal that commands the compressor outlet valve. When it is active, it means that the compressor is working under load and when it is not active, it means that the compressor is off or working off loaded.
3. TOWERS - Defines which tower is drying the air and which tower is draining the humidity removed from the air. When it is not active, it means that tower one is working and when it is active, it means that tower two is working.
4. MPG - Is responsible for activating the intake valve to start the compressor under load when the pressure in the APU is below 8.2 bar. Consequently, it will activate the sensor COMP, that assumes the same behavior as MPG sensor.
5. LPS - Is activated when the pressure is lower than 7 bars.
6. Oil Level - Detects the level of the oil on the compressor and is active (equal to one) when the oil is below the expected values.

The sensors installed in two different compressors will be called APU01 and APU02. They communicate with a server that receives the data from the sensors with one second of sampling frequency. Every second, the system stores the data collected from the sensors and respective timestamps to a data logger file. Every five minutes, the file is sent to the server using the TCP/IP protocol application. The data received from the two compressors, during two months, was processed and analyzed. The data contains three identified anomalies on APU01, and one identified anomaly on APU02.

In this paper, we will analyze the data and understand the compressed air system dynamic. Additionally, we will use the information that we have about the failures that have occurred on both equipments to understand the behavior of each sensor when they occur and how it deviates from the normal behavior of the APU. By applying analytic approaches based on data, it is possible to find results for strategic decision-making, providing advantages such as maintenance cost reduction, APU components fault reduction, and improvements in the equipment operation. Having a predictive maintenance plan for the components of the APU is vital to avoid unplanned shutdowns, maintaining higher availability and shorter lead-time, decreasing costs for the companies.

3   Related Work

The transformation of industrial manufacturing with computers and automation with smart systems lead us to use sensors to monitor industrial equipment events. In this section, we will present some studies developed in the context of predictive maintenance and anomaly detection that consider different approaches and obtained good results.

3.1   Predictive Maintenance

Some of the maintenance and repair procedures are only applied in response to not predicted maintenance issues. However, failures in equipment affect the safety, availability, and the environment [10]. Since 1940, maintenance techniques are evolving, and new goals are being achieved [14], with the implementation of Reliability Centered Maintenance (RCM) policies in an attempt to address a host of reliability issues to balance improvement in overall equipment. Reliability Centered Maintenance (RCM) is an elaborate seven-step structured process that regulates equipment maintenance strategies and might be inclusive of condition-based, predictive, and planned maintenance [9]. Also, the RCM aims to determine the maintenance processes required to ensure equipment performance expected. There are several maintenance techniques used by RCM models, such as Preventive Maintenance (PM), Run to Failure (RTF), and Condition-based Maintenance (CBM). CBM contains two elements, Predictive Maintenance (PdM) and Real-time Monitoring (RTM). Ideally, CBM techniques are implemented during design and development phases and matured throughout the life cycle. Preventive Maintenance (PM) works through periodical inspections where equipment parts are replaced based on a fixed timetable [3]. Run to failure (RTF), also referred to as Corrective Maintenance, waits for the failure and then proceeds to repair it [17]. Condition Based Maintenance (CBM) is a maintenance strategy, which conducts the maintenance process using the information gathered via condition monitoring. This strategy is responsible for reducing the maintenance cost through maintenance actions when the machine failure process is approaching. A Real-Time Monitor (RTM) [10] is employed to schedule tasks with random execution times in a real-time computing system. Predictive Maintenance (PdM) measures the condition of the equipment, determines when it will fail in a specified future period, and then proceeds to take action to avoid system failure.

3.2   Anomaly Detection

Over the last years, several studies [1,2,4,6,10,12,14] have been carried out regarding the application of machine learning methods to predictive maintenance, failure, and anomaly detection. The aim is to find the best methodologies to detect failure and anomalies on equipment by analyzing the data received from sensors. Anomaly detection is also a well-rated approach to detect failure on equipment and is applied to predictive maintenance problems. An anomaly is an occurrence that deviates from what is standard, typical, or expected. Detecting the presence of anomalies can provide valuable insights into the industry to prevent unexpected equipment faults and to apply predictive maintenance. The detection of anomalies relies on different behaviors that occur after the model is built. Rabatel et al. [16] focused on the field of train maintenance, using sensors positioned on the main train components. They have extracted normal behavior using a set of sequential patterns applying those patterns in normal and abnormal data to evaluate the conformity score. Manco et al. [13], developed an application to predict and explain door failures on metro trains. The authors used an outlier detection method to predict failure, considering the data that does not share common patterns as a failure. Benedetti et al. [4] designed a learning approach to detect possible anomalies in photovoltaic (PV) systems, based on the comparison between the measured and the predicted values of the AC power production. In [8], the goal was to detect anomalies on train speed for intelligent railway systems. The authors adopted a Bayesian statistical learning model to represent normal behavior of train speed changes and detect anomalies based on them. Wan-Jui Lee [11] applied Linear Regression to model two different classes of compressor behavior for each train separately, defining the boundary separating the two classes under typical situations and models the distribution of the compressor idle time and run time separately using logistic functions. Pereira et al. [15] developed a failure detection system to predict train door breakdowns before they happen using data from the logging system. The authors developed a system for classifying irregular open/close cycles within trains, based on the difference between the inlet and outlet pressure in specific intervals of the cycle.

All of these works were developed with the goal of extract the normal behavior of the system, considering as anomalies the data that does not share common patterns. To achieved this goal, different machine learning methods were applied, depending on the context and characteristics of the work.

Our approach is based on the definition of the normal behavior of the compressor and the definition of rules when the behavior of the compressor does not share common patterns with the defined normal behavior. Our dataset is unlabeled, making it difficult to apply predictive machine learning models. The definition of rules for anomaly detection can be useful to label the dataset and predict anomalies based on them.

4   Our Proposal

Our work was developed at an early stage of the project, where the main goal was to get familiar with the dataset, distinguish the compressor's working modes, and characterize them.

By the analysis of the values' evolution returned by each sensor through one day, we verified that all of them reach maximum and minimum peaks. For the analogical sensors, this means that their values increase over a time window until they reach a maximum peak. From there, they start to decrease until they reach a minimum peak, and so on. For the digital sensors, which only have two values, zero or one, the maximum peaks reach when the sensor is active, and they last for a certain period until they are inactive again. Every time the algorithm detects a peak, it means that the compressor turns off. The goal is to monitor how many times the compressor has turned off on a specific period. The frequency of the peaks can vary from day to day and during the day. Some of those variations are minimal and might be caused by small perturbations on the environment where the machine is working. However, some of the variations are higher and they are visible during the anomalies on the compressor components. Figure 1 represents the behavior of each sensor installed on both APU01 and APU02.

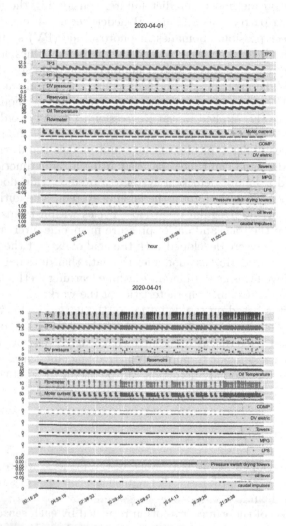

Fig. 1. Daily sensor readings: APU01 (top) APU02 (bottom)

Define the normal number of peaks in a period of time, and monitor them in real-time might be a solution to detect anomalies. To define the normal behavior of both APU01 and APU02, we decided to monitor the number of peaks on a time window of two hours, where it is possible to verify a significant number of peaks on both APUs. The periods start at every hour of the day, with the first period starting from midnight until 2 AM, the second period starting from 1 AM until 3 AM, and so on. This analysis occurs when the equipment where the compressor is installed is in operation.

The developed algorithm for peak detection updates the maximum value when the difference between the value and the current local maximum is higher than δ, with $\delta = 0.01$.

The sensor readings are very sensitive to environmental noise and perturbations, and the returned decimal values can also be noisy. The sensor data have an extensive range of values, and consecutive readings can have insignificant differences between them. The only peaks that should be considered on analogical sensors are the maximum values that they present in the specified period. We have tried different values of δ to ignore the noisy values and to fit with our goal. However, we have noticed that this technique discards some significant peaks.

Low-pass filtering is a solution that is often applied to eliminate the effects of environmental noise. This approach eliminates the perturbation of the sensors reading. Thus, we have applied a low-pass filter on our data set, to attenuate the peaks and only consider the maximum peaks that are relevant to our study. In previous studies [5, 7, 15] low-pass filters have been applied before the analysis of the signals, to remove perturbation. This filter passes signals with a frequency lower than the selected cutoff frequency and attenuates signals with frequencies higher than the cutoff frequency. The function *butter* of the class *signal* of the library *scipy* on Python, with filter order equal to 1 and cutoff frequency equal to 0.001. Those parameters were defined after a set of experiences and satisfy the needs of the data set.

The analogical peaks are counted as shown in Fig. 2 for the TP3 sensor in a period of two hours. Without the low pass filter, more than 10 peaks were identified. However, it is visible that only with the low pass filter, the real number of 5 peaks was identified, considering a peak when the sensor reaches a maximum value.

The goal is to estimate the mean number of times the sensor reaches its maximum value on a period of 2 h, as its normal behavior. We propose the analysis of the frequency of peaks on two hours, considering only the days that do not have reports of failure or anomaly. Then, the calculation of the mean frequency considering all the days without anomalies and the definition of the standard frequency of peaks. Some rules will be defined to detect anomalies taking into consideration a reasonable deviation from the standard frequency of peaks.

The digital sensors, since they can only assume two values (0 or 1), give the possibility to understand the time required to reach the peak. With this approach, it is possible to compare the time the compressor works under load

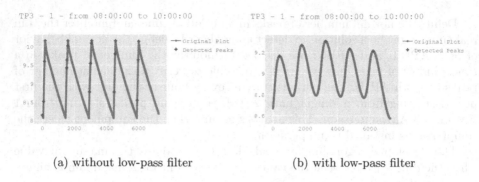

(a) without low-pass filter   (b) with low-pass filter

Fig. 2. TP3 sensor readings

and try to understand the standard duration for each of the compressors. It is necessary to split the duration into ranges, and then compute the mean for each range. The mean inside each range will help distinguish different normality modes. After, some rules should be defined to detect anomalies, considering the different normality modes. The digital sensors considered were COMP, DV electric, TOWERS, MPG, LPS and Oil Level.

5   Experimental Evaluation

The analysis of the peak frequency should only consider the data from the days when the compressor did not present any anomalies or failures. The days with reported anomalies were removed from the dataset and will be used to compare the peak frequency on days without failure and the peak frequency on days with failure.

The algorithm computes the number of peaks on each period of each day for both APUs. The results were analyzed separately, to understand if APU01 and APU02 present different behaviors since they are operating on distinct environments. Table 1 presents the results for the mean peak frequency for each analogical sensor of each APU. The sensors TP2, TP3, H1, Oil Temperature, and Motor Current, have a close peak frequency, which means that those variables present some degree of correlation on both compressors. When they present significant differences in the number of peaks, it can be an indicator of an anomaly.

Table 1. Mean peaks in two hour period for each compressor system (APU01 and APU02) for analogic sensors

APU	TP2	TP3	H1	DVPressure	OilTemperature	MotorCurrent
APU01	4	5	5	2	4	4
APU02	7	7	7	2	6	6

To understand how the distribution of peak frequency ranges, we have decided to analyze the peaks on TP3, because they are easier to identify with less chance of error. Also, in Fig. 1, we can relate that TP3 reflects the behavior of most of the sensors.

Figure 3 shows the evolution of the variable TP3 during a day and the differences that occur on its peak frequency throughout the day.

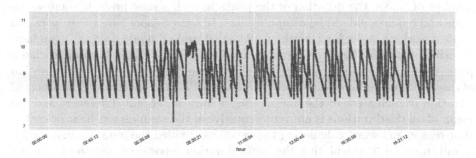

Fig. 3. Evolution of TP3 during a day

Figure 4 represents the amount of samples of each value of peak frequency on APU01 and APU02. The axis x represents the peak frequency on TP3 sensor (the number of peaks found), and the axis y represents the number of periods of two hours when that number of peaks frequency has been verified.

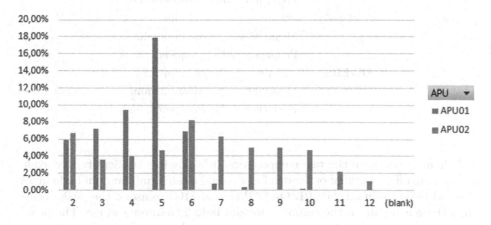

Fig. 4. Frequency of the mean number of peaks on APU01 and APU02

Is it possible to observe in the number of peaks detected on APU01 varies between 2 and 9, with the mean number of peaks rounded to 5. It is also possible to notice that the number of peaks observed on the analogical sensors of APU02 is higher than APU01, varying between 2 and 12. On APU01, the mean number of 4 and 5 peaks have an higher frequency, comparing to the others. However, on APU02, the frequency of each number of peaks more distributed, but it is possible to distinguish 6 and 7 as the mean number of peaks with higher frequency.

The approach used to analyze the frequency of digital sensors was different. We can compute the duration of the peak on digital sensors considering the 0 to 1 transition on the signal. Although it is possible to obtain the total number of peaks, the duration of the peaks in each sensor presents some variations and requires individual computation. The compressors have three operation modes: working under load, working off loaded, and off mode. In Sect. 2, we have described which of the three operation modes when each digital sensor reaches a peak, changing its value from 0 to 1. Tables 2 and 3 represent the mean duration of the peaks on digital sensors, for APU01 and APU02, respectively. The reported duration of each state of the digital sensors have significant differences and the mean of all the durations is not representative of the compressors behaviour. For that reason and when calculating the mean, we divided the duration in duration 1 and duration 2, calculating the mean duration separately and the frequency of each duration.

Table 2. Peak duration on digital signals APU01

APU01	Duration 1	Duration 2
COMP/MGP	<2 min	>2 min
	Mean: 4 s	Mean: 22 min
	Frequency: 40%	Frequency: 60%
DV electric	<2 min	≈2 min
	Mean: 35 s	Mean: 2 min
	Frequency: 20%	Frequency: 80%
TOWERS	<2 min	>2 min
	Mean: 40 s	Mean: 23 min
	Frequency: 75%	Frequency: 35%

When we compare the two compressors, it is possible to identify that compressors are off or working off loaded for a period close 20 min and under load for a period close 2 min on APU01. On COMP and MGP sensors, the peak occurs when there is no air on the compressors and lasts 22 min on average. The peaks on DV electric occurs when the compressor is working under load and last for 2 min. The digital signal TOWERS gives us information about the duration of the peak when the compressor is off or working off loaded. They usually last for less than 1 min, on average 40 s, and it has moments when the compressor starts to work at no load. When the compressor starts to work again, the compressor reaches a minimum peak (equal to zero) with a mean duration equal to 40 s. On the other hand, when the APU02 is switched off or working in an offload

Table 3. Peak duration on digital signals APU02

APU02	Duration 1	Duration 2
COMP/MGP	<2 min Mean: 4 s Frequency: 40%	>2 min Mean: 12 min Frequency: 60%
DV electric	≈ 2 min Mean: 2 min Frequency: 98%	>2 min Mean: 15 min Frequency: 2%
TOWERS	<2 min Mean: 1 min Frequency: 35%	> 2 min Mean: 13 min Frequency: 65%

mode, the duration is readings with a mean duration of 13 min. On COMP and MGP the peaks last for periods 7 min and 15 min, 13 min of mean duration. The peaks on DV electric last for 2 min. Both APU01 and APU02 have registered some peaks with a duration close to 1 min. However, these peaks are recurrent on APU01 and rare on APU02. It can be explained with the moments that the compressor is working under load when tower one is drying the air, and tower two is draining humidity.

Although the two compressors operate in the same context, some differences in their working environment can be the cause of the difference detected in the frequency of peaks and their duration. This difference can also be explained by an undetected failure in one of the compressors. In any case, the analysis of the behavior of the two compressors allows us to define rules to detect anomalies on the compressors. The rules definition is based on the behavior of the sensor on the days when a failure occurred and the previous days. On the previous days of failure, the mean number of peaks has suffered some deviations and some extreme values such as 15 peaks per period or no peaks per period. The period when the compressor was working in charge has also increased until periods 5 min mean.

Based on those deviations, the rules defined to detect anomalies using the analogical sensors, and its severity are:

- Rule 1 - periods without peaks detected (critical);
- Rule 2 - periods with less than 2 peaks detected (medium);
- Rule 3 - periods with more than 10 peaks detected (medium);
- Rule 4 - differences between the number of peaks on TP2, TP3, H1 and Motor Current higher than 2 (medium).

The rules defined to detect anomalies using the digital sensors were based on the digital sensors COMP, to detect the period when the compressor is off and DV electric, to detect the period when the compressor was working under load. The rules defined and its severity are:

- Rule 5 - periods when the compressor is working under load for more than 5 min, with COMP sensor inactive (critical);
- Rule 6 - periods when the compressor is off for more than 30 min, with COMP sensor active (medium).

As we described in Sect. 2, the data is sent to the server every five minutes using the TCP/IP protocol. Every two hours, the server runs a script that verifies if the rules were displayed and will send an email with the description of the behaviour of the APU on the previous two hours.

We are still on a preliminary phase of the project, the knowledge of the behavior of the compressor system is still limited, and there are still several uncertainties about the anomalies on the system. For this reason, the evaluation of this anomaly detection method is difficult and does not allow us to be absolutely sure of the detected faults. However, we know that the compressor system had two identifies moments of fault when the equipment had to go to maintenance, so we decided to run the rules on the previous days of fault. We have monitored the behavior of the compressor ten days before each failure and the number of times each rule was triggered is represented in Table 4. The defined rules were identified before the known failures, making this a good method to predict anomalies.

Table 4. Rules triggered before failure

Failure	Rule 1	Rule 2	Rule 3	Rule 4	Rule 5	Rule 6
Failure 1	2	11	8	3	23	26
Failure 2	2	7	3	4	12	90

6 Conclusions

Several works have been done in the context of predictive maintenance, where different machine learning models have been applied. However, the analysis of the peak frequency is not a commonly used approach in the context of predictive maintenance and anomaly detection. Although we are still in the first phrase of this project, in which the knowledge of the data is still limited, we have considered the frequency of peaks a reliable method of detecting anomalies. This method is based on the visual analysis of the peaks and is less subject to errors. With this method, it was possible to detect different modes of operation in the two APUs, making it difficult to define boundaries of normality for the compressor operating modes. On the other hand, it was possible to define some effective rules that could be applied to both compressors and that are useful anomaly indicators.

Those rules have been verified on the failure days and on the days previous to the failure. For future work, we want to improve the anomaly detection rules and to apply predictive maintenance techniques. Most of the work is related with the prediction of the values of TP3, to predict the peak frequency, and with the prediction of the values of COMP, to predict the duration of each working mode.

Acknowledgments. This research was Funded from national funds through FCT - Science and Technology Foundation, I.P in the context of the project FailStopper (DSAIPA /DS/0086/2018).

This work is financed by National Funds through the Portuguese funding agency, FCT - Fundação para a Ciência e a Tecnologia, within project UIDB/50014/ 2020.

References

1. Allah Bukhsh, Z., Saeed, A., Stipanovic, I., Doree, A.G.: Predictive maintenance using tree-based classification techniques: a case of railway switches. Transp. Res. Part C Emerg. Technol. **101**(February), 35–54 (2019). https://doi.org/10.1016/j.trc.2019.02.001
2. Aremu, O.O., Palau, A.S., Parlikad, A.K., Hyland-Wood, D., McAree, P.R.: Structuring data for intelligent predictive maintenance in asset management. IFAC-PapersOnLine **51**(11), 514–519 (2018). https://doi.org/10.1016/j.ifacol.2018.08.370
3. Bengtsson, M.: Condition Based Maintenance Systems–An investigation of technical constituents and organizational aspects. Ph.D. thesis (2004)
4. De Benedetti, M., Leonardi, F., Messina, F., Santoro, C., Vasilakos, A.: Anomaly detection and predictive maintenance for photovoltaic systems. Neurocomputing **310**, 59–68 (2018). https://doi.org/10.1016/j.neucom.2018.05.017
5. Fridolfsson, J., et al.: Effects of frequency filtering on intensity and noise in accelerometer-based physical activity measurements. Sensors **19**(9), 2186 (2019). https://doi.org/10.3390/s19092186
6. Fumeo, E., Oneto, L., Anguita, D.: Condition based maintenance in railway transportation systems based on big data streaming analysis. Procedia Comput. Sci. **53**, 437–446 (2015). https://doi.org/10.1016/j.procs.2015.07.321, http://www.sciencedirect.com/science/article/pii/S1877050915018244, iNNS Conference on Big Data 2015 Program San Francisco, CA, USA 8-10 August 2015
7. Hook, J.: Smoothing non-smooth systems with low-pass filters. Physica D: Nonlinear Phenomena **269**, 76–85 (2014). https://doi.org/10.1016/j.physd.2013.11.016, http://www.sciencedirect.com/science/article/pii/S0167278913003254
8. Kang, S., Sristi, S., Karachiwala, J., Hu, Y.: Detection of anomaly in train speed for intelligent railway systems. In: 2018 International Conference Control Automation Diagnosis, ICCAD 2018 (2018)
9. Kennedy, R.: Examining the Processes of RCM and TPM: Group (January) 1–15 (2006)
10. Koons-Stapf, A.: Condition based maintenance: Theory, methodology, & application (2015)
11. Lee, W.J.: Anomaly detection and severity prediction of air leakage in train braking pipes. Int. J. Prognostics Health Manag. 21 (2017)
12. Lopes Gerum, P.C., Altay, A., Baykal-Gürsoy, M.: Data-driven predictive maintenance scheduling policies for railways. Transp. Res. Part C Emerg. Technol. **107**(October 2018), 137–154 (2019). https://doi.org/10.1016/j.trc.2019.07.020

13. Manco, G., et al.: Fault detection and explanation through big data analysis on sensor streams. Expert Syst. Appl. **87**, 141–156 (2017). https://doi.org/10.1016/J.ESWA.2017.05.079, https://www.sciencedirect.com/science/article/pii/S0957417417304074
14. Moubray, J.: Reliability-centered Maintenance. Industrial Press (2001). https://books.google.pt/books?id=bNCVF0B7vpIC
15. Pereira, P., Ribeiro, R.P., Gama, J.: Failure prediction – an application in the railway industry. In: Džeroski, S., Panov, P., Kocev, D., Todorovski, L. (eds.) DS 2014. LNCS (LNAI), vol. 8777, pp. 264–275. Springer, Cham (2014). https://doi.org/10.1007/978-3-319-11812-3_23
16. Rabatel, J., Bringay, S., Poncelet, P.: Anomaly detection in monitoring sensor data for preventive maintenance. Expert Syst. Appl. **38**(6), 7003–7015 (2011). https://doi.org/10.1016/j.eswa.2010.12.014
17. Wang, Q., Zheng, S., Farahat, A., Serita, S., Gupta, C.: Remaining Useful Life Estimation Using Functional Data Analysis, April 2019

IoT Streams 2020: Feature Learning

Enhancing Siamese Neural Networks Through Expert Knowledge for Predictive Maintenance

Patrick Klein[1]([✉]) [iD], Niklas Weingarz[1] [iD], and Ralph Bergmann[1,2] [iD]

[1] Business Information Systems II, University of Trier, 54296 Trier, Germany
{kleinp,s4niwein,bergmann}@uni-trier.de
[2] German Research Center for Artificial Intelligence (DFKI), Branch University of Trier, Behringstraße 21, 54296 Trier, Germany
ralph.bergmann@dfki.de

Abstract. The data provided by cyber-physical production systems (CPPSs) to monitor their condition via data-driven predictive maintenance is often high dimensional and only a few fault and failure (FaF) examples are available. These FaFs can usually be detected in a (small) localized subset of data streams, whereas the use of all data streams induces noise that could negatively affect the training and prediction performance. In addition, a CPPS often consists of multiple similar units that generate comparable data streams and show similar failure modes. However, existing approaches for learning a similarity measure generally do not consider these two aspects. For this reason, we propose two approaches for integrating expert knowledge about class or failure mode dependent attributes into siamese neural networks (SNN). Additionally, we present an attribute-wise encoding of time series based on 2D convolutions. This enables that learned knowledge in the form of filters is shared between similar data streams, which would not be possible with conventional 1D convolutions due to their spatial focus. We evaluate our approaches against state-of-the-art time series similarity measures such as dynamic time warping, NeuralWarp, as well as a feature-based representation approach. Our results show that the integration of expert knowledge is advantageous and combined with the novel SNN architecture it is possible to achieve the best performance compared to the other investigated methods.

Keywords: Siamese neural network · Predictive maintenance · Expert knowledge · 2D convolution · Time series similarity

1 Introduction

The current transition to Industry 4.0 transforms production environments into complex cyber-physical production systems (CPPSs) consisting of several separate cyber-physical systems (CPSs) [20]. Each CPS contains a large number of different sensors and actuators, whereby instances of the same type can occur

J. Gama et al. (Eds.): ITEM 2020/IoT Streams 2020, CCIS 1325, pp. 77–92, 2020.
https://doi.org/10.1007/978-3-030-66770-2_6

multiple times in the CPPS. The data recorded by these sensors is enriched with the control commands of the actuators and provides the opportunity to monitor the current condition in order to detect faults and failures (FaFs). For prognostic and health management in a CPS, Lee et al. [19] proposed a similarity-based approach which is generally favored if numerous run-to-failure (R2F) recordings are available [14]. The architecture of siamese neural networks (SNNs) is able to learn a similarity measure by distinguishing training examples of similar pairs from dissimilar ones, even if only few examples are available [10]. However, recent surveys on data-driven predictive maintenance (PredM) approaches [8, 12, 24] do not consider the use of SNNs, although they are well suited for additional challenges, such as the need of explainability. To the authors' best knowledge, only Zhang et al. [27] applied SNNs on vibration data of ball bearings for similarity-based PredM. While effects resulting from long-term degradation processes can be well monitored at the component level, sensor faults or incorrect control commands due to unexpected situations which are typical for CPSs [21] can only be analyzed by considering the CPPS as a whole. Thus, unlike monitoring a single component, a large number of data streams from the CPPS is potentially relevant. Still, for identifying a specific failure mode, only a relatively small, specific subset is useful. Although SNNs or deep learning, in general, have their strength in learning expressive representations from high-dimensional data, this requires a large amount of examples for each failure mode, which are often not available for most FaFs. However, an engineer is usually able to identify (or at least restrict) the relevant data streams w.r.t. a failure mode, based on general knowledge about the design and mechanics of the CPS. We expect that integrating this knowledge can support an SNN during training and inference. For this reason, we investigate how to infuse prior expert knowledge about the detectability of a failure mode in the form of a restriction on relevant data streams of sensors and actuators into an SNN model, which is also the main contribution of our work. Therefore, we present two approaches for infusing manually defined expert knowledge and compare them with various state-of-the-art methods for time series similarity-based classification on a data set generated by a physical model factory that imitates relevant characteristics of a CPPS.

In the following section the foundations regarding distance-based time series classification with different representations, similarity measures, and SNNs for PredM are presented. Then, our approaches for infusing expert knowledge are introduced in Sect. 3. Next, we evaluate them against various other approaches on a self-created CPPS research data set. Finally, Sect. 5 concludes the results and discusses future work.

2   Foundations and Related Work

2.1   Distance-Based Time Series Classification

In a distance-based time series classification scenario, let $D_{train}\{(X_i, y_i)\}$ be our labeled training data set with pairs consisting of an input $X_i \in \mathbb{R}^{a \times t}$ in the form of a multivariate time series with a attributes (streams) and length t as well as its respective label $y_i \in \{1, ..., c\}$. The classification of a k-nearest neighbour (NN) classifier with $k = 1$ for an input $Q \in D_{test}$ is the label y_j of X_j which has the minimal distance from all examples in D_{train}. More formally,

$$y_j \text{ with } j = \arg\min_i \{d(Q, X_i)\}, \tag{1}$$

where $d(\cdot, \cdot)$ is a distance function. Since simple measures – such as any form of Minkowski distance functions – cannot handle the alignment of contraction and expansion along the time axis, typically elastic measures such as dynamic time warping (DTW) [4] are used on raw time series data [15]. Therefore, a distance matrix between each time step of Q and X_i is computed in order to find a path with the minimal cumulative distance under some constraints. It has been shown that a k-NN classifier combined with DTW results in the best accuracy on various benchmark data sets [1]. This method can also be used for establishing a similarity-based PredM approach by using the k most similar NNs between a time window Q and a stored time series X_i from previous R2F recordings to estimate the condition of a system. For example, Mai and Chevalier [22] developed a complex similarity function that includes DTW for time series comparison to support diagnosis, corrective actions, and remaining useful life estimations in case of an abnormal event.

2.2   Feature-Based Time Series Representation

A well-known problem of DTW, however, is its relatively bad run time behaviour, making it unsuitable for analyzing sensor data of a CPPS in real time. For this reason, it is often preferable to transform the input from the problem space into a more suitable representation in terms of its utility for solving the given problem [3]. A common transformation of time series consists of the automatic computation of a large number of predefined features and the selection of significant ones, e.g. through usage of the TSFresh algorithm [6]. We denote this representation as $f_{TSF}(X) \in R^n$ where n is the number of computed features for a time series X. This type of representation intends to take advantage of the fact that similar time series are represented by similar features, resulting in a small distance between similar instances. For example, kurtosis and root mean square are typical features for monitoring the vibration of bearings and higher values are generally associated with a worse condition.

Other work has shifted to the usage of deep neural networks to learn f in order to extract relevant features that result in an expressive representation of a time series. Typically, autoencoders (AEs) are used to generate a latent representation $H = f_{AE}(X)$ that fuses and compresses multi-sensory data and is learnt by reconstruction of its input [24].

2.3   Siamese Neural Networks for Time Series Similarity

In general, an SNN architecture [5] consists of two deep neural networks that both share the same parameters θ as shown in Fig. 1. These networks are referred to as an encoder that extracts (deep) features $H = f_{SNN}(X)$ from an input X by a neural network $f_{SNN}(\cdot)$. In contrast to AEs, an encoder $f_{SNN}(\cdot)$ learns its parameters θ by distinguishing training examples of similar (X_q, X_p) from dissimilar (X_q, X_n) pairs of time series as shown by Pei et al. [23].

A pair is considered to be semantically similar $y = 1$, if both instances are of the same class and otherwise $y = 0$ for dissimilar pairs. The encoder of the SNN $f_{SNN}(\cdot)$ is trained to produce discriminative representations for X_q, X_p, X_n by minimizing the distance between positive pairs $d(f_{SNN}(X_q), f_{SNN}(X_p))$ and maximizing the distance between negative pairs $d(f_{SNN}(X_q), f_{SNN}(X_n))$. Usually, the distance measure $d(\cdot, \cdot)$ can be any simple distance measure such as a Minkowski or cosine distance. The loss is usually computed for a mini batch of size b which consists of half positive and half negative pairs. Thereby, binary cross entropy (BCE) is used as follows to compute the loss value:

$$L(X_a, X_b, y) = -\frac{1}{b} \sum \big(y * log(sim(X_a, X_b)) + (1 - y) * log(1 - sim(X_a, X_b)) \big),$$
(2)

where X_a, X_b are two time series and $sim(\cdot)$ is a function transforming the distance produced by the SNN into a similarity and $y \in \{0, 1\}$ is the labeled similarity of this pair.

2.4 Related Work

The closest to our work regarding SNNs is the approach by Zhang et al. [27] for bearing fault diagnosis using limited training data. Related to the integration of expert knowledge into deep neural networks is the work of Huang et al. [13] that replicates the hierarchical structure of a production system by the way layers are connected in a neural network. Somewhat related to our idea of manually restricting attributes is the work of Guan et al. [11], in which they included an additional branch to a deep neural network that only focuses on an excerpt of medical images since the most relevant information is located in a small part of the overall image. However, they do not use a manual restriction approach, which means that there is no guarantee that irrelevant noise from the whole image is excluded and that the focus of the analysis is performed on the most relevant excerpt. In contrast to approaches that transform time series into images as input for applying 2D convolutions [8], we use the approach proposed by Assaf and Schumann [2] so that each filter is applied only to one data stream at the same time.

3 Infusing Expert Knowledge About Attribute Relevance

If the amount of data per class is large, a neural network is expected to find meaningful relationships between input and output by itself. However, if the amount of examples per class is relatively small, we expect that – as previously shown on images by Lapuschkin et al. [18] – spurious or artifactual correlations learned from training data can negatively influence the usefulness in real-world

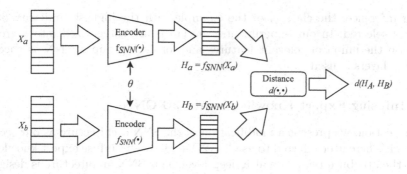

Fig. 1. Typical SNN architecture

applications where these are not present. With a manually defined attribute restriction – referred to as MAR throughout this paper – we want to minimize the influence of noise through irrelevant attributes and support the SNN to focus on the relevant aspects. Our two proposed approaches are driven by the idea that each failure mode has only a small subset of relevant attributes, i.e. sensor data streams, that are necessary for determining its existence. We assume that manually defining this subset and excluding irrelevant attributes should improve performance, robustness and trust of a deep learning model. Moreover, this predefined subset can be further specified into: i) attributes that contain directly measurable patterns which indicate a FaF and ii) attributes that are necessary to establishing the relevant context in the sense of broader situational awareness, e.g. actuator commands and additional sensors. With regard to Turney's classification of attributes [25], we can think of i) as primary ones, ii) as contextual ones and the excluded ones as irrelevant ones.

In the following, we present two approaches that are developed with the purpose to infuse expert knowledge about the attribute relevance by forcing neural networks to use only relevant attributes. Our first approach is more generally applicable regarding the used types of neural network layers and it applies the MAR at the input level, whereas the second one is based on a specialized architecture to apply MAR at a later stage in the architecture.

3.1 Infusing Expert Knowledge at the Input Level

This approach – hereafter referred to as MS-SNN – is based on the assumption that, firstly, many failure modes have common characteristics and, secondly, that prior expert knowledge allows them to be grouped regarding their relevant attributes. More precisely, each label $y_i \in \{1, ..., c\}$ with similar relevant attributes is merged into a group $g_j \in \{1, ..., l\}$ so that $l \ll c$. Then for each group g_j, a separate SNN encoder $f_{SNN,g_j}(\cdot)$ is trained only receiving attributes as input that are manually defined as relevant for each label y_i of group g_j. Each encoder can be of a different type (e.g. LSTM, CNN) and uses different hyperparameters based on the characteristics of group g_j. To estimate the current state during inference, the class y_i of the example with the highest similarity of all SNNs is selected. In our experiments, the labels are categorized into 8 groups based on the union of relevant features and for each group a CNN as encoder with FC layers is used.

3.2 Infusing Expert Knowledge with 2D CNNs

In this section, we present a modification of the SNN architecture as our second approach – hereafter referred to as CNN2D + MAR – to infuse expert knowledge about the attribute relevance at a deep level. This SNN architecture is designed to ensure two objectives: firstly, preserve the attribute dimension as long as possible to enable attribute-wise access at deep layers. Secondly, to ensure that only manually defined attributes are considered for generating the encoding and assessing the similarity. The modifications conducted on input, encoder, and distance measure w.r.t. a standard SNN are presented below.

Input. The normal input of a time series $X_1 \in \mathbb{R}^{a \times t}$ is extended by $x_2 \in \{0,1\}^{2a}$ such that $x = \{X_1, [x_{2_1}, x_{2_2}]\}$. This additional input is based on the training example's label y_i and consists of two vectors $x_{2_1}, x_{2_2} \in \{0,1\}^a$ indicating the manually defined attribute's relevance for a failure mode. The vector x_{2_1} defines which attributes should be compared in a univariate way, whereas x_{2_2} defines which attributes are taken into account for defining the context which ensures that also multivariate aspects are considered.

Encoder. The encoder consists of two distinct branches. The first branch encodes time series and the second one learns a weighting value z between both outputs of the first branch.

The first branch applies 2D convolutions (convs) to $X_1 \in \mathbb{R}^{a \times t}$. Therefore, l layers of 2D convs with a filter size of $(1 \times k)$ followed by batch normalization and a ReLU activation function are applied. The filter size causes that each filter is applied on k time steps of 1 attribute at the same time. The lth layer uses a (1×1) convolution to reduce the number of generated feature maps to 1 which means that we finally get a feature map $M^l \in \mathbb{R}^{a \times t_y}$ at layer l where t_y is the length of the time dimension. If strides $s > 1$ are used in the convs, then $t_y < t$ holds, which corresponds to a compressed time dimension. Traditionally, the conv layers are followed by one or more fully connected (FC) layers to connect the different features (from the feature maps). Since we want to obtain a separate feature representation for each attribute, so-called time-distributed FC layers are applied attribute-wise which means that each row $m_l^i \in M^l$ is processed by the same FC layers. Finally, this results in our first output $H_1 \in \mathbb{R}^{a \times n}$ where n is the number of units of the last FC layer. The purpose of this transformation is to obtain a representation for each attribute i which corresponds to the row vector of H_1, denoted as $h_1^i \in \mathbb{R}^n$, and enables the use of an attribute-weighted distance measure.

A remaining deficiency of H_1 is that this representation does not consider patterns that occur across different attributes which is typically computed by 1D convs. Especially in CPPSs where a lot of failures can only be determined in its context, i.e. in relation of several data streams, this perspective on the data is important. For this purpose, H_1 is multiplied element-wise ($\odot$) with the relevance vector $x_{2_2} \in \{0,1\}^a$, which serves as a gate so that only features of relevant attributes are considered for generating a "contextual" representation. This "contextual" representation $h_2 = g(H_1 \odot x_{2_2})$ is obtained by processing the gated input with several FC layers that are referred to as $g(\cdot)$. This results in the second output $h_2 \in \mathbb{R}^j$ where j is the size of the last FC layer. In summary, the first branch generates two outputs of which the first $H1$ allows an association to the input attributes and the second h_2 only considers the attributes that are manually defined as relevant.

The second branch is responsible for a further output z, which is used to weight the distances resulting from both previous outputs based on the failure mode of the training example used for comparison. Therefore, z is obtained by $z = k(x_{2_2})$ where k represents several FC layers. The last layer consists of one neuron with a sigmoid activation function so that $z \in [0,1]$. Since both encoders receive the same input x_{2_2} based on the known training example, both encoders generate the same value for z.

Distance. The distance between a pair (a,b) using the output of the encoder $f_{SNN}(X_1, [x_{2_1}, x_{2_2}]) = \{H_1, h_2, z\}$ where $H_1 \in \mathbb{R}^{a \times n}$, $h_2 \in \mathbb{R}^j$, $z \in [0,1]$ is calculated as follows:

$$d(a,b) = z * d_1(H_{1,a}, H_{1,b}) + (1-z) * d_2(h_{2,a}, h_{2,b}). \tag{3}$$

The distance function $d_1(\cdot, \cdot)$ is an attribute weighted distance and would be calculated for the Manhattan distance as follows:

$$d_1(H_{1,a}, H_{1,b}) = \frac{1}{r} \sum_{i=1}^{r} |w_i * (H_{1,a}^i - H_{1,b}^i)|, \tag{4}$$

with $\sum_{i=1}^{r} w_i = 1$ and $r = a * n$ is the number of entries of output matrix H_1. The weighting is based on x_{2_1} of the training example and restricts the distance calculation to only relevant attributes. Since the amount of attributes to be considered can vary greatly, we normalize each weight $w_i = \frac{1}{m \times n}$ where m is the sum of relevant attributes multiplied by the length n of each attribute vector h_1^i. In the case of an irrelevant attribute, we use $w_i = 0$ so that this distance does not influence our assessment.

For the Manhattan distance, $d_2(\cdot, \cdot)$ would be calculated as follows:

$$d_2(h_{2,a}, h_{2,b}) = \frac{1}{j} \sum_{i=1}^{j} |(h_{2,a}^i - h_{2,b}^i)|. \tag{5}$$

Since the input $h_{2,a}$ and $h_{2,b}$ are vectors that represent the current context, $d_2(\cdot, \cdot)$ has the purpose of a contextual distance measure that considers the multivariate aspects. This corresponds to the typically used distance measure for

SNNs, but with the difference that its input $h_{2,a}$ and $h_{2,b}$ is exclusively generated of features from attributes that have been manually classified as relevant.

4 Evaluation

4.1 Fischertechnik Model Factory Data Set

We use the Fischertechnik (FT) factory model presented in [16] for the simulation of a CPPS. It consists of five workstations (WSs) such as a sorting line with colour recognition, a high-bay warehouse, two processing stations and a vacuum gripper robot, which are connected to each other in order to simulate the processing of workpieces. Each of these WSs is made up of FT parts, which means that actuators and sensors of the same type occur multiple times within the factory. A detailed description of the relation and structure is available in form of an ontological knowledge base [17]. The raw data is generated by multiple runs of this factory model, in which one (or no) failure mode is simulated at a time. During each run, 61 attributes are recorded, representing sensor data streams and actuator control commands. The data set contains 29 classes that correspond to different failure modes, components and conditions, which can be summarized into four groups:

- False signals from control sensors are simulated over a period of approx. 10 s continuously or intermittently for light barriers and position switches at five different positions.
- Wear is simulated by artificially induced vibrations on two conveyor belt motors with intermittent or exponential progression over random durations. For the simulation of an exponential degradation progression, a state deviating from normal is classified as degraded first and then critical before the failure occurs, while the intermittent failure mode simulation only has the critical phase. The motors are monitored by three-axis acceleration sensors.
- Leakages are simulated in pneumatic systems, which are monitored by differential pressure sensors.
- Other FaFs such as a broken tooth of a gear or slippage on the conveyor belt were fabricated. Additionally, incorrect transport processes of the vacuum gripper due to a missing workpiece were simulated.

For processing the raw data into examples, a sliding window approach with a time window of 4 s, a step size of 1 s, and a sampling rate of 4 ms is used, resulting in a shape of $X \in R^{61 \times 1000}$. Our training data set consists of 25,550 examples, of which 24,908 are labeled as a normal state and 642 labeled as FaFs. The test data set is composed of 18 classes and consists of 3,389 examples, of which 2907 are labeled as normal state and 482 labeled as FaFs. The splitting into both sets was done in a way that all examples labeled as FaF are separated based on a complete R2F recording, so that all examples of single R2F are either only included in the test or training data set. A detailed overview of the classes and their distribution in the data sets can be found in Appendix A.

The selection of relevant attributes for each failure mode is based on expert knowledge with an average of about 4 attributes per FaF label for x_{2_2} and around 1.4 for x_{2_1}. In our case, this knowledge was obtained by examining the (visualized) data streams. Alternatively, this could be acquired by means of a failure mode effect analysis (FMEA) [7]. For example, to monitor a leakage in our pneumatic systems, we have identified its differential pressure and the control parameters of their valves and compressors as relevant attributes. For the healthy state (no failure simulated), the union of features selected for all failures modes is used, resulting in a count of 41 used for x_{2_1} as well as x_{2_2}.

4.2 Approaches for Measuring Time Series Similarity

Baseline Methods. We report three baseline methods that are not based on neural networks. The first one combines a feature-based representation $f_{TSF}(X_1)$ with 27,969 significant features with the Euclidean distance. The other variants are based on DTW using a FastDTW implementation, whereby i) DTW is directly applied to X_1 or ii) X_1 is reduced to the relevant attributes according to x_{2_2} of the labeled training example before DTW is applied.

Siamese Neural Networks. As part of the evaluation, we use three encoder types, namely a standard CNN with 1D convs, 2D convs with a filter size of $(1 \times k)$ and one with LSTM layers. Each conv operation used valid padding and is followed by batch normalization and processed by a ReLU activation function. A dropout regularization function is added as final layer. For all CNN2D variants (except CNN2D + MAR) an additional 1D conv operation with 61 filters, a filter size and stride of 1 on the input X_1 is used to obtain a feature map $m \in R^{a \times t}$. This feature map contains (contextual) information across a time step which is then concatenated with X_1 so that the input into the 2D conv encoder is $R^{a \times t \times 2}$. Additionally to these core encoders, we considered two extensions which are applied subsequently. First, FC layers which are typically used in CNNs to merge different features into a feature vector that is then passed to the distance measure. Second, the approach of NeuralWarp (NW) [9] that uses an additional feed forward neural network for similarity determination between each time step of two time series based on their deep representations instead of a standard distance measure. In both extensions, the input to each FC layer is batch normalized and ReLU is used as activation function, except the last neuron of NW, which uses a sigmoid activation function. The configurations which (to the best of our knowledge) yield the highest performance are shown in Table 1.

4.3 Experimental Setup and Training Procedure

Across all variants, a batch size of 64 is used, meaning that 128 (64 positive and 64 negative) pairs are processed in each batch. Due to high VRAM requirements, the batch size for the LSTM encoder has to be reduced to 16 though. The composition of batches follows the approach that each one should contain one example

Table 1. Models selected for evaluation

		CNN1D	CNN1D FC	CNN1D NW	CNN2D	CNN2D FC	CNN2D + MAR	LSTM NW
Training	Batch Size	64	64	64	64	64	64	16
	Learning Rate	0.001	0.00001	0.001	0.001	0.001	0.001	0.001
	Dropout	0.05	0.05	0.05	0.05	0.05	0.1	0.05
Encoder	Layer Type	Conv1D	Conv1D	Conv1D	Conv2D	Conv2D	Conv2D	LSTM
	Units per Layer	256, 64, 32	256, 64, 32	256, 64, 32	128, 64, 16, 1	128, 64, 16, 1	128, 64, 16, 1	128, 64, 32
	Filter Size	7, 5, 3	7, 5, 3	7, 5, 3	5,5,3,1	5,5,3,1	5,5,3,1	-
	Stride	2, 2, 1	2, 2, 1	2, 2, 1	2,2,2,1	2,2,2,1	2,2,2,1	-
	FC-Layer	-	1024, 768, 512	-	-	1024, 768, 512	(128, 64, 32) (256, 128, 64)	-
NW	Units per Layer	-	-	32, 16, 1	-	-	-	32, 16, 1
Dis.	Distance	MH	MH	NW	MH	MH	Weighted MH & MH	NW

of all 29 classes and reflect the data distribution. For this reason, 32 pairs are sampled according to the data set distribution, which therefore mostly leads to pairs of healthy condition while the remaining 32 pairs are selected equally distributed over all classes. Furthermore, if not stated otherwise, the Manhattan (MH) Distance is applied.

The selection of hyper parameters, such as layer size, learning and dropout rate, is performed manually by expert knowledge by means of achieving a steep loss during the first 300 epochs of training. We use early stopping to determine the termination of the training process if there is no improvement to the loss in an interval of i) 500 or ii) 1000 epochs. Among all models saved every 10 epochs in a single training, the one with the best loss is selected. To avoid overfitting of the CNN2D + MAR variant due to the attribute restrictions, the dropout rate is increased from 0.05 to 0.1 in contrast to CNN2D and CNN2D FC. In addition to the early stopping described above, a fixed limit of 0.03 is set for the loss and the number of epochs is limited to a maximum of 2500.

The evaluation is conducted on a partial section (case base) of the training data set, which is identical for all experiments. It contains a maximum of 150 examples per class that are randomly selected and only reached by the class representing the healthy state. In total, the case base therefore consists of 792 examples. All approaches are evaluated using the k-NN method with $k = 1$, which is consistent with the procedure of related work [1,9,15].

4.4 Predictive Maintenance Related Quality Measures

In order to examine the suitability of our approaches for the application in PredM, we propose several quality measures that are shown in Table 2. First of all, we consider the standard measures Precision (Prec.), Recall (Rec.) as well as the F1-Score (F1) as weighted average based on the number of examples per class. In the context of PredM, it makes sense to take a closer look at the normal condition class because too many false positives would lead to unnecessary inspections and too many false negatives would result in undetected FaFs. Therefore, we report the F1-Score of this class – referred to as Health F1 – as major criterion for distinguishing between normal and faulty states and indicating the overall utility of an approach.

A disadvantage of these standard measures, however, is that they do not consider the value of a wrong prediction. In the case of the real world application of PredM, a wrong classification could still be useful for a human maintenance engineer in order to locate the source of an issue, even if the specific failure mode is classified wrongly. For this reason, we report self-defined quality measures that evaluate the usefulness of a prediction based on the factors location, condition and failure mode. Location (Loc.) assesses the position in the factory at which a deviation from the normal state is detected. Condition (Cond.) distinguishes between different stages of the fault progression and is divided into normal, degraded, critical and failure, whereby a subset of these is used for different failure modes. The diagnosis (Diag.) score represents the similarity between different ways in which a component may fail. In case of a label that diverges from normal condition, the quality of each factor is calculated as $\frac{\sum_i^n u_i}{n}$ where n is the number of test examples labeled as FaFs and u_i is the predefined usefulness for humans corresponding to the label of the test example i. If the classified class is equal to the label of example i then $u_i = 1$, otherwise $u_i \in [0, 1)$. Moreover, the measure H+F is an extension of the previously described measures by also considering examples with normal condition in the calculation described above. The resulting three factors are averaged to provide a more comprehensive measure.

4.5   Results

For each SNN, we perform multiple training runs with variation of the loss function and early stopping limit (as per Sect. 4.3). Using an additional validation set for parameter optimization and model selection was not possible due to the restricted amount of available examples of failures. Hence, we selected the parameter combination with the highest overall Health F1 score (as per Sect. 4.4). If these scores are equal, the decision is made according to the overall F1 score, since it weights precision and recall equally. In most cases the variants with BCE as loss and an early stopping limit of 1000 epochs are selected (except NeuralWrap (CNN1D) with a limit of 500 epochs and NeuralWarp (LSTM) with a mean squared error as loss function), although there are only slight deviations in the scores of the other combinations. In contrast, the CNN2D + MAR SNN showed larger deviations for the performance measures, which we could not resolve by hyperparameter tuning, so the average of six consecutive training runs is reported. The aim was to ensure that an appropriate reference point for comparison is used, which does not overstate the results but also does not disadvantageously reflect them. Our evaluation results are shown in Table 2.

In the evaluation we especially focus on the consideration of two hypotheses:

H1 The integration of expert knowledge about the relevance of individual attributes (MAR) can improve similarity-based classification if for each failure mode only a small subset of attributes is relevant.

H2 Learning methods (e.g. SNNs) are superior compared to static methods (e.g. DTW) because of their ability to adapt to the problem domain.

We can confirm H1 with the exception of the MS-SNNs approach. Both DTW + MAR and CNN2D + MAR provide better results compared to their respective variants without attribute relevance knowledge. The results also confirm H2 since approaches without learning capabilities (1st block of Table 2) generally achieve worse results than those with learning capabilities (2nd and 3rd block of Table 2), again with the exception of MS-SNNs. Another disadvantage of these static approaches is their poor run time behaviour, which reduces their applicability in real-time applications. For instance, in our computing environment the classification of an example with DTW takes about 18.63 s (using multithreaded computation) and is therefore slower than our CNN2D + MAR approach (1.36 s/example, using a single NVIDIA Tesla V100 GPU) by a factor of about 13.7.

Furthermore, the results show that joint learning of all classes performs significantly better than using several specialized SNNs (MS-SNNs approach). It can be assumed that the larger number of classes to be delimited requires the learning of more distinct representations. Overall, our proposed CNN2D + MAR architecture is able to achieve the best performance by leveraging expert knowledge about the attribute relevance. For validating the significance of our results we used a non-parametric stratified shuffling test [26] with $p < 0.01$ for Prec., Rec. and F1 against CNN1D FC and CNN2D FC, since these also achieve high Health F1 values of 0.97. Considering the results of the six trained CNN2 + MAR models, a significance is shown especially in comparison to the CNN1D FC. The best two trained models show significantly better results compared to the other two models for all metrics. Only the recall is not sufficiently significant compared to CNN2D FC.

Furthermore, CNN2D and CNN2D + MAR provide the best results for locating fault locations (see Loc. score, Table 2). A possible explanation might be that the deep representations used for similarity comparisons always retains the attribute dimension. The CNN2D FC variant loses this link in the FC layer, which could explain the weaker performance for this measure.

Table 2. Evaluation results of different time series similarity measures and standard deviation of multiple runs for CNN2D + MAR

Approach	Health F1	Failure Diag.	Failure Loc.	Failure Cond.	H+F	Overall Prec.	Overall Rec.	Overall F1
Feature-based + Eucl.	0.76	0.48	0.44	0.59	0.62	0.81	0.57	0.67
DTW	0.85	0.70	0.66	0.74	0.76	0.87	0.70	0.77
DTW + MAR	0.94	0.44	0.39	0.57	0.87	0.85	0.84	0.84
CNN1D	0.96	0.73	0.64	0.76	0.91	0.89	0.85	0.87
CNN1D FC	**0.97**	0.66	0.55	0.73	0.92	0.88	0.87	0.87
NeuralWarp (CNN1D)	0.96	0.70	0.64	0.79	0.91	0.87	0.84	0.85
NeuralWarp (LSTM)	0.95	0.71	0.59	0.77	0.90	0.88	0.83	0.85
CNN2D	0.95	0.75	**0.76**	0.79	0.90	0.89	0.85	0.87
CNN2D FC	**0.97**	0.72	0.59	0.75	0.92	0.89	0.87	0.88
CNN2D + MAR	**0.97** ±0.00	**0.78** ±0.04	**0.76** ±0.05	**0.84** ±0.03	**0.93** ±0.01	**0.91** ±0.01	**0.88** ±0.01	**0.89** ±0.01
MS-SNN + MAR	0.68	0.60	0.51	0.76	0.54	0.86	0.47	0.60

5   Conclusion and Future Work

This research has shown that the integration of expert knowledge about relevant attributes (data streams) can enhance the performance of similarity-based deep learning approaches for high-dimensional time series classification. Additionally, restricting the similarity-based classification to manually defined attributes could help to improve confidence into the predictions. Furthermore, a general suitability for applying 2D convolutions on multivariate time series consisting of data streams with similar characteristics has been shown. Our proposed model, which combines these two approaches, is able to achieve the best results compared to all other methods.

Future work could examine the usefulness of our attribute-wise time series representations for transfer learning purposes, e.g. for comparing the same failure modes between different instances of similar components. Furthermore, it could be investigated whether the integration of more knowledge through the use of different 2D CNNs based on sensor data properties, such as sampling rate or attribute value range, could further enhance performance. Finally, to promote further research of time series analysis for PredM, we provide our implementation, data set as well as supplementary resources at https://github.com/PredM/SiameseNeuralNetwork.

A   Dataset

An overview of the classes and their distribution contained in the data set is shown in Table 3. Note that the case base used for evaluation, as described in Sect. 4.3, contains up to 150 examples from the training data set for each class, i.e. 150 for no_failure and every example of all other classes. The "txt" part of the label indicates the location of the component, i.e. the CPS, where the failure was simulated.

Table 3. Data set overview

Failure mode	Train	Test	Total
no_failure	24908	2907	27815
txt15_conveyor_failure_mode_driveshaft_slippage...	11	0	11
txt15_i1_lightbarrier_failure_mode_1	7	0	7
txt15_i1_lightbarrier_failure_mode_2	6	18	24
txt15_i3_lightbarrier_failure_mode_2	8	5	13
txt15_m1_t1_high_wear	82	88	170
txt15_m1_t1_low_wear	112	79	191
txt15_m1_t2_wear	42	58	100
txt15_pneumatic_leakage_failure_mode_1	11	0	11
txt15_pneumatic_leakage_failure_mode_2	12	0	12
txt15_pneumatic_leakage_failure_mode_3	10	0	10
txt16_conveyor_failure_mode_driveshaft_slippage...	11	12	23
txt16_conveyor_big_gear_tooth_broken_failure	13	11	24
txt16_conveyor_small_gear_tooth_broken_failure	3	0	3
txt16_i3_switch_failure_mode_2	9	0	9
txt16_i4_lightbarrier_failure_mode_1	31	42	73
txt16_m3_t1_high_wear	42	26	68
txt16_m3_t1_low_wear	12	20	32
txt16_m3_t2_wear	63	43	106
txt17_i1_switch_failure_mode_1	17	15	32
txt17_i1_switch_failure_mode_2	24	11	35
txt17_pneumatic_leakage_failure_mode_1	24	9	33
txt17_workingstation_transport_failure_mode_wou...	20	18	38
txt18_pneumatic_leakage_failure_mode_1	11	9	20
txt18_pneumatic_leakage_failure_mode_2	27	10	37
txt18_pneumatic_leakage_failure_mode_2_faulty	11	8	19
txt18_transport_failure_mode_wout_workpiece	6	0	6
txt19_i4_lightbarrier_failure_mode_1	9	0	9
txt19_i4_lightbarrier_failure_mode_2	8	0	8
Total	25550	3389	28939

References

1. Abanda, A., Mori, U., Lozano, J.A.: A review on distance based time series classification. Data Mining Knowl. Discov. **33**(2), 378–412 (2018). https://doi.org/10. 1007/s10618-018-0596-4
2. Assaf, R., Schumann, A.: Explainable deep neural networks for multivariate time series predictions. In: Proceedings of the Twenty-Eighth International Joint Conference on Artificial Intelligence, IJCAI-19, pp. 6488–6490 (2019)
3. Bergmann, R.: Experience Management: Foundations, Development Methodology, and Internet-Based Applications. Springer, Heidelberg (2002). https://doi.org/10. 1007/3-540-45759-3
4. Berndt, D.J., Clifford, J.: Using dynamic time warping to find patterns in time series. In: KDD: Papers from AAAI Workshop, pp. 359–370. AAAI Press (1994)
5. Bromley, J., et al.: Signature verification using a "siamese" time delay neural network. IJPRAI **7**(4), 669–688 (1993)
6. Christ, M., Braun, N., Neuffer, J., Kempa-Liehr, A.W.: Time series feature extraction on basis of scalable hypothesis tests. Neurocomputing **307**, 72–77 (2018)
7. Goodman, D., James, P., Hofmeister, F.S.: Prognostics and Health Management: A Practical Approach to Improving System Reliability Using Condition-Based Data. Wiley (2019)
8. Fink, O., Wang, Q., Svensén, M., Dersin, P., Lee, W.J., Ducoffe, M.: Potential, challenges and future directions for deep learning in prognostics and health management applications. Eng. Appl. Artif. Intell. **92**, 103678 (2020)
9. Grabocka, J., Schmidt-Thieme, L.: NeuralWarp: Time-Series Similarity with Warping Networks. CoRR abs/1812.08306 (2018)
10. Koch, G., Richard Zemel, R.S.: Siamese neural networks for one-shot image recognition. In: ICML, Lille, France (2015)
11. Guan, Q., Huang, Y., Zhong, Z., Zheng, Z., Zheng, L., Yang, Y.: Thorax disease classification with attention guided convolutional neural network. Pattern Recog. Lett. 131 (2019)
12. Guo, J., Li, Z., Li, M.: A review on prognostics methods for engineering systems. IEEE Trans. Reliab. **69**(3), 1110–1129 (2020). https://doi.org/10.1109/TR.2019. 2957965
13. Huang, X., Zanni-Merk, C., Crémilleux, B.: Enhancing deep learning with semantics: an application to manufacturing time series analysis. Procedia Comput. Sci. **159**, 437–446 (2019)
14. Jia, X., Cai, H., Hsu, Y.M., Li, W., Feng, J., Lee, J.: A novel similarity-based method for remaining useful life prediction using kernel two sample test. In: Proceedings of the Annual Conference of the PHM Society (2019)
15. Jiang, W.: Time series classification: nearest neighbor versus deep learning models. SN Appl. Sci. **2**(4), 1–17 (2020). https://doi.org/10.1007/s42452-020-2506-9
16. Klein, P., Bergmann, R.: Generation of complex data for ai-based predictive maintenance research with a physical factory model. In: 16th International Conference on Informatics in Control Automation and Robotics, pp. 40–50. SciTePress (2019)
17. Klein, P., Malburg, L., Bergmann, R.: FTOnto: a domain ontology for a Fischertechnik simulation production factory by reusing existing ontologies. In: Proceedings of the Conference LWDA, vol. 2454, pp. 253–264. CEUR-WS.org (2019)
18. Lapuschkin, S., Wäldchen, S., Binder, A., Montavon, G., Samek, W., Müller, K.-R.: Unmasking Clever Hans predictors and assessing what machines really learn. Nat. Commun. **10** (2019). https://doi.org/10.1038/s41467-019-08987-4

19. Lee, J., Bagheri, B., Kao, H.A.: A cyber-physical systems architecture for industry 4.0-based manufacturing systems. Manuf. Lett. **3**, 18–23 (2015)
20. Lezoche, M., Panetto, H.: Cyber-Physical Systems, a new formal paradigm to model redundancy and resiliency. Enterprise Information Systems, pp. 1–22 (2018)
21. Luo, Y., Xiao, Y., Cheng, L., Peng, G., Yao, D.D.: Deep Learning-Based Anomaly Detection in Cyber-Physical Systems: Progress and Opportunities. CoRR abs/2003.13213 (2020)
22. Mai, C.K., Chevalier, R.: Equipment diagnostics based on comparison of past abnormal behaviors using a big data platform. In: Proceedings of the Annual Conference of the PHM Society (2016)
23. Pei, W., Tax, D.M.J., van der Maaten, L.: Modeling Time Series Similarity with Siamese Recurrent Networks. CoRR abs/1603.04713 (2016)
24. Ran, Y., Zhou, X., Lin, P., Wen, Y., Deng, R.: A Survey of Predictive Maintenance: Systems, Purposes and Approaches. CoRR abs/1912.07383 (2019)
25. Turney, P.D.: The Management of Context-Sensitive Features: A Review of Strategies. CoRR abs/cs/0212037 (2002)
26. Yeh, A.: More accurate tests for the statistical significance of result differences. arXiv preprint cs/0008005 (2000)
27. Zhang, A., Li, S., Cui, Y., Yang, W., Dong, R., Hu, J.: Limited data rolling bearing fault diagnosis with few-shot learning. IEEE Access **7**, 110895–110904 (2019)

Explainable Process Monitoring Based on Class Activation Map: Garbage In, Garbage Out

Cheolhwan Oh, Junhyung Moon, and Jongpil Jeong[✉]

Department of Smart Factory Convergence, Sungkyunkwan University,
Suwon, Jangan-gu, Gyeonggi-do 16419, Republic of Korea
{dhdldzhkf13,mjh7345,jpjeong}@skku.edu

Abstract. Process monitoring at industrial sites contributes to system stability by detecting and diagnosing unexpected changes in a system. Today, as the infrastructure of industrial sites is advanced due to the development of communication technology, various and vast amounts of data are generated, and the importance of a methodology to effectively monitor these data to diagnose a system is increasing daily. As a deep neural network-based methodology can effectively extract information from a large amount of data, methods have been proposed to monitor processes using this methodology to detect any system abnormalities. Neural network-based process monitoring is effective in detecting anomalies but has difficulty in diagnosing due to the limitations of the black-box model. Therefore, this paper proposes a process monitoring framework that can detect and diagnose anomalies. The proposed framework performs post-processing based on the class activation map to perform the diagnosis of data that are considered outliers. To verify the performance of the proposed method, experiments were conducted using industrial public motor datasets, demonstrating that the proposed method can effectively detect and diagnose abnormalities.

Keywords: Class activation map · Garbage in · Garbage out · Statistical process control · Deep neural network · Fault detection and diagnosis

1 Introduction

With recent advancements in the industry, the use of machinery has diversified to the point at which it can be found anywhere in life, and with the proliferation of the internet of things, it is possible to collect data that could not have been previously collected from the existing systems. Accordingly, the need for a technique to effectively prevent faults in a system by effectively managing the collected data has increased.

In various industries, statistical process control (SPC) technology is effective in improving the process through fault detection and diagnosis (FDD). However,

© Springer Nature Switzerland AG 2020
J. Gama et al. (Eds.): ITEM 2020/IoT Streams 2020, CCIS 1325, pp. 93–105, 2020.
https://doi.org/10.1007/978-3-030-66770-2_7

problems, such as multicollinearity and false alarms, occur when high correlation and nonlinearity exist in the data [1]. Therefore, large-scale complex industrial processes require appropriate monitoring techniques to process large-scale process data efficiently. Thus, studies have been proposed that combine the traditional SPC methodology with machine learning and deep learning techniques that effectively analyse large datasets [2].

The general focus of machine learning is the representation of input data and the generalisation of learned patterns for use in future unknown data. The excellence of the data representation dramatically affects the performance of the machine learning model on the data. That is, if the data representation is not good, even the advanced model may exhibit degraded performance. If the data representation is good, a relatively simple model may exhibit high performance. Therefore, feature engineering, which focuses on constructing shapes and data representations from raw data, is an essential component of machine learning [3]. However, feature engineering consumes much effort in machine learning tasks, is generally domain-specific, and involves significant human labour.

On the other hand, deep learning is a method in which the model automatically extracts features from raw data. Deep learning, which mimics the way the human brain works, consists of a hierarchical architecture that builds a hierarchy. Moreover, stacked layers automatically extract features from raw data [4]. Furthermore, like the human brain, deep learning mimics the brain's excellent performance in image processing and speech recognition even when it receives raw images and sounds. For this reason, deep learning-based methodologies have been attracting attention in the process monitoring field where raw sensor data are handled [5].

However, deep learning methods are considered black-box models and cannot explain the internal calculation mechanism. Due to these limitations, insight from deep learning models can be confirmed through the visualisation of the learned representation [6]. However, because this method does not provide clear evidence to end users, it is not easy to trust the results. In addition, in the case of real-time sensor data that are not composed of images, trusting the visualization of the diagnostic results is more challenging because the results are not visually intuitive compared to images.

This paper proposes an explainable neural network-based process monitoring framework that can detect and diagnose system faults. The proposed framework performs post-processing based on the class activation map (CAM) [7] to perform the diagnosis of data that are considered outliers.

The rest of this paper is organised as follows. Section 2 discusses the related work. Section 3 explains the control chart in SPC. Section 4 describes the proposed method. Section 5 presents the conducted experiments to evaluate the performance of the proposed approach and describes the experiment result. Section 6 discusses conclusions and future work.

2   Related Work

In the manufacturing process, accident prevention and product defect reduction are among the most important goals. Thus, it is important to detect and diagnose machine defects. For decades, FDD has been actively researched. First, fault detection evaluates whether the process operates under normal circumstances. Then, fault diagnosis determines the characteristics and cause of the defect.

The FDD method can be broadly classified into two categories: model-based and data-based methods. The model-based approach develops and applies process models in fault detection. The method has strong reliability and has been widely researched, developed, and applied in process systems. However, it is difficult to capture system complexity and nonlinear models, and early fault detection in complex processes cannot be easily implemented [8].

In contrast, data-driven methods are measured based on minimal process knowledge. Data-driven FDD methods can be classified qualitatively or quantitatively. The expert system and qualitative trend analysis are representative qualitative techniques [9].

Quantitative methods can be categorised into statistical or non-statistical categories. As a statistical method, the SPC-based process monitoring technique monitors a process by setting a control limit based on data collected from a stable state [10]. Support vector machines and artificial neural networks are the most commonly used non-statistical supervised learning methods, and both construct a learning model of recorded data with labels and perform FDD by comparing the model with the current process data. The downside of this FDD technique is that it requires numerous labelled data samples for training [11].

In particular, because process monitoring using a neural network is a black-box model, it is difficult to interpret the relationship between input data and output results in the actual manufacturing process despite high classification performance [6]. Accordingly, the problem arises that end users in a system with FDD based on neural networks must rely on models that can make mistakes. In this situation, the end user may become unreliable and suspicious of the system [12].

To improve this, research has been conducted to overcome the limitations of the neural network's black-box model and to propose a fault diagnosis through an explainable artificial intelligence model [13]. Among them, the CAM, which can be applied to convolutional neural network (CNN)-based deep learning models is effective in improving the black-box problem [7].

The CAM is a method to provide the model with explanatory power by visualising which part of the image the CNN model predicted. The CAM uses the weight of the target class in the last convolutional layer to highlight an important region as a localisation map when predicting a class in an image. However, the CAM has the restriction that the global average pooling (GAP) layer must be enforced rather than the fully connected (FC) layer in the last layer. The recently proposed Grad-CAM improved this using the gradient of the target class in the last convolutional layer [14]. Accordingly, the Grad-CAM can be used in CNN models, such as VGG with FCN. Moreover, the CAM and

Grad-CAM have been used in several fields to improve the explanatory power of deep learning models. In addition, in FDD, the CAM or Grad-CAM can be used for a visual explanation [15].

3 Control Chart in Process Monitoring

Rather than monitoring the process with a guess, SPC is a methodology that finds solutions or improvements by identifying and interpreting problems based on data. It is primarily used for quality control [10].

This section describes the control chart technique, the technique used to perform process monitoring in this paper. In general, the control chart technique is divided into univariate or multivariate control charts depending on the number of data features to be monitored. As this paper proposes a method to implement a control chart using multivariate latent variables extracted from a deep learning model, this section primarily describes the multivariate control chart technique.

3.1 Multivariate Control Charts

The advantage of using the univariate control chart is that a mathematical model is unnecessary; instead, it can be easily applied and interpreted by directly using operation data. However, the main drawback of these univariate SPC methods is that they can cause erroneous results when applied to multivariate data with a high correlation between variables, and it is inefficient to draw a control chart for each variable [16].

To efficiently manage two or more related data or to simultaneously monitor a process, a multivariate control chart capable of simultaneously observing changes in two or more management items is required. To this end, several multivariate control charts have been proposed, such as Hotelling's T^2 chart, the multivariate EWMA chart, and the multivariate CUSUM chart [16]. The most widely used of these is Hotelling's T^2 [17]. The T^2 statistic is calculated using Eq. (1):

$$T^2 = (x - \bar{x})^T S^{-1} (x - \bar{x}), \tag{1}$$

where $\bar{x}$ and S are the sample mean vector and sample covariance matrix, respectively, which are determined from the past data $X \in R^{n \times m}$ collected in the control state, where n and m are the numbers of samples and variables, respectively. This is used as a statistic to determine how similar the data collected in the control state are to the newly measured data. Hotelling's T^2 statistic refers to the mahalanobis distance between the historically collected data in the control state and the new measurements. The upper control limit of the T^2 chart assumes normality and follows the F-distribution [10]. Equation (2) calculates the upper control limit, which is the critical value:

$$UCL_{T^2} = \frac{m(n+1)(n-1)}{n(n-m)} F_{(m,n-m,\alpha)}, \tag{2}$$

In Eq. (2), the significance level α is the type 1 error rate. This is the maximum allowable limit for false alarms that misjudge a positive as a negative. Moreover, $F_{(m,n-m,\alpha)}$ is the upper α th quantile of the F-distribution with m and $(n-m)$ degrees of freedom.

However, the multivariate process control based on Hotelling's T^2 is not useful for data with numerous correlated variables. If numerous correlation variables exist, it is challenging to invert the covariance matrix S because the covariance matrix becomes an almost singular matrix, which leads to problematic results [18]. In addition, when numerous highly correlated variables are included in the data, this may cause multicollinearity; thus, the ability to detect a progress shift may deteriorate [1]. Therefore, various latent variable-based control charts for extracting features from raw data have been proposed.

3.2   Latent Variable Based Multivariate Control Charts

Hotelling's T^2 chart, which is based on the principal component analysis (PCA), is a representative case among latent variable-based control chart methodologies. In addition, PCA is a technique that determines the axes that are orthogonal to each other while preserving the variance of the data as much as possible and transforms the data in the high-dimensional space into a low-dimensional space without linear correlation [19]. This is similar to the T^2 chart without PCA described in the previous Eqs. (1) and (2), but the main difference is that a Q chart for performing residual analysis is added and used together. To do this, first, the data matrix X is decomposed into individual elements through PCA, and the individual elements are further divided into principal component subspace (PCS) and residual subspace (RS) according to the number of principal components selected, which is expressed in Eq. (3).

$$X = \hat{X} + \tilde{X} = \hat{T}\hat{P}^T + \tilde{T}\tilde{P}^T = \begin{bmatrix} \hat{T} & \tilde{T} \end{bmatrix} \begin{bmatrix} \hat{P} & \tilde{P} \end{bmatrix}^T = TP^T, \tag{3}$$

where $T = \begin{bmatrix} \hat{T} & \tilde{T} \end{bmatrix}$ and $P = \begin{bmatrix} \hat{P} & \tilde{P} \end{bmatrix}$ are the score and loading matrices, respectively. $\hat{T} \in R^{n \times p}$ and $\tilde{T} \in R^{n \times m-p}$ are score matrices belonging to PCS and RS, respectively, and $\hat{P} \in R^{m \times p}$ and $\tilde{P} \in R^{m \times m-p}$ are also loading matrices belonging to PCS and RS, respectively. As for the number of principal components p, after drawing the scree plot, the number of principal components corresponding to the elbow point or that can explain the variance is selected as desired by the user. After determining the number of principal components p, the PCA-based T^2 statistic can be calculated using Eqs. (4) and (5):

$$\hat{t} = x\hat{P}, \tag{4}$$

$$T^2_{PCA} = \hat{t}\hat{\Lambda}^{-1}\hat{t}^T, \tag{5}$$

where $\hat{t}$ is the score vector of x in the PCS, $\hat{\Lambda}$ is the diagonal matrix of the largest eigenvalues of the covariance matrix of $\hat{X}$. The upper control limit of PCA-based T^2 is calculated as Eq. (6), which is almost the same as Eq. (2) mentioned above.

$$UCL_{T^2_{PCA}} = \frac{p(n+1)(n-1)}{n(n-p)} F_{(p,n-p,\alpha)}, \tag{6}$$

However, because the T^2 statistic calculated in Eq. (5) uses only the information in the PCS, the concern exists that variations in the RS cannot be detected [20]. Therefore, the Q chart is also used to detect shifts that cannot be explained by only the information contained in the PCS. The Q chart can be constructed using the residuals obtained from the RS. The PCA-based Q statistics monitor the squared error between the true vector x and the vector $\hat{x}$ estimated using the PCA. The PCA-based Q statistic is calculated in Eq. (7):

$$Q_{PCA} = (x - \hat{x})(x - \hat{x})^T = \tilde{x}\tilde{x}^T, \tag{7}$$

Assuming that the Q statistic, squared prediction error, follows a normal distribution, we can calculate the upper control limits of the Q chart with the following approximation based on the weighted chi-squared distribution [21].

$$UCL_{Q_{PCA}} = \frac{v}{2m}\chi^2_{(2m^2/v,\alpha)}, \tag{8}$$

In Eq. (8), m and v are the sample mean and variance of Q_{PCA}, respectively, and the α means are the type 1 error rate, as mentioned above. Moreover, this works well even when the prediction error does not follow a normal distribution [22].

However, the PCA-based SPC technique is a method based on the linearity of data. Therefore, using PCA as it is without removing non-linearity certainly does not correctly reflect the information in the data and limits the accuracy of detecting anomalies. To address this, researchers have proposed various methodologies to reflect nonlinearity. Moreover, the most popular method is the kernel method. Accordingly, in [23], the researchers proposed Kernel PCA (KPCA), which removes nonlinearity by mapping data to a high level using a kernel function to achieve the linearity of data. Furthermore, it is a methodology to extract latent variables considering nonlinearity by applying PCA to linearized data. KPCA has been favored in many fields because it is simple to use and can adequately consider the nonlinearity of data. Also, in the field of process monitoring, several studies have been proposed in which latent variables are extracted using KPCA and applied to multivariate control charts, and its effectiveness has been proven [24–26].

Recently, a technique of applying the latest deep learning method to extract latent variables for use in a multivariate control chart has been proposed. In [2], the authors proposed a method of extracting latent variables and applying them to a multivariate control chart using an unsupervised learning algorithm, one of the deep learning methods. The latent variables were extracted using a variational autoencoder (VAE) model capable of extracting the features of the independent variable X, and it was proved that the performance of the proposed method is superior to that of the existing PCA- and KPCA-based multivariate control charts.

4   Proposed Method

This section describes the method we propose. The proposed methodology follows a three-step process:

- Fault detection by 1D-CNN
- Fault diagnosis by CAM
- Process monitoring based on VAE

In the first process of our proposed framework, the collected industrial time-series data are analysed using neural network-based techniques to detect whether the current system has reached a fault condition. After the neural network-based fault detection is performed, diagnosis is performed by calculating the CAM of the time-series data detected as a fault to determine whether the fault is caused by data generated at a certain time. To calculate the CAM, the neural network model for fault detection has a CNN-based architecture, and a 1D convolutional computation is performed to analyse the time-series data.

When the FC layer is used as the last layer for feature extraction in a time-series classification for performing fault detection, the temporal information is damaged while unfolding without considering the extracted temporal information. Thus, the FC layer is not used well in the neural network for time-series classification; instead, the GAP layer is widely adopted and used. In fact, in a study that proposed a time-series classifier model that indicates the latest performance, the last layer primarily uses the GAP layer; so there is no need to use Grad-CAM, a follow-up study that improves the short-comings of the CAM that the last layer of the CNN model must be forced to the GAP layer [27].

Therefore, in the framework proposed in this paper, the fault detection process was performed using the latest inception-resnet model [28] that uses GAP features while the time-step length of the last 1D-CNN layer is equal to the input time-series length. Consequently, the length of the CAM generated through the detection model is the same as the length of the input time series. For this reason, a specific pattern of CAM can be identified in the diagnosis process through the CAM, which has the advantage of including the timing of the pattern in the diagnosis.

In the final process monitoring step, the end user is provided with a dashboard to monitor the FDD results. This monitoring dashboard performs VAE-based process monitoring to prevent misdiagnosis and provide easy diagnosis results. The proposed process monitoring is performed according to the garbage in, garbage out (GIGO) logic.

Whereas GIGO-based process monitoring is based on the assumption that the CAM corresponding to a well-predicted true positive (TP) and true negative (TN) in the preceding fault detection has similar manifolds, the CAM corresponding to the incorrectly predicted false positive (FP) and false negative (FN) exhibits anomalies. This starts from the point at which the predicted label data, which are the output of the fault detection model, are needed to calculate the

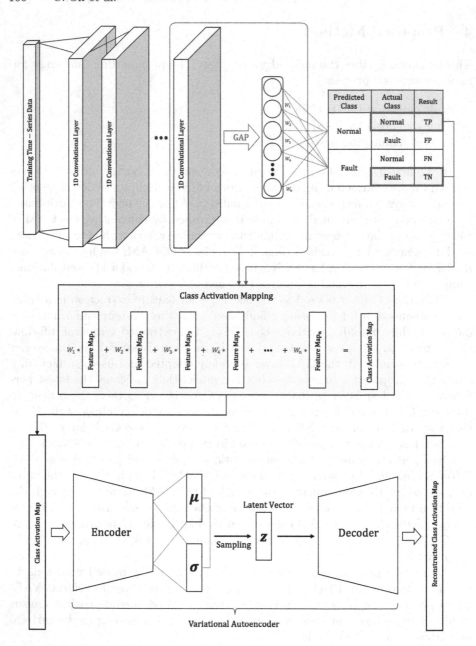

Fig. 1. The training phase of the proposed method. VAE is trained by generating CAM only with training data corresponding to TP and TN.

CAM. Initially, when fault detection of the 1D-CNN model is performed incorrectly, the predicted label data input to calculate the CAM becomes garbage; thus, the output CAM is also assumed to be garbage data.

Process monitoring is performed by training the VAE model, which learns the manifolds of CAM only corresponding to the TP and TN produced in the fault detection and diagnosis process. After completing the training of the VAE model, the latent variable z containing the manifold of the CAM corresponding to the TP and TN is calculated using the encoder of the VAE to set the upper control limit $UCL_{T_{PCA}^2}$ and $UCL_{Q_{PCA}}$ of the PCA-based T_{PCA}^2 and Q_{PCA} charts introduced in Sect. 3. The z extracted through the VAE model is robust in the T_{PCA}^2 and Q_{PCA} charts based on the normality assumption because they follow a normal distribution [2]. Finally, in the test step, the CAM generated through misclassification and misdiagnosis that may occur in FDD is subjected to post-processing through VAE-based T_{PCA}^2 and Q_{PCA} charts to perform process monitoring.

In other words, the control chart implemented as a latent variable z of the VAE model that learned only the manifolds of the CAM corresponding to the TP and TN does not judge this as an outlier when receiving the CAM generated with well-classified label information. Conversely, when the CAM generated with misclassified label information is received, it is diagnosed as an anomaly.

If the last step of process monitoring is not performed, because the reliability of the diagnosis results has not been verified, an end user may have doubts regarding whether the diagnosis results provided in the form of the CAM can be trusted. However, in the proposed method, VAE-based process monitoring can effectively identify the CAM that is considered garbage so that end users can trust the diagnosis results provided to them.

Figure 1 illustrates the model training phase to perform the proposed method. Among the training data used in the learning process, the CAM is generated using only data classified as TP and TN. That is, the VAE is learned using only the normal CAM that is not considered garbage. Moreover, the VAE, which has learned only the normal CAM, treats the garbage CAM input during the test process to be performed later as an outlier.

5 Experiment and Performance Analysis

To evaluate the performance of the proposed method, the Ford Motor Dataset, a public industrial dataset, was used in this paper. These data were originally used in a competition at the IEEE World Congress on Computational Intelligence in 2008 [29]. The classification problem is to diagnose whether a certain symptom exists or does not exist in an automotive subsystem. Each case consists of 500 measurements of engine noise and a classification. There are two separate problems:

- FordA: Train and test data set were collected in typical operating conditions, with minimal noise contamination.
- FordB: Training data were collected in typical operating conditions, but the test data samples were collected under noisy conditions.

These data are suitable for experimenting with the proposed method in that they include a dataset that is difficult to diagnose because it is noisy and an industrial dataset that is relatively easy to diagnose because of low noise.

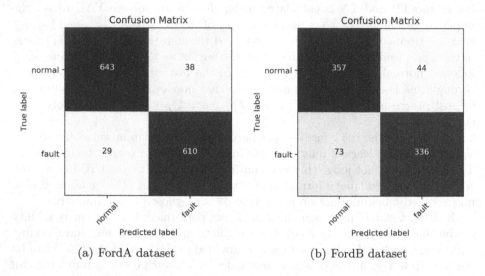

(a) FordA dataset   (b) FordB dataset

Fig. 2. Fault detection result using inceptionTime [28] classifier

Fault detection was performed using the inceptionTime classifier known to have the latest performance in the Ford Motor Dataset, and the result is depicted in Fig. 2. For Ford A and Ford B datasets, the model accuracy was 94.9% and 85.6%, respectively.

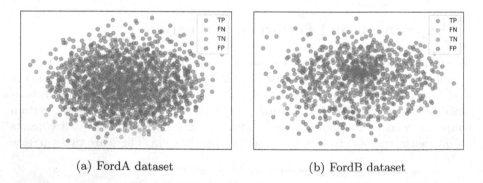

(a) FordA dataset   (b) FordB dataset

Fig. 3. Result of visualization using MDS representation for garbage and normal CAM

We assumed that normal CAM corresponding to TP and TN and garbcage CAM corresponding to FP and FN would have different manifolds. To check this, we visualize after reducing the dimensions of the normal CAM and the garbage CAM using Multi-dimensional scaling (MDS). MDS is a method to locate structures or relationships between objects by placing them in a space of a lower dimension (usually two-dimensional) than the original dimension by using distance or dissimilarity between the objects [30]. Figure 3 shows the results of the visualization using MDS. As a result of the visualization, it was confirmed that the CAM generated with label information corresponding to FN and FP considered as garbage CAM can be separated almost linearly from the normal CAM.

Lastly, VAE training was performed using only normal CAM to implement a latent variable-based control chart for proactively identifying garbage CAM that may provide misdiagnosis information to end users. The α used to perform the experiment was 1%. The outlier classification rule was set to the case where an alarm occurred in both the T^2_{PCA} and Q_{PCA} charts. The number of principal components was set to the point where the explained variance exceeds 90%.

Table 1. Results of a latent variable-based control chart experiment

Metrics	FordA	FordB
Number of outliers	70	128
Number of garbage CAM	67	117
Number of true alarm	65	109
Number of Type 1 Errors	5	19
Number of Type 2 Errors	2	8
Type 1 Error Rate	7.1%	14.8%
Type 2 Error Rate	2.9%	6.8%
Accuracy: only 1D-CNN	94.9%	85.6%
Accuracy: with VAE	99.5%	96.7%
Increased Accuracy	4.6%	11.1%

Table 1 lists the results of applying the latent variable-based control chart extracted from the VAE. After checking the CAM classified as outliers through the process monitoring step, the newly calculated accuracy increased to 99.5% and 96.7%, respectively, based on the CAM that generated the true alarm and the data that caused the false alarm.

6   Conclusion and Future Work

In this paper, we proposed a process monitoring framework that can detect and diagnose faults occurring in the system based on GIGO logic. In the proposed framework, FDD is performed using a 1D-CNN-based model. In the previous step, we trained a VAE that only learns the manifold of a normal CAM to perform reliability verification on the CAM generated for diagnosis. By identifying the garbage CAM that may provide misdiagnosis information to the end user through a latent variable-based control chart extracted through VAE, misdiagnosis information can be prevented from reaching the end user. The advantage of this is that it can achieve higher fault detection accuracy than before while providing end users with diagnosis results that have been verified for reliability, so that end users can trust the system.

As future work, studies that increase the generalisation performance of the proposed method by applying it to a wide range of industrial site data are needed. In addition, in this study, after confirming that the manifolds of the normal and garbage CAM were linearly separated, a control chart-based monitoring method was applied to separate them. However, in future work, research can be conducted on a technique to properly separate the garbage CAM using a simple boosting-based ensemble model.

Acknowledgments. This work was supported by the Smart Factory Technological R&D Program S2727115 funded by Ministry of SMEs and Startups (MSS, Korea).

References

1. Ku, W., Storer, R.H., Georgakis, C.: Disturbance detection and isolation by dynamic principal component analysis. Chemometr. Intell. Lab. Syst. **30**(1), 179–196 (1995)
2. Lee, S., Kwak, M., Tsui, K.-L., Kim, S.B.: Process monitoring using variational autoencoder for high-dimensional nonlinear processes. Eng. Appl. Artif. Intell. **83**, 13–27 (2019)
3. Domingos, P.: A few useful things to know about machine learning. Commun. ACM **55**(10), 78–87 (2012)
4. Bengio, Y., Courville, A., Vincent, P.: Representation learning: a review and new perspectives. IEEE Trans. Pattern Anal. Mach. Intell. **35**(8), 1798–1828 (2013)
5. Wang, J., Ma, Y., Zhang, L., Gao, R.X., Wu, D.: Deep learning for smart manufacturing: methods and applications. J. Manuf. Syst. **48**, 144–156 (2018)
6. Zhao, R., Yan, R., Chen, Z., Mao, K., Wang, P., Gao, R.X.: Deep learning and its applications to machine health monitoring. Mech. Syst. Signal Process. **115**, 213–237 (2019)
7. Zhou, B., Khosla, A., Lapedriza, A., Oliva, A., Torralba, A.: Learning deep features for discriminative localization. In: Proceedings of the IEEE Conference on Computer Vision and Pattern Recognition, pp. 2921–2929. IEEE (2016)
8. Venkatasubramanian, V., Rengaswamy, R., Yin, K., Kavuri, S.N.: A review of process fault detection and diagnosis: Part I: quantitative model-based methods. Comput. Chem. Eng. **27**(3), 293–311 (2003)
9. Hwang, I., Kim, S., Kim, Y., Seah, C.E.: A survey of fault detection, isolation, and reconfiguration methods. IEEE Trans. Control Syst. Technol. **18**(3), 636 653 (2009)
10. Montgomery, D.C.: Introduction to Statistical Quality Control. Wiley, Hoboken (2007)
11. Zhu, X., Goldberg, A.B.: Introduction to semi-supervised learning. Synth. Lect. Artif. Intell. Mach. Learn. **3**(1), 1–130 (2009)

12. Gehrmann, S., Strobelt, H., Krüger, R., Pfister, H., Rush, A.M.: Visual interaction with deep learning models through collaborative semantic inference. IEEE Trans. Vis. Comput. Graph. **26**(1), 884–894 (2019)
13. O'Shea, T.J., Roy, T., Erpek, T.: Spectral detection and localization of radio events with learned convolutional neural features. In: 2017 25th European Signal Processing Conference (EUSIPCO), pp. 331–335 (2017)
14. Selvaraju, R.R., Cogswell, M., Das, A., Vedantam, R., Parikh, D., Batra, D.: Grad-CAM: visual explanations from deep networks via gradient-based localization. In: Proceedings of the IEEE International Conference on Computer Vision, pp. 618–626. IEEE (2017)
15. Kim, J., Kim, J.-M.: Bearing fault diagnosis using grad-CAM and acoustic emission signals. Appl. Sci. **10**(6), 2050 (2020)
16. Lowry, C.A., Montgomery, D.C.: A review of multivariate control charts. IIE Trans. **27**(6), 800–810 (1995)
17. Hotelling, H.: Multivariate Quality Control. Techniques of Statistical Analysis. McGraw-Hill, New York (1947)
18. Seborg, D.E., Mellichamp, D.A., Edgar, T.F., Doyle III, F.J.: Process Dynamics and Control. Wiley, Hoboken (2010)
19. Wold, S., Esbensen, K., Geladi, P.: Principal component analysis. Chemometr. Intell. Lab. Syst. **2**(1–3), 37–52 (1987)
20. Mastrangelo, C.M., Runger, G.C., Montgomery, D.C.: Statistical process monitoring with principal components. Qual. Reliab. Eng. Int. **12**(3), 203–210 (1996)
21. Box, G.E.P., et al.: Some theorems on quadratic forms applied in the study of analysis of variance problems, I. Effect of inequality of variance in the one-way classification. Ann. Math. Stat. **25**(2), 290–302 (1954)
22. van Sprang, E.N.M., Ramaker, H.-J., Westerhuis, J.A., Gurden, S.P., Smilde, A.K.: Critical evaluation of approaches for on-line batch process monitoring. Chem. Eng. Sci. **57**(18), 3979–3991 (2002)
23. Schölkopf, B., Smola, A., Müller, K.-R.: Nonlinear component analysis as a kernel eigenvalue problem. Neural Comput. **10**(5), 1299–1319 (1998)
24. Lee, J.-M., Yoo, C., Choi, S.W., Vanrolleghem, P.A., Lee, I.-B.: Nonlinear process monitoring using kernel principal component analysis. Chem. Eng. Sci. **59**(1), 223–234 (2004)
25. Ge, Z., Yang, C., Song, Z.: Improved kernel PCA-based monitoring approach for nonlinear processes. Chem. Eng. Sci. **64**(9), 2245–2255 (2009)
26. Mansouri, M., Nounou, M., Nounou, H., Karim, N.: Kernel PCA-based GLRT for nonlinear fault detection of chemical processes. J. Loss Prev. Process Ind. **40**, 334–347 (2016)
27. Ismail Fawaz, H., Forestier, G., Weber, J., Idoumghar, L., Muller, P.-A.: Deep learning for time series classification: a review. Data Min. Knowl. Disc. **33**(4), 917–963 (2019). https://doi.org/10.1007/s10618-019-00619-1
28. Fawaz, H.I., et al.: InceptionTime: Finding AlexNet for Time Series Classification. arXiv preprint arXiv:1909.04939 (2019)
29. Abou-Nasr, M., Feldkamp, L.: Ford classification challenge (2007). Zip Archive http://www.timeseriesclassification.com/description.php
30. Kruskal, J.B.: Multidimensional scaling by optimizing goodness of fit to a nonmetric hypothesis. Psychometrika **29**(1), 1–27 (1964)

AutoML for Predictive Maintenance: One Tool to RUL Them All

Tanja Tornede[1,2,3(✉)], Alexander Tornede[1,2], Marcel Wever[1,2], Felix Mohr[4], and Eyke Hüllermeier[1,2,3]

[1] Department of Computer Science, Paderborn University, Paderborn, Germany
{tanja.tornede,alexander.tornede,marcel.wever,eyke}@upb.de
[2] Heinz Nixdorf Institute, Paderborn University, Paderborn, Germany
[3] Software Innovation Campus Paderborn, Paderborn, Germany
[4] Universidad de La Sabana, Chía, Cundinamarca, Colombia
felix.mohr@unisabana.edu.co

Abstract. Automated machine learning (AutoML) deals with the automatic composition and configuration of machine learning pipelines, including the selection and parametrization of preprocessors and learning algorithms. While recent work in this area has shown impressive results, existing approaches are essentially limited to standard problem classes such as classification and regression. In parallel, research in the field of predictive maintenance, particularly remaining useful lifetime (RUL) estimation, has received increasing attention, due to its practical relevance and potential to reduce unplanned downtime in industrial plants. However, applying existing AutoML methods to RUL estimation is non-trivial, as in this domain, one has to deal with varying-length multivariate time series data. Furthermore, the data often directly originates from real-world scenarios or simulations, and hence requires extensive preprocessing. In this work, we present ML-Plan-RUL, an adaptation of the AutoML tool ML-Plan to the problem of RUL estimation. To the best of our knowledge, it is the first tool specifically tailored towards automated RUL estimation, combining feature engineering, algorithm selection, and hyperparameter optimization into an end-to-end approach. First promising experimental results demonstrate the efficacy of ML-Plan-RUL.

Keywords: AutoML · Predictive maintenance · Remaining useful lifetime

1 Introduction

In industry, a predictable and continuous production is an important step towards efficiency. Unplanned downtime due to a lack of maintenance usually causes problems such as a waste of resources or dangers for employees. The food industry is a good example, where whole batches of food have to be disposed due to legal constraints in cases of an unplanned downtime. On the other side,

J. Gama et al. (Eds.): ITEM 2020/IoT Streams 2020, CCIS 1325, pp. 106–118, 2020.
https://doi.org/10.1007/978-3-030-66770-2_8

performing maintenance too frequently may cause unnecessary costs. To optimize maintenance intervals, it is useful to predict the time left until the next failure, called remaining useful lifetime (RUL) [18]. This way, the jobs of the plant can be scheduled such that they do not run into an unplanned downtime, and the lifetime of the components of the plant can be exploited to a maximum. However, even if the plant is sufficiently digitized and equipped with sensors for condition monitoring, creating a system to predict the remaining useful lifetime of a component still requires expert knowledge from several domains, which is not always available.

To alleviate this situation, it is quite natural to consider the use of AutoML [9] tools, which partially automate the creation of such a system, making it cheaper as well as more accessible. More specifically, AutoML tools seek to find a complete machine learning pipeline optimized for a given dataset. Here, a pipeline is a (often sequential) composition of different machine learning algorithms optionally starting with one or multiple preprocessing algorithms and ending with a learning algorithm for making predictions. In addition to the composition, the tools also automatically optimize the hyperparameters exposed by the respective components with regard to the given dataset.

However, most AutoML tools are specifically tailored to either tabular data or structured data such as images, but cannot immediately handle time series data as input. This type of data is relevant for RUL estimation, however, since sensors in plants mostly produce varying-length multivariate time series as measurements, which cannot be directly fed into standard regression algorithms—at least not without further preprocessing such as padding. But even with such simple preprocessing, a reasonable performance cannot be expected, since the sensor values on their own cannot be considered valuable features. Moreover, the data collected is often unlabeled, as it directly comes from run-to-failure scenarios. Here, the time series simply end when the machine ran into a failure and thus stopped working. However, as will be detailed in Sect. 4.1, transforming this data into labeled data for supervised learning can greatly influence the difficulty of the underlying learning problem. Thirdly, as the data often directly comes from real-world scenarios or simulations, preprocessing is of key importance, even more so than for standard ML settings. Last but not least, special asymmetric loss functions need to be optimized, as failing to replace a component due to an overestimated RUL is normally worse than replacing it too early.

In this paper, we present an AutoML tool for remaining useful lifetime estimation, called ML-Plan-RUL, extending the existing tool ML-Plan [14]. To the best of our knowledge, it is the first AutoML tool specifically tailored to this problem.

2   Remaining Useful Lifetime Estimation

One way to schedule maintenance is to predict the next time of failure and adapt the tasks and maintenance plan accordingly. This prediction is also known as remaining useful lifetime (RUL) estimation. In general, a RUL estimator $\mathbf{h}$ is mapping historical sensor data x of a system to a value $y \in \mathbb{R}_{\geq 0}$ denoting the point in time at which the next failure of the system is supposed to occur.

Formally, given historical data $x \in \mathcal{X}$, the goal is to learn a remaining useful lifetime estimator $\mathbf{h} : \mathcal{X} \to \mathcal{Y}$ predicting the residual lifetime y of a system or component. The input space $\mathcal{X}$ corresponds to the set of instances, i.e., maintenance cycles. One maintenance cycle consists of the time series of all S sensors, beginning at the moment the system is set up and ending when a failure occurs. Training data of the form $\mathcal{D}_{train} = \{x_i\}_{i=1}^{N}$ is given, containing N instances (i.e., maintenance cycles), where x_i represents the recorded history data of instance i until a failure occurred. This kind of data is called run-to-failure data. Each instance i consists of a sequence of time-stamped data for every sensor $s \in \mathcal{S}$:

$$x_i = \left[x_{i,1}, \ldots, x_{i,|\mathcal{S}|} \right], \qquad x_{i,s} = \left[\left(t_{i,s}^{(j)}, v_{i,s}^{(j)} \right) \right]_{j=1}^{T(i,s)} \tag{1}$$

The frequency of the recordings can differ from sensor to sensor, as sensors can either deliver values with a fixed sensor-specific frequency, or only at points in time whenever a value changes. Thus, data is collected from different sensors at different time steps, which can additionally result in time series of varying length. The sensor values $x_{i,s}$ for the ith history of a sensor $s \in \mathcal{S}$ are defined as in (1), where $t_{i,s}^{(j)} \in \mathbb{N}_0$ is the jth time step at which a sensor value is recorded for the given sensor s. These values are sorted in increasing order, i.e., $t_{i,s}^{(j-1)} < t_{i,s}^{(j)}$. Furthermore, $v_{i,s}^{(j)} \in \mathcal{V}(s)$ is the sensor value recorded at that time, where $\mathcal{V}(s)$ denotes the domain of readings from sensor s. Note that the number $T(i,s)$ of sensor values recorded for instance i can be different for every sensor $s \in \mathcal{S}$.

Test data is of the form

$$\mathcal{D}_{test} = \{(x_i, y_i)\}_{i=1}^{N}, \tag{2}$$

where x_i represents the recorded history data of an instance i until some end time $T_i = \max_{s \in S} t_{i,s}^{(T(i,s))}$, and y_i is the corresponding remaining useful lifetime that is left after the recorded data ends.

The performance of $\mathbf{h}$ for $\mathcal{D}_{test}$ is measured via a loss function. In general, underestimation of the RUL is less problematic than overestimation, as the latter would result in a failure, which in practice is more costly than replacing a component too early. Thus, the use of an asymmetric loss function is important to penalize late predictions more severely than early ones. One commonly used asymmetric loss function (depicted in Fig. 1) is proposed in [15]:

$$\mathcal{L}(\mathcal{D}_{test}) := \frac{1}{N} \sum_{i=1}^{N} 1 - a_i, \tag{3}$$

where the accuracy a_i of the RUL estimation for an instance i is defined as

$$a_i := \begin{cases} \exp\left(- \ln(1/2) \cdot (p_i/5) \right) & \text{if } p_i \leq 0 \text{ (late prediction)} \\ \exp\left(+ \ln(1/2) \cdot (p_i/20) \right) & \text{if } p_i > 0 \text{ (early prediction)} \end{cases}, \tag{4}$$

with $p_i = (y_i - \mathbf{h}(x_i))/y_i$ the error in percentage.

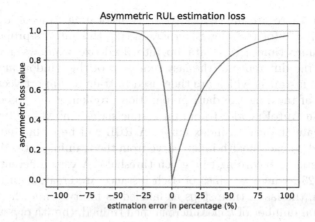

Fig. 1. Asymmetric loss function for RUL estimation, where late predictions correspond to a percentage error < 0 (left) and early predictions to a percentage error > 0 (right).

In order to allow for a better interpretation of the results, and to be comparable to other work, we additionally evaluate the performance on the test set with respect to the Mean Absolute Percentage Error (MAPE) defined as

$$MAPE(\mathcal{D}_{test}) := \frac{1}{N} \sum_{i=1}^{N} |p_i|. \tag{5}$$

3   Related Work

In this section, we first give an overview of the AutoML field discussing which learning problems have already been tackled in the past. This is followed by an overview of different data preparation approaches for RUL estimation.

A plethora of different approaches to AutoML have been proposed in the recent literature. However, those tools are usually tailored towards a specific learning problem, e.g., binary and multinomial classification [5,7,14,16,24,26, 29], or multi-label classification [19,25,27]. Some AutoML tools are even more specialized, focusing on the configuration of a single type of model only [1,4], or being restricted to a special case of a learning problem, such as image classification via neural architecture search [3]. Other approaches in turn aim for automating feature engineering tasks [10,11,13].

While most AutoML tools for standard classification tasks can typically deal with regression problems as well, to the best of our knowledge, all of these tools require datasets in a tabular format. More specifically, none of these tools employ machine learning models naturally capable of dealing with time series data, nor include the necessary algorithms for transforming time series data into a tabular format to make the data amenable to standard regression methods. Consequently, none of the aforementioned tools can be used in the context of RUL estimation.

In general, there are multiple ways of transforming time series data, so as to make it suitable for training a learner. In [12], the authors propose to divide the run-to-failure time series data up into fixed-size windows and label each window with the difference of the last time step of the window and the length of the original instance, which are then used to train a support vector machine. Another way of tackling the data preparation problem is proposed in [8]. The authors use an AutoEncoder to obtain a time series embedding, which is then used to estimate the health index curve. A RUL will be estimated for the test instance based on each health index curve from the training data, that is similar to the test instance according to a given threshold. A very different approach is proposed in [23], where k copies of each instance are created. In the ith copy, $i \in \{1, \ldots, k\}$, the last i time steps as labeled as faulty, while the rest remains healthy. A total number of k classifiers is then trained, the ith one with the data in which the last i time steps are labelled as faulty.

4   Combined Feature Engineering and Model Selection

In this paper, an extension of ML-Plan [14] specifically tailored to RUL estimation is proposed. The tool builds a pipeline of algorithms (ML pipeline) including feature engineering on time series data, standard feature preprocessing, e.g., feature selection or components analysis, and regression models, while simultaneously tuning the hyperparameters of the employed algorithms.

ML-Plan leverages Hierarchical Task Network (HTN) Planning [6] to automatically combine and parameterize different machine learning algorithms into an ML pipeline that optimizes a given performance metric. The idea is to recursively decompose an initial complex task into new sub-tasks that can either be simple or again complex, until a fully specified pipeline is reached that solely consists of simple tasks. While complex tasks are a means for structuring the search space, simple tasks represent concrete decisions, e.g., a specific algorithm or a concrete value for a hyperparameter. Figure 2 illustrates the construction of a complete pipeline including hyperparametrization via the means described above.

The pipeline resulting from this construction is depicted in Fig. 3. Here, a feature generator is firstly used to transform the multivariate time series data into a tabular format. Second, a preprocessor is applied to achieve dimensionality reduction. Last, a regressor is applied predicting the remaining useful lifetime of the system.

The problem of finding a complete pipeline yielding high quality performance is reduced to a standard search problem with an underlying search graph, where the nodes represent either partially (inner nodes) or fully specified pipelines (leaf nodes). This graph is traversed using an informed best-first search, where the fitness of an inner node is evaluated by drawing several random completions of this partially specified pipeline, evaluating them and aggregating their results taking the minimum loss observed. The minimum aggregation is chosen as a

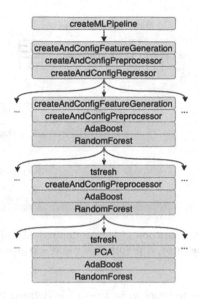

Fig. 2. Example of the search graph with complex tasks of the planning problem in blue and simple tasks in green. (Color figure online)

natural upper bound on the true minimum that can be achieved in this subtree. For a more detailed description of the search procedure used in ML-Plan we refer to [14].

4.1 Extending ML-Plan for RUL Estimation

The training data $\mathcal{D}_{train}$ typically associated with RUL estimation describes a whole maintenance cycle, i.e., from setting up the system until a failure occurs. As already discussed at the end of Sect. 3, the lack of labels in this kind of data implies that we cannot train a standard predictor in a supervised manner. Therefore, we need to transform the training data $\mathcal{D}_{train}$ into a labeled dataset $\mathcal{D}'_{train}$. A simple way is to cut off the last part of each instance and use the remaining time steps until the end of life as RUL label. Formally, the transformed training dataset is defined as $\mathcal{D}'_{train} = \{(\boldsymbol{x}'_i, y_i)\}_{i=1}^{N}$, where $\boldsymbol{x}'_i := \left[\boldsymbol{x}'_{i,1}, \dots, \boldsymbol{x}'_{i,|\mathcal{S}|}\right]$ denotes a shortened instance and

$$\boldsymbol{x}'_{i,s} = \left[\left(t_{i,s}^{(j)}, v_{i,s}^{(j)}\right) \mid \left(t_{i,s}^{(j)}, v_{i,s}^{(j)}\right) \in \boldsymbol{x}_{i,s} \wedge t_{i,s}^{(j)} \leq T'_i\right]_{j=1}^{T(i,s)} \tag{6}$$

denotes one sensor time series. The new length $T_{lb} \leq T'_i \leq \min(T_i, T_{ub})$ of the time series of instance $\boldsymbol{x}'_i$ is chosen uniformly at random between a predefined lower bound T_{lb} and a predefined upper bound T_{ub}. The upper bound is less or equal to the length of the longest instance $T_{max} = \max_{j \in [N]} T_j$ found in the dataset, where the original length of instance $\boldsymbol{x}_i$ is defined as $T_i = \max_{s \in S} t_{i,s}^{(T(i,s))}$, which is the largest time step found in any sensor time

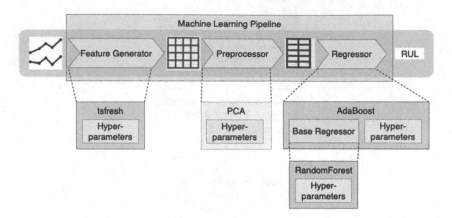

Fig. 3. A hierarchical representation of the configured ML pipeline's shape is shown, consisting of a feature generator, a preprocessor and a regressor.

series of that instance. The label $y_i = T_i - T_i'$ is defined by the difference of the original and the new instance length.

In spite of its advantage of not requiring extra parametrization or optimization, this is of course a very simple way to transform run-to-failure data into time-to-event data. In practice, other options are conceivable, such as windowing the data [12]. Furthermore, note that this procedure can highly influence the difficulty of the learning task, as cutting a time series too early might lead to removing the relevant part indicating a possible problem of the component. The main motivation for using a random split is that the new length is an arbitrary parameter that can have high impact on the quality, and a poor choice can produce bad results while random splits are more robust in this regard. Hence, it would be desirable to integrate the transformation into the AutoML pipeline, allowing for different types of transformation and optimizing the associated hyperparameters. However, this would result in varying validation data, making the results between different pipelines incomparable. In addition, this may result in optimizing the training data instead of the pipeline, which is of course not desirable. We leave further investigation of this highly relevant but non-trivial problem for future work.

At this point, a standard regression learner is still not applicable for solving the problem, due to varying length feature vectors, which are caused by the following properties of time series data. First, each instance can have a different length (final time step). Second, the frequencies of the recordings differ from sensor to sensor.

One possibility to tackle this problem is to automatically generate fixed-size feature vectors from these time series. To this end, we use tsfresh [2], which is a Python-based library automatically generating several such features for time series data. We parameterized tsfresh, so that each of the 62 possible features are *eligible*. Those features include the length of the time series, minimum and maximum, the number of peaks, the sample entropy, the kurtosis and the variance.

ML-Plan-RUL perceives each of the 62 features as one binary parameter, which can be enabled or disabled respectively. An example is given in Fig. 4. In general, other means of automatic feature construction, as the use of AutoEncoders, are of course also conceivable.

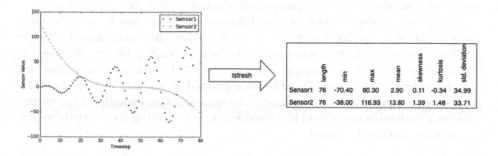

Fig. 4. On the left-hand side time series data is given containing 2 sensors. The fixed-size feature vector resulting from the application of tsfresh is shown on the right-hand side, where the following features are enabled: the length of the time series, minimum and maximum values, the mean, the skewness, the kurtosis and the standard deviation. The remaining features of tsfresh are disabled, i.e. not computed, and consequently also not listed.

In this first version of ML-Plan-RUL, we apply the same transformation to all sensors, which is, however, presumably not optimal, as time series coming from different sensors are likely to exhibit different characteristics to be captured. As future work, it is planned to test individual time series transformations for each sensor, combined with multiple preprocessing steps afterwards, as we suspect the performance of RUL estimation to strongly depend on the feature representation of the time series.

Once the feature representation has been generated, the problem is essentially reduced to a standard regression problem, allowing us to apply standard preprocessing and regression techniques. An example of a complete pipeline is shown in Fig. 3. Each pipeline consists of three steps: a feature generation step using tsfresh, followed by a preprocessing step such as PCA, and finally a regressor. The current version of ML-Plan-RUL[1] includes time series feature generation (provided by tsfresh [2]), 16 preprocessors, and 21 regressors (both provided by scikit-learn [17]), where some preprocessors or regressors use base learners, resulting in 1,000 unparameterized solutions.

In order to effectively search the space of candidate pipelines defined above, we also adapted the way ML-Plan trades off exploration and exploitation. To cope with this trade-off, the standard variant of ML-Plan starts with a breadth-first search spawning inner nodes of the search tree for every possible pipeline in terms of algorithm choices, before moving on to the best-first search.

---

[1] https://github.com/tornede/IoTStreamPdM2020Workshop.

As the number of possible pipelines is significantly larger for RUL estimation than for the previous version of ML-Plan, we organized the search graph in such a way that the selection of the regressor is made first, followed by the choice of feature generation and feature selection. On this graph, we use breadth-first search as expansion step for the regressors only in order to ensure a minimum degree of diversity across the considered pipelines. Obviously, this adaptation antedates the heuristic search via the informed best-first search, resulting in a more greedy exploitative search behavior. Note that the evaluation of a single pipeline is also usually quite costly, which is the reason why a breadth-first search spawning and initially evaluating every of the 1,000 unparametrized pipelines would consume most if not all of the time granted by the user for the AutoML process. Consequently, for any dataset, the same solution candidates (given the same randomization seed) would be considered, degenerating the heuristic search to a deterministic grid search.

5   Experiments

Due to a lack of existing methods that may serve as a baseline (cf. Sect. 3), we compare the performance of ML-Plan-RUL to a random search (RS) on the same search space.

5.1   Experimental Setup

Here, random search randomly draws parameterized pipelines, evaluating them and accepting them as a new incumbent if their validation performance improves over previously drawn pipelines. The random sampling is performed by first selecting an unparameterized pipeline uniformly at random followed by uniform random selection of the value of each hyperparameter exposed by the pipeline.

Due to the lack of publicly available data for RUL estimation, we use a selection of 5 datasets created by the C-MAPSS algorithm, which simulates a realistic large commercial turbofan engine. Four of these datasets are generated by Sazena et al. [22] and published in [21], and the fifth one has been published later for the PHM08 Data Challenge [20]. All datasets come with a fixed train/test split, where the training data of [21] and all data from [20] are run-to-failure data.

The run-to-failure data was transformed once in the beginning into time-to-event data as described in Sect. 4.1, with T_i' selected uniformly at random from [6, 190] according to the test data generation described in [22]. Optimization is performed w.r.t. the asymmetric loss as defined in Eq. 3, and the test data is additionally evaluated w.r.t. MAPE as defined in (5).

All experiments were repeated with 10 different seeds and executed on nodes equipped with 8 cores (Intel Xeon E5-2670) and 32 GB main memory with an overall timeout of 4 h. Each candidate pipeline was evaluated for up to 20 min via Monte Carlo cross-validation featuring 5 splits, each having a 70/30% train/test distribution.

5.2   Results

The results, averaged over 10 different seeds, of the experiments are shown in Table 1. If one run of ML-Plan-RUL or RS was not able to find any pipeline within 4 h, this final pipeline is assumed to be a predictor which always predicts a RUL of 0, suggesting maintenance immediately. According to the definition of the asymmetric loss in (3) and the according plot in Fig. 1 its performance value is 1, and the same holds for MAPE as defined in (5). This effected only the performance values of RS, as there were no solutions found for 4 seeds of the CMAPSS FD002 dataset, for 5 seeds of the CMAPSS FD004 dataset and for 1 seed of the PHM08 dataset. The significance is determined by the Wilcoxon Signed Rank Test [28], where a pairwise comparison of the performance value of ML-Plan-RUL and RS is done for each seed. If ML-Plan-RUL is determined to be significantly better than RS, a black circle will be shown in the according row of the performance measure.

As one can see, ML-Plan-RUL consistently outperforms RS across all four CMAPSS datasets w.r.t. the asymmetric loss and is slightly worse than RS on the PHM08 dataset.

Table 1. Performance of ML-Plan-RUL and Random Search (RS) after a 4 h run averaged over 10 seeds. Best results are printed in bold for each dataset. Standard deviation is given additionally to the performance metrics. The datasets on which ML-Plan-RUL is significantly better than RS are marked with a black circle.

	Asymmetric		MAPE	
	ML-Plan-RUL	RS	ML-Plan-RUL	RS
CMAPSS FD001	**0.6717 ± 0.06**	0.6841 ± 0.02	**0.3152 ± 0.13** •	0.3931 ± 0.12
CMAPSS FD002	**0.7458 ± 0.02**	0.8492 ± 0.12	**1.0343 ± 0.23**	1.1511 ± 0.26
CMAPSS FD003	**0.6562 ± 0.03**	0.6814 ± 0.04	**0.3515 ± 0.07**	0.5748 ± 0.30
CMAPSS FD004	**0.7273 ± 0.01** •	0.8897 ± 0.11	**0.6874 ± 0.07** •	1.2095 ± 0.27
PHM08	0.8909 ± 0.01	**0.8880 ± 0.04**	2.3271 ± 0.10	**2.2140 ± 1.03**

6   Conclusion

In this paper, we presented ML-Plan-RUL, an AutoML tool specifically tailored to RUL estimation in predictive maintenance. We proposed a way to transform run-to-failure data into RUL labeled data. Building on the existing AutoML tool ML-Plan, we integrated an automated feature engineering process transforming time series data into a standard feature representation. Thus, the RUL problem is amenable to standard preprocessing and regression methods. Our experimental evaluation demonstrates that ML-Plan-RUL consistently outperforms RS on the majority of the considered datasets w.r.t. the optimized asymmetric loss.

As future work, we plan to integrate feature engineering methods other than tsfresh. Furthermore, we will include additional RUL estimation methods, so as to liberate ML-Plan-RUL from the need to reduce the problem to standard regression, and instead also allows for leveraging other approaches such as health index curves.

Acknowledgements. This work was partially supported by the German Research Foundation (DFG) within the Collaborative Research Center "On-The-Fly Computing" (SFB 901/3 project no. 160364472), the German Federal Ministry of Economic Affairs and Energy (FLEMING project no. 03E16012F), and the German Federal Ministry of Education and Research (ITS.ML project no. 01IS18041D). The authors gratefully acknowledge support of this project through computing time provided by the Paderborn Center for Parallel Computing (PC^2).

References

1. Chen, B., Wu, H., Mo, W., Chattopadhyay, I., Lipson, H.: Autostacker: a compositional evolutionary learning system. In: Proceedings of the Genetic and Evolutionary Computation Conference, GECCO 2018, Kyoto, Japan, 15–19 July 2018, pp. 402–409 (2018)
2. Christ, M., Braun, N., Neuffer, J., Kempa-Liehr, A.W.: Time series feature extraction on basis of scalable hypothesis tests (tsfresh - a python package). Neurocomputing **307**, 72–77 (2018)
3. Elsken, T., Metzen, J.H., Hutter, F.: Neural architecture search: a survey. J. Mach. Learn. Res. **20**, 55:1–55:21 (2019)
4. Erickson, N., et al.: AutoGluon-tabular: robust and accurate AutoML for structured data. CoRR abs/2003.06505 (2020)
5. Feurer, M., Klein, A., Eggensperger, K., Springenberg, J.T., Blum, M., Hutter, F.: Efficient and robust automated machine learning. In: Advances in Neural Information Processing Systems 28: Annual Conference on Neural Information Processing Systems 2015, Montreal, Quebec, Canada, 7–12 December 2015, pp. 2962–2970 (2015)
6. Ghallab, M., Nau, D., Traverso, P.: Automated Planning: Theory and Practice. Elsevier, Amsterdam (2004)
7. Gijsbers, P., Vanschoren, J.: GAMA: genetic automated machine learning assistant. J. Open Source Softw. **4**(33), 1132 (2019)
8. Gugulothu, N., Tv, V., Malhotra, P., Vig, L., Agarwal, P., Shroff, G.M.: Predicting remaining useful life using time series embeddings based on recurrent neural networks. CoRR abs/1709.01073 (2017)
9. Hutter, F., Kotthoff, L., Vanschoren, J. (eds.): Automated Machine Learning - Methods, Systems, Challenges. The Springer Series on Challenges in Machine Learning. Springer, Heidelberg (2019). https://doi.org/10.1007/978-3-030-05318-5
10. Kanter, J.M., Veeramachaneni, K.: Deep feature synthesis: towards automating data science endeavors. In: 2015 IEEE International Conference on Data Science and Advanced Analytics, DSAA 2015, Campus des Cordeliers, Paris, France, 19–21 October 2015, pp. 1–10 (2015)

11. Kaul, A., Maheshwary, S., Pudi, V.: AutoLearn - automated feature generation and selection. In: 2017 IEEE International Conference on Data Mining, ICDM 2017, New Orleans, LA, USA, 18–21 November 2017, pp. 217–226 (2017)
12. Khelif, R., Chebel-Morello, B., Malinowski, S., Laajili, E., Fnaiech, F., Zerhouni, N.: Direct remaining useful life estimation based on support vector regression. IEEE Trans. Ind. Electron. **64**(3), 2276–2285 (2017)
13. Khurana, U., Turaga, D.S., Samulowitz, H., Parthasrathy, S.: Cognito: automated feature engineering for supervised learning. In: IEEE International Conference on Data Mining Workshops, ICDM Workshops 2016, Barcelona, Spain, 12–15 December 2016, pp. 1304–1307 (2016)
14. Mohr, F., Wever, M., Hüllermeier, E.: ML-Plan: automated machine learning via hierarchical planning. Mach. Learn. **107**(8), 1495–1515 (2018). https://doi.org/10.1007/s10994-018-5735-z
15. Nectoux, P., et al.: Pronostia: an experimental platform for bearings accelerated degradation tests (2012)
16. Olson, R.S., Moore, J.H.: TPOT: a tree-based pipeline optimization tool for automating machine learning. In: Automated Machine Learning - Methods, Systems, Challenges, pp. 151–160 (2019)
17. Pedregosa, F., et al.: Scikit-learn: machine learning in python. J. Mach. Learn. Res. **12**, 2825–2830 (2011)
18. Ran, Y., Zhou, X., Lin, P., Wen, Y., Deng, R.: A survey of predictive maintenance: systems, purposes and approaches. CoRR abs/1912.07383 (2019)
19. de Sá, A.G.C., Freitas, A.A., Pappa, G.L.: Automated selection and configuration of multi-label classification algorithms with grammar-based genetic programming. In: Auger, A., Fonseca, C.M., Lourenço, N., Machado, P., Paquete, L., Whitley, D. (eds.) PPSN 2018. LNCS, vol. 11102, pp. 308–320. Springer, Cham (2018). https://doi.org/10.1007/978-3-319-99259-4_25
20. Saxena, A., Goebelt, K.: Phm08 challenge data set. vol. NASA Ames Prognostics Data Repository. NASA Ames Research Center, Moffett Field, CA (2008). http://ti.arc.nasa.gov/project/prognostic-data-repository. Accessed 20 May 2020
21. Saxena, A., Goebelt, K.: Turbofan engine degradation simulation data set. vol. NASA Ames Prognostics Data Repository. NASA Ames Research Center, Moffett Field, CA (2008). http://ti.arc.nasa.gov/project/prognostic-data-repository. Accessed 20 May 2020
22. Saxena, A., Goebel, K., Simon, D., Eklund, N.: Damage propagation modeling for aircraft engine run-to-failure simulation. In: International Conference on Prognostics and Health Management, pp. 1–9. IEEE (2008)
23. Susto, G.A., Schirru, A., Pampuri, S., McLoone, S.F., Beghi, A.: Machine learning for predictive maintenance: a multiple classifier approach. IEEE Trans. Ind. Inform. **11**(3) (2015)
24. Thornton, C., Hutter, F., Hoos, H.H., Leyton-Brown, K.: Auto-Weka: combined selection and hyperparameter optimization of classification algorithms. In: The 19th ACM SIGKDD International Conference on Knowledge Discovery and Data Mining, KDD 2013, Chicago, IL, USA, 11–14 August 2013, pp. 847–855 (2013)
25. Wever, M., Mohr, F., Hüllermeier, E.: Automated multi-label classification based on ML-Plan. CoRR abs/1811.04060 (2018)
26. Wever, M.D., Mohr, F., Hüllermeier, E.: ML-Plan for unlimited-length machine learning pipelines. In: ICML 2018 AutoML Workshop (2018)
27. Wever, M.D., Mohr, F., Tornede, A., Hüllermeier, E.: Automating multi-label classification extending ML-Plan. In: ICML 2019 AutoML Workshop (2019)

28. Wilcoxon, F.: Individual comparisons by ranking methods. Biometrics Bull. **1**(6), 80–83 (1945)
29. Yang, C., Akimoto, Y., Kim, D.W., Udell, M.: OBOE: collaborative filtering for AutoML model selection. In: Proceedings of the 25th ACM SIGKDD International Conference on Knowledge Discovery & Data Mining, KDD 2019, Anchorage, AK, USA, 4–8 August 2019, pp. 1173–1183 (2019)

Forklift Truck Activity Recognition from CAN Data

Kunru Chen[1,2]($\boxtimes$), Sepideh Pashami[1,2], Sławomir Nowaczyk[1,2],
Emilia Johansson[1,2], Gustav Sternelöv[1,2], and Thorsteinn Rögnvaldsson[1,2]

[1] Center for Applied Intelligent Systems Research, Halmstad University,
Halmstad, Sweden
kunru.chen@hh.se
[2] Toyota Material Handling Europe, Mjölby, Sweden

Abstract. Machine activity recognition is important for accurately estimating machine productivity and machine maintenance needs. In this paper, we present ongoing work on how to recognize activities of forklift trucks from on-board data streaming on the controller area network. We show that such recognition works across different sites. We first demonstrate the baseline classification performance of a Random Forest that uses 14 signals over 20 time steps, for a 280-dimensional input. Next, we show how a deep neural network can learn low-dimensional representations that, with fine-tuning, achieve comparable accuracy. The proposed representation achieves machine activity recognition. Also, it visualizes the forklift operation over time and illustrates the relationships across different activities.

Keywords: Machine Activity Recognition · Learning representation · Autoencoder · Forklift truck · CAN signals · Unsupervised learning

1 Introduction

In recent years, a field of study has emerged as Machine Activity Recognition (MAR), i.e. the study of how to label machine activities from data streams (video, audio, or other types of data). MAR enables monitoring machine productivity, understanding customer needs better, and designing improved maintenance schemes. So far, work on MAR has almost exclusively been applied to construction equipment. A recent overview of the field is provided by Sherafat et al. [7], who categorize the approaches into kinematic methods, computer vision based methods, and audio based methods. The first two are the most common approaches. The approaches tend to be based on external sensors placed on (or nearby) the machine for the sole purpose of activity recognition. It is rare to use the streaming on-board data on the controller area network (CAN), which is multidimensional and consist of control and sensor signals to and from different parts of the equipment. We are only aware of some early works by Vachkov et al. [8,9], who used CAN data and different variants of self-organizing maps for

© Springer Nature Switzerland AG 2020
J. Gama et al. (Eds.): ITEM 2020/IoT Streams 2020, CCIS 1325, pp. 119–126, 2020.
https://doi.org/10.1007/978-3-030-66770-2_9

this. There have been important developments in the last decade, both regarding the volume of on-board data and the capacity of machine learning algorithms. Thus, it is worthwhile to explore how well MAR can be done using more recent machine learning techniques and CAN data.

In this paper we present ongoing work on MAR for forklift trucks, a type of equipment that is widely used in the industry, but rare in MAR research. Forklift trucks are considered exceptionally challenging, even "unrecognizable", due to few "articulated moving parts" [7]. We show that the situation is not poor when one uses multidimensional CAN data.

A contribution of this work concerns learning nonlinear representations from unlabeled data. Representation learning [1] is a way to make use of large unlabeled data sets to visualize relations, and improve classification performance. This can lead to deep learning classifiers that significantly outperform shallow classifiers. We have used autoencoders to learn the CAN data embedding, and then fine-tune it with supervised learning, in order to visualize the forklift operations. We are not aware of any work, prior to our study, that has approached this visualization question for MAR.

2   Definition of the Task

The task is to recognize the activities of forklift trucks. Forklift experts defined expected actions and grouped them into six levels of detail. The top level includes engine off and on. The next level contains 1) engine off, 2) engine on but forklift idle, and 3) engine on and forklift working. This activity breakdown was continued to level six. The complexity in the activities depend on the number and order of signals, driver behavior, and time. The same activity can vary in duration. The top activity levels can be recognized with rules and a single signal; the actions in levels 4–6 are much more complex. The results in this paper are reported for the fifth level, with five different activities, excluding engine off.

3   The Data

The forklift trucks used in this study were reach forklifts with 1.6-ton load capacities and 10-meter maximum lift height. Data collection was made with a Vector GL1000 compact Logger and signals from two CAN buses were saved. The original frequency of the CAN bus data is 50 Hz, but the data was extracted with a frequency of 10 Hz. Data were collected from two different warehouse sites, one in Sweden and one in Norway. During the data collection at the Swedish site, the operators' hand actions were filmed for later activity labeling.

Two data sets were collected with the same driver at the Swedish site: one with 58 min and one with 27 min. The long represented normal operation, including picking up orders and waiting, whereas the short focused on load handling operations. Another data set collected at the Norway site spanned two weeks of normal operation, with different drivers. However, no labels could be created for forklift activities, due to the lack of videos.

Each second of the videos from the Swedish site was labeled manually by an expert from watching the operators' actions. The fifth level activity recognition has five categories. The recognition of each activity was evaluated with one-against-all, presenting data imbalance. In the 58-min data set, the class proportions are 35.6%, 24.3%, 15.8%, 15.1%, and 9.1%, corresponding to the five labels *other, drive without load, take load, drive with load*, and *leave load*. In the 27-min data set, the corresponding proportions are 2.5%, 31.1%, 21.8%, 23.1%, and 21.6%.

The collected data contained more than 260 signals, of which 14 were selected by the experts as especially relevant for recognizing the activities. These 14 signals were also available in the data from the Norwegian site. These 14 signals contain information about the fork adjustment functions, the fork height, the weight on the fork, the speed and the heading of the vehicle.

4 Methods

The goal is to recognize the activities from these 14 signals. Our idea is to use time window snapshots by the size of two seconds to define the activities. Two seconds correspond to 20 time samples, so the total size of each pattern was 280 (14 signals × 20 time steps). The activity label for each pattern was determined by the label for the last second in the time window snapshot. The overlap between sliding windows is 50% (10 time steps). Random forests (RF) [3] was applied as the baseline classifier model.

The choice of a two-second time window was made after plotting the data with t-Distributed Stochastic Neighbor Embedding [5] with different time window lengths. Data corresponding to different activities became more separated when increasing the window size, which is reasonable since data points should become more and more unique as the time window is increased. However, there is a trade-off where a large window can give more information about the corresponding activity while can also increase the difficulty in finding the patterns of

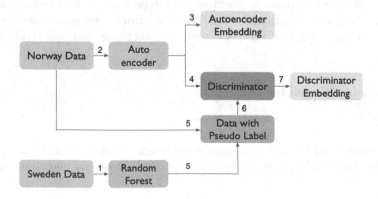

Fig. 1. Flow chart for forklift truck activity recognition.

the data in the window, i.e., more than one activities can be captured in a single window.

Figure 1 shows a flow chart of the method, divided into seven steps: (1) training a baseline RF with the Sweden (labeled) data sets, (2) training an autoencoder [4] with the Norway (unlabeled) data, (3) extracting the output of the bottleneck layer of the trained autoencoder, this embedding is named *autoencoder embedding*, (4) transforming the autoencoder into a discriminator by removing the decoder and adding one layer as the output layer connected to the bottleneck layer, (5) generating pseudo-labels on the Norway data by using the baseline RF trained at step 1, (6) training the discriminator using the data with pseudo-labels from step 5, (7) extracting the output of the last hidden layer of the discriminator, which is named *discriminator embedding*.

In this case, overly optimistic values can be given by reporting the result using, e.g., the area under the receiver-operating curve (AUC), or the accuracy. We therefore report the recognition results using two measures that are more suitable with imbalanced data: the balanced accuracy (BA) and the area under the precision-recall curve (APRC) [6]. The BA is the average of the true positive rate (TPR) and the true negative rate (TNR). The precision-recall curve describes the trade-off between precision and recall, which are measurements focusing on the true positive (TP), hense it is more appropriate for imbalanced data [2]. The APRC has similar characteristics as the AUC: it is a score across different probability thresholds, and it needs to be compared with the lower bound from a random classifier. For a classifier that makes random decisions, its AUC score will be 0.5 while its APRC value will be the ratio of positive samples over all samples. In the result section, for each activity, we report the APRC value achieved with a random classifier as "Random APRC".

5   Results

Throughout the experiments in this paper, the 27-min labeled data set was used as a hold-out test set. The 58-min labeled data set was used for supervised training. All hyper-parameter selection was done with 10-fold cross validation on the training set. Additionally, for the results from deep neural networks, the loss into training and validation was checked to confirm that overfitting did not happen.

5.1   Baseline Classifier

The best RF model was selected by doing a randomized grid search on three significant hyper-parameters. The final RF model was generated with 00 trees, a maximum depth of 11, and maximum 2 features to consider while looking for the best split. The baseline classifier's results on the test set are shown in Table 1.

Table 1. One-against-all recognition performance of baseline RF classifier (BA is Balanced Accuracy, and APRC is Area under the Precision-Recall Curve). For comparison, the performance of a random classifier is shown in the bottom row.

Measure	Other	Drive w/out load	Drive w load	Take load	Leave load
BA	0.858 ± 0.022	0.811 ± 0.026	0.715 ± 0.026	0.684 ± 0.042	0.601 ± 0.078
APRC	0.661 ± 0.380	0.602 ± 0.156	0.535 ± 0.032	0.546 ± 0.036	0.636 ± 0.042
"Random" APRC	0.025	0.311	0.218	0.231	0.216

5.2   Classifiers Trained from Unlabeled Data

The experiment processed to train classifiers from unlabeled data according to Sect. 4. Autoencoders of different sizes (breadth and depth) were trained to obtain a stable signal reconstruction performance. The results reported in this paper use an encoder with the 280 dimensional input and three layers connecting the input layer and the bottleneck layer, with 128, 64, and 32 units, respectively. The decoder had a symmetric structure with three layers. The total autoencoder architecture can be described as $280-128-64-32-N-32-64-128-280$, where N denotes the number of bottleneck units. The activation function in the bottleneck layer is linear while the other layers have ReLu units. Each autoencoder was trained with backpropagation and early stopping.

The first findings were that an autoencoder trained on the unlabeled data set was efficient also for encoding the labeled data sets, and the reconstruction of the signals improved as the number of bottleneck units increased, see the left panel in Fig. 2. This showed that data from one site could be used to learn a representation applicable to other sites. It also showed that the data is so complex that it requires a high-dimensional manifold to be represented accurately.

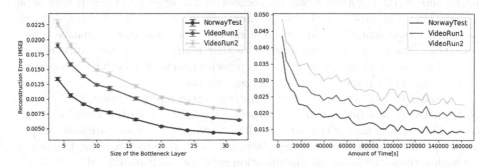

Fig. 2. The left panel shows the reconstruction error (MSE) when changing the size of the bottleneck layer, for all three data sets. The right panel shows how the reconstruction error decreased when the amount of data used for training increased. In both cases the autoencoders were trained only on the large unlabeled data set.

Another finding was that having more data is helpful in learning better representations for reconstructing the signal. The right panel in Fig. 2 shows how the reconstruction performance improved as adding the training set size.

Table 2. Balanced accuracy (BA) with different representations

	Other	Drive w/out load	Drive w load	Take load	Leave load
Baseline (280D)	0.858 ± 0.022	0.811 ± 0.026	0.715 ± 0.026	0.684 ± 0.042	0.601 ± 0.078
Autoencoder (3D)	0.722 ± 0.286	0.684 ± 0.042	0.597 ± 0.044	0.624 ± 0.030	0.609 ± 0.022
Discriminator (3D)	0.848 ± 0.024	0.818 ± 0.040	0.718 ± 0.022	0.689 ± 0.016	0.615 ± 0.018

Table 3. Area under the precision-recall curve (APRC) with different representations

	Other	Drive w/out load	Drive w load	Take load	Leave load
Baseline (280D)	0.661 ± 0.380	0.602 ± 0.156	0.535 ± 0.032	0.546 ± 0.036	0.636 ± 0.042
Autoencoder (3D)	0.125 ± 0.136	0.557 ± 0.070	0.390 ± 0.036	0.382 ± 0.050	0.551 ± 0.042
Discriminator (3D)	0.256 ± 0.286	0.722 ± 0.054	0.507 ± 0.048	0.529 ± 0.024	0.528 ± 0.044

Tables 2 and 3 summarize the recognition results on the test set, for the baseline RF classifier with 280-dimensional input, and classifiers built using autoencoder and discriminator representations. We used three-dimensional representations in both cases (i.e. $N = 3$). However, when an RF classifier was constructed using the learned autoencoder representation, its recognition performance was worse than the one from the baseline RF model. Figure 3a shows the recognition performance (BA) plotted versus the reconstruction error and there is very little correlation (a negative correlation is expected). It shows that the most variance preserving representation did not coincide with the most discriminative representation. The results are concluded with that training a "better" autoencoder did not produce a more discriminative representation for the activity recognition task, indicating a misalignment of the two criteria.

In order to instead build a more discriminative representation, the autoencoder network was fine-tuned in a supervised manner with the pseudo-labeled data. The decoder part of the autoencoder was removed and an additional output layer was placed after the bottleneck layer (see Sect. 4). Since there are five target activities, the structure of the classification network was $280-128-64-32-3-5$, where the activation function in the output layer is softmax. After the training, the 3-dimensional bottleneck before the output layer is extracted to be the discriminator representation. Figure 3b is a visualization of the 3D-representation applied to the 58-min labeled data set. In this space, different activities are better separated from each other and it is possible to see the relationships between neighbors activities.

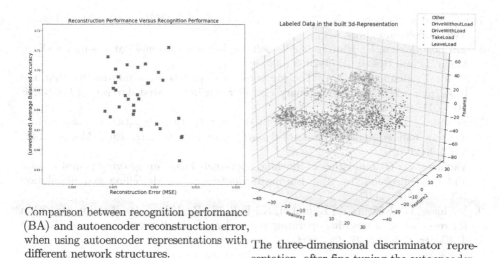

Comparison between recognition performance (BA) and autoencoder reconstruction error, when using autoencoder representations with different network structures.

The three-dimensional discriminator representation, after fine-tuning the autoencoder.

Fig. 3. Performance comparison between reconstruction and recognition (left) and visualization of the discriminator representation (right).

6 Conclusions

It was shown that streaming CAN data can be used to achieve machine activity recognition for a forklift truck. It was also presented that forklift activities at different sites are similar, i.e. autoencoders trained on one site data were also good for encoding data from another site, but that several hours of activity data are needed to build a good autoencoder for the signals. However, autoencoder representations yielded poor activity recognition, and there is a weak connection between reconstruction performance and recognition performance. It was shown how discriminative encoders could be trained with pseudo-labeled data, making it possible to construct a three-dimensional representation that achieved equal recognition results to the 280-dimensional baseline. This representation allowed a better visualization of the learned activities and their relationships.

A future work is to explore if a general supplementary criterion for representation learning for MAR can be inferred from comparing the autoencoder representation and the discriminative representation, avoiding the need for a pseudo labeled data set.

References

1. Bengio, Y., Courville, A., Vincent, P.: Representation learning: a review and new perspectives. IEEE Trans. Pattern Anal. Mach. Intell. **35**, 1798–1828 (2013)
2. Branco, P., Torgo, L., Ribeiro, R.: A survey of predictive modelling under imbalanced distributions (2015)
3. Breiman, L.: Random forests. Mach. Learn. **45**, 5–32 (2001)

4. Goodfellow, I., Bengio, Y., Courville, A.: Deep Learning. MIT Press (2016). http://www.deeplearningbook.org
5. van der Maaten, L., Hinton, G.: Visualizing high-dimensional data using t-SNE. J. Mach. Learn. Res. **9**, 2579–2605 (2008)
6. Saito, T., Rehmsmeier, M.: The precision-recall plot is more informative than the ROC plot when evaluating binary classifiers on imbalanced datasets. PLoS ONE **10**, e0118432 (2015)
7. Sherafat, B., et al.: Automated methods for activity recognition of construction workers and equipment: state-of-the-art review. J. Constr. Eng. Manag. **146**, 03120002 (2020)
8. Vachkov, G.: Classification of machine operations based on growing neural models and fuzzy decision. In: 21st European Conference on Modelling and Simulation (ECMS 2007) (2007)
9. Vachkov, G., Kiyota, Y., Komatsu, K., Fujii, S.: Real-time classification algorithm for recognition of machine operating modes by use of self-organizing maps. Turkish J. Electr. Eng. **12**, 27–42 (2004)

Embeddings Based Parallel Stacked Autoencoder Approach for Dimensionality Reduction and Predictive Maintenance of Vehicles

Vandan Revanur, Ayodeji Ayibiowu, Mahmoud Rahat,
and Reza Khoshkangini$^{(\boxtimes)}$

Center for Applied Intelligent Systems Research (CAISR), Halmstad University,
Halmstad, Sweden
{vanrev18,ayoayi18}@student.hh.se
{mahmoud.rahat,reza.khoshkangini}@student.hh.se

Abstract. Predictive Maintenance (PdM) of automobiles requires the storage and analysis of large amounts of sensor data. This requirement can be challenging in deploying PdM algorithms onboard the vehicles due to limited storage and computational power on the hardware of the vehicle. Hence, this study seeks to obtain low dimensional descriptive features from high dimensional data using Representation Learning. The low dimensional representation can then be used for predicting vehicle faults, in particular a component related to powertrain. A Parallel Stacked Autoencoder based architecture is presented with the aim of producing better representations when compared to individual Autoencoders with focus on vehicle data. Also, Embeddings are employed on Categorical Variables to aid the performance of the Artificial Neural Networks (ANN) models. This architecture is shown to achieve excellent performance, and in close standards to the previous state-of-the-art research. Significant improvement in powertrain failure prediction is obtained along with reduction in size of input data using our novel deep learning ANN architecture.

Keywords: Dimensionality reduction · Autoencoder · Artificial Neural Network · Embeddings · Powertrain · Predictive maintenance

1 Introduction

Rise in customer demand for "intelligent" functionality in vehicles has led to the increased deployment and usage of sensors in automobiles.

Automobiles, and even bicycles are becoming equipped with more sensors in the last two decades. An average car currently contains around 60–100, but as vehicles become "smarter," the number of sensors might reach as many as 200 sensors per vehicle [1]. The sensor information is used to provide insights about the mechanical and structural health of vehicles while observing physical

© Springer Nature Switzerland AG 2020
J. Gama et al. (Eds.): ITEM 2020/IoT Streams 2020, CCIS 1325, pp. 127–141, 2020.
https://doi.org/10.1007/978-3-030-66770-2_10

phenomenon like temperature, pressure, acoustics, strain, etc. The huge amount of information generated by sensors poses a challenge because of the high dimension of the generated data. A single data-point from a vehicle possibly comprises of hundreds to thousands of independent and dependent features. The nature of this data leads us to the curse of dimensionality for machine learning applications since it induces sparsity. So, the challenge is clear: how do we efficiently manage all that data produced by the vehicle?

PdM is one area of application [2] of this kind of data for forecasting vehicle health status [10,11]. In the automotive domain, breakdowns of vehicles in an unwanted situation can be expensive, and in the worst-case scenario, can also be fatal. These breakdowns and failures could be avoided with continuous vehicle-specific online monitoring. PdM requires a lot of system modelling, feature selection or engineering and data analysis, but the high dimensionality and large amounts of the data can make this task challenging. It is important that the representation learning models generate generic representation since PdM is applicable to multiple components of vehicles.

Engineers develop PdM tend to ask themselves "Which features are important to analyze and store?." Mostly, because data collection and transmission is expensive, picking the right features helps with better insights, and gives us a better chance of building a more powerful PdM model.

This work addresses the problem of finding a low dimensional good representation of the data that can be used for predictive maintenance purposes. We attempt to find a balance between data compression (i.e transformation to low-dimensional) and good representation (i.e few or no significant information loss). This work further investigates the impact of continuity on structured data, and how continuity can potentially lead to the generation of better representation, which can improve the performance of Artificial Neural Network based Artificial Neural Network based PdM models and also insights analysis.

Dimensionality reduction helps in selecting and transforming features in the high dimensional data to a new set of features. A great deal of research has been done in dimensionality reduction especially using deep learning in [3,7] which our focus is on. The idea of having a generic low dimensional representation that can be used for specific goals and possibly predictive maintenance has been studied by [6], where the representation learning suffers from information loss.

Feature selection can be used to address information loss if properly modelled as shown in [8]. Feature selections can be implemented for PdM [9,12], which can help decide what features to use or keep. Most deep learning based representation learning, especially serial autoencoder based models tend to translate the data into a new representation without taking into consideration the possibility of various feature dynamics. Parallel AutoEncoder (PAE) approach is one way to address this issue as studied in [13–15]. PAE makes it possible to potentially address different dynamics of the feature composition separately, keeping the structural properties of the data, thereby reducing information loss. A great deal of research in PAE are applied in the computer vision and health domains, but not in automotive domain. This research focuses on the application of PAE on vehicle data compared to other literature targeted to other industries.

In order to improve representation learning, as well as the performance of PdM models, introducing continuity (because Neural Networks are continuous in nature) into the data might be a good idea. This ideology was studied in [16,17], where they use embeddings as a way of introducing continuity in the data. For PAE to be able to generate a strong low-dimensional representation, we need to ensure that the input data exhibits some level of dependence especially on discrete features.

Embeddings can learn the representation of categorical features, text, and non-continuous features in a multi-dimensional space. This new representation can expose the essential continuity of the input data to improve neural network models. This paper shows the use of embeddings on categorical features in the data for representation learning and comparing it with traditional methods like one-hot encoding. Most literature studying PdM in the automotive domain tend to lay less emphasize on the vehicle discrete characteristics, but instead focusing on the sensor/numerical characteristics of the vehicle without taking into consideration that the general vehicle configuration is as important as the numerical information (sensor readings). They can be a potential discriminator in detecting and predicting vehicle faults.

This paper aims to obtain low dimensional meaningful (i.e features that improve prediction performance) representation and validating the parallel architecture and the use of embeddings. The focus is not on optimizing the machine learning model used for the predictive maintenance aspect. The evaluation took place by measuring the prediction performance of each representation learning methods against each other.

The contributions of this paper are two-fold. First is the methodology we propose, which is using a parallel stacked representation learning models for generating a low dimensional and meaningful representation on vehicle data. Second is the idea of deploying embeddings that would aid neural networks to learn continuity in categorical features found in-vehicle data as well as allowing the embeddings to learn the relationship between various vehicle configurations for future discrimination.

The rest of the paper is organised as follows; In Sect. 2 we describe the data used in this work. Problem Formulation and Proposed Approach are described in Sect. 3 and Sect. 4 covers the methodology of our approach. Section 5 describes the experimental evaluation and the results, which are followed by a discussion and conclusion of the work in Sect. 6.

2   Data Representation and Pre-processing

In this study, Logged Vehicle Data (LVD), provided by Volvo is utilized. This data contains sensor data collected periodically from 2016 to 2019. The data exists in two formats such as Readout Data (LVD) and Repair Data, which are described as follows:

The readout data contains the raw sensor readings collected from heavy duty trucks during their operations. This data includes both numerical and categorical features. We refer to the readout data as **Raw Data** from here on. The readout includes information such as the vehicle identification number, the day the vehicle is serviced at the workshop. Various combinations of truck configurations can be found in the data. These configurations are available as sensor readings, height configuration, axle arrangement, and many others. These configurations also called features, have been categorised into numerical and categorical features. There are a total of 446 configurations. Thus, the raw data has a total of 446 dimensions.

The Repair Data data includes of a history of powertrain component repairs of various Volvo trucks.

Pre-processing of the Raw data involves annotating the raw data with the Remaining Useful Life (RUL) labels and performing feature engineering operations such as missing value imputation and filtering operations such as removing features with no variance and removing duplicate features. The RUL tells us how much time a component, device, or object has left before it fails. There are two existing methods to estimate RUL, they are:

1. Sliding Box Approach: The idea is to define if a failure has happened within a predefined time interval from the current time step t. [9,18] Each time step is assigned a binary label as shown in Eq. 1. Here τ is the window or the box of time that slides in order to determine the label L_t for current time step.

$$L_t = \begin{cases} 1 & if \ there \ is \ failure \ in \ [t, t + \tau) \\ 0 & if \ there \ is \ NO \ failure \ in \ [t, t + \tau) \end{cases} \quad (1)$$

2. Time To Next Event (TTE) approach: The idea is that instead of assigning binary labels, at each point in time, we assign time to the next event as the label [12]. More formally, the labelling is shown in Eq. 2.

$$L_t = t_m - t \quad (2)$$

Here L_t is the label of the time step at time t , and t_m is the time at which the vehicle malfunctioned (event). In our case, since we do not possess the exact date of malfunctioning of the vehicle, we use the date of repair as t_m.

Similar to [12], we follow a TTE based methodology for estimating the RUL for the trucks.

3 Hypothesis

Massive amounts of sensor data are generated during the functioning of an autonomous vehicle. Predictive maintenance aims to leverage the data generated to predict vehicle faults. However, the high dimensional nature of the data is a serious problem since it demands increased storage capacities and processing power to be available on-board the vehicles. Hence it is important to obtain meaningful low-dimensional representations of the sensor data.

Our **first hypothesis** is that employing a novel Dimensionality Reduction Pipeline based on parallel stacking of autoencoders will provide better results. The reasoning behind this hypothesis is that Autoencoders can learn low dimensional representations of numerical data. The raw data contains both categorical and numerical features. Hence, using a single serial autoencoder dimension reduction might not be able to capture relationships between the features property accurately. A parallel approach provides scope for learning the intrinsic properties of the categorical and numerical variables separately [13,15].

Our **second hypothesis** is that the application of Embeddings to transform categorical variables into numerical values will lead to the improved utility of categorical features for prediction performance. As shown in [17], Embeddings can capture the intrinsic relationships between the categorical variables, and provide superior performance compared to One-Hot Encoding approach. All the research concerning the LVD, up to our best knowledge, utilizes One-hot Encoding for the transformation. One-Hot Encoding poses a few issues such as the linear increase of dimensionality of the input matrix due to creation of the transformed categorical values. The intrinsic relationships between the categorical variables are not captured in One-Hot Encoding since it creates n independent features from each categorical feature, where n is the levels of that particular feature. Embeddings, on the other hand, reduces the dimensionality of the categorical features by creating a dense matrix, in contrast to a sparse matrix by One-Hot Encoding. For instance, in the LVD, One Hot Encoding (OHE) generates a sparse matrix with 200 features, whereas the Embeddings yield 169 dense features. In addition, unlike unstructured data found in nature, structured data with categorical features may not have continuity at all, and even if it has, it may not be so obvious. The core of our dimensionality reduction is based on neural networks. Neural networks are continuous, and hence they might not perform well with raw categorical data. Thus, we hypothesize that Embeddings would aid neural networks to learn continuity in categorical features, thereby improving model performance.

4 Proposed Method

The system architecture of our methodology for transforming high dimensional vehicle data to low dimensional vehicle data for a predictive goal is shown in Fig. 1.

The pre-processed data can be mathematically represented as

$$X = [x_1, ..., x_N]^T \in R^{NxD},$$

where N is the number of rows of data records, and D the feature dimensionality. Here N = 19954 and D = 446. The 446 features contain 362 numerical features (Fn) and 74 Categorical features (Fc). The numerical features are passed

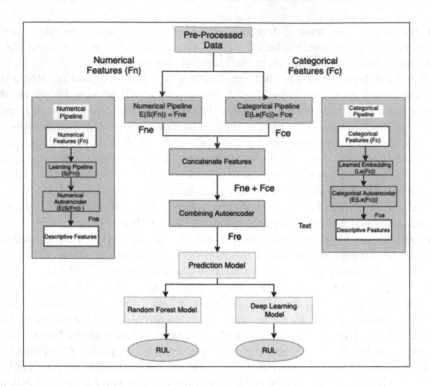

Fig. 1. System architecture

through a learning pipeline, and the categorical features are passed to a learned embeddings block.

The numerical pipeline performs the following:

1. Feature Selection (Learning Pipeline): $S(f)$
2. Feature Extraction (Numerical Autoencoder): $E(f)$

The Categorical Pipeline performs the following:

1. Embedding Transformation (Learned Embeddings): $Le(f)$
2. Feature Extraction (Categorical Autoencoder): $E(f)$

Here, f represents features that are input to a transformation function. S represents selection of features, E represents extraction of features. Le represents Learned Embedding transformation. In Fig. 1, $S(Fn)$ represents the process of selecting a feature subspace of the numerical features (Fn) using filter and embedded selection approaches. $Le(Fc)$ represents the process of obtaining vector encodings of the categorical features (Fc) using the learned embeddedings. The pre-processed data is split into training and testing sets using 'GroupShuffleSplit' algorithm of SciKit-Learn with a 'test_size' of 0.2 and 'n_splits' set to 5, whilst supplying the 'groups' function of the 'split' method with the Chassis_ID of the vehicles. In this way, we ensure that there is no overlap of data belonging to any particular vehicle in the train data and the test data. $E(S(Fn))$ represents feature extraction performed on a selected set of features, and $E(Le(Fc))$ represents feature extraction performed on the embedded vectors.

A neural network is used to learn the embedding (numerical vector representation) of the categorical variables. Given a set of categorical features Fc, the neural network transforms the features into a numerical vector, which is mathematically represented in Eq. 3.

$$y = Le(Fc) \tag{3}$$

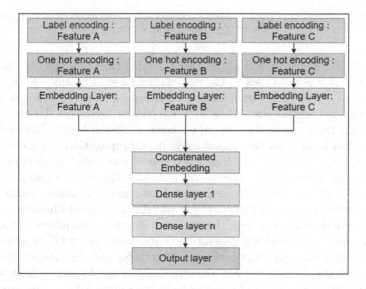

Fig. 2. Illustration that learned embedding layers are equivalent to extra layers on top of each label encoding and one hot encoding input.

To learn the numerical vector shown in Eq. 3, a mapping M_i is required to represent each state x_i of the categorical feature as a vector of numerical features X_i as shown in 4

$$M_i : x_i \rightarrow X_i \tag{4}$$

The transformation mapping is done in three steps. Firstly, each state x_i of the discrete categorical feature is label encoded L_i; that is, each state is mapped to an integer value. This label encoding process is shown in Eq. 5 represents the top-most layer in Fig. 2

$$L_i : x_i \rightarrow l_i \tag{5}$$

Secondly, the label encoded states of the categorical variables are one hot encoded O_i. Given z_i is the number of unique categorical variable l_i states, then

γ_{a,z_i} is the one-hot encoding of l_i. The one hot encoding γ_{a,z_i} is a vector of length of z_i, where the element is only non-zero when $a = l_i$ is represented in Eq. 6

$$O_i : l_i \rightarrow \gamma_{a,z_i} \tag{6}$$

Thirdly, the one hot encoded categorical states γ_{a,z_i}, are mapped to a numerical vector X_i using an embedding layer E_i, as shown in Eq. 7

$$E_i : \gamma_{a,z_i} \rightarrow X_i \tag{7}$$

The numerical vector X_i can be represented with the Eq. 8.

$$X_i \equiv \sum_a \omega_{a,\beta} \cdot \gamma_{a,z_i} = \omega_{x_i,\beta} \tag{8}$$

In Eq. 8, $\omega_{a,\beta}$ is the weight connecting the label encoding layer to the embedding layer, and β is the index of the embedding layer. The embeddings are just the weights $\omega_{x_i,\beta}$ of the layer, and can be learned like every other dense layer in the neural network layers. All of the embedding layers can be concatenated together and then treated as an input layer to dense layers. The weights of the embedding layers can be trained using back-propagation. By combining the embedding layers, as shown in Fig. 2, we can learn special properties between categorical variables and also the intrinsic relationship of each category itself.

The categorical variables transformed into numerical values using Embeddings as stated above, generates a dense matrix of reduced dimension, by capturing the relationship between the various categorical variables. This in turn transforms the categorical features into a continuous stream of numerical values which are better for neural networks. These transformed features are then fed to then categorical autoencoder. Fce denotes the extracted features from the categorical pipeline, and extracted features from the numerical pipeline are denoted by Fne. The extracted features from both the pipelines are concatenated and fed to a Combining Autoencoder. The features extracted from this Autoencoder are represented by Fre, representing the extracted features of a reduced dimension. These reduced dimensionality features are passed to a prediction model to predict the RUL. The regression is evaluated using the Mean Absolute Error (MAE) metric.

5   Experimental Evaluation and Results

In this section, the results are presented in sections, such that each section describes the results of a particular stage in the architecture shown in Fig. 1.

1. Embeddings Evaluation: Embeddings comparison with One Hot Encoding.
2. Parallel Stacked Autoencoder Regression: The features from the Numerical Autoencoder and the Categorical Autoencoder are concatenated and fed to

the regressor for RUL prediction. Since we decided to label the data according to RUL labeling, the results of a corresponding regression problem are reported. Also, the results of incorporation of categorical feature transformation using Embeddings along with numerical features are presented. Results comparing OHE and Embeddings are also presented.

3. Combining Autoencoder Regression: Evaluation of the combining autoencoder, which combines the features from both the numerical and categorical pipelines.

5.1   Embeddings Evaluations

The advantages of the inclusion of the Embeddings are presented in Table 1. Important inferences can be made from this table by comparing different rows of the Table. Row 1 and row 2 of the table present, the MAE from using only the features from the numerical pipeline and MAE with the inclusion of features from the Categorical Pipeline (the features from the Embeddings). We observe a better performance with both the Random Forest as well the Deep Network. Row 3 and 4 show the benefits of the embeddings at the Feature selection stage of the Numerical pipeline. Finally, row 5 and row 6 show that learned embeddings have the potential to improve even just the pre-processed data without any feature selection. This Table basically vindicates the improvement in performance with the inclusion of Embeddings for Categorical Variables. The performance of the Embeddings is compared with OHE in Table 2. Here in row 1 and row 2, we can observe that the embeddings yield a better MAE with the pre-processed data without any feature selection. Furthermore, row 3 and row 4 show that this behavior is also seen as we proceed down the Numerical Pipeline, that is, the embeddings provide a better result even with the extracted features from the numerical pipeline.

Table 1. Embeddings vs. No Embeddings

Row no	Numerical features	Categorical features	Random forest MAE	Deep network MAE
1	50 (AE)	–	168.98	156.34
2	**50 (AE)**	**169 (Embeddings)**	**154.81**	**145.74**
3	100 (learned)	–	156.41	173.41
4	100 (learned)	169 (Embeddings)	155.2	152.65
5	362 (Full)	–	157.92	187.82
6	362 (Full)	169 (Embeddings)	157.65	158.54

5.2   Parallel Stacked Autoencoder Regression

The problem of predicting time to failure is formulated as a regression task using RUL labeling. Our primary evaluation is based on evaluating model performance

Table 2. Embeddings vs OHE

Row no	Numerical features	Categorical features	Random forest MAE	Deep network MAE
1	362 (Full)	169 (Embeddings)	157.65	158.54
2	362 (Full)	200 (OHE)	157.67	190.05
3	50 (AE)	200 (OHE)	160.49	175.23
4	**50 (AE)**	**169 (Embeddings)**	**154.81**	**145.74**

for the predictive regression task. For evaluating the model performance, we used the MAE metric. Table 3 and Table 4 show the MAE of different models, including the parallel stacked approach and baseline of both Random Forest and Deep Network models, respectively. The first row in both tables is a naive estimation of RUL, namely the average RUL across all vehicles, used as the baseline for comparison.

Table 3. Model comparison based on MAE of the RUL predictions - Random Forest Model.

Model	MAE of RUL prediction
Mean Time to Failure (Baseline)	230.81
Best Numerical Pipeline	168.98
Best Categorical Pipeline	166.21
Parallel Stacked Model	**160.55**
Combining Autoencoder with input from Parallel Stacked Model	168.38

Table 4, which is based on the Neural Network model performed better than the Random Forest Model. Basically, it shows that continuity can improve model performance of Neural Networks.

5.3   Combining Autoencoder Regression

The features from the parallel stacked pipeline are finally passed to a combining autoencoder, to capture relationships between both the pipelines.

The Combining Autoencoder generates different subsets of output dimension that are evaluated: 2D, 5D, 10D, 20D, 30D, 40D, 50D, and 80D. Since the generated features in this stage are in low dimensional, there is a consequent reduction in data size that is observed.

The features from the Combining Autoencoder are passed to both the Random Forest and Neural Network model. Also, the feature subset are compared with other dimensionality reduction methods as shown below:

1. PCA with OHE
2. PCA with Embeddings
3. UMAP with OHE
4. UMAP with Embeddings

Table 4. Model comparison based on MAE of the RUL predictions - Deep Network Model.

Model	MAE of RUL prediction
Mean Time to Failure (Baseline)	230.81
Best Numerical Pipeline	156.35
Best Categorical Pipeline	148.51
Parallel Stacked Model	148.24
Combining Autoencoder with input from Parallel Stacked Model	**146.29**

The result of this comparison is shown in Fig. 3 and 4. From this, we can observe that our approach with the parallel stacked autoencoder, fares better than all the other dimensionality approaches at all the dimensions.

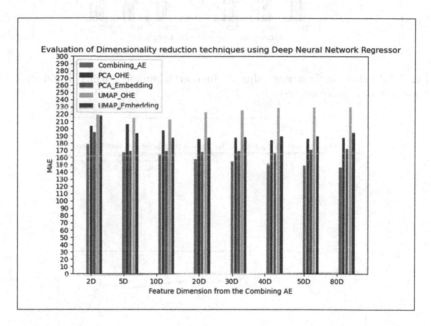

Fig. 3. Evaluation of Dimensionality reduction techniques using Deep Neural Network (Color figure online)

The performance improvement obtained using the parallel Autoencoder approach can be seen in Figs. 5 and 6. Here we observe that even with 86.99% of data size reduction, we are still able to improve the MAE prediction by 23.03%, and even with extreme data size reduction of 99.7%, we still see a significant performance improvement of 6.31%. Here it must be noted that the performance improvement of 6.31% from 99.7% data size reduction does not mean that only 0.3% of the original data is sufficient to predict the RUL. Here the 0.3% does not correspond to a direct removal of data from the original data. This data obtained

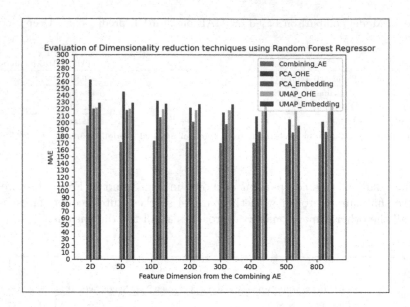

Fig. 4. Evaluation of Dimensionality reduction techniques using Random Forest Regressor. (Color figure online)

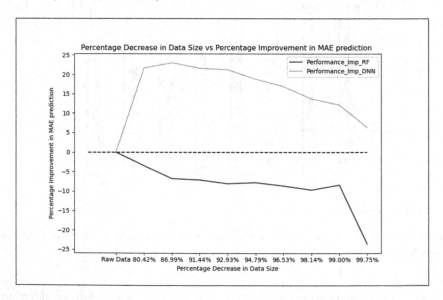

Fig. 5. Percentage Decrease in Data Size vs Percentage Improvement in MAE prediction (Color figure online)

as a result of various transformations as described in Sect. 4. And similarly with the prediction improvement of 23.03% with 86.99% data size reduction. The blue line shows the performance change for the Random forest model and the Yellow

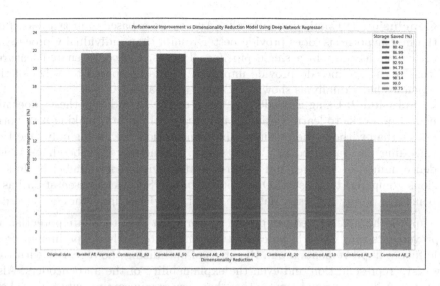

Fig. 6. Performance Improvement and Storage Saved with relationship to the reduction model Using the Deep Network Regressor (Color figure online)

line shows the performance change for the Deep Learning Model. These percentage improvement scores are calculated with results from raw data without any data reduction (Baseline Model) as the basis; that is, the Baseline Model is treated as 0% improvement (which is basically when we use the whole data before compression).

Although, the Neural Network model increases in performance as the dimensional reduces, the Random Forest starts getting worse. This observation can as a result that the approach developed favours Neural Network models.

In Fig. 6, we show how much compression we can achieve with the Deep Network Model and the percentage of storage saved without information loss.

6   Conclusion

In this paper, a parallel stacked autoencoder methodology is proposed for dimensionality reduction and feature generation which are used for predicting the upcoming failures in trucks. We address two shortcomings in existing state-of-the-art: Implementation of PAE architecture for numerical and categorical features, and employing embeddings on categorical features to generate continuity. We demonstrate experimentally, using real-world data from the vehicles, that the proposed approach leads to significant performance improvement compared to individual autoencoder models. We also demonstrate the practical advantages such as the reduction in size combined with improvement in prediction performance using our methodology. In turn, we validate that both our hypotheses to be true and present two important conclusions.

1. **Conclusion 1:** Employing a Parallel Autoencoder based approach based on the first hypothesis, does provide better results than individually processing the whole features in a single pipeline. That is, the concatenated features from both pipelines do provide improved results compared to either of the pipelines individually as shown in Table 3 and Table 4.
2. **Conclusion 2:** Using Embeddings, based on the second hypothesis, does aid neural networks to learn continuity in categorical features making it perform better than without the continuity implementation (i.e., using only One Hot Encoding), as validated in Table 1 and 2. Furthermore, Embeddings yields dense numerical features and a representation with lesser number of dimensions compared to those of One Hot Encoding. Such a representation has a benefit of occupying lesser data size, which alleviates data storage concerns.

The approach implemented has proven to work, but still, there are potentials of improvements that can still be carried out and more further experiments. Possible future improvements are in the areas of optimizing the regressor with this new data representation and even the explainability of the autoencoders. Also predicting failures of components other than powertrain components and see how it fares. We also consider evaluating the impact of embeddings in learning multidimensional relationship and see if embeddings can help in discriminating faulty and non-faulty vehicles. Furthermore, we consider calculating the explained variance of both the random forest model and neural network regressor model to see if there is any significant difference and lastly evaluating the impact of overhead this new feature transformation might cost the system especially in terms of computational cost and operational runtime. A good idea will be to see if the overhead incurred does or does not makes the model improvements negligible.

References

1. Automotive Sensors and Electronics Expo 2017 (2017). http://www.automotivesensors2017.com/. Accessed 13 June 2020
2. Big data and Analytics in the Automotive Industry - Automotive Analytics Thought Piece. The Creative Studio at Deloitte, London (2015)
3. Hinton, G.: Reducing the dimensionality of data with neural networks. Science **313**(5786), 504–507 (2006). https://doi.org/10.1126/science.1127647
4. Bengio, Y., Lamblin, P., Popovici, D., Larochelle, H.: Greedy layer-wise training of deep networks. In: Advances in Neural Information Processing Systems 19 (2007). https://doi.org/10.7551/mitpress/7503.003.0024
5. Maggipinto, M., Masiero, C., Beghi, A., Susto, G.: A convolutional autoencoder approach for feature extraction in virtual metrology. Procedia Manuf. **17**, 126–133 (2018). https://doi.org/10.1016/j.promfg.2018.10.023
6. Vaiciukynas, E., Ulicny, M., Pashami, S., Nowaczyk, S.: Learning low-dimensional representation of bivariate histogram data. IEEE Trans. Intell. Transp. Syst. **19**(11), 3723–3735 (2018). https://doi.org/10.1109/tits.2018.2865103
7. Xu, B., Ding, X., Hou, R., Zhu, C.: A feature extraction method based on stacked denoising autoencoder for massive high dimensional data. In: 2018 14th International Conference on Natural Computation, Fuzzy Systems and Knowledge Discovery (ICNC-FSKD), Huangshan, China, pp. 206–210 (2018). https://doi.org/10.1109/FSKD.2018.8687138

8. Pirbazari, A.M., Chakravorty, A., Rong, C.: Evaluating feature selection methods for short-term load forecasting. In: 2019 IEEE International Conference on Big Data and Smart Computing (BigComp), Kyoto, Japan, pp. 1–8 (2019). https://doi.org/10.1109/BIGCOMP.2019.8679188
9. Prytz, R., Nowaczyk, S., Rögnvaldsson, T., Byttner, S.: Predicting the need for vehicle compressor repairs using maintenance records and logged vehicle data. Eng. Appl. Artif. Intell. **41**, 139–150 (2015). https://doi.org/10.1016/j.engappai.2015.02.009
10. Khoshkangini, R., Pashami, S., Nowaczyk, S.: Warranty claim rate prediction using logged vehicle data. In: Moura Oliveira, P., Novais, P., Reis, L.P. (eds.) EPIA 2019. LNCS (LNAI), vol. 11804, pp. 663–674. Springer, Cham (2019). https://doi.org/10.1007/978-3-030-30241-2_55
11. Khoshkangini, R., Mashhadi, P., Pashami, S., Nowaczyk, S., et al.: Early prediction of quality issues in automotive modern industry. Information **11**(7), 354 (2020)
12. Mashhadi, P., Nowaczyk, S., Pashami, S.: Stacked ensemble of recurrent neural networks for predicting turbocharger remaining useful life. Appl. Sci. **10**(1), 69 (2019). https://doi.org/10.3390/app10010069
13. Du, T., Liao, L.: Deep neural networks with parallel autoencoders for learning pairwise relations: handwritten digits subtraction. In: 2015 IEEE 14th International Conference on Machine Learning and Applications (ICMLA) (2015). https://doi.org/10.1109/icmla.2015.175
14. Ledesma, D., Liang, Y., Wu, D.: Adaptive generation of phantom limbs using visible hierarchical autoencoders. arXiv preprint arXiv:1910.01191 (2019)
15. Wang, R., Li, L., Li, J.: A novel parallel auto-encoder framework for multi-scale data in civil structural health monitoring. Algorithms **11**(8), 112 (2018). https://doi.org/10.3390/a11080112
16. Cerda, P., Varoquaux, G.: Encoding high-cardinality string categorical variables (2019)
17. Guo, C., Berkhahn, F.: Entity embeddings of categorical variables. arXiv, abs/1604.06737 (2016)
18. Dong, G., Liu, H.: Feature Engineering for Machine Learning and Data Analytics. CRC Press (2018)

IoT Streams 2020: Unsupervised Machine Learning

Unsupervised Machine Learning Methods to Estimate a Health Indicator for Condition Monitoring Using Acoustic and Vibration Signals: A Comparison Based on a Toy Data Set from a Coffee Vending Machine

Yonas Tefera[1]([✉]), Maarten Meire[1], Stijn Luca[2], and Peter Karsmakers[1]

[1] Department of Computer Science, DTAI-ADVISE, KU Leuven,
Kleinhoefstraat 4, 2440 Geel, Belgium
{yonas.tefera,maarten.meire,peter.karsmakers}@kuleuven.be
[2] Department of Data Analysis and Mathematical Modelling, Ghent University,
Coupure Links 653, 9000 Gent, Belgium
stijn.luca@ugent.be

Abstract. Automating the task of assessing an asset's status based on sensor data would not only relieve trained engineers from this time intensive task, it would also allow a continuous follow-up of assets, potentially resulting in a fine-grained view on the asset's status. In this work three unsupervised machine learning approaches that define a Health Indicator (HI) based on acoustic and vibration signals were empirically assessed. Such a HI indicates the similarity of the current measured state to the baseline/normal operational state. The lower the HI score the worse the asset's condition. In this way the condition of an asset can be automatically monitored. Gaussian mixture models, Variational Autoencoders (VAE) and One Class Support Vector Machine (OC-SVM) were considered for this task. To enable the empirical assessment, a toy data set was created in which vibration and acoustic data was recorded simultaneously from a coffee vending machine with rotating elements in the bean grinder and water pump with relatively fast changing levels in the water and bean containers, and several stages in the coffee making cycle. Experiments were performed to analyse whether subtle changes in the sensor data due to changing container levels could be automatically detected and discriminated. Moreover, it was studied if a change could be rooted back to a cause (being a low level in the water or bean container). A set of temporal and spectral domain features were extracted and considered, while experiments were also performed by fusing the acoustic and vibration signals. The applied models achieved a comparable performance in terms of detecting low and empty container levels, with VAE using convolutional layers and OC-SVM achieving a further better discrimination of the different container levels when using the fused signals. It was also determined that the root cause of a level change can be determined by looking at the HI in the various stages.

© Springer Nature Switzerland AG 2020
J. Gama et al. (Eds.): ITEM 2020/IoT Streams 2020, CCIS 1325, pp. 145–159, 2020.
https://doi.org/10.1007/978-3-030-66770-2_11

Keywords: Gaussian Mixture Models (GMMs) · One Class Support
Vector Machine (OC-SVM) · Variational Autoencoder (VAE) ·
Condition monitoring · Health Indicator · Data driven modeling

1   Introduction

In condition monitoring assets are continuously tracked by sensors to follow-up
their operational status and identify possible changes that might indicate future
faults. In this way interruption due to failure of the asset is prevented and
maintenance can be applied only when it is required which reduces the down
time.

Nowadays, a multitude of sensors are installed to monitor an assets condition. This work focuses on the use of an acoustic sensor, which is contactless and
retrofittable, and a vibration sensor, which requires contact with the asset. Such
sensors are typically applied when the asset contains rotating elements. Manually
inspecting the large amount of data these sensors generate is not feasible. Therefore, robust algorithms that automatically identify anomalous behavior within
the data are required.

When data-driven modeling (machine learning) techniques are used to detect
faulty conditions in most cases example data from both normal as anomalous
cases are assumed. For example, in [6] the authors propose a feature learning model for condition monitoring based on convolutional neural networks and
vibration signals for rotary machinery. However, in practice the type of anomalies that can occur is not clearly defined and when data of anomalies is available
it is scarce. Other approaches define a Health Indicator (HI) which uses a model
that was estimated only (or mainly) based on data acquired when the asset
operated in a normal way. Such HI should indicate the similarity of the current
measured state to the baseline/normal operational state. A low HI relates to a
poor asset's condition while a high HI points to a healthy condition. In [7] the
authors defined a HI based on the Mahalanobis distance of vibration signals to
indicate the health condition of a cooling fan and induction motor. Deep statistical feature learning based on Gaussian-Bernoulli deep Boltzmann machine
from vibration measurements of rotating machinery was used in [9] as a fault
diagnosis technique. In [11] acoustic signals were used to define a HI based on the
residual errors of an autoencoder to detect abnormalities in a Surface-Mounted
Device. Other examples that use acoustic signals are found in [3, 4, 12].

The main contributions of this work focus on an empirical assessment of three
unsupervised machine learning approaches to generate a HI based on acoustic,
vibration and fused signals. Two generative methods, Gaussian Mixture Models
(GMM) and Variational Autoencoders (VAE), and a discriminative method,
One Class Support Vector Machines (OC-SVM), were considered. Moreover,
different types of features were compared. In case of VAE, convolutional layers
were added to let the model automatically discover higher level features based
on the handcrafted lower level features. Using the models built, a root cause
analysis that pin points a change in HI to a specific operational state of the asset

(where specific parts are being used) was performed. As an input to the models, a toy data set is collected that enables the empirical assessment. To the best of our knowledge no data set is publicly available that recorded both vibration and acoustic data simultaneously from an asset that has rotating elements as well as relatively fast behavioral changes and contains several operational states (or contexts). In this work, a coffee vending machine with rotating elements in the bean grinder and water pump, relatively fast changing levels in the water and bean containers, and several stages in the coffee making cycle were used to generate the data set.

The remaining part of the paper is organized as follows. Section 2 discusses the collected toy data set, the feature extraction, modeling algorithms and model formulation. Sections 3 discusses the experimental setup. In Sect. 4 the obtained results are discussed in detail. Finally, Sect. 5 concludes the paper by summarizing the results obtained from the set of experiments.

2 Toy Data Set for Condition Monitoring of Assets

In order to study the machine learning methods that generate an asset's HI based on vibration, acoustic or both signals, a toy data set from a coffee vending machine, was recorded in an office environment that has:

a) synchronized recordings of both vibration and acoustic signals to capture the dynamics of rotating elements in the bean grinder and water pump,

b) relatively fast changes in the underlying physics (the change in levels of the bean and water container),

c) several operational states or contexts (different stages in the coffee making cycle).

First, the operational characteristics of the coffee vending machine will be introduced. Then, the sensing mechanisms used to collect a toy data set and the models built to calculate the HI will be briefly reviewed.

2.1 The Coffee Vending Machine

The coffee vending machine used in this research work is a **Bosch-TCA53**. It is a fully automatic espresso machine with desirable characteristics suitable for the planned experiments. The important concepts and components in the condition monitoring of the coffee vending machine are:

Fig. 1. Coffee preparation states of the vending machine.

1) **Process States:** The coffee preparation process of Bosch-TCA53 vending machine goes through the set of states shown in Fig. 1 from start to finish, when the machine is operating in normal conditions.

   In the grinding state, the machine will grind enough coffee beans to prepare a cup of coffee. Then it progresses to the rinsing state which will wash the brewing tank and make it ready to brew the coffee. After brewing, the final state is finishing where optional operations are performed (like adding sugar and/or cream). Each input data stream from the sensors is annotated in the pre-processing phase to extract the different states.

2) **Sensors used for data collection:** The two sensors used are:

   (i) *Accelerometer*: A three axis-accelerometer is used to collect the vibration data generated by the vending machine. This sensor is attached to the side of the machine in direct contact with the bean container. The sampling rate of the sensor is 1037 Hz.

   (ii) *Microphone*: is used to collect the acoustic data generated by the vending machine. This sensor was positioned next to the machine roughly in 2 cm distance without being in direct contact with it. The sampling rate of the sensor is 48 kHz.

   Figure 2 shows the acoustic and vibration signals acquired during a normal coffee preparation process.

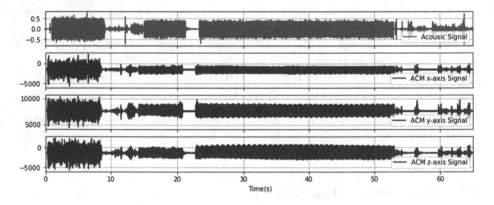

Fig. 2. Acoustic and vibration signals during a normal coffee preparation process.

3) **Monitored Tasks:** The main interest of using the coffee vending machine in an experimental setup originates from detecting subtle changes in signals received from the sensors which correspond to a change in operating behavior. Two tasks were defined based on the sensor data:

   a) to discriminate the situation of above half-full bean and water containers from all other situations where at least one container is below half level;

   b) to output a HI that correlates with the different container levels.

   Lower container levels should correspond to lower HI meaning the condition of the machine is further apart from the normal situation.

4) **Data collection:** To ease the analysis three discrete container levels were defined:
   - **Normal Set:** This data set represents a condition when the bean and water in the containers are above half of the respective tank levels.
   - **Low Level Set:** This data set represents a low, below half, bean and/or water container level condition.
   - **Empty Set:** This data set represents an empty bean or water container level condition.

Table 1. Collected training and test data set

Cycle combinations	# of cycles
Normal Bean/Normal Water	9
Low Water /Normal Bean	6
Low Bean/Normal Water	7
Low Bean/Low Water	4
Empty Bean/Normal Water	1
Empty Water/Normal Bean	4

In total 31 full cycle espresso coffee samples were collected for experimental purpose. The toy data collected from the coffee vending machine tried to capture all possible combinations of the specified status conditions as shown in Table 1. For the sake of having a more balanced number of abnormal cycles to be used in the test phase, the bean and water containers were filled, unfilled and refilled with no-specific order in the collection procedure.

2.2   Feature Extraction

When extracting features from sensor data, one should try to capture the relevant information from the input data as much as possible. The features are extracted to capture both the time and spectral domain signal properties of the input data, collected from the sensors. Prior to calculating the features, the sensor signals first pass through a framing operation, which transforms the raw signals into short overlapping segments or frames. In this work the following set of features are assessed:

1. **Time Domain Energy**
   For a sequence of samples in a frame, its energy is calculated as a sum of the squares of the samples in the frame [2].
2. **Spectral Centroid**
   The spectral centroid measures the spectral position of a signal. This measure is obtained by evaluating the "center of gravity" using the Fourier transform's frequency and magnitude information. The individual centroid of a spectral

frame is defined as the average frequency weighted by their corresponding amplitudes, divided by the sum of the amplitudes [2].

3. **Linear and mel spectra**
   After transforming the signal from the time to the frequency domain, the resulting spectra generally have too high dimensionality. These spectra are then further compacted by passing them through a number of linear or mel filter banks. Mel spectra are commonly used in acoustic signal processing, as can be seen in [1]. Linear spectra are chosen for the accelerometer signal since less dimensionality reduction is needed, due to a lower signal bandwidth.

4. **Mel-frequency cepstral coefficients**
   Mel-frequency cepstral coefficients (MFCCs) are used in the representation of acoustic and low frequency dominant signals. The MFCC feature extraction technique basically includes windowing the signal, applying the DFT, taking the log of the magnitude, and then warping the frequencies on a Mel scale, followed by applying the inverse DCT as can be seen in detail from [15].

2.3 Modeling Algorithms

Normal profiles are created using the data obtained from baseline operating conditions of the machine, reflecting the fact that no faulty condition occurs in the coffee making cycles. A model is built from the normal profiles using unsupervised algorithms to automatically label significant deviations. The algorithms used are:

1. **Gaussian Mixture Model**
   A Gaussian mixture model (GMM) is a weighted sum of M component Gaussian densities as given by [13],

$$p(\mathbf{x}|\lambda) = \sum_{i=1}^{M} w_i g(\mathbf{x}|\boldsymbol{\mu}_i, \boldsymbol{\Sigma}_i) \tag{1}$$

where $\mathbf{x}$ is a D-dimensional data vector (i.e. measurement or features), w_i, $i = 1, \ldots, M$, are the mixture weights, and $g(\mathbf{x}|\boldsymbol{\mu}_i, \boldsymbol{\Sigma}_i)$, $i = 1, \ldots, M$, are the Gaussian densities of each component that have the following D-variate form,

$$g(\mathbf{x}|\boldsymbol{\mu}_i, \boldsymbol{\Sigma}_i) = \frac{1}{(2\pi)^{D/2}|\boldsymbol{\Sigma}_i|^{1/2}} exp\left\{ -\frac{1}{2}(\mathbf{x} - \boldsymbol{\mu}_i)^T \boldsymbol{\Sigma}_i^{-1}(\mathbf{x} - \boldsymbol{\mu}_i) \right\} \tag{2}$$

with mean vector $\boldsymbol{\mu}_i$ and covariance matrix $\boldsymbol{\Sigma}_i$.
   The HI (h_{gmm}) of an observation is directly tied to it's weighted log probability ($\log(p(\mathbf{x}|\lambda))$).

2. **One-Class Support Vector Machine**
   One-Class Support Vector Machine (OC-SVM) [14] is a variant of SVM method trained on data from only a single class by computing a bounding hypersphere that encompasses as much of the training data as possible. Given training vectors $\mathbf{x}_i \in R^n$, $i = 1, \ldots, l$ without any class information, OC-SVM is defined as:

Primal problem:

$$\min_{w,\xi,\rho} \quad \frac{1}{2}\mathbf{w}^T\mathbf{w} - \rho + \frac{1}{\nu l}\sum_{i=1}^{l}\xi_i \tag{3}$$

$$\text{subject to} \quad \mathbf{w}^T\phi(\mathbf{x}_i) \geq \rho - \xi_i,$$

$$\xi_i \geq 0, i = 1,\ldots,l.$$

Dual problem:

$$\min_{\alpha} \quad \frac{1}{2}\alpha^T Q \alpha \tag{4}$$

$$\text{subject to} \quad 0 \leq \alpha_i \leq \frac{1}{\nu l}, i = 1,\ldots,l,$$

$$\alpha^T\alpha = 1.$$

where $Q_{ij} = K(\mathbf{x}_i,\mathbf{x}_j) = \phi(\mathbf{x}_i)^T\phi(\mathbf{x}_j)$ is the kernel function. Then an RBF kernel $(\exp(-\gamma \parallel \mathbf{x}_i - \mathbf{x}_j \parallel^2), \gamma > 0)$ is used, which is a popular and mostly used kernel in practice. The decision function is defined as:

$$f(\mathbf{x}) = sgn((w^T\phi(\mathbf{x}_i)) - \rho) = sgn(\sum_{i=1}^{l}\alpha_i K(x,x_i) - \rho) \tag{5}$$

The resulting HI (h_{OCSVM}) of an observation is measured by the score of each sample.

3. **Variational Autoencoder**

As described in [10], the goal of a standard autoencoder (AE) is to use an encoding network ($\mathcal{E}$) to create a compact representation $\mathbf{z}$ from an input $\mathbf{x}$ and then use a decoding network ($\mathcal{D}$) to make a reconstruction $\hat{\mathbf{x}}$.

$$\mathbf{z} = \mathcal{E}(\mathbf{x}|\theta_E), \tag{6}$$

$$\hat{\mathbf{x}} = \mathcal{D}(\mathbf{z}|\theta_D). \tag{7}$$

Variational autoencoders are a modification of this AE to a generative model. This is done by replacing the representation $\mathbf{z}$ of an input $\mathbf{x}$ by a posterior distribution $q(\mathbf{z}|\mathbf{x})$, $\mathbf{z}$ will then be sampled from this distribution.

$$q(\mathbf{z}|\mathbf{x}) = \mathcal{E}(\mathbf{x}|\theta_E), \tag{8}$$

This posterior is usually chosen as a Gaussian, where the mean and variance are the output of the encoder. To ensure valid outputs when sampling from the posterior, the Kullback-Leibler (KL) divergence from a prior distribution p(z) is used as regularization. During inference the sampling of $\mathbf{z}$ is fixed to the mean of the posterior distribution q(z|x), to remove randomness in the reconstruction. Using this reconstruction, the error with the original input can be calculated using Eq. 9, we will call this error the HI h_{VAE}.

$$h_{VAE} = -\Sigma_{i=1}^{n}(\mathbf{x}_i - \hat{\mathbf{x}}_i)^2 \tag{9}$$

2.4 Sensor Data Fusion

Observational data collected by sensors can be combined, or fused, at a variety of levels for an improved performance of the detection system. This fusing can take place at the raw data (or observation) level, feature level, or at the decision level [5]. Raw sensor data can be directly combined if the sensors are commensurate (i.e. if the sensors are measuring the same physical phenomena). Conversely, if the sensors data are noncommensurate, the data can be fused at a feature or decision level. In this work, since we are using two sensor data streams that are not necessarily commensurate, fusing is performed at the feature level for performance comparison purposes with the individual sensor HI results.

3   Experimental Setup

This section presents and discusses the empirical results obtained by using GMM, OC-SVM and VAE models for HI estimation and related fault detection on the acoustic and vibration data sets. A comprehensive set of experiments are performed to compare and demonstrate the detection accuracy and asset change trends in HI by the models using vibration, acoustic and fused features.

3.1 Experimental Settings

From the acoustic and vibration data collected in different operating conditions, two categories of features are extracted to be used as input to the developed models.

Category 1: uses higher level features of time domain energy, spectral centroid and MFCCs. For this category, frames of size 500 ms equating to a window size of 24000 for the acoustic signal and 518 for the accelerometer signal, with an overlap of 50% were used. For the MFCC features, 128 mel bands are used with the first 13 cepstral coefficients being retained.

Category 2: uses linear and mel spectra as an input to the models. The window size is reduced to 100 ms and the overlap remained 50%. This reduction was done to provide a more detailed input to the convolutional network, since it will discover its own features. A total of 64 mel and linear bands were used for acoustic and accelerometer signals respectively. In this category the spectrograms are divided into frames of 32 timesteps, which roughly equates to 1.5 s of data, and are then used as input for the machine learning model, allowing it to automatically discover features.

The extracted features are standardized to have a zero mean and unit variance so that they will have an equally weighted effect in the modeling phase. For the second category features this is done before the division into frames. Since we have 9 coffee making cycles in the normal data set, a 9-fold split is created with each fold containing 6 cycles in the training, 2 in the validation and 1 in the test set. This approach prevents data from the same cycle to appear in the different sets.

When applying GMM models, the optimal number of components are obtained by calculating the Bayesian Information Criterion (BIC) value which achieved a minimum for 4 number of components. For OC-SVM, the hyper-parameter settings which consistently gave a better performance for the different experiments are a 0.1, 1/30 for the fused signals and 1/15 for the other signals and RBF kernel values for nu, gamma and the kernel type respectively. The evaluation will be done both on a frame level, for each separate input, and on a run level, for a complete coffee making cycle. The run level results are obtained by averaging the frame level results.

3.2   Autoencoder Architectures

In this research two kinds of VAE will be used: one with convolutional layers (VAE-Conv) and one without (VAE-FC). Due to these layers, VAE-Conv will be able to automatically discover features from low level features (e.g. mel spectra).

The VAE-FC uses only fully connected layers on the first category of features. The model consists of 6 fully connected layers, 3 in the encoder and 3 in the decoder, with 16, 8, 4 neurons and 4, 8, 14 neurons respectively. The neurons are doubled when using the fused signal.

In the architecture that uses the second category of features, convolutional and deconvolutional layers are needed. This VAE model consists of 5 2D convolutional layers and a fully connected layer in the encoder and a fully connected layer and 5 2D deconvolutional layers in the decoder, with 8, 16, 32, 64, 128, 32 and 256, 64, 32, 16, 8, 1 neurons in the encoder and decoder respectively.

In both models, the activation functions are relu in all but the final layers of the encoder and decoder, where linear functions are used instead. L2 regularization and the adam [8] optimizer are used with a factor of $1e^{-4}$ and $1e^{-3}$ respectively.

4   Results and Discussion

In this section the results obtained with the various models will be discussed. Initially, the performance of individual and fused sensor input is evaluated with respect to discriminating normal and abnormal conditions. The performance in terms of correct classifications is given on the frame and complete run level. Then additional analysis is done to further discriminate between the various container levels on a chosen model. Finally, a frame level analysis of the HI outcomes is performed to determine the root cause of the observed trends.

4.1   Model Comparison

As explained in Sect. 3.1 two categories of features are used. The results of the experiments are summarized in Table 2. All results shown are calculated by taking the mean and standard deviation of the AUC score across the 9 folds. Looking at the results from the models, on the frame level a quite good distinction can be made between the normal and abnormal cycles using acoustic signals, while the accelerometer signals provide a weaker distinction. However, by fusing both signals the majority of the models attained a slight performance increase. On the run level, an even better distinction is achieved compared to the frame level. This difference is likely attributed to the lowered HI in the grinding phase compared to the other phases. This will be discussed in more detail in Sect. 4.3. In general we see that using only the acoustic signal provides a close performance compared to the fused signal, while the accelerometer signal has a lower performance.

Table 2. Status prediction results where the models in an orange cell use the category 1 features and the model in the green cell uses category 2 features.

		Sensors		
		ACM	Audio	Fused
GMM	Frame Level	0.703 ± 0.082	0.826 ± 0.081	0.854 ± 0.071
	Run Level	0.871 ± 0.043	0.945 ± 0.060	0.945 ± 0.060
OC-SVM	Frame Level	0.774 ± 0.079	0.885 ± 0.056	0.874 ± 0.032
	Run Level	0.894 ± 0.141	0.990 ± 0.019	0.994 ± 0.027
VAE-FC	Frame Level	0.660 ± 0.061	0.827 ± 0.081	0.855 ± 0.046
	Run Level	0.919 ± 0.093	0.990 ± 0.019	1.000 ± 0.000
VAE-Conv	Frame Level	0.704 ± 0.117	0.811 ± 0.123	0.802 ± 0.058
	Run Level	0.904 ± 0.087	0.939 ± 0.171	0.995 ± 0.014

4.2   Level/Trend Analysis

This section investigates whether there is a correlation between the HIs delivered by the considered models and the levels of the bean and water containers. Focusing on the results from OC-SVM and VAE-Conv, with the remaining algorithms showing similar trends, the accelerometer performed poorly in distinguishing abnormal data when compared to the acoustic signals as shown in Table 2. Based on these results, one may be inclined to conclude that using only the acoustic signals might be enough or better to purely determine if the current situation deviates from the normal operation.

However, when considering the HI in relation with the container levels no clear correlation is observed for the acoustic signals, however the accelerometer seems to perform slightly better in this task, as can be seen on Fig. 3 and 4. Another interesting aspect of the result is observed from the fused signal of Fig. 4, revealing a better correlation with the container levels, meaning that the cycles are becoming more anomalous as the container levels decrease.

A more detailed view of the HI for the different cycles is shown in Fig. 5 and 6.

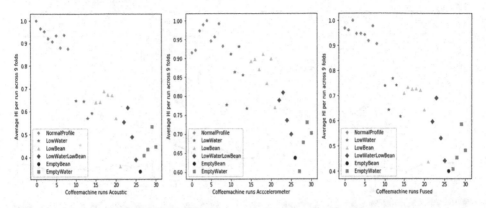

Fig. 3. OC-SVM: average of the run level results for category 1 features across all folds

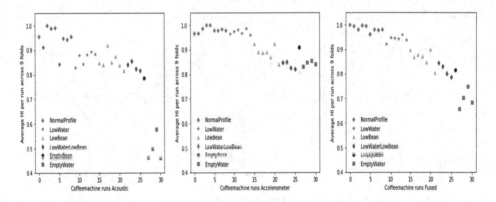

Fig. 4. VAE-Conv: average of the run level results for category 2 features across all folds

The most noticeable observations are:

- For OC-SVM model with category 1 features, there is an overlap between the three low container level runs of the acoustic signal. When we look at the accelerometer signals, we notice a better discrimination of the various levels compared to the acoustic signals. Looking at the fused signals, they achieve a much better discrimination between almost all the various cycles, with an overlap only in between the LowBean and LowWater scenarios.
- For VAE-Conv model with category 2 features, there is an overlap between four low and empty container level runs of the acoustic signal. This indicates that the acoustic signal is less correlated with the container level. When we look at the accelerometer signals, we notice a clear difference in HIs for the various levels. However, the accelerometer is not able to properly separate whether the resulting conditions are due to the water or bean container levels. Finally, when looking at the fused signals, they achieve a much better discrim-

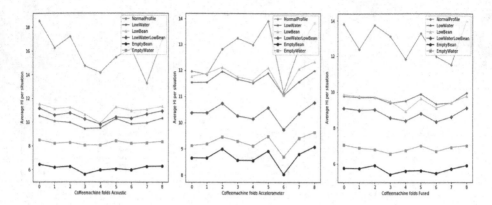

Fig. 5. OC-SVM: average HI of all cycles per scenario for each fold

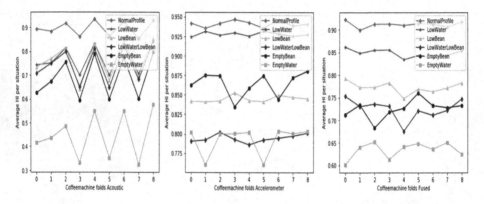

Fig. 6. VAE-Conv: average HI of all cycles per scenario for each fold

ination between almost all the various cycles, with only an overlap between the EmptyBean and LowWaterLowBean scenarios. A possible explanation could be found in the in-depth analysis of the HIs in Sect. 4.3.

In conclusion, the fusion of both signals provides a complementary solution in achieving a high performance in normal/abnormal cycles separation and a clearer discrimination between the abnormal cycles in both models and feature categories.

4.3   Causality

In the previous sections we discussed both a quantitative comparison of the performance of our models based on the AUC score and an analysis of the ability to differentiate the various abnormal cycles on the run level. However, another way to approach this problem is to examine if the root cause of the abnormal cycle (e.g. a low bean container) can be found based on the shift in HI in the states on the frame level. The VAE-Conv model will be used for

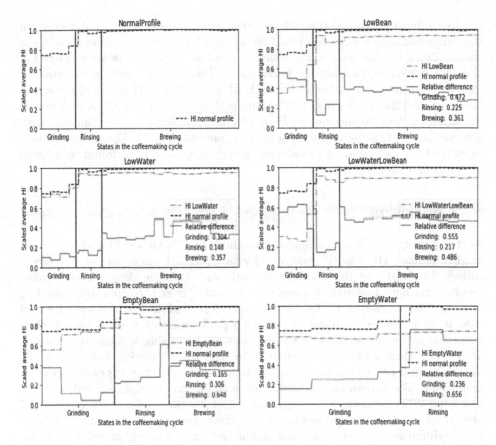

Fig. 7. Average HI across folds per container situation, compared to the normal situation. The black lines indicate the state changes. The average relative distance in HI between the normal and selected situation is shown in the legend.

this examination. In Fig. 7, a comparison between the different abnormal and normal container situations is shown. The first image shows the average HI of the cycles in the normal situation, and the other images show how the average HI of these situations compares to the normal situation. These HIs are all scaled by dividing them by the maximum of the HI of the normal situation. Firstly, we noticed that the HI for the first state "grinding" is noticeably lower than for the other states. This can likely be attributed to two factors. The first factor could be the imbalance in the data, with the brewing phase being roughly five times as long as the grinding phase. Due to this imbalance, the VAE will train more on the brewing phase and be able to reconstruct it better compared to the grinding phase, resulting in a difference in HI. A second factor is the amount of energy in the different states, with the grinding state features having more energy compared to the brewing state, which could contribute to the lower HI.

Secondly we examined the different states in these situations to determine if the correct container situation could be selected based on the average HIs in the states. These HIs are once again scaled, so we can calculate a relative instead of absolute difference, to achieve a fairer comparison. For this scaling we attached more importance to deviations on a high HI, so we flipped $(1 + h_{VAE})$ the scores before scaling them. One noticeable thing is that for both situations with empty containers a clear distinction can be made. When looking at the situations with low containers, this distinction is less clear, but still visible. These observations show that the root cause of the abnormal cycle can possibly be found by looking at the frame level results.

5   Conclusion

In this paper, three machine learning methods GMM, OC-SVM and VAE were used to define a HI. The HI generated by each method was analyzed on a newly collected toy data set that includes acoustic and vibration signals from a coffee vending machine. Different features were extracted from the input data enabling in identifying a behavior that deviates from the normal situation. It was observed that in most cases an improved detection performance can be achieved when vibration and acoustic data was fused compared to using a single modality. A sensor can have a robust performance in detecting deviating behavior, while another sensor can give a good discrimination of the different types of abnormal conditions. The experimental results obtained on this toy data set indicate this property. While acoustic signals enable a better discrimination of the normal and abnormal operational conditions, the vibration signals are better in identifying subtle differences in the abnormal signals leading to an enhanced root cause analysis. Furthermore, leveraging on the use of both sensors, a sensor fusion approach consistently outperformed the case when a single sensor was used.

Acknowledgment. We are grateful to Magics Instruments for providing the platform to collect the data used in this experiment and for their thoughtful and detailed feedback which has helped greatly in improving this work. This research received funding from the Flemish Government under the "Onderzoeksprogramma Artificiële Intelligentie (AI) Vlaanderen" programme.

References

1. Cao, Y., Kong, Q., Iqbal, T., An, F., Wang, W., Plumbley, M.: Polyphonic sound event detection and localization using a two-stage strategy. In: Proceedings of the Detection and Classification of Acoustic Scenes and Events 2019 Workshop (DCASE2019), pp. 30–34. New York University, NY, USA, October 2019
2. Giannakopoulos, T., Pikrakis, A.: Introduction to Audio Analysis: A MATLAB Approach. Elsevier (2014). https://doi.org/10.1016/C2012-0-03524-7
3. Gong, C.S.A., et al.: Design and implementation of acoustic sensing system for online early fault detection in industrial fans. J. Sens. **2018** (2018)

4. Gu, D.S., Choi, B.K.: Machinery faults detection using acoustic emission signal. In: Beghi, M.G. (ed.) Acoustic Waves, Chap. 8. IntechOpen, Rijeka (2011). https://doi.org/10.5772/22892
5. Hall, D.L.D.L., Member, S., Llinas, J.: An introduction to multisensor data fusion. Proc. IEEE **85**(1), 6–23 (1997). https://doi.org/10.1109/5.554205
6. Janssens, O., et al.: Convolutional neural network based fault detection for rotating machinery. J. Sound Vibr. **377** (2016). https://doi.org/10.1016/j.jsv.2016.05.027
7. Jin, X., Chow, T.W.: Anomaly detection of cooling fan and fault classification of induction motor using Mahalanobis-Taguchi system. Expert Syst. Appl. **40**(15), 5787–5795 (2013). https://doi.org/10.1016/j.eswa.2013.04.024
8. Kingma, D., Ba, J.: Adam: a method for stochastic optimization. In: International Conference on Learning Representations, December 2014
9. Li, C., Shanchez, R.V., Zurita, G., Cerrada, M., Cabrera, D.: Fault diagnosis for rotating machinery using vibration measurement deep statistical feature learning. Sensors (Switzerland) **16**(6) (2016). https://doi.org/10.3390/s16060895
10. Meire, M., Karsmakers, P.: Comparison of deep autoencoder architectures for real-time acoustic based anomaly detection in assets. In: 2019 10th IEEE International Conference on Intelligent Data Acquisition and Advanced Computing Systems: Technology and Applications (IDAACS), vol. 2, pp. 786–790, September 2019. https://doi.org/10.1109/IDAACS.2019.8924301
11. Oh, D.Y., Yun, I.D.: Residual error based anomaly detection using auto-encoder in SMD machine sound. Sensors 1–14 (2018). https://doi.org/10.3390/s18051308
12. Oh, H., Azarian, M., Pecht, M.: Estimation of fan bearing degradation using acoustic emission analysis and Mahalonabis distance. In: Proceedings of the Applied Systems Health Management Conference, pp. 1–12 (2011)
13. Reynolds, D.A.: Gaussian mixture models. Encycl. Biometric Recogn. **31**(2), 1047–1064 (2008). https://doi.org/10.1088/0967-3334/31/7/013
14. Schölkopf, B., Platt, J., Shawe-Taylor, J., Smola, A.J., Williamson, R.C.: Estimating the support of a high-dimensonal distribution. Microsoft Research, Redmond, WA **TR 87**(November) (1999)
15. Zheng, F., Zhang, G., Song, Z.: Comparison of different implementations of MFCC. J. Comput. Sci. Technol. **16**(6), 582–589 (2001). https://doi.org/10.1007/BF02943243

Unsupervised Anomaly Detection for Communication Networks: An Autoencoder Approach

Pieter Bonte[1]([✉])[iD], Sander Vanden Hautte[1][iD], Annelies Lejon[2],
Veerle Ledoux[2], Filip De Turck[1][iD], Sofie Van Hoecke[1][iD],
and Femke Ongenae[1][iD]

[1] IDLab, Ghent University - imec, Technologiepark-Zwijnaarde 126,
9052 Gent, Belgium
pieter.bonte@ugent.be
[2] Skyline Communications, Ambachtenstraat 33, 8870 Izegem, Belgium

Abstract. Communication networks are complex systems consisting of many components each producing a multitude of system metrics that can be monitored in real-time. Anomaly Detection (AD) allows to detect deviant behavior in these system metrics. However, in communication networks, large amounts of domain knowledge and huge manual efforts are required to efficiently monitor these complex systems. In this paper, we describe how AutoEncoders (AE) can elevate the manual effort for unsupervised AD in communication networks. We show that AE can be applied, without domain knowledge or manual effort and evaluate different types of AE architectures and how they perform on a variety of anomaly types found in communication networks.

Keywords: Anomaly detection · Time series · Communication networks · AutoEncoders

1 Introduction

Anomaly Detection (AD) in communication networks is a challenging task as these systems consist of many components that produce various real-time system metrics. The sheer scale and the dynamic nature of these systems make traditional AD inadequate as these techniques require knowledge about the domain, information about the environment the components are deployed in, or the actual configuration of the network and its components that are being used. As many traditional AD techniques are threshold-based, this becomes infeasible to manually configure and maintain thresholds for anomalies and leads to high rates of false alarms [4].

Skyline Communications[1] monitors communication networks for various providers worldwide. The company provides solutions for monitoring the broadcast, satellite, cable, telco, and mobile industry. When the network is showing

---

[1] https://skyline.be/.

© Springer Nature Switzerland AG 2020
J. Gama et al. (Eds.): ITEM 2020/IoT Streams 2020, CCIS 1325, pp. 160–172, 2020.
https://doi.org/10.1007/978-3-030-66770-2_12

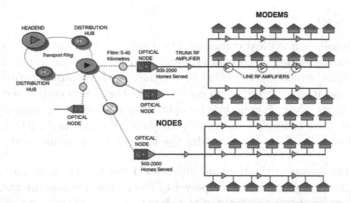

Fig. 1. Overview of the communication network use case: on the right we see various modems capturing system metrics regarding the state of the network. On the left, we see that multiple of these modems are connected to one node.

anomalous behavior, it needs to be detected early on, preventing communication downtime and financial loss. Skyline employs AD to detect network failures early-on and informs its customers of potential system risks. However, these customers typically only want to be notified about anomalies having a major influence on the health of their systems. Being notified about non-critical anomalies is finan-cially expensive due to the high maintenance costs. It is thus important to reduce the number of false positives, and to not overload the customers. Skyline also requires a generic approach, as each of their customers can have slightly different system metrics, different network configurations or completely different compo-nents. Furthermore, their customers typically do not want to share their data due to the sensitivity of the data. This requires the training and deployment of on-premise AD. As the models are trained and deployed on the hardware of the customer, these models should thus not require too much preprocessing. Most importantly, it is typically unknown in advance what could be considered an anomaly, requiring unsupervised approaches for detecting system failures.

In this paper, we aim to show how AutoEncoders (AE) can ideally be employed to perform AD in communication networks. We describe how AEs can learn normal behavior in communication networks, without the need for large amounts of preprocessing or domain expertise. We show how AE can pre-dict anomalies when the behavior deviates from normal behavior. In the next section, we go deeper into the specific AD use case in communication networks and define the requirements for the system. We then describe related work and more details regarding AEs. We describe the differences between various AE architectures and evaluate their AD performance on both synthetic as real-life data.

2   Use Case and Requirements

This Section describes the use case and requirements.

2.1   Use Case

Figure 1 visualizes a typical communication network. On the right we see various modems positioned at certain households. These modems capture real-time system metrics, which are retrieved by Skyline. In the communication network, these modems are connected to an optical node, that takes care of serving up to 2000 households. Even though data is captured at modem-level, anomalies should be reported at node-level, as network providers are concerned with more global system failures. Each modem provides the following system metrics:

- status: the status of the modem, indicates if the modem is online or not.
- US Tx: the upstream transmit power of the received communication signal.
- SNR: the signal-to-noise ratio of the signal.
- CR: the corrected ratio that was necessary to correct the received data fragments.
- UR: the ration of uncorrected data fragments.
- CS: a metric indicating various timeouts.
- PreMTTER: total energy ratio measured before combining the signals of various modems.
- PostMTTER: total energy ratio measured after combining the signals of various modems.

The status metric is categorical, while the other metrics are continuous. It is important to note that these various systems metrics can be considered as data streams or time-series and that they describe the metrics for their own system, i.e. the modem. As AD needs to be performed on a node-level, these metrics are aggregated. The aggregation is done by taking the mean of metrics of the available modems under each node. Note that some modems might be offline.

2.2   Anomaly Types

In communication networks, four types of anomalies can occur, each type is visualized in Fig. 2 and described below:

- Outliers: an abrupt spike of a certain signal, e.g. due to a temporal communication loss with a satellite.
- Trend changes: the signal (slowly) changes to a different kind of behavior, typically for a longer time period, e.g. due to wrongly configured modem.
- Variance changes: the variance of the signal changes, e.g. due to malfunctioning cable.
- Level shifts: the signal temporally takes a different kind of behavior, due to temporally downtime of upstream components.

We note that the trend changes and level shifts are depicted in Fig. 2 in an increase of signal fashion, however, a decrease in signal is also possible.

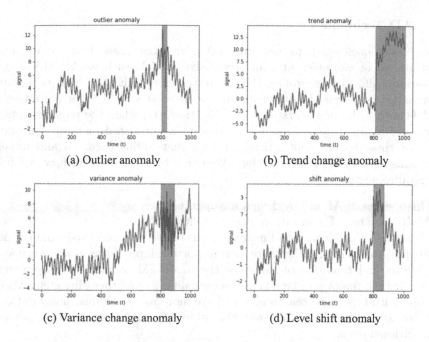

Fig. 2. The different type of communication network anomalies indicated in red. (Color figure online)

2.3 Requirements

Based on the description of the use case and the different types of anomalies the following requirements can be extracted:

1. Unsupervised: as there are no labels available, the AD should be unsupervised.
2. Multi-variate: each modem is producing multiple data streams that might need to be correlated.
3. Generic: applicable in many use cases without the need for much manual effort such as extensive preprocessing. This is important such that the same techniques can be used for different customers.
4. Accurate: as the number of false positives should be minimal.
5. Context-aware: to reduce the number of false positives, it should be possible to add additional context. For example, modems can have different hardware versions, resulting in different behavior. Taking this context into account allows to better differentiate the data.
6. Adaptable: as trends and seasonality in data might change, the AD should be able to adapt in order to reduce the number of false positives.
7. Efficiency: as the AD should happen on-premise, learned AD should be able to be transferred to other scenarios to reduce learning.

These requirements will allow us to narrow the search for applicable AD techniques.

2.4   AD Techniques

Many techniques exist to perform AD over time-series data, some of the most prevalent examples are, autoregressive models such as ARIMA and all its variants [9], matrix profiles [12], AutoEncoders (AE) [13], clustering-based approaches, one-class classifications such as one-class SVM [8] or discrete-state models such as hidden Markov models [5]. However, when the requirements set above are mapped upon these techniques, many proposed methods fail one or more of these requirements. However, one that fulfills them all and appears promising here is the AutoEncoder. We give a brief overview of how AE fulfill the requirements:

- Unsupervised: AE are by design unsupervised.
- Multi-variate: AE can take multiple inputs.
- Generic: AE can learn non-linear relations between features reducing the need for preprocessing. Furthermore, non-important input features are given lower weights and thus do not influence the model. Many statistical approaches require the removal of trends and seasonality, as preprocessing step. AE can cope with trend and seasonality and are more robust against noisy data.
- Context-aware: AE can take any kind of input and can extend the input with additional data.
- Adaptable: the weights of an AE can be updated with new data.
- Transferable: AE allow transfer learning by reusing some of the layers.

3   Related Work

There is abundant literature on the topic of AD. We focus on approaches related to AD for communication networks. Pawling et al. describe a one-pass clustering-based approach for AD in wireless communication networks [11]. It is an optimization of the k-means clustering algorithm that allows efficient updating of the clusters. However, the approach requires heavy preprocessing and there is no support to use easily transfer the models to other scenarios. Brutlag et al. propose an extension of Holt-Winters Forecasting, which supports incremental model updates through exponential smoothing [3], for detecting aberrant behavior in time series for network monitoring. Oki et al. propose a solution for detecting mobile network failure by combining both operator and social data [10]. They use an ensemble model consisting of logistic regression, random forest, and an AE. However, they assume a labeled dataset. Dornel et al. describe a solution for monitoring computer networks using traffic forcasting [6]. They employ Exponential Smoothing and ARIMA models to detect possible future abnormal behavior of network usage. Ageev et al. elaborate on a technique using fuzzy logics to detect abnormal traffic in IoT networks [1]. Liu et al. focus on a network monitoring platform that allows to easily label detected anomalies [7]. A random forest model is then used to classify the anomalies. However, the technique is not unsupervised and is thus out-of-scope for this research as there are no labels available.

In conclusion, previous research has mainly focused on fixed models for specific cases that typically only take into account data streams without any support for additional context data or easily using the models in different scenarios. We are interested in an approach that can be easily deployed in various scenarios and take additional context data into account to reduce false positives. We are the first to study how AEs can be utilized in communication networks for efficient AD.

4 Autoencoders for Unsupervised Anomaly Detection

In order to explain how we can use AEs for the generic processing of multivariate datastreams, we first define what a stream is:

Definition 1. *A **Stream** $\mathscr{S}$ is a possible unbounded ordered sequence of data, i.e. $\mathscr{S} = \{s_0, s_1, s_2, ...\}$ with s_i the data occurring at timestamp i.*

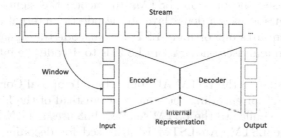

Fig. 3. Overview of the AE architecture. The encoder takes the windowed data stream and transforms it into the internal representation of lower dimension and the decoder predicts the input again from this internal representation.

As it is not possible to process unbounded streams of data (as it has no end), we define a time-based windowing function that can chunk the stream in processable parts:

Definition 2. *A (time-based) **window** function $\mathscr{W}_i$ over a Stream $\mathscr{S}$, is a function that splits the stream in processable chunks of data of size i.*
$\mathscr{W}_i(\mathscr{S}) = \{(s_0, .., s_i), (s_{i+1}, .., s_{2i}), ...(s_j, ..s_{j+i}), ...\}$.

An AE is a neural network that learns to reconstruct its input by enforcing a bottleneck on the dimension of the latent space that represents the compressed representation of the data. Figure 3 shows how the AE takes the windowed data stream as input and converts it to an internal representation of a lower dimension. The decoder then reconstructs the input from this internal representation. As the internal representation is a bottleneck in the network, it needs to summarize the most important characteristics. Thus an AE can be seen as a function that reconstructs its input from the input itself, i.e. $f_{ae}(x) = x'$ while reducing the internal representation in f_{ae}.

Definition 3. *The **reconstruction error** (RE) calculates how different the reconstructed input is from the input itself, i.e. $d(x, x')$ with d a distance function.*

An anomaly can be flagged when the RE is above a certain threshold. In AD, an AE can learn the normal behavior of the data stream, as it represents the stream characteristics in its internal representation. This assumption is valid when one does feed normal data, i.e. data without anomalies, to the network. As it is often not possible to know what normal behavior is, the assumption still holds when the dataset is unbalanced, i.e. the number of anomalies is much lower than the normal data.

Many different architectures of AE exist, we list some of the most prominent configurations:

– Dense AE: a neural network with at least three dense layers, where the hidden layers decrease in size on the encoder part and increase in size on the decoder part, enabling a bottleneck in the middle hidden layer. Figure 3 visualizes the Dense AE.
– LSTM AE: uses one or more LSTMs to encode the signal to an internal representation and uses a dense layer to decode the internal representation.
– LSTM seq2seq: uses one or more LSTMs to encode the signal to an internal representation and uses one or more LSTMs to decode the internal representation.
– TCN AE: similar to the LSTM AE, but uses a Temporal Convolutional Network (TCN) [2] for encoding the time series instead of the LSTM cell.
– TCN seq2seq: similar to the LSTM seq2seq, but uses a TCN [2] for encoding instead of the LSTM. An LSTM is still used for decoding as there is no upsampling variant for the temporal convolutions of the TCN.

In the next section, we describe how the different architectures compare and how AEs, in general, can deal with the set requirements.

5   Evaluation

In the next section, we investigate which of the architectures can ideally be used for AD in communication networks and how well AEs meet the set requirements from Sect. 2.3. First we evaluate the different AE architectures on generated data and then we evaluate on the Skyline use case.

5.1   AE Architecture Evaluation

First, we will evaluate if the different types of AE architectures are able to detect the variety of anomaly types described in Sect. 2.2. The time series for this evaluation and their anomalies were generated using the time series anomaly generator AGOTS[2]. We have trained each AE architecture on a series of 1000

---

[2] https://github.com/KDD-OpenSource/agots.

samples without anomalies and evaluated on a modified version of the series that includes the anomalies.

We used a window of size 10 and 100 epochs to train each architecture. First, we visually show the behavior of the different architectures for the selected anomalies from Sect. 2.2. We evaluated this behavior over more than 30 different generated time series for each anomaly type and verified the visualized behavior of each architecture depicted below. Table 1 also summarizes the averaged precision-recall characteristics, using the average area under the curve (AUC) of the precision-recall curve. These curves calculate the precision and recall when employing different thresholds on the REs in order to flag an anomaly. For each anomaly type, we first show the RE of each architecture. In order to detect the anomaly, the RE should visually peak on the location of the anomaly. This means that the RE is higher for the anomalous behavior, indicating that the AE had difficulties reconstructing the signal, as it is not part of the learnt normal behavior.

We now discuss how the different architecture perform on the different AD types:

Outlier Anomalies: Figure 4 depicts the REs for each architecture on the outlier anomaly. We see that all of the architectures reasonably detect the outliers.

Trend Anomalies: Figure 5 depicts the REs for each architecture on the outlier anomaly. We see that the dense AE produces a spike when at the changing point, however, fails to detect that the trend has changed. We see that the seq2scq approaches are more robust to changes in the normal signal, even though they have generally a much higher RE, even for the normal behavior. The LSTM AE and TCN AE are more prone to show higher REs due to high values in the input signal.

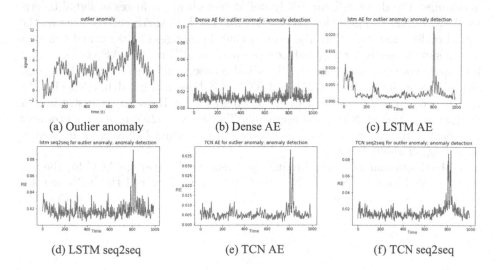

(a) Outlier anomaly   (b) Dense AE   (c) LSTM AE

(d) LSTM seq2seq   (e) TCN AE   (f) TCN seq2seq

Fig. 4. Visualization of the RE for outlier anomaly.

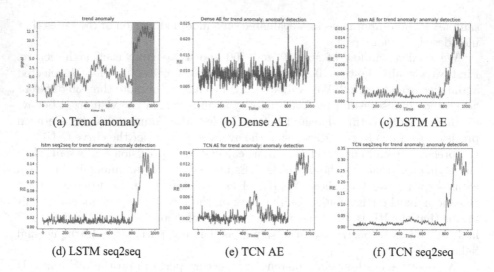

(a) Trend anomaly   (b) Dense AE   (c) LSTM AE

(d) LSTM seq2seq   (e) TCN AE   (f) TCN seq2seq

Fig. 5. Visualization of the RE for trend anomaly.

Variance Anomalies: Figure 6 shows the results for the variance anomly type. We can see that all architectures produce reasonable results.

Shift Anomalies: Figure 7 shows the results for the shift anomaly type. All architectures detect the shift, however, the dense AE only detects the outer changes. This can be seen as the RE during the shift drops again. The other architectures are less prone to this behavior. We see that the LSTM AE is again reacting to the subtle changes in normal behavior.

We have shown the performance for the different architectures on 4 types of anomalies. The dense AE can really well detect abrupt changes in signal behavior, however, fails to more long term changes. The LSTM AE can reconstruct the signal really good, however, it is prone to subtle changes in the normal behavior of the signal, causing it to produce false positives. The TCN AE shows similar behavior, however, more subtle. This is because, compared to the dense and seq2seq approaches, the LSTM and TCN AE have a limited bottleneck. The LSTM seq2seq is more robust even with higher REs. However, it is still noisier compared to the TCN seq2seq approach. The TCN seq2seq approach produces the least variance on the reconstruction of the normal behavior while clearly detecting all anomaly types.

Table 1 summarizes these findings and reports the average AUC for the different evaluations for each architecture. We see that overall the TCN seq2seq performs best, even though its RE is higher for the normal behavior than the other approaches.

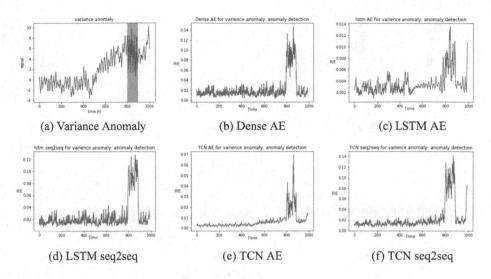

(a) Variance Anomaly   (b) Dense AE   (c) LSTM AE

(d) LSTM seq2seq   (e) TCN AE   (f) TCN seq2seq

Fig. 6. Visualization of the RE for variance anomaly.

Table 1. Comparison the different AE architectures. ('+': detects the anomalies, '−': does not detect or only partly detects the anomalies; RE = Reconstruction Error.)

	Outliers		Trend		Variance		Shift		Low variance normal behaviour	Low RE normal behaviour
	Score	Avg AUC	Score	Avg AUC	Score	Avg AUC	Score	Avg AUC		
Dense AE	+	0.86	−	0.39	+	0.98	−	0.43	+	−
LSTM AE	−	0.29	+	0.81	+	0.65	+	0.65	−	+
LSTM seq2seq	+	0.74	+	0.83	+	0.97	+	0.76	+	−
TCN AE	+	0.53	+	0.81	+	0.74	+	0.72	−	+
TCN seq2seq	+	0.80	+	0.86	+	0.97	+	0.81	+	−

5.2 Skyline Use Case Evaluation

As we operate in an unsupervised environment with no labels available, it is not trivial to evaluate the correctness of the anomaly detection approach. Skyline provided us with anomaly scores that were based on thorough investigation of the time series, heavily preprocessing and expert knowledge.

Dataset: We evaluated the data of 25 nodes. Each data stream describes the aggregated data from the underlying modems contained in 16 features. Each data stream contains 4000 samples, i.e. data over a period of two weeks at a frequency of 5 min. We used the first 60% of the time series to train upon and the remainder for validation and testing purposes.

Evaluation: We have performed hyper-parameter tuning for each node, optimizing the architecture, the number of used neurons, the size of the window, the optimizer, and the dropout rate. Table 2 shows the performance of the dif-

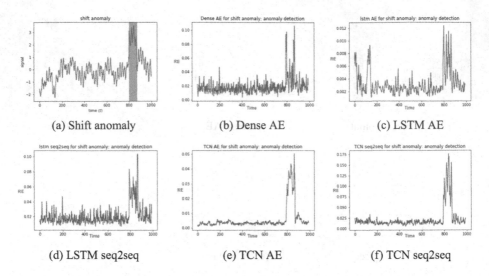

(a) Shift anomaly   (b) Dense AE   (c) LSTM AE

(d) LSTM seq2seq   (e) TCN AE   (f) TCN seq2seq

Fig. 7. Visualization of the RE for shift anomaly.

ferent AE architectures. On the left table, we report for a random selection of 10 nodes the architecture that achieved the best AUC scores for the Receiver Operator Curves (ROC). The ROC curve gives an indication of the true positives compared to the false positives when varying the thresholds on the REs. When using a very low threshold, all anomalies would be found, however, some normal events will be flagged as well. We see that the AUC values are pretty high, indicating that the selected models are doing a great job at identifying the anomalies, without triggering too many false positives. We do not achieve perfect scores, as the baseline we compare with is also not perfect. We have validated that we can detect all baseline anomalies, however, typically reporting more anomalies depending on the chosen threshold. Varying the threshold allows to differentiate between the severity of the detected anomalies.

Table 2 shows that different architectures are chosen for the different nodes and there is no clear winner. On the right of Table 2 we report the percentage each architecture is chosen as the best model, together with the average AUC they report. We see that there is a tie between the Dense AE, LSTM seq2seq, and the TCN AE. However, in the cases that the Dense AE performed best, it also reports the highest achieved AUC values. From Table 1 we already showed that the Dense AE is good at detecting outliers and the skyline case contains many outlier anomalies. We also report the AUC for a model that has been trained on all the node training data and evaluated on their combined test sets. In this case, the Dense AE also performs best, surprisingly with a larger window. All models that were trained on a single node achieved the best performance using a window of 5, while the model for all nodes combined achieved the best results using a larger window of 10. Furthermore, this Dense AE was a deeper model, i.e. 5 layers, compared to the shallow dense models with a single hidden layer

Table 2. Evaluation of the AE architectures on the skyline use case. Left the AUC of the ROC for a selection of 10 nodes. We report the best AUC for the best architecture. Right we report the percentages of nodes in the dataset each architecture performed best, with their average AUC.

nodeID	AUC	Architecture
node1	0.75	LSTM seq2seq
node2	0.90	LSTM AE
node3	0.69	TCN AE
node4	0.99	Dense AE
node5	0.84	TCN seq2seq
node6	0.93	LSTM seq2seq
node7	0.90	LSTM AE
node8	0.97	Dense AE
node9	0.99	Dense AE
node10	0.94	LSTM seq2seq
All nodes	0.81	Dense AE

Architecture	Selection percentage	AVG AUC
Dense AE	24%	0.96
LSTM AE	8%	0.90
LSTM seq2seq	28%	0.90
TCN AE	28%	0.83
TCN seq2seq	12%	0.86

that performed best for the single nodes. This can be explained by the fact that the model needs to extract many more different types of time series behavior over multiple nodes, requiring deeper models to extract and generalize these different behaviors. We can see that the AEs are able to detect the anomalies in complex communication networks without preprocessing, domain expertise or large manuel efforts. The only preprocessing required is differentiating between continuous and categorical features.

6   Conclusion

We have shown that AEs can detect anomalies in communication networks in a generic fashion, i.e. without the need for large amounts of preprocessing[3], by learning the normal behavior of the time series. We have evaluated the performance of different AE architectures on 4 types of anomalies commonly found in communication networks. Furthermore, we have evaluated these architectures on a real communication network dataset. We showed that TCN seq2seq architectures perform best on the artificial datasets, however, the dense AE showed best results on the real use case data. In future work, we will investigate the theoretical foundation of the different architectures to theoretically explain their behavior for different anomaly detection problems and investigate ensembles to combine their strengths. We will also investigate a method for automatically extracting

---

[3] We note that the technique does require some hyperparameter tuning.

the best threshold in an unsupervised manner. Furthermore, we will investigate the best ways to exploit context in AEs to further increase the accuracy.

Acknowledgement. This research was funded by the imec.icon project RADIANCE, which was co-financed by imec, VLAIO, Barco, ML6 and Skyline.

References

1. Ageev, S., et al.: Abnormal traffic detection in networks of the internet of things based on fuzzy logical inference. In: 2015 XVIII SCM, pp. 5–8. IEEE (2015)
2. Bai, S., et al.: An empirical evaluation of generic convolutional and recurrent networks for sequence modeling. arXiv preprint arXiv:1803.01271 (2018)
3. Brutlag, J.D.: Aberrant behavior detection in time series for network monitoring. In: LISA, vol. 14, pp. 139–146 (2000)
4. Chandola, V., et al.: Anomaly detection: a survey. ACM Comput. Surv. (CSUR) **41**(3), 15 (2009)
5. Cho, S.B., et al.: Efficient anomaly detection by modeling privilege flows using hidden Markov model. Comput. Secur. **22**(1), 45–55 (2003)
6. Dornel, H., et al.: Traffic forecasting for monitoring in computer networks using time series. Int. J. Adv. Eng. Res. Sci. **6**(7) (2019)
7. Liu, D., et al.: Opprentice: towards practical and automatic anomaly detection through machine learning. In: Proceedings of the 2015 Internet Measurement Conference, pp. 211–224. ACM (2015)
8. Manevitz, L.M., et al.: One-class SVMs for document classification. J. Mach. Learn. Res. **2**(Dec), 139–154 (2001)
9. Mehrotra, K.G., et al.: Anomaly Detection Principles and Algorithms. Springer, Heidelberg (2017). https://doi.org/10.1007/978-3-319-67526-8
10. Oki, M., et al.: Mobile network failure event detection and forecasting with multiple user activity data sets. In: Thirty-Second AAAI Conference on Artificial Intelligence (2018)
11. Pawling, A., et al.: Anomaly detection in a mobile communication network. Comput. Math. Organ. Theory **13**(4), 407–422 (2007)
12. Yeh, C.C.M., et al.: Matrix profile I: all pairs similarity joins for time series: a unifying view that includes motifs, discords and shapelets. In: 2016 ICDM, pp. 1317–1322. IEEE (2016)
13. Zhou, C., et al.: Anomaly detection with robust deep autoencoders. In: Proceedings of the 23rd ACM SIGKDD, pp. 665–674. ACM (2017)

Interactive Anomaly Detection Based on Clustering and Online Mirror Descent

Lingyun Cheng, Sadhana Sundaresh, Mohamed-Rafik Bouguelia$^{(\boxtimes)}$, and Onur Dikmen

Department of Intelligent Systems and Digital Design, Halmstad University, Halmstad, Sweden
{linche18,sadsun18}@student.hh.se,
{mohamed-rafik.bouguelia,onur.dikmen}@hh.se

Abstract. In several applications, when anomalies are detected, human experts have to investigate or verify them one by one. As they investigate, they unwittingly produce a label - true positive (TP) or false positive (FP). In this paper, we propose a method (called OMD-Clustering) that exploits this label feedback to minimize the FP rate and detect more relevant anomalies, while minimizing the expert effort required to investigate them. The OMD-Clustering method iteratively suggests the top-1 anomalous instance to a human expert and receives feedback. Before suggesting the next anomaly, the method re-ranks instances so that the top anomalous instances are similar to the TP instances and dissimilar to the FP instances. This is achieved by learning to score anomalies differently in various regions of the feature space. An experimental evaluation on several real-world datasets is conducted. The results show that OMD-Clustering achieves significant improvement in both detection precision and expert effort compared to state-of-the-art interactive anomaly detection methods.

Keywords: Interactive anomaly detection · Outlier detection · User feedback · Expert effort

1 Introduction

Anomaly detection allows us to find instances that deviate significantly from the majority of data, indicating e.g., a system fault. Usual unsupervised anomaly detection methods are purely data-driven and do not benefit from valuable expert knowledge. However, many of the anomalies that real-world data exhibits are irrelevant to the user as they represent atypical but normal events. For example, as illustrated in Fig. 1, in domestic hot water heat-pump systems, the water reaches abnormally high temperatures once in a while to kill potential Legionella bacteria; this is an atypical but normal event. Moreover, anomalies are often subjective and depend on the application purpose and what the user considers as abnormal. For example, an abnormal train delay, which is due to a passenger

© Springer Nature Switzerland AG 2020
J. Gama et al. (Eds.): ITEM 2020/IoT Streams 2020, CCIS 1325, pp. 173–186, 2020.
https://doi.org/10.1007/978-3-030-66770-2_13

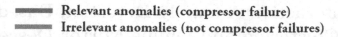

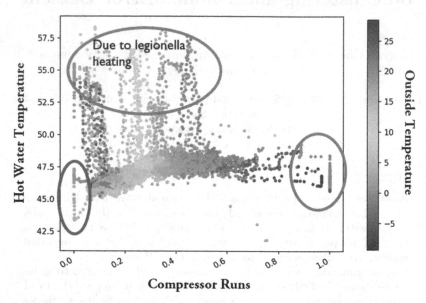

Fig. 1. Data from a real heat-pump system, where the goal is to detect compressor failures. Several anomalies are irrelevant as they are not related to compressor failure. These are just atypical (but reasonable) events. Nevertheless, they appear as abnormal.

who blocked the door, is not interesting for a diagnosis purpose. However, it can be interesting for planning purposes.

In order to distinguish between relevant and irrelevant anomalies, this paper proposes an interactive anomaly detection algorithm that proactively communicates with an expert user to leverage her/his feedback and learn to suggest more relevant anomalies. The objective here is two-fold: (i) maximizing the precision on the instances verified by the expert (i.e., ideally, only relevant anomalies are presented to the user), and (ii) minimizing the effort spent by the expert to verify these instances.

Recently, several methods such as AAD [10], OMD [12], and OJRank [13] have been proposed to incorporate user feedback into anomaly detectors, to achieve the objective (i). All these methods learn to combine anomaly scores from members of an ensemble of anomaly detectors (e.g., trees in an Isolation Forest [2]). The method proposed in this paper differs from the existing interactive anomaly detection methods in two ways. First, instead of only considering an ensemble of anomaly detectors, the proposed method aims to learn regions of the feature space where relevant anomalies are present. Second, existing methods focus on achieving a good precision (objective (i)) with less attention towards minimizing the expert effort required to investigate anomalies (objective (ii)).

The energy and the time of the expert user are often limited, and every opportunity to interact with her/him should be fully utilized. Our proposed method aims to achieve both objectives by learning to score anomalies differently in various regions of the feature space.

The remainder of this paper is organized as follows. In Sect. 2, we present the related work and discuss the similarity and differences between the proposed method and the existing ones. In Sect. 3, we formalize our goals and describe our proposed method. In Sect. 4, we present the experimental evaluation where the proposed method is compared against stare-of-the-art methods on several real-world datasets. In Sect. 5, we conclude and discuss future work.

2   Related Work

Since the work proposed in this paper involves interactions with a human expert, it is related to, but different from, *active learning* (which selects informative instances to be labeled, according to a query strategy). It is also closely related to interactive learning methods designed to learn from the *top-1 feedback* (which selects the top instance to be labeled, without a query strategy). In this section, we discuss how our work relates to and differs from state-of-the-art methods in these categories.

Active Learning Methods

Usual active learning (AL) techniques such as [3, 4] aim to minimize the labeling cost required to train a high-performance classification model. This is achieved by sampling a small number of informative instances (according to a query strategy) which are presented to an expert for labeling. We refer the reader to [5] for a survey of AL strategies for classification. AL techniques have also been used for anomaly and novelty detection in [6–8]. In all these AL methods, the goal is to minimize the final error of the model (after querying ends) on new unseen instances. This is in contrast to our proposed method, which aims to minimize the number of irrelevant anomalies presented to the expert during querying (i.e., while she/he is investigating them). In this case, each query is about the most anomalous yet-unlabeled instance.

In [9], a method for detecting errors in insurance claims was proposed. The method aims at reducing the expert effort required to verify the insurance claim errors. It assumes that a classifier has been trained to predict errors in claims and use it to score new unlabelled claims. The top-scoring claims are then clustered, and the clusters are ranked. Insurance claims from the top cluster are presented to the expert for investigation. Presenting instances from the same cluster avoids switching between contexts and therefore reduces the expert effort. The method moves to the next cluster when the precision for the current cluster falls below a threshold. However, this method does not update the model based on user feedback. In contrast, our proposed method incorporates each user-feedback so that the next suggested anomaly is more likely relevant.

Interactive Learning Based on the Top-1 Feedback

In contrast to the above-mentioned methods, there have been a limited number of interactive anomaly detection methods based on the top-1 feedback. Here the goal is to maximize the number of true/relevant anomalies presented to the expert user. These methods can be summarized according to the general process described in Algorithm 1. The method we propose in this paper falls under this category.

Algorithm 1: Interactive Anomaly Detection from the Top-1 Feedback.

Input: raw dataset, budget of b queries;
Initialize an anomaly detection model h;
for $t \leftarrow 1$ **to** b **do**
  Rank instances in the descending order of their anomaly scores;
  Present the top-1 (most anomalous) instance x to the expert;
  Get a feedback label $y \in \{1, -1\}$ (i.e., TP or FP);
  Update the model h based (x, y) (or all instances labelled so far);
end

In [10], a method called AAD (Active Anomaly Detection) was proposed to maximize the number of correct anomalies presented to the user. At each iteration, the instance having the highest anomaly score is presented to the expert, and label feedback is obtained. The set of all instances labeled so far is used to solve an optimization problem that combines anomaly scores from an ensemble of anomaly detectors. AAD initially used an ensemble of one-dimensional histogram density estimators (LODA) [1], and was extended later to use a tree-based ensemble such as Isolation Forest [2]. Some drawbacks of ADD are: (i) the fact that it does not care about minimizing the expert effort, and (ii) as the number of labeled instances grows with each new feedback, the optimization problem takes more and more time to solve (i.e., it is not updated in an online fashion). Later, the authors of AAD suggested a method referred to as FSSN (feature space suppression network) [11]. The method uses an ensemble of global anomaly detectors and learns their local relevance to specific data instances, using a neural network trained on all labeled instances. FSSN improves the precision over AAD, but suffers from the same drawbacks as AAD.

Most recently, two methods OJRank [13] (On-the-Job learning to Re-rank anomalies) and OMD [12] (using Online Mirror Descent) have been proposed to learn to score anomalies from the top-1 feedback. Both learn to combine scores of an ensemble of anomaly detectors and optimize a loss function in an online fashion based on each received feedback. In OMD, a convex point-wise loss function is optimized using online mirror descent, while in OJRank, a pair-wise loss function is optimized using stochastic gradient descent. Both OMD and OJRank aim to maximize the number of correct anomalies presented to the expert. However, only OJRank emphasizes minimizing expert effort. Nonetheless, OMD depends on way fewer hyper-parameters than OJRank (i.e., only one hyper-parameter representing the learning rate). This is an interesting criterion as there is usually no way to fine-tune the value of hyper-parameters when labeled data is scarce.

Based on these observations, we propose an extension of OMD (called OMD-Clustering), which splits the feature space into various regions (using several clusterings) and learns (online from each feedback) to score anomalies differently in these different regions of the feature space. We show that the proposed method improves the precision (i.e., detects more relevant anomalies within a budget) and significantly reduces the effort spent by the expert to verify these instances.

3 Proposed Method

3.1 Preliminaries and Goals

We are given an unlabeled dataset $X \in \mathbb{R}^{n \times d}$ of n instances in a d-dimensional space, as well as an unsupervised anomaly detection model A that scores instances according to their abnormality, i.e. $A(X) = \{s_1, s_2, \ldots, s_n\}$. The proposed method can use any base anomaly detection model A, however, to be consistent with the methods presented in Sect. 2, Isolation Forest [2] is used as a base model in this paper.

We consider a limited budget of b, which is the number of instances the expert can verify (i.e., the total number of feedbacks). For example, this could correspond to the number of faulty systems that experts can diagnose within a period or the number of potentially erroneous invoices that could be manually analyzed within a day of work [13].

Following the general process presented in Algorithm 1, the proposed method proceeds iteratively. At each iteration $1 \ldots b$, instances are scored, the instance with the highest anomaly score is presented to the expert for verification, expert feedback is obtained, and the model is updated based on the obtained feedback. The goal here is to update the model such that:

1. The **precision** at the given budget b is maximized: This corresponds to the total number of genuinely anomalous instances (i.e., relevant anomalies) verified by the expert within the budget b. Ideally, we want the expert to only verify relevant anomalies. This metric is defined as:

$$\text{precision@b} = \frac{TP_b}{a}, \tag{1}$$

   where TP_b is the number of true positives (relevant anomalies) among the b verified instances, and a is the total number of true anomalies in the dataset (constant).

2. The overall **expert effort** is minimized: This corresponds to the cost or effort that the expert spends (due to switching context) when verifying consecutive instances. If consecutive instances presented to the expert are very different (resp. similar), she/he would switch context more often (resp. less often). We

use the same definition of *expert effort* as in [13]; this is the distance between consecutive instances presented to the expert:

$$\text{expert effort} = \sum_{t=1}^{b-1} (1 - \text{cosim}(x_t, x_{t+1})), \tag{2}$$

where $\text{cosim}(.,.)$ denotes the cosine similarity, and x_t denotes the instance presented to the expert at the tth iteration.

3.2 OMD-Clustering

As shown in Fig. 1, instances that are anomalous for the same reason (e.g., compressor failure) are usually located in a similar region of the feature space. Therefore, instead of learning to combine anomaly scores given by members of the ensemble (i.e., trees of the Isolation Forest) such as in [10–13], the proposed method learns to score anomalies differently in different regions of the feature space. To do this, we first split the feature space into diverse and potentially overlapping regions, as illustrated in Fig. 2(a). Such regions are obtained by applying clustering several times based on various numbers of clusters, various combinations of features, and initial clustering conditions. A total of m overlapping clusters resulting from the different clusterings are obtained.

Next, a sparse scores matrix $Z \in \mathbb{R}^{n \times m}$ is defined where the n rows correspond to the instances and the m columns correspond to the clusters (i.e., regions). Each entry $Z_{i,j}$ is set to s_i if x_i belongs to cluster c_j, otherwise to 0, i.e.,

$$Z_{i,j} = \begin{cases} s_i & \text{if } x_i \in c_j \\ 0 & \text{otherwise} \end{cases} \tag{3}$$

where x_i is the ith instance in dataset X, s_i is the score assigned by the anomaly detection model A to instance x_i (i.e., $s_i = A(x_i)$), and c_j is the jth cluster. The process of clustering and the construction of the Z scores matrix are described in Algorithm 2. Note that the Z matrix needs only to be constructed once at the beginning (i.e., before starting the interactions with the expert).

Now that $Z \in \mathbb{R}^{n \times m}$ is defined, the remaining of this section explains how to incorporate the expert feedback at each iteration of the interaction loop.

Let $\mathbf{1}$ be a vector of all ones (i.e. m ones). It is worth noting that $(\frac{1}{m} Z.\mathbf{1}) \in \mathbb{R}^n$ corresponds exactly to the original anomaly scores we get with the unsupervised anomaly detector $A(X) = \{s_1, s_2, \ldots, s_n\}$. By using $\frac{1}{m} Z.\mathbf{1}$ to compute the final scores, the same weight (i.e., $\frac{1}{m}$) is being used for to all the m regions of the feature space. Instead of this, we propose to assign different weights to the m regions and define the final anomaly scores based on a weighted sum of the regions scores. That is, we replace the sum $\frac{1}{m} Z.\mathbf{1}$ with

$$\left(\text{scores} = \frac{1}{m} Z.\boldsymbol{w} \right) \quad \in \mathbb{R}^n \tag{4}$$

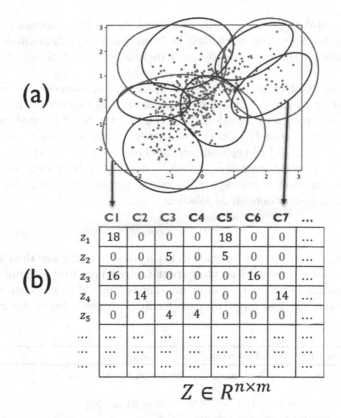

(a)

(b)

	C1	C2	C3	C4	C5	C6	C7	...
z_1	18	0	0	0	18	0	0	...
z_2	0	0	5	0	5	0	0	...
z_3	16	0	0	0	0	16	0	...
z_4	0	14	0	0	0	0	14	...
z_5	0	0	4	4	0	0	0	...
...	...	...	...	...	...	...	...	...
...	...	...	...	...	...	...	...	...
...	...	...	...	...	...	...	...	...

$$Z \in R^{n \times m}$$

Fig. 2. Illustration of the process of splitting the space into various regions and the construction of the sparse scores matrix $Z \in \mathbb{R}^{n \times m}$. The n rows correspond to the instances and the m columns correspond to the clusters. Each entry $Z_{i,j}$ is set to the anomaly score s_i if x_i belongs to cluster c_j, otherwise to 0.

Algorithm 2: Construction of the Z scores matrix.

Input: dataset X, anomaly scores $A(X) = \{s_1, \ldots, s_n\}$, number of clusterings C to perform;
$m \leftarrow 0$; // *total number of clusters*
for $i \leftarrow 1$ **to** C **do**
    Pick a random subset of p features, and a random number of clusters k;
    Perform k-means clustering on the subset of X induced by the p features;
    $m \leftarrow m + k$;
end
Construct a sparse scores matrix $Z \in \mathbb{R}^{n \times m}$ according to eq. 3.;
return Z;

---

and we learn $w \in \mathbb{R}^m$ based on subsequent expert feedbacks. This formulation of the anomaly scores allows us to assign lower weights to the regions of the feature space containing nominal instances or irrelevant anomalies, and higher weights to the regions containing true/relevant anomalies. As a result, successive anomalies presented to the expert will more likely be from the same truly anomalous region, hence minimizing the expert effort and increasing the precision at the given budget.

In order to learn w, we use the same optimization procedure (online mirror descent) and we minimize the same simple linear loss function as in OMD [12]. Consider that the current iteration is t. Let x_t be the top-1 anomalous instance in X based on the anomaly scores given by the current weights w (according to Eq. 4); let $y_t \in \{+1, -1\}$ be the feedback label provided by the expert for instance x_t (with $+1$ = relevant anomaly, and -1 = nominal or irrelevant anomaly); let z_t be row vector from Z corresponding to the instance x_t. Then, the (convex) loss function is simply defined as follows:

$$f(w) = -y_t(z_t.w) \tag{5}$$

Note that when $y_t = +1$, the function in Eq. 5 gives a smaller loss than if $y_t = -1$, since the instance presented to the expert (scored based on weights w) was a relevant anomaly. Finally, the main interactive anomaly detection algorithm, which minimizes the loss based on each feedback, is provided in Algorithm 3.

Algorithm 3: OMD-Clustering

Input: dataset $X \in R^{n \times d}$, model A, budget b, learning rate η ;

Construct the scores matrix $Z \in \mathbb{R}^{n \times m}$ using Algorithm 2;
$\theta \leftarrow 1$;   (initialize weights to ones, $\theta \in \mathbb{R}^m$)
for $t \leftarrow 1$ **to** b **do**
    $w \leftarrow \arg\min_{\hat{w} \in \mathbb{R}^+} ||\hat{w} - \theta||$;   (constrains the weights to be positive)
    scores $\leftarrow \frac{1}{m} Z.w$;   (scores $\in \mathbb{R}^n$, see eq. 4)
    Let x_t be the instance with the maximum score in scores;
    Get feedback $y_t \in \{+1, -1\}$ for x_t from the expert;
    $X \leftarrow X - \{x_t\}$;
    $\theta \leftarrow \theta - \eta \partial f(w)$;   (take a gradient step to minimize the loss)
end

---

4   Evaluation

In this section, we assess the performance of the proposed method OMD-Clustering on several real-world datasets. We compare the proposed method to two state-of-the-art interactive anomaly detection methods OJRank [13] and OMD [12], as well as an unsupervised anomaly detector (Isolation Forest [2]) as a reference. The evaluation is done on a set of 13 datasets with available ground truth (true label consisting of "*nominal*" and "*anomaly*"). Eleven of these are real-wold outlier detection datasets from a publicly available repository [14], and two of them (toy and toy2) were artificially generated. Details of the datasets are summarized in Table 1. The performance of the methods is evaluated in terms of:

- The precision at a given budget (precision@b) as described in Eq. 1. In this case, we produce curves that show how the precision of the different methods changes according to various values of the budget b.
- The expert effort as described in Eq. 2. Here, we also produce curves to show how the expert effort changes according to various values of the budget b.
- The area under the precision and the expert effort curves (resp. AUC_{prec} and AUC_{effort}).

In all experiments, we use the hyper-parameter values recommended (for the same datasets) in the original papers of OJRank [13] and OMD [12]. For the proposed method, the number of clusterings (used in Algorithm 2) is set to $C = 30$ for all datasets.

Table 1. Details of the benchmark datasets

Name	Size	Nbr. Features	Nbr. Anomalies	Anomalies %
Abalone	1920	9	29	1.51
ann_thyroid_1v3	3251	21	73	2.25
cardiotocography	1700	21	45	2.65
covtype_sub	2000	54	19	0.95
kddcup_sub	2000	91	77	3.85
Mammography	11183	6	260	2.32
Mammography_sub	2000	6	46	2.30
shuttle	12345	9	867	7.02
shuttle_sub	2000	9	140	7.00
weather	13117	8	656	5.00
yeast	1191	8	55	4.62
toy	485	2	20	4.12
toy2	485	2	35	7.22

The precision and expert effort curves obtained by the four methods (OJRank, OMD, OMD-Clustering, and Unsupervised) are shown in Fig. 4(a–b) and Fig. 5(a–c). Figure 4(a–b) shows the results of the two artificial datasets illustrated in Fig. 3, while Fig. 5(a–c) shows the results on three of the real-world datasets (cardiotocography, abalone, and mammography). As one expects, we can see from these figures that, in general, all the interactive anomaly detection methods achieve a higher precision at budget compared to the unsupervised anomaly detection method, which confirms that interacting with the expert help to get more relevant anomalies. The proposed method (OMD-Clustering)

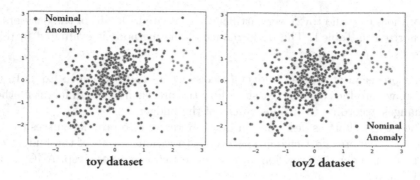

Fig. 3. Simple artificial datasets: toy (with a single anomalous region), and toy2 (with two different anomalous regions).

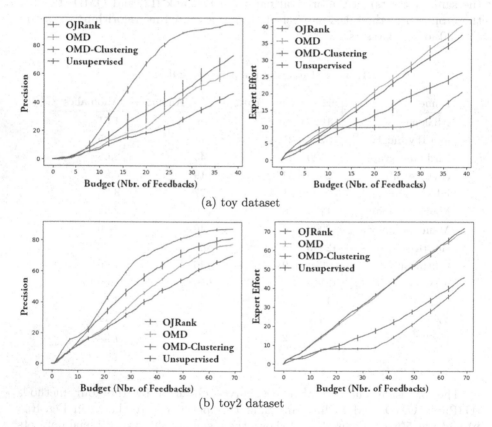

Fig. 4. Evaluation of the precision and expert effort according to various values of the budget, on the two synthetic datasets: toy and toy2.

achieves a precision which is higher than or equal to the other interactive methods, while always resulting in a significantly smaller expert effort. This indicates that clustering helps to aggregate similar instances from which relevant anomalies can be more easily detected.

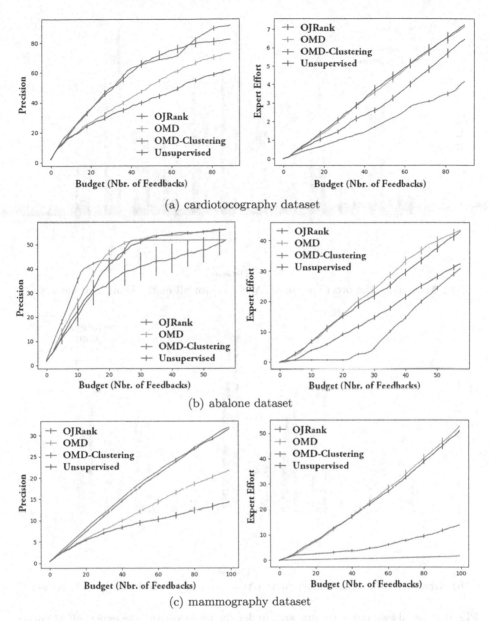

Fig. 5. Evaluation of the precision and expert effort according to various values of the budget, on three real-world datasets: cardiotocography, abalone, and mammography.

The results on all the remaining datasets are summarized more compactly in Fig. 6(a–b). Figure 6(a) shows bars plots corresponding to the area under the precision curves (AUC_{prec}). Figure 6(b) shows bars plots corresponding to the area under the expert effort curves (AUC_{prec}). The same observations can be

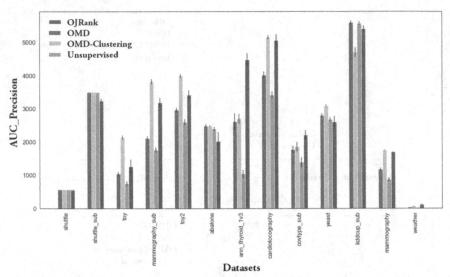

(a) Area under the precision curve (AUC_{prec}) for all methods on each dataset.

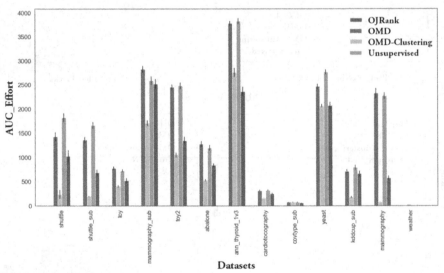

(b) Area under the expert effort curve (AUC_{effort}) for all methods on each dataset.

Fig. 6. Overall evaluation results: area under the precision and the expert effort curves for all methods and datasets.

made from these figures. Once again, we can see that all the interactive methods outperform the unsupervised one, highlighting the importance of interacting with a human expert. Moreover, the proposed OMD-Clustering method usually achieves a higher precision with a lower effort than the other methods on most of the datasets.

5   Conclusion and Future Work

In this paper, we developed an interactive anomaly detection method, where a human expert can provide feedback while verifying/investigating anomalies. The proposed method incorporates each feedback in an online fashion and learns to assign weights to various regions of the feature space. As a result, regions of the feature space with irrelevant anomalies would contribute less to the final anomaly score, while regions with more relevant anomalies would contribute more. The proposed method was evaluated on various real-world datasets and compared to state-of-the-art interactive anomaly detection methods. The results show that the proposed method is more precise at detecting relevant anomalies within a budget, while at the same time, reducing the expert effort significantly.

The existing interactive anomaly detection methods (including the one proposed in this paper) require a fixed dataset and re-rank all instances after each incorporated feedback. As future work, it would be interesting to investigate how such interactive methods can be extended to a streaming setting where data is continuously arriving and need to be processed as soon as it is available.

References

1. Pevný, T.: Loda: lightweight on-line detector of anomalies. Mach. Learn. **102**(2), 275–304 (2015). https://doi.org/10.1007/s10994-015-5521-0
2. Liu, F.T., Ting, K.M., Zhou, Z.-H.: Isolation forest. In: 2008 Eighth IEEE International Conference on Data Mining, pp. 413–422. IEEE (2008)
3. Bouguelia, M.-R., Nowaczyk, S., Santosh, K.C., Verikas, A.: Agreeing to disagree: active learning with noisy labels without crowdsourcing. Int. J. Mach. Learn. Cybern. **9**(8), 1307–1319 (2018). https://doi.org/10.1007/s13042-017-0645-0
4. Bouguelia, M.-R., Belaid, Y., Belaid, A.: An adaptive streaming active learning strategy based on instance weighting. Pattern Recogn. Lett. **70**, 38–44 (2016)
5. Settles, B.: Active Learning. Synthesis Lectures on Artificial Intelligence and Machine Learning, vol. 6. Morgan & Claypool, San Rafael (2012)
6. Görnitz, N., Kloft, M., Rieck, K., Brefeld, U.: Toward supervised anomaly detection. J. Artif. Intell. Res. **46**, 235–262 (2013)
7. Nissim, N., et al.: ALPD: active learning framework for enhancing the detection of malicious pdf files. In: 2014 IEEE Joint Intelligence and Security Informatics Conference, pp. 91–98. IEEE (2014)
8. Pelleg, D., Moore, A.W.: Active learning for anomaly and rare-category detection. In: Advances in Neural Information Processing Systems, pp. 1073–1080 (2005)
9. Ghani, R., Kumar, M.: Interactive learning for efficiently detecting errors in insurance claims. In: Proceedings of the 17th ACM SIGKDD International Conference on Knowledge Discovery and Data Mining, pp. 325–333 (2011)
10. Das, S., Wong, W.-K., Dietterich, T., Fern, A., Emmott, A.: Incorporating expert feedback into active anomaly discovery. In: 2016 IEEE 16th International Conference on Data Mining (ICDM), pp. 853–858. IEEE (2016)
11. Das, S., Doppa, J.R.: GLAD: GLocalized anomaly detection via active feature space suppression. arXiv preprint arXiv:1810.01403 (2018)

12. Siddiqui, M.A., Fern, A., Dietterich, T.G., Wright, R., Theriault, A., Archer, D.W.: Feedback-guided anomaly discovery via online optimization. In: Proceedings of the 24th ACM SIGKDD International Conference on Knowledge Discovery & Data Mining, pp. 2200–2209 (2018)
13. Lamba, H., Akoglu, L.: Learning on-the-job to re-rank anomalies from top-1 feedback. In: Proceedings of the 2019 SIAM International Conference on Data Mining, pp. 612–620. Society for Industrial and Applied Mathematics (2019)
14. Rayana, S.: ODDS library, Stony Brook University, Department of Computer Sciences (2016). http://odds.cs.stonybrook.edu

ITEM 2020: Hardware

`hxtorch`: PyTorch for BrainScaleS-2

Perceptrons on Analog Neuromorphic Hardware

Philipp Spilger[(✉)], Eric Müller, Arne Emmel, Aron Leibfried,
Christian Mauch, Christian Pehle, Johannes Weis, Oliver Breitwieser,
Sebastian Billaudelle, Sebastian Schmitt, Timo C. Wunderlich,
Yannik Stradmann, and Johannes Schemmel

Kirchhoff-Institute for Physics, Ruprecht-Karls-Universität Heidelberg,
Heidelberg, Germany
{pspilger,mueller}@kip.uni-heidelberg.de

Abstract. We present software facilitating the usage of the BrainScaleS-2 analog neuromorphic hardware system as an inference accelerator for artificial neural networks. The hardware is transparently integrated into the PyTorch machine learning framework. In particular, we support vector-matrix multiplications and convolutions; corresponding software-based autograd functionality is provided for hardware-in-the-loop training. The software provides support for automatic partitioning and scheduling of neural networks onto one or multiple chips. We discuss the implementation including optimizations, analyze runtime overhead, measure performance and evaluate the results in terms of the hardware design limitations. As an application of the introduced framework, we present a model that classifies activities of daily living with smartphone sensor data.

Keywords: Machine learning · Analog accelerator · Neuromorphic · Convolutional neural networks · PyTorch · Human activity recognition

1 Introduction

Modern machine learning (ML) frameworks such as PyTorch or Tensorflow provide interfaces and tools to easily define and evaluate ML models [1]. They aim to reduce development effort and increase interoperability by providing a large collection of operators, algorithms, optimizers and analysis tools. Using a high-level specification of the complete model, these packages construct a corresponding computational graph that is fundamentally agnostic to the substrate on which it is executed and optimized. State-of-the-art ML frameworks support CPU and GPU-based backends that accelerate inference and training. Compared to typical CPUs, GPUs are capable of processing data in a highly parallel fashion and are well-suited to the abundance of vector-matrix or matrix-matrix multiplications in artificial neural networks (ANN).

P. Spilger and E. Müller—Contributed equally.

© Springer Nature Switzerland AG 2020
J. Gama et al. (Eds.): ITEM 2020/IoT Streams 2020, CCIS 1325, pp. 189–200, 2020.
https://doi.org/10.1007/978-3-030-66770-2_14

While GPUs represent a traditional approach to accelerating the execution of ANNs, neuromorphic chips mimic biological neural networks and provide a research platform for computational neuroscience and beyond-Von-Neumann computation. BrainScaleS-2 (BSS-2) is such a neuromorphic system; it includes analog neurons and can operate in both a spiking and non-spiking mode. The non-spiking mode can be used to implement analog vector-matrix multiplication [2] while the spiking mode provides neuron dynamics accelerated relative to biology and CPU-based digital simulations [3]. In this work, we present software that allows BSS-2 to be used as an accelerator backend for PyTorch.

Figure 1 shows the BSS-2 hardware setup providing 512 neurons per chip, see [4]. Synapses are arranged in a matrix above the neurons, containing 256 rows for inputs, and connecting to the neurons in columns. Vector entries control how long a synapse row is activated. The charge reaching the neurons is then the product of the vector entry and the matrix weight, as it is the product of time and current. Neurons accumulate charge emitted by a column of synapses on the membrane

Fig. 1. BSS-2 setup (left); a white dust cap covers the chip (right).

capacitance, which completes the vector-matrix multiplication. All neuron membrane voltages are digitized in parallel. The resulting operation is $x^\mathsf{T} W = y$, where the inputs $x_i \in [0, 31]$ are transposed multiplied by the weight matrix $W_{ij} \in [-63, 63]$ for signed and $W_{ij} \in [0, 63]$ for unsigned weights, resulting in outputs $y_j \in [-128, 127]$. The available resolution of vector entries therefore is 5 bits, synapse weights are 6 bits (plus a sign for signed weights), the result is 8 bits. Two embedded SIMD microprocessors provide additional flexibility and support vector access to the synapse array. In the current lab setup, host connectivity is provided by a 1GBit-Ethernet (GbE) link to an FPGA providing buffer memory and managing real-time access to the BSS-2 chip. Details on the hardware architecture can be found in [2].

2   Methods and Tools

Simple and user-friendly interfaces are key components affecting the success of custom hardware accelerators. Especially the PyTorch and Tensorflow machine learning frameworks are widely known and established in both, research and industry, cf. [1]. Compared to Tensorflow, we experienced a simpler integration of the PyTorch build flow into our software environment: the build flow relies on standard cmake, and out-of-tree dependencies are tracked using standard mechanisms. In conjunction with sufficient documentation, this is the reason we chose PyTorch [5] as a frontend for our accelerator hardware. However, a similar integration into Tensorflow is possible.

In terms of artificial neural networks, the BSS-2 system provides support for a limited set of operations: matrix multiplications and convolutions can be mapped onto analog multiplication and accumulation units. Two embedded SIMD micro-processors can be used to perform additional digital operations. However, the processors are not optimized for number crunching but rather serve as programmable controllers for the analog compute units.

The software we present in the next section builds upon the "BrainScaleS Operating System", a software stack providing multiple hardware access layers. We make use of a register-level abstraction layer, other components provide a reliable GbE-based communication channel to the hardware system or integrate multiple hardware systems into the SLURM resource manager. We provide an overview over the software components in [6, 7].

3 Implementation

In this section we give an overview of our software implementation providing a BSS-2 hardware backend for PyTorch. We start with the PyTorch integration and considerations regarding data and computational flow. Afterwards, we describe our graph-based approach for describing and handling control and data flow on-chip as well as off-chip. We partition operations into chunks fitting onto the available hardware and schedule hardware using just-in-time-based (JIT) execution. Finally, we focus on hardware-specific aspects.

3.1 PyTorch Integration

PyTorch provides an extensions interface which allows us to implement new custom operations without modifying the core source code. Integration of the computation executed on the accelerator hardware into PyTorch can be split into two parts. Firstly, low-level operator primitives written in C++ and wrapped to `Python` implementing the `torch.autograd.Function` interface provide means to execute the operation directly. Since BSS-2 is geared towards accelerating two-dimensional matrix multiplication, the low-level operator primitive implemented with direct hardware access is adhering to the interface of the `matmul` and `conv{1,2,3}d` operation. Secondly, layers using the `torch.nn.Module` interface provide the ability to integrate the computation into an abstract model, a representation of the computation to be done without eagerly executing it.

Forward Pass. The forward pass of the `matmul` operation is comprised of a linear sequence of transformations to and from the hardware. Figure 2 shows its internal implementation. Tensors from PyTorch are preprocessed to match types and shape of the hardware. A partitioner then places the operation onto available hardware resources, cf. Sect. 3.3. The resulting custom data flow graph is then traversed by JIT execution, cf. Sect. 3.2. Measured activations are postprocessed to resemble the expected shape and type and returned.

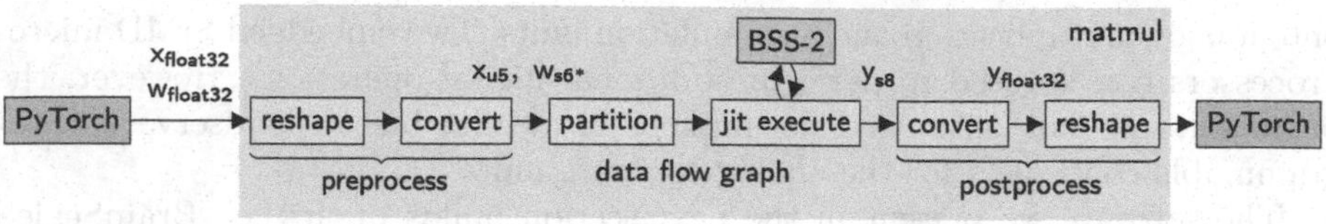

Fig. 2. Implementation of the `matmul` operation executed on BSS-2. Inputs and weights of type `float32` are reshaped such that the input batch space is one dimensional; types are converted to 5-bit unsigned inputs and 6-bit "signed" weights ($[-63, 63]$). A partitioner performs splitting and placement of the weight matrix onto the hardware resources. The resulting data flow graph is then used for JIT execution, which constructs an instruction stream sent to the hardware, see [2], and decodes the result data received from the hardware using the software architecture described in [7]. The resulting digitized 8-bit neuron membrane potential values are converted to `float32`, reshaped to match the originally provided type/shape from PyTorch and returned as the result of the operation.

Backward Pass. PyTorch features intrinsic support for automatic differentiation of a sequence of operations via the `torch.autograd.Function` interface, which is used for the low-level operations on BSS-2. Supply of a `backward()` function allows integration of custom operations into this framework. The output gradient as well as saved state of the forward pass of the operation is used to compute a gradient for the inputs. The analog accelerator's usability for computing the gradient of an operation is limited due to fixed-pattern and temporal noise. This noise could be considered a source of randomness but as it is not configurable by the user, its applicability for modeling is nontrivial. However using the results obtained from the hardware execution of the forward pass together with a software model to calculate the gradients allows mitigation of hardware distortions and resolution limitations during training. This method is adapted from [8], where a combination of a software model and the forward pass data from BSS-1 hardware runs are used to train a spiking network, thereby training with *hardware in the loop*. This approach is also suited for spike-based modeling, e.g., [9]. The software model employed here is much simpler in that it only resembles the backward pass of the conventional `matmul` operation scaled by a factor.

Mapping Convolutions. In order to support convolutions, a `convNd` operation is implemented using the `matmul` operation. The convolution is transformed to a matrix multiplication by unrolling the kernel into the vertical dimension, placing all kernel channels horizontally aside each other and traversing the input such that each operation is equivalent to the original kernel applied at a certain position. Figure 3 shows the transformation exemplary for a conv2d operation. The transformations are implemented using the C++-API of PyTorch, which allows most operations to be in-place modifications of tensor shapes only.

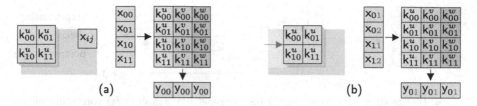

(a)   (b)

Fig. 3. Transformation of a 2-d convolution ((a) left, (b) left) of inputs x_{ij} with kernel k_{ij} to a multiplication ((a) right, (b) right). The kernel has three channels (u, v, w) and is moved from (a) to (b) with a stride of 1. The resulting matrix is constant for all kernel positions, which is efficient in terms of reconfiguration of the weights while leading to overlapping inputs for different kernel positions.

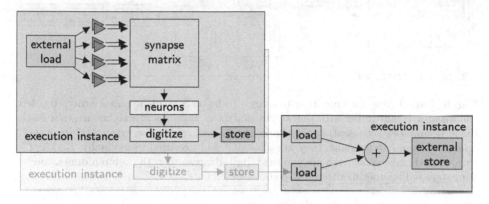

Fig. 4. Graph representation of two matrix multiplications (left) followed by an addition (right). Each multiplication as well as the addition are separately executed. The data flow between execution instances (gray boxes) comprises stores and loads of measured neuron activations. Vertices within the individual execution instances represent the on-chip data flow and hardware configuration.

3.2 Graph Representation and Just-in-time Execution

A major task of neural network accelerator operation is the tracking of data flow to and from the host as well as on the hardware substrate itself. In the case of BSS-2 and in addition to general input and output properties, heterogeneous entities, e.g., synapses and neuron circuits, need to be configured. Limited hardware resources require a temporal reuse of hardware substrate to compute a larger operation over the course of multiple inter-dependent executions.

These demands are met by a hardware-centric data flow graph. It describes the on-chip data flow as well as input and output. While the former is used for hardware configuration, the latter links individual execution instances in a *dependency graph*. Vertices represent statically configurable computation or hardware circuits. A heterogeneous set of edge types allows to express analog and digital signal/data flow in a unified interface. Support of batched input data mitigates comparably long static configuration times. A static-single-assignment

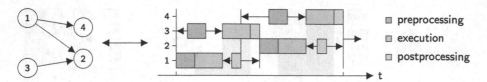

Fig. 5. Just-in-time execution (right) of a dependency graph (left) consisting of four execution instances. Four runs are scheduled onto the accelerator hardware. Pre- and postprocessing of independent execution instances can overlap in time.

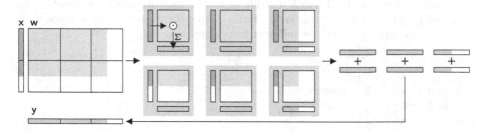

Fig. 6. Partitioning an operation too large to fit on a single synapse array. Top left: the input x is multiplied with the weight matrix w. Inputs and weights are split at the black boundaries representing the shape of a hardware synapse array. Middle: as split operations are independent, they are allocated and executed individually. Right: split results in the row dimension are summed digitally, results in the column dimension are concatenated leading to the result y (bottom left).

builder pattern facilitates correct configuration. Figure 4 shows an exemplary graph.

Individual execution instances in the dependency graph are executed just in time. Every instance can be split into a sequence of tasks: preprocessing, build of the instruction stream, execution on the accelerator hardware and postprocessing of the received results. Assuming that concurrency on the host computer is not a limiting factor, pre/postprocessing of non-sequentially-dependent execution instances can be parallelized leading to a saturation of the accelerator hardware usage. Figure 5 exemplifies an dependency graph and a possible execution flow.

3.3 Partitioning

The physical dimensions of each of the two the synapse arrays on the hardware is fixed to $N = 256$ rows (128 for signed weights) and $M = 256$ columns limiting the shape of a single multiply-accumulate (MAC) operation. Temporal reuse of the synapse array allows larger operations. The operation is split into parts which fit on a single synapse array and are placed individually with a round-robin allocation scheme on the available synapse arrays. Figure 6 visualizes the partitioning scheme.

In order to support more columns, the results of the split operations are to be concatenated. To the contrary, to support more rows the results of the split operations are to be summed up digitally:

$$y_j = \sum_i^N x_i w_{ij} = \left(\sum_i^{N_1} x_i w_{ij} \right) + ... + \left(\sum_i^{N_R} x_i w_{ij} \right), \quad N = \sum_r^R N_r \quad (1)$$

where the input size N is split into R ranges N_r of analog computation $\sum_i^{N_r} x_i w_{ij}$, which are then summed digitally. This approach is expected to be comparable to computation on a larger physical synapse array if no boundary effects—like analog saturation or digital overflow—occur.

For weight matrices large in both dimensions compared to the synapse array this partitioning scheme leads to a optimal chip area usage, because the number of partial synapse array allocations scales with the edges like $\mathcal{O}(N + M)$ while the number of full synapse array allocations scales with the area like $\mathcal{O}(N \cdot M)$.

3.4   Parallel Execution of Convolutional Layers

In convolutional layers, the size of the transformed weight matrix (cf. Fig. 3) often is a lot smaller than the synapse array of our accelerator. Especially in the one dimensional case, it is possible to perform multiple such operations in one step, a possible layout on the chip is sketched in Fig. 7. The downside of this approach is the increase of independent parameters, since the weights of each expansion have to be learned individually due to fixed pattern noise and other deviations, cf. [2]. To overcome this problem, we add

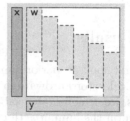

Fig. 7. Expanded `Conv1d` layer maximizing usage of the synapse array.

modified versions of the data set to the training data, shifted by the stride of the convolution operation. However, this is only applicable for a single layer or an equal number of parallel executions, since it can only be tuned to the hyperparameters of one layer. Nevertheless, the execution time while evaluating the model is reduced up to a factor of the number of parallel executions and the energy consumption is nearly decreased by the same factor.

3.5   Handling Hardware Setup, Initialization and Parameters

The accelerator hardware setup and initialization routine is time-consuming compared to a single computation. Hence, initialization of the hardware is only performed once. We also allow users to modify the hardware initialization process. Exclusive access to hardware resources is handled via free functions utilizing a singleton pattern. Inside the execution of an operation, the JIT executor, cf. Sect. 3.2, then uses available hardware acquired previously via the singleton.

Using BSS-2 involves choice of parameters affecting the available dynamic range. Two such parameters, described in [2], are the interval duration between successive input events, and sending the same input multiple times. Both parameters were introduced to increase the precision of the analog computation on first-version chips. As such parameters possibly have to be tuned for each layer we supply them side-by-side to other operation parameters already present in the equivalent CPU operation. The following listing shows the implemented scheme at the example of a conv1d operation:

```
conv1d(x, kernel, stride=1, num_sends=6, wait_between_events=25)
```

While these parameters are in principle differentiable, a model is yet to be developed. Therefore they are treated as non-differentiable hyperparameters.

Since the hardware specific parameters are not present for CPU/GPU operations, care has to be taken when converting such operations to accelerator hardware execution. We provide replacements for the PyTorch layers Linear and Conv{1,2}d, which take these additional parameters as keyword arguments. Since these layers use the same state as their counterparts, pre-trained weights can easily be loaded into a model that uses them. Placing these operations and layers aside the PyTorch counterparts allows their simultaneous usage.

4   Results

We first look at performance figures for speed of execution and utilization of the accelerator hardware in order to evaluate imposed software overhead. Afterwards, we demonstrate usability of the presented software framework by an application on the human activity recognition dataset [10].

4.1   Performance Evaluation

Hardware Limitations and Measurement Setup. The currently used first hardware version (v1) contains a bug which requires rewriting the synapse array for each sent input. As a consequence, the input data volume increases by a factor of ≈100. To increase the precision of the analog calculations, inputs are repeated. In addition, successive events are spaced over time, cf. [2]. The second hardware version (v2) is currently in the commissioning process and expected to be free of these limitations. Performance estimations for v2 are given by disabling these workarounds on v1. This only affects the quality of the computation.

The available hardware setup consists of the BSS-2 chip connected to an FPGA which provides one GbE link to the host computer. This connection poses a severe communication limitation as the chip features full-duplex 8 Gbit/s interconnects. To evaluate software performance against the chip hardware design limitation, we use a software simulation providing a fast mock-up communication partner. This is a valid approach for software performance evaluation since the postprocessing of response data is content-agnostic.

Results. We evaluate the performance in terms of multiply-accumulate (MAC) operations per time for square-shaped weight matrices with fixed batch size and varying batch size for a fixed weight matrix in Fig. 8. The left panel shows that the current implementation is able to saturate v2 in combination with a 1-GbE host connection in the limit of large matrix multiplications. Furthermore, the current implementation reaches up to the hardware design limitation within a factor of two. Given the static configuration necessary for a matrix multiplication, the right panel shows the achieved performance for v2 and the design limitation simulation is within 50% of the saturation speed for batch sizes larger than ≈200.

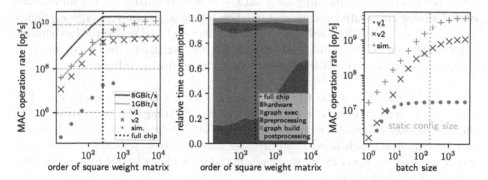

Fig. 8. Performance measurement for square matrices with sizes ranging from 1^2 to $(2^{14})^2$ elements (batch size: 2000). The dotted line marks the matrix size of a single BSS-2 chip (left and center). *Left*: Rate of MAC operations for real and simulated hardware: the yellow line illustrates the limiting speed for setups using 1 Gbit/s links (host link); the gray line shows this for 8 Gbit/s links (chip I/O); disregarding a constant configuration overhead, the rate of operations increases linearly for matrices smaller than a chip; for matrices larger than the full chip area, individual runs can overlap in the pre- and postprocessing step thereby increasing the speed further; the red dots and blue crosses show measurements using the real hardware setup. *Center*: Distribution of execution times for the 8 Gbit/s case (cf. Fig. 2 for details on the categories); the chip utilization increases for matrices larger than the full chip area. *Right*: Measurement for varying batch sizes (matrix size: 256^2); rates are plotted for different chip versions and simulated design-goal hardware; the dotted line marks the batch size where the static configuration overhead matches the variable data volume; this coincides with the point where ≈50% of the maximum performance is reached.

4.2 Application Example: Human Activity Recognition

Our application example uses the smartphone acceleration data from [10]. The dataset contains recordings of 30 subjects carrying a waist-mounted smartphone while walking straight ahead, up or down, sitting, standing or lying on their backs. The data is already split in training and test data, containing 9 channels of sensor data with a length of 2.56 s sampled at 50 Hz, each.

Table 1. Model parameters for "Human Activity Recognition" example.

Layer	Activation	Input shape	Output shape	# of Params
Conv1d	ReLU	[−1, 9, 128]	[−1, 16, 16]	4'624
Linear-1	ReLU	[−1, 256]	[−1, 125]	32'125
Linear-2	Softmax	[−1, 125]	[−1, 6]	756

The Model. We use a 1-d convolution layer with kernel size 32, stride 6 for feature detection, followed by two dense layers. The model topology is defined by Table 1. The hyper-parameters of all layers are optimized for the dimensions of the analog substrate to achieve a balance between accuracy, energy efficiency and execution speed. The software model is quantized and scaled to the dynamic range of the hardware. In addition, we add Gaussian noise to the output of every layer to adapt to the conditions on hardware, even during inference.

Training. First, we trained the model in software without our accelerator. The resulting confusion matrix is shown in Fig. 9a. Running the very same model on our analog substrate shows results that are quite off (cf. Fig. 9b), which can be explained with fixed pattern noise and non-linearities. With additional hardware-in-the-loop training we come significantly closer to our software results as is depicted in Fig. 9c.

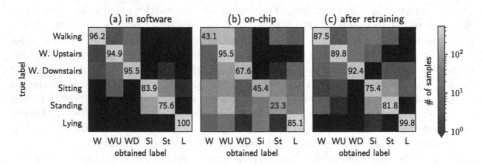

Fig. 9. Confusion matrices and recall accuracies for the separate test set, (a) after training in software, (b) executed on BSS-2 without retraining, and (c) after training with hardware in the loop.

Results. The achieved overall accuracy is 90.7% in software and 87.8% on-chip. As already found in [10,11] there is a noticeable misclassification between sitting and standing. This can be explained by the similar orientation of the smartphone and the non-dynamic nature of these activities. More words about the drop of accuracy on hardware, as well as another example that classifies the MNIST dataset and can be found in [2].

5   Discussion and Outlook

This work presents software integrating analog vector-matrix multiplication on BSS-2 into the PyTorch framework. Using the PyTorch extension interface, hxtorch provides support for convolutional and dense layers. The hardware backend builds upon the BrainScaleS operating system [6,7] and utilizes a configuration and runtime flow that is essentially identical to the spiking operation of the system. We describe the underlying implementation comprising data flow representation, operator mapping, hardware partitioning, system setup and execution. We evaluate end-to-end runtime performance and show that the best possible performance, in terms of hardware design limitations, is reached within a factor of two for sufficiently large matrix multiplications. We obtain 14.7 Gop/s for a single simulated accelerator. In conjunction with the single GbE host link, this surpasses the speed of v2 by a factor of $\approx$5. The static configuration of a 256-by-256 matrix matches a batch size of around 200 256-wide inputs in terms of data volume and computation time. Finally, we demonstrate an end-to-end application example on "Human Activity Recognition" with software results comparable to [11] but obtain a drop in the classification quality for the hardware backend. We expect the result to improve for v2.

Although we focused here on an interface to the non-spiking functionality of the accelerator, it is possible to extend PyTorch to model the spiking operation of the chip as well. In the simplest case input spikes are represented as sparse binary tensors, with one of the axes being the time dimension. For efficient hardware operation this time dimension is identified with the time dimension of the intrinsic temporal dynamics of the analog circuitry. This implies that recurrent spiking neural networks with up to $N = 512$ neurons per chip can be implemented. A simulation can be run concurrently to estimate the gradients. By performing the forward pass through chip and backward pass through the simulation like in [8,9,12], hardware parameters can be adjusted based on simulation parameter updates. Ideally, gradient estimation would be independent of analog measurements on the chip, which introduce additional memory bandwidth requirements. Finally, deeper integration into ML frameworks facilitates compute graph analysis. Consequently, network topologies can be described natively; the compute graph still allows for the specification of arbitrary computation—e.g., plasticity rules in spiking neural networks—that can be offloaded to the embedded microprocessors.

Contributions and Acknowledgments
PS is the main developer of the software extensions of this work. EM is the lead developer and architect of the BSS-2 software stack. AE contributed to the PyTorch extension and the experiment. AE, AL, CM, OB, TCW and YS contributed to the software implementation. CP contributed to the initial implementation of the extension. JW is a main contributor to hardware commissioning and contributed to the extension. SB contributed to the hardware design, commissioning and the software implementation. SS contributed to core software components and the software design. JS is the lead designer and architect of

the BSS-2 neuromorphic system. All authors discussed and contributed to the manuscript.

The authors wish to thank all present and former members of the Electronic Vision(s) research group contributing to the BSS-2 hardware platform. The authors express their special gratitude towards: J. Klähn, D. Stöckel and S. Friedmann for earlier software contributions. We especially express our gratefulness to the late Karlheinz Meier who initiated and led the project for most if its time. This work has received funding from the EU (H2020/2014-2020: 720270, 785907, 945539 (HBP)), from the BMBF (16ES1127), and from the Lautenschläger-Forschungspreis 2018 for Karlheinz Meier.

References

1. He, H.: The State of Machine Learning Frameworks in 2019. The Gradient (2019)
2. Weis, J., et al.: Inference with artificial neural networks on analog neuromorphic hardware. In: Gama, J., et al. (eds.) ITEM 2020/IoT Streams 2020. CCIS, vol. 1325, pp. 201–212. Springer, Cham (2020). https://doi.org/10.1007/978-3-030-66770-2_15
3. Wunderlich, T., et al.: Demonstrating advantages of neuromorphic computation: a pilot study. Front. Neurosci. **13**, 260 (2019). https://doi.org/10.3389/fnins.2019.00260
4. Schemmel, J., Billaudelle, S., Dauer, P., Weis, J.: Accelerated analog neuromorphic computing. arXiv preprint (2020). arXiv: 2003.11996 [cs.NE]
5. Paszke, A., et al.: PyTorch: an imperative style, high-performance deep learning library. In: Wallach, H., Larochelle, H., Beygelzimer, A., d'Alché-Buc, F., Fox, E., Garnett, R. (eds.) Advances in Neural Information Processing Systems, vol. 32 (2019)
6. Müller, E., et al.: The operating system of the neuromorphic BrainScaleS-1 system. arXiv preprint (2020). arXiv: 2003.13749 [cs.NE]
7. Müller, E., et al.: Extending BrainScaleS OS for BrainScaleS-2. arXiv preprint (2020). arXiv: 2003.13750 [cs.NE]
8. Schmitt, S., et al.: Classification With deep neural networks on an accelerated analog neuromorphic system. In: Proceedings of the 2017 IEEE International Joint Conference on Neural Networks (2017). https://doi.org/10.1109/IJCNN.2017.7966125
9. Cramer, B., et al.: Training spiking multi-layer networks with surrogate gradients on an analog neuromorphic substrate. arXiv preprint (2020). arXiv: 2006.07239 [cs.NE]
10. Anguita, D., Ghio, A., Oneto, L., Parra, X., Reyes-Ortiz, J.L.: A public domain dataset for human activity recognition using smartphones. In: Esann (2013)
11. Ronao, C.A., Cho, S.-B.: Human activity recognition with smartphone sensors using deep learning neural networks. Expert Syst. Appl. **59**, 235–244 (2016)
12. Le Gallo, M., et al.: Mixed-precision in-memory computing. Nat. Electron. **1**(4), 246–253 (2018). https://doi.org/10.1038/s41928-018-0054-8

Inference with Artificial Neural Networks on Analog Neuromorphic Hardware

Johannes Weis(✉), Philipp Spilger, Sebastian Billaudelle, Yannik Stradmann,
Arne Emmel, Eric Müller, Oliver Breitwieser, Andreas Grübl,
Joscha Ilmberger, Vitali Karasenko, Mitja Kleider, Christian Mauch,
Korbinian Schreiber, and Johannes Schemmel

Kirchhoff-Institute for Physics,
Ruprecht-Karls-Universität Heidelberg, Heidelberg, Germany
johannes.weis@kip.uni-heidelberg.de

Abstract. The neuromorphic BrainScaleS-2 ASIC comprises mixed-signal neurons and synapse circuits as well as two versatile digital microprocessors. Primarily designed to emulate spiking neural networks, the system can also operate in a vector-matrix multiplication and accumulation mode for artificial neural networks. Analog multiplication is carried out in the synapse circuits, while the results are accumulated on the neurons' membrane capacitors. Designed as an analog, in-memory computing device, it promises high energy efficiency. Fixed-pattern noise and trial-to-trial variations, however, require the implemented networks to cope with a certain level of perturbations. Further limitations are imposed by the digital resolution of the input values (5 bit), matrix weights (6 bit) and resulting neuron activations (8 bit). In this paper, we discuss BrainScaleS-2 as an analog inference accelerator and present calibration as well as optimization strategies, highlighting the advantages of training with hardware in the loop. Among other benchmarks, we classify the MNIST handwritten digits dataset using a two-dimensional convolution and two dense layers. We reach 98.0% test accuracy, closely matching the performance of the same network evaluated in software.

Keywords: Analog accelerator · Neural network processor · Neuromorphic hardware · Convolutional neural networks · Machine learning · In-memory computing · MNIST

1 Introduction

Artificial neural networks (ANN) find application in a wide variety of fields and problems. With networks growing in depth and complexity, the increase of computational cost becomes more and more significant [1]. In fact, execution time and power consumption often represent the crucial limiting factors in further scaling and in the application of ANNs [2].

© Springer Nature Switzerland AG 2020
J. Gama et al. (Eds.): ITEM 2020/IoT Streams 2020, CCIS 1325, pp. 201–212, 2020.
https://doi.org/10.1007/978-3-030-66770-2_15

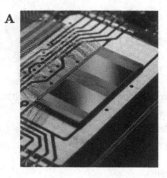 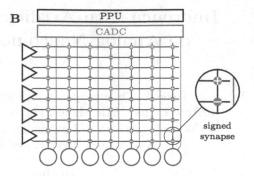

Fig. 1. Overview of the BrainScaleS-2 system. A: Block diagram of the analog core, showing synapse drivers (triangles), neurons (large circles), and synapses (small circles in matrix). Signed weights are achieved by using two synapse rows for positive and negative weights. Figure adopted from [12]. B: Chip photograph.

A large fraction of the computational cost for neural network-based inference is spent on vector-matrix multiplications [3]. With their massive parallelization of floating point calculations, GPUs already cut runtime significantly compared to CPUs. Computational complexity can often be cut by representing and processing data with reduced precision [4]. Specialized digital inference accelerators have been presented [5,6] that offer further efficiency improvements over implementations on general-purpose hardware. Potentially even more efficient ASICs could be based on mixed-signal circuit designs by exploiting physical processes for computational purposes [7]. Drawbacks of such systems can include vulnerability to fixed-pattern and trial-to-trial variations, resulting in distorted network configurations and reduced reproducibility. Similar to digital solutions with reduced precision, networks have to cope with limited weight resolution, which can be as low as one bit [8].

In this work, we demonstrate BrainScaleS-2 [9] as an analog inference accelerator. We describe the hardware configuration and operating principle of analog vector-matrix multiplication on the ASIC and benchmark the system's performance by training and classifying the MNIST dataset of handwritten digits [10]. We further discuss calibration and the benefits of training with hardware in the loop as strategies to counter chip-specific fixed-pattern variations [11,12].

2   Methods

BrainScaleS-2 is a mixed-signal ASIC fabricated in a 65 nm CMOS process by TSMC that has originally been designed as an accelerator for biologically plausible spiking neural networks. It features analog circuits emulating neurons and synapses as well as digital periphery for communication, parameter storage, and realtime control. Recent additions to the system allow for in-memory computation of multiply-accumulate operations within the chip's analog core, thereby making the system applicable for inference with artificial neural networks [9].

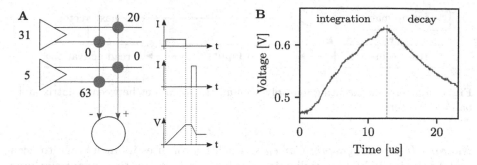

Fig. 2. A: Illustration of a multiply-accumulate operation. The vector value controls the length of the current pulses, the matrix weight their amplitude. The currents are integrated on the neuron's membrane. B: The recorded membrane trace clearly shows the integration phase where the synaptic inputs are integrated, after which the result is digitized (dotted line). Afterwards, the voltage decays exponentially towards the resting potential.

Matrix multiplication can also be combined with spiking operation, enabling seamless hybrid operation. High-dimensional input data can be preprocessed in traditional convolutional networks before being evaluated in sparse, energy efficient spiking networks. The chip contains 512 analog neurons arranged in two blocks, each neuron receives input from 256 synapses. Thus, BrainScaleS-2 can be used to multiply a vector with 256 entries to a matrix comprising 512 columns. An architectural overview of the circuitry for processing vector-matrix multiplications on BrainScaleS-2 is depicted in Fig. 1. Digitally encoded input vectors are injected from the left, converted to the analog domain and multiplied within the central synapse array. Each neuron accumulates values from its corresponding synapse column. The resulting vector of neuron activations is read out in parallel via a columnar analog-to-digital converter (CADC).

Multiplication in Analog Synapse Circuits. Within the synapse array, the multiplication of an input value with the synaptic weight is modelled as the electrical charge $Q = I \cdot \Delta t$ emitted during a current pulse of variable length and amplitude. The current I is determined by a 6 bit weight stored locally in each synapse. The time window Δt during which that current is emitted is modulated by circuitry in the synapse drivers (triangles on the left in Fig. 1). The value is set by the payload of input events, which is otherwise used to select a subset of synapses from a row. More specifically, we use 5 bit of this label to encode the pulse length Δt.

Each row of synapses can be connected to the afferent neurons with either positive or negative sign. To achieve signed weights, two rows of synapses can be combined to represent a single logical row. This configuration, however, reduces the number of available vector entries from 256 to 128. When using signed weights, the remaining input label bit is still available to differentiate two sets of synapses, therefore two different multiplications can be executed side by side.

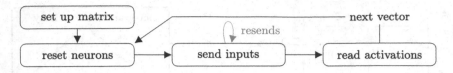

Fig. 3. Pattern for executing multiply-accumulate operations between a matrix and a batch of vectors.

Neurons Integrate Synaptic Currents. Each neuron uses its membrane to accumulate the individual multiplication results from its respective synaptic column. They integrate the positive and negative charge contributions, as sketched in Fig. 2A. Motivated by spiking operation, the input signals are low-pass filtered with finite time constant. To speed up integration and for reduction of synaptic input saturation, the minimum time constant of approximately 1 μs was configured.

The neurons' dynamics are based on a leaky integrator model commonly used for spiking networks [13]: A resistor continuously pulls the membrane voltage, which is physically represented across a capacitor, towards a resting potential. The resulting dynamics constitute a crucial part for the emulation of spiking networks. In contrast, they can lead to distortions in the accumulation of vector matrix multiplication results which do not contain implicit timing information. In order to stabilize the accumulated voltages and reduce the effect of noise, we configured a rather large but finite resistance. The leak resistance leads to an exponential decay of the integrated charge, which can be seen in Fig. 2B.

Digitization of Results. The membrane potentials are digitized in parallel for all 256 neurons connected to a synapse matrix, using the CADCs, and stored via the on-chip microprocessors. The resulting 8 bit values represent the neuron activations and are the result of the multiply-accumulate (MAC) operation.

By aligning the choice of the resting potential with the dynamic range of the ADC, two operating modes can be selected: In case the lower end of the ADC range coincides with the resting potential, negative activations are cut off. In this configuration, the neurons behave as hardware rectified linear units (ReLU).

In case the inputs a neuron receives exceed the size of the synapse matrix, the network can be partitioned into smaller matrices which are evaluated in a time multiplexed fashion [14]. Since the activation function needs to be applied after combining the individual results, negative activations must be representable. For this purpose, the resting potential can be chosen centered in the ADCs' dynamic ranges.

2.1 Structure of a Multiply-Accumulate Operation

To compile a MAC operation from the elements outlined above, the sequence shown in Fig. 3 can be applied.

1. To begin with, the weight matrix is written to the synapses. Writing all 256×512 values takes about 5 ms. Batched execution can minimize the amount of expensive reconfiguration.
2. A reset of the membrane potentials removes any previous state accumulated by the neurons. An immediate read of the voltages establishes a baseline activation to suppress low frequency noise. Resetting all neurons takes approximately 1 μs.
3. The vector inputs are sent sequentially to the chip. Between events, wait times of 8–200 ns are inserted. These mitigate saturation effects in the neurons' synaptic inputs, which can occur in case multiple inputs of large amplitude are sent in a short period of time. To improve the signal-to-noise ratio, the activations on the membranes can be increased by incorporating resends of the input vectors within a single integration phase. Wait times as well as the number of resends must be optimized considering the neurons' decay times, which limit the maximum integration time. Alternatively, the membrane capacitance can be reduced, yielding higher activations, but also shorter decay time constants. Skipping inputs of zero reduces the overall runtime, especially in conjunction with ReLU activation functions.
4. The activations are digitized after the accumulation of charges. Considering the finite time constant of the synaptic inputs, a waiting period of 2 μs is inserted for the membrane potential to settle. The ADC conversion takes 1.5 μs.

2.2   Calibration

Transistor-level mismatch in the manufacturing process of an ASIC leads to inhomogeneous electrical properties of the fabricated circuits. Due to the analog nature of BrainScaleS-2, the resulting fixed-pattern variations cause each neuron and synapse to behave differently when presented with similar input. Without calibration, networks sensitive to such perturbations can not perform up to their full potential on the analog substrate, as weights and activations would be distorted. BrainScaleS-2 therefore provides a substantial amount of digitally controlled parameters that allow equalization of all computational units through calibration.

The operating point of the neuron circuits is determined by a set of internal parameters and references. Some parameters are of technical nature and need to be calibrated to ensure correct operation. Others directly influence the circuit dynamics, e.g. the neurons' time constants and resting potentials. Most importantly, the strength of the synaptic currents has to be equalized across neurons: It determines the increment of the membrane potential as a response to the synaptic stimulation. The response of all 512 neurons to constant stimuli is shown in the histograms of Fig. 4A, separately for the calibrated and uncalibrated states. For both, positive and negative contributions, the synaptic strength has been calibrated to a precision of 7%.

Calibration is also applied to the pulse generation circuits in the synapse drivers. The length of the current pulses encoding the 5 bit input values is subject to row-wise random offsets. Calibration registers allow to strongly reduce these variations to 0.3 ns.

We developed a collection of optimization routines for BSS-2, which automate such calibration steps and allow to set the hardware up for matrix multiplication usage. The code is based on the Python API of [15] and may also be used for configuring the system for spiking neural networks.

2.3   Training with Hardware in the Loop

Remaining imperfections after calibration can still lead to a loss of performance when directly transferring trained network models to an analog computing substrate. In the context of spiking neural networks, it has been previously shown that integrating the analog hardware into the training loop can restore the original performance [11,12]. For some parameters, such training in the loop can in fact replace explicit calibration [16]. For the analog matrix multiplication described in this manuscript, the gradients are calculated based on measured activations, only assuming linearity of the synaptic weights. A detailed description of the implementation and integration into PyTorch [17] is given by [14].

3   Results

3.1   Characterization

We first evaluated the performance of BrainScaleS-2's matrix multiplication mode by configuring a synthetic test matrix. In the left half, weights increased linearly from left to right, all synapses in column i were set to weight $w = i - 63$. In the right half, each synapse was set to a random weight, drawn uniformly from -63 to 63. Multiple homogeneous vectors of different amplitude were used to characterize the linearity of both vector entries and matrix weights (Fig. 4B).

For lower weights and inputs, the multiplication followed the expected linear behavior. For higher activations, saturation occurred, which is most clearly observable for the vector with entries of 15. However, we expect most real-world networks to use sparser matrices with more balanced excitatory and inhibitory weights than this test. In the right part of the matrix, the random weights resulted in activations close to zero. It is notable that per column this activation was either positive or negative, depending on the exact mean of the associated weights and scaling with the injected vectors' values. This suggests that both, positive and negative inputs can be summed correctly and have been tuned to the same strength.

3.2   MNIST Benchmark

The above measurements indicate that the analog substrate can indeed be used to perform MAC operations. To investigate its performance on a common benchmark, the MNIST [10] dataset is used. [14] additionally trained and classified the Human Activity Recognition dataset on BrainScaleS-2.

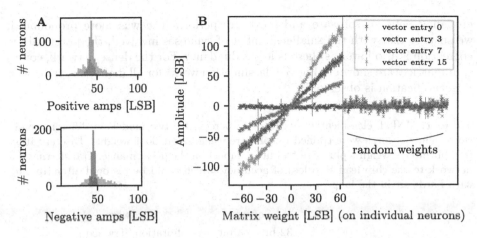

Fig. 4. A: Histogram of amplitudes received on all neurons for equal inputs. After calibration (colored) the width of the distribution is decreased compared to the uncalibrated state (gray). B: Characterization of analog multiplication results, sweeping both matrix weights and vector entries. The left half of the synapse matrix was configured such that weights increased from a value of −63 in the leftmost column to +63 in the 127th column with an increment of one. Within each column, all weights were set to the same value. The right half was set to random weights for each synapse. We injected four constant input vectors, each consisting of 128 entries of 0, 3, 7 and 15. Error bars indicate the standard deviation within 30 runs. (Color figure online)

Models. We examined the performance of two different network models. Both relied on ReLU activation functions for the hidden layers and a softmax for the output layer. The two networks did not incorporate a bias. They were trained with the Adam optimizer [18] in TensorFlow [19] using 32 bit float weights.

The *convolutional model* was based on images zero-padded by one to 30 × 30 pixels. It consisted of a two-dimensional convolutional layer, a dense layer of 128 neurons and 10 label units. The convolution layer used 20 10 × 10 filters with a stride of 5 × 5.

The *dense model* consisted of two fully connected layers of 64 and ten neurons, respectively. Due to its small size, this model directly fits into the on-chip weight matrix and does not require reconfiguration.

Accuracy. As a first step in transferring the models to BrainScaleS-2, we discretized the weights to 6 bit integers plus sign. Evaluating both networks in software showed only slight drops in performance (Table 1).

When executing the convolutional network on BrainScaleS-2, the classification performance on held-out test data dropped to 92.1%, indicating a non-ideal calibration of and temporal noise in the analog circuits. After a continued training with hardware in the loop, an accuracy of 98.0% could be restored, closely matching the results obtained in software. A similar behavior was observed for the smaller dense model, with 96.3% after training in the loop. Here, the discrepancy between software and hardware performance was more pronounced, we suspect that with the smaller number of synapses involved, the potential for correction is also lower as there is less redundancy. For the dense network, confusion matrices are shown in Fig. 5. Classification works for all digits, no systematic misclassification is observable.

Table 1. MNIST classification accuracy in percent for two models in different conditions. The networks were trained in software using 32 bit float weights. Discretization to 6 bit integer weights plus sign had little impact on the performance. Transferring the network to the chip lead to a loss of accuracy, which could be restored after training with hardware in the loop.

	Software		Hardware	
	32 bit float	6 bit int	Calibration only	Trained in the loop
Convolutional model	98.29 %	98.10 %	92.13 %	98.01 %
Dense model	97.43 %	97.36 %	92.46 %	96.30 %

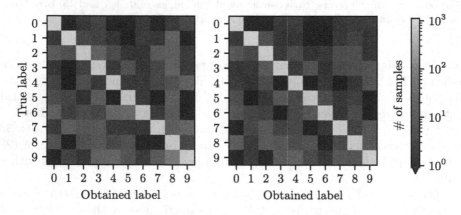

Fig. 5. Confusion matrix of the dense network running MNIST. Left: Executed pre-trained model on hardware, no re-training. Right: Results after training one epoch with hardware in the loop. Note the logarithmic colorbar in both plots. (Color figure online)

Energy Consumption. A bug in the current chip revision requires constant reconfiguration of the synapse matrix for each input vector. It yields a drastically increased runtime and energy consumption, far off the targeted performance for BrainScaleS-2. The bug was fixed in the next chip revision, increasing performance by three orders of magnitude.

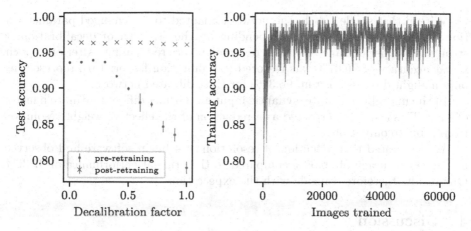

Fig. 6. MNIST accuracy when detuning the calibrated neuron parameters, shown for the dense network. Left: Accuracy before and after training one epoch with hardware in the loop. Results show the mean and standard deviation of 10 runs classifying the 10000 test images with unchanged parameters. Right: Accuracy per batch during the one epoch of training. 200 images per batch, 300 batches per epoch. Colors indicate the state of calibration, corresponding to the left plot. (Color figure online)

Currently, when fully utilizing the resources on hardware, vectors of up to 256 entries can be multiplied with matrices of up to 512 columns. One of these vector-matrix multiplications takes 5 ms, and at a power consumption of approximately 0.3 W [12], takes 1.5 mJ. The measurement was taken on the chip's supply rails and therefore includes all analog and digital circuitry on the ASIC. This estimation leads to an energy efficiency of 175 MOPS/W, counting multiplication and addition as two operations. The next chip generation will provide circa 0.2 TOPS/W, while state of the art digital solutions reach efficiencies in the order of 2 TOPS/W (Google Edge-TPU [20]). In contrast to BrainScaleS-2, these alternatives however lack the ability of processing hybrid networks containing spiking and non-spiking units.

Assuming parallelized and batched execution, inference with the convolutional network takes 40 ms per image, resulting in an energy consumption of 12 mJ. The smaller dense network, again assuming parallel execution, requires 10 ms and therefore 3 mJ per image.

Calibration vs. Learning. It has previously been shown that, to a certain degree, learning can replace the need for explicit calibration [16]. To analyze such effects for the presented models, we started with a software-trained network and then detuned the calibration of the neurons' leak conductance and synaptic input amplitudes by continuously transitioning between the calibrated and uncalibrated state. The latter resulted from taking the median of the respective parameter distribution across all neurons (Fig. 4A). For multiple configurations on this spectrum, we continued training with hardware in the loop for one epoch.

Within that single epoch, the network adapted to the changed parametrization of the substrate (Fig. 6): Depending on the strength of decalibration, a strong loss of performance could be observed before re-training. After one epoch, a test accuracy of 96.07% was restored (decalibration factor: 1.0), representing only a slight drop down from 96.31% for the calibrated network.

In the uncalibrated state, synaptic input amplitudes differed by up to a factor of four. This can be interpreted as a reduction of the effective weight resolution from 6 bit to only 4 bit.

We replicated this reduction of resolution to 4 bit in software and observed a reduced accuracy of 96.99% compared to the original performance of 97.36%. Our results therefore coincide with the expectations.

4 Discussion

In this publication, we have shown that BrainScaleS-2 can be successfully used for vector-matrix multiplication, especially in the context of deep convolutional neural networks. We have presented a set of calibration mechanisms to set up the analog system and equalize fixed-pattern variations of the computational units. Improvements upon a pre-trained and directly transferred network could be reached through training with hardware in the loop, compensating for remaining imperfections. Since calibration data can be generated once and then be re-used for multiple networks, calibration can still prove valuable compared to task-specific training.

Compared to the same network evaluated in software, we reached state-of-the-art classification performance on the MNIST dataset. Shortcomings of the current hardware generation were fixed in the next chip revision and yield efficiency improvements by a factor of 1000, as early results show.

5 Contributions

J. Weis developed calibration routines, conducted the presented experiments and evaluations and wrote the initial manuscript. P. Spilger is the main developer of the software extensions providing support for BrainScaleS' non-spiking operation mode. S. Billaudelle designed neuron and synapse driver circuits and contributed to commissioning of the chip. Y. Stradmann contributed to hardware design and commissioning and gave conceptual advice. A. Emmel contributed to experiment code. E. Müller is the lead developer and architect of the BrainScaleS-2 software stack. C. Mauch and O. Breitwieser contributed to the software architecture and implementation. A. Grübl was responsible for chip assembly and implemented the digital front- and backend. J. Ilmberger contributed to host-side communication infrastructure. V. Karasenko is the main developer of the FPGA firmware and developed the communication infrastructure between FPGA and ASIC. M. Kleider contributed to FPGA firmware development as well as initial commissioning of the system. K. Schreiber designed and implemented the CADC and the physical ASIC test setup. J. Schemmel is the lead designer and architect of the BrainScaleS-2 neuromorphic system. All authors discussed and contributed to the manuscript.

Acknowledgments. The authors wish to thank all present and former members of the Electronic Vision(s) research group contributing to the BrainScaleS-2 hardware platform, software development as well as operation methodologies. We especially express our gratefulness to the late Karlheinz Meier who initiated and led the project for most if its time. This work has received funding from the EU ([H2020/2014-2020]) under grant agreements 720270, 785907 and 945539 (HBP), from the BMBF (16ES1127 (HD-BIO-AI)) and from the Lautenschläger-Forschungspreis 2018 for Karlheinz Meier.

References

1. Brown, T.B., et al.: Language models are few-shot learners (2020). arXiv: 2005.14165 [cs.CL]
2. Schwartz, R., Dodge, J., Smith, N.A., Etzioni, O.: Green AI. (2019). arXiv: 1907.10597 [cs.CY]
3. Oh, K.-S., Jung, K.: GPU implementation of neural networks. Pattern Recogn. **37**(6), 1311–1314 (2004)
4. Micikevicius, P., et al.: Mixed precision training. arXiv preprint arXiv:1710.03740 (2017)
5. Jouppi, N.P., et al.: In-datacenter performance analysis of a tensor processing unit. In: Proceedings of the 44th Annual International Symposium on Computer Architecture, pp. 1–12 (2017)
6. Yin, S., et al.: A 1.06-to-5.09 TOPS/W reconfigurable hybrid-neural-network processor for deep learning applications. In: 2017 Symposium on VLSI Circuits, pp. C26–C27 (2017)
7. Boser, B.E.: An analog neural network processor with programmable topology. IEEE J. Solid-State Circ. **26**, 2017–2025 (1991)
8. Yamaguchi, M., Iwamoto, G., Tamukoh, H., Morie, T.: An energy-efficient time-domain analog VLSI neural network processor based on a pulse-width modulation approach. arXiv preprint (2019). arXiv: 1902.07707 [cs.ET]
9. Schemmel, J., Billaudelle, S., Dauer, P., Weis, J.: Accelerated analog neuromorphic computing. arXiv preprint (2020). arXiv: 2003.11996 [cs.NE]
10. LeCun, Y., Cortes, C.: The MNIST database of handwritten digits (1998)
11. Schmitt, S., et al.: Classification With deep neural networks on an accelerated analog neuromorphic system. In: Proceedings of the 2017 IEEE International Joint Conference on Neural Networks (2017). https://doi.org/10.1109/IJCNN.2017.7966125
12. Cramer, B., et al.: Training spiking multi-layer networks with surrogate gradients on an analog neuromorphic substrate. arXiv preprint (2020). arXiv: 2006.07239 [cs.NE]
13. Brette, R., Gerstner, W.: Adaptive exponential integrate-and-fire model as an effective description of neuronal activity. J. Neurophysiol. **94**, 3637–3642 (2005). https://doi.org/10.1152/jn.00686.2005
14. Spilger, P., et al.: **hxtorch**: PyTorch for BrainScaleS-2 — perceptrons on analog neuromorphic hardware. In: Gama, J., et al. (eds.) ITEM 2020/IoT Streams 2020. CCIS, vol. 1325, pp. 189–200. Springer, Cham (2020). https://doi.org/10.1007/978-3-030-66770-2_14

15. Müller, E., et al.: Extending BrainScaleS OS for BrainScaleS-2. arXiv preprint (2020). arXiv: 2003.13750 [cs.NE]
16. Wunderlich, T., et al.: Demonstrating advantages of neuromorphic computation: a pilot study. Front. Neurosci. **13**, 260 (2019). https://doi.org/10.3389/fnins.2019.00260
17. Paszke, A., et al.: PyTorch: an imperative style, high-performance deep learning library. In: Wallach, H., Larochelle, H., Beygelzimer, A., d'Alché-Buc, F., Fox, E., Garnett, R. (eds.) Advances in Neural Information Processing Systems, vol. 32, pp. 8024–8035. Curran Associates Inc. (2019)
18. Kingma, D.P., Ba, J.: Adam: a method for stochastic optimization (2014). arXiv: 1412.6980 [cs.LG]
19. Abadi, M., et al.: TensorFlow: large-scale machine learning on heterogeneous distributed systems (2015)
20. Edge TPU performance benchmarks (2020). https://coral.ai/docs/edgetpu/benchmarks/

Search Space Complexity of Iteration Domain Based Instruction Embedding for Deep Learning Accelerators

Dennis Rieber[1]($\boxtimes$) and Holger Fröning[2] (iD)

[1] Robert Bosch GmbH, Stuttgart, Germany
DennisSebastian.Rieber@de.bosch.com
[2] Computing Systems Group, Heidelberg University, Heidelberg, Germany
holger.froening@ziti.uni-heidelberg.de

Abstract. With the success of deep learning applications in many domains, the number of new deep learning operators and hardware accelerators increased significantly in recent years. Building efficient deep learning kernels from complex machine instructions like matrix-multiply is a task not yet automated by tools. Deciding which loop and memory transformations to perform and which part of the computation to implement with which machine instruction is mostly done by a human expert. Automating this task presents two challenges: 1) finding the right combination of transformations and 2) deciding where to embed which available instruction. Current work, such as ISAMIR [16] or TVM [3], offer some degree of automation for this task on iteration domain granularity and report results competitive with performance libraries. In this work we explore the search space complexity of this task with a novel graph-based Intermediate Representation (IR) that allows a hierarchical description of the n-dimensional tensor computations performed by Deep Learning operators. We create an extensive search space across possible transformations of a given computation and then try to find possible implementations in a state of the art Deep Learning instruction set using pattern matching. Our results show that further research into the design of embedding methods for specialized instruction is required to gracefully handle the vast search space of possible transformations.

Keywords: Intermediate representation · Instruction selection · Tensor computations · Neural networks · Deep learning accelerators

1 Introduction

Deep learning methods are computationally demanding, which particularly in resource-constrained settings requires specialized hardware. For such specialized hardware, among others, tooling is required to automate the mapping step from abstract problem description, e.g. using computational graphs, like TensorFlow [1] or Pytorch [11]. to the available instructions of the underlying hardware.

© Springer Nature Switzerland AG 2020
J. Gama et al. (Eds.): ITEM 2020/IoT Streams 2020, CCIS 1325, pp. 213–228, 2020.
https://doi.org/10.1007/978-3-030-66770-2_16

However, most tools in this context focus on the network operator level, e.g. convolution, with library implementations of the individual operators.

Recent work, such as ISAMIR[16] or TVM [3], addresses this task with more flexibility by providing tools to embed complex instructions, for example a dedicated General Matrix Multiply (GEMM) instruction, into loop-order-invariant and dependency-free computations, which represent a large portion of current deep learning workloads. With respect to performance, ISAMIR and TVM report results similar to those of hand-optimized libraries for convolution or GEMM workloads. To find an embedding, it is often necessary to transform the original operator implementation into equivalent forms. These transformations can include loop transformations, memory transposition or algebraic rewrites. In this work, we explore the search space complexity created by such transformations.

The contributions of this work include:

- A graph-based Intermediate Representation (IR) to describe tensor computations and specialized tensor instructions. The IR represents the performed computation and data dependencies, allowing fast transformations and pattern matching.
- A method to generate a search space of legal kernels variants through graph transformations.
- A search space exploration of this embedding problem. Insights from this exploration can be used to aide in the design of novel approaches to the embedding problem.

The decision to implement our own IR is based on the fact that TVM is missing some of the necessary transformations to create a mapping, such as loop fission or memory transformations. For ISAMIR we could not find a publicly available implementation.

2   Related Work

Existing deep learning frameworks like TensorFlow [1] or Pytorch [11] focus on application-level interfaces to describe artificial neural networks with a set of operators, like convolutions, pooling or activations. These operators are mapped to libraries like cuDNN [4] for NVIDIA GPUs or NNPack[1] for x86 architectures. These libraries offer handcrafted kernels with high performance for a specific hardware target. The specificity of these approaches provides near-optimal performance on a specific hardware, but increases the engineering effort when introducing new operators or hardware architectures.

More flexibility is offered by TVM [3], an open source compiler stack for neural networks. A front end describes a network in Relay [13], a functional language. TVM performs rule-based operator fusion before the individual or fused operators are lowered to a scheduling language based on Halide [12]. For every instance of a lowered operator, an auto-tuner tries to find a well performing

---

[1] https://github.com/Maratyszcza/NNPACK, accessed 06.2020.

schedule. To target custom hardware backends, TVM embeds custom instructions into the schedule with *tensorization*. TVM can tensorize a kernel when a compute statement and its surrounding loops are an exact match to the custom instruction. The user decides which instruction to use at which location.

ISAMIR [16] provides even more automation in the instruction embedding. It is designed to map tensor instructions to compute kernels and after that, perform optimizations for performance. Like TVM, it operates on loop-order-invariant and dependency-free computations. The basic approach is to identify a mapping in what they call a "haystack" of possible transformations. ISAMIR tries to establish a mapping between an iteration domain in the workload and the instruction through tensor access functions. If the system cannot establish a mapping, a non-deterministic search uses algebraic rewrites, like factorization, to create new variants of the same computation. This process is repeated until a mapping is found or the search is exhausted.

The approach to use a graph rewrite system to create different kernels for same computation is used by LIFT [17] to create efficient GPU kernels. The possibility to use the rewrite system to implement deep learning kernels with specialized instructions was also explored [10].

MLIR [8] is an IR for deep learning and is designed to designed to be a platform and create portability between different optimizations and hardware targets.

3   Tensor Compute Graphs

Modern neural networks operate on multi-dimensional arrays, called tensors. Each output element is computed by the same set of operations, but with a different input interval. The kernels exhibit static control flow, meaning there are no if-statements and iteration domains only depend on parameters known at compile time. The following example is part of the computation used in a scaled dot-product attention module[18]:

$$R_{ij} = s \cdot \sum_k Q_{ik} K_{kj}^T \tag{1}$$

where R is the result tensor, Q and K^T the operand tensors, and s a scalar operand.

Our work captures these computational properties, together with data dependency and program flow information in a graph-based IR, called TENSOR COMPUTE GRAPHS (TCG). A TCG has nodes of several types: *tensor*, *reduction*, *compute*, *input* and *access* nodes. The nodes form a directed multigraph and each node has multiple child and one parent node. Additional edges represent data dependencies and index-variable definitions. The semantic meaning of nodes and a constructed graph is described in the following section.

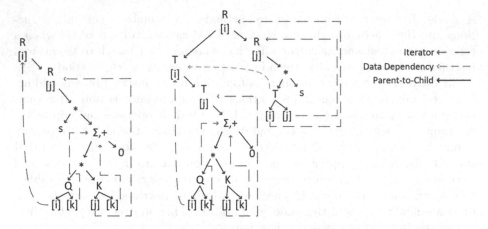

Fig. 1. The right-hand graph corresponds to Eqs. (2) and (3), while the graph on the left-hand expresses Eq. (1). For brevity, we left out the child-to-parent edges. Nodes with a capital letter followed by an interval ($T[i]$) are *tensor* nodes. Nodes with capital letter (T) represent tensor *inputs*, lowercase letters are scalar *inputs*. Algebraic symbols ($+, *$) are *compute* nodes, nodes with a $\sum$ are *reductions*. Lowercase letters and symbols in brackets ($[i]$) are *access* nodes.

3.1 Semantics of Tensor Compute Trees

- **Tensor** nodes describe the formation of a tensor dimension and the compute flow. The child to the right of each *tensor* node describes how each of the dimension's elements is computed. The child to the left of a *tensor* node is the preceding computation in the program flow, the parent is the succeeding one. This does not reflect data dependencies, only the order of computations.
- **Reduction** nodes describe reductions of an input dimension over an operation. The child to the right is the initial value, the left-hand child the input. Such a node computes one result that can be used by the parent for its own computation.
- **Compute** nodes represent elementwise unary or binary functions. Children are inputs or preceding computations. They are ordered according to the needs of the function. For example, a subtraction has a strict operand ordering, while an addition has a relaxed ordering due to its commutative nature.
- **Input** nodes represent an input tensor with n children of type *access*, one for each tensor dimension. The children are ordered right-to-left, with the rightmost representing the innermost dimension. If a dependency exists, an edge points to the *tensor* node computing the dimension.
- **Access** nodes form an expression tree to describe memory access functions for a tensor dimension. They either carry a reference to a node defining an iterator or an arithmetic operation. Iterators are defined by either *tensor* or *reduction* nodes and describe the traversal of the dimension.

On the left-hand side graph in Fig. 1 we explain the fundamental concepts. It shows the TCG representation of Eq. 1. A graph is always connected and rooted in a *tensor* node with no *parent*, in this case $R[i]$. The nodes $R[i]$ and $R[j]$ are *tensor* nodes defining the shape of the computed tensor, which is two-dimensional here. Generally, the shape can be inferred by recursively following the path of right-hand children, until a non-*tensor* node is encountered. Each additional *tensor* node adds an inner dimension to the tensor. Assuming a linear memory address space, the innermost dimension is continuous in memory. This nesting creates a rectangular iteration space. Following the parent-to-child connection, the next node is a *compute* node, multiplying the result of the *reduction* and the static *input* s. The *reduction* sums up the result of the scalar multiplication of different values in Q and K^T. Which input values are used is determined by the *access* nodes and iterators, represented by edges connected to the defining node.

Note that a different notation of the problem leads to a different TCG representation. The right-hand side graph in Fig. 1 corresponds to the following Eqs. (2) and (3).

$$T_{ij} = \sum_k Q_{ik} K_{kj}^T \tag{2}$$

$$R_{ij} = s \cdot T_{ij} \tag{3}$$

In this case, Eq. (2) computes a temporary matrix T, which Eq. (3) uses to compute the final output. Multiple computations in the same kernel form a sequence of compute subgraphs along the left-hand children of *tensor* nodes. Because $T[i]$ is the left-hand child of $R[i]$, it is the predecessor of $R[i]$ and computed first. In this case, there is also data dependency defined by the edge between the computation of *tensor* $T[i]$ and its use at *input* T. This edge enforces the ordering between $T[i]$ and $R[i]$.

In general, every graph and subgraph represent the shape of a computed tensor, followed by the *compute* and *reduction* nodes describing how each element is calculated. Since every element of a *tensor* node is computed independently by the same subgraph, each element has implicitly computational parallelism.

Similar to the family of IRs in Static Single Assignment (SSA) form, the value of a computed tensor cannot be manipulated after its computation. However, since this IR only allows static control flow, the ϕ functions used by SSA are not necessary. To implement zero padding and similar operations, *inputs* can be predicated. Details on the construction rules, memory access functions and data dependency representation can be found in Appendix A.

3.2   Instruction Selection

Instructions and kernels are both described by a TCG, which make instruction selection a pattern matching problem. After a preprocessing step that creates a graph with tree property, we use the top-down tree matching algorithm by Hoffmann and O'Donnel [5] to find matching instructions in a kernel. A similar approach is used in the TWIG framework [2].

If the matching finds overlapping instructions, we select the instruction that globally maximizes the number of covered nodes. Details on the preprocessing and instruction selection can found in Appendix B.

4   Kernel Transformations

The composable nature of kernels and freedom provided by commutative and data-independent operations makes transformations necessary to expose computations that fit to an instruction. Computational correctness is maintained by only performing transformations that are not violating data dependencies.

Transformations are implemented as a graph rewrite operation $S \xrightarrow{f_n(x)} R_n$, where S is a source graph, f_n is a transformation function, x is the set of affected nodes and edges in S, and R_n is the graph created by f_n. Two transformations are independent from one another, if they do not operate on the same set of nodes and edges. This creates flexibility in the ordering of transformations.

We choose a set of transformations that changes the computational structure of a kernel. These transformations allow flexibility in balancing the granularity of computations, the amount of intermediate results needing storage, and the amount of data required per instruction. An exception is the *input masking* transformation, as it is necessary to generate matching patterns for any kernel. The used transformations are as follows:

- **Input Masking:** select input tensor dimensions if the number of dimensions in the kernel is higher than in the instruction. This is similar to the deterministic part of the ISAMIR approach.
- **Operand Swap:** this transformation swaps the two child nodes of a *compute* node. This covers the operations where operand ordering is commutative. If possible, we order the inputs of *compute* nodes into a canonical form, reducing the number of required permutations.
- **Compute Fission:** moves a *compute* into a new subgraph that only performs the computation described by the moved node.
- **Reduction Fission:** moves a *reduction* into a new subgraph that only performs the reduction described by the moved node. The *reduction* in the source tree is replaced with an additional *tensor* dimension which is reduced in the subsequent reduction.
- **Fusion:** reduces the distance between two computations, by fusing the left-hand child of a *tensor* node into the parent. This is similar to the fusion of loop nests and allows the use of computed data before all dimensions of a tensor are computed.
- **Inlining:** replaces an input with the preceding computation. Because multiple inputs could use this computation, inlining is performed at every input consuming the computation selected for inlining.
- **Transpose:** transposes the dimensions of an input or output tensor.

5   Search Space Exploration

We evaluate the embedding problem's search space by mapping typical neural network layers to an Instruction Set Architecture (ISA) similar to proposed architectures like VIP [6] or Cambricon [9]. In particular, the evaluation ISA

Table 1. List of available instructions

Type	Operands	Result	Operations
Vector-Scalar	V, S	V	[add,mul,sub,div,max,exp]
Vector-Vector	V, V	V	[add,mul,sub,div,max,exp]
Reduction	V	S	[add, mul, max]
Dot	V, V	S	[add,mul,sub,div,max,exp][add,mul,max]
Matrix-Vector	M, V	V	[add,mul,sub,div,max,exp][add,mul,max]

provides different classes of scalar, vector and matrix operations. Table 1 defines our instruction set, where V is a vector, M is matrix and S a scalar value. Dot and matrix-vector instructions each perform two operations. The first is for the elementwise operation, the second for the reduction. All instructions support variable sizes for input and output dimensions.

On the application side we use a representative set of deep learning kernels as shown in Table 2. They range from simple operators like a fully-connected layer to complex kernels like the Capsule Routing algorithm [15]. The *Attention* kernel is implemented according to Eqs. (2) and (3).

We start our exploration of the solution space by looking at possible loop-level transformations in Subsect. 5.1. The additional influence of memory transformations is explored in Subsect. 5.4, where we use tensor layout transposition as a proxy for all memory transformations to study the influence this kind of transformation on the solution space.

In this work, we will not study the effects of tiling, as these decisions also heavily influence the performance aspect of the implementation, which falls into the realm of scheduling optimization rather than instruction embedding. If an instruction cannot cover a full iteration domain, these tiling factors can be inferred after the mapping and thus do not contribute to the search space. In addition, we will not work with specific data types [14], as this approach can be utilized on any data type.

5.1 Search Space

Starting from the original kernel, different sequences of transformations lead to a large number of different candidates. First, we create an exhaustive search space from the transformations presented in Sect. 4. The search starts with the canonicalization of inputs using the swap transformation. Then, we use reduction fission and compute fission to fully distribute the workload, such that each subgraph contains only one compute or reduction node. Conceptually, this is similar to a series of loop nests, each performing one operation and creating a new, intermediate tensor until the result is computed. This offers many possibilities to fuse and inline different computations. We exhaustively generate all possible combinations of fusions. For each resulting candidate, we create all possible combinations of masking. Since the highest number of input dimensions in

Table 2. List of evaluated kernels. Hit rate is the ratio of solutions to candidates. Number of transformations (#trans) is reported as median. Search configuration 4 in Table 3 is used.

No.	Kernel	#nodes	#candidates	#solutions	Hit rate	#trans
1	FC + Bias	16	24	4	16.6%	7
2	FC + Bias + Sigmoid	29	144	4	2.7%	12
3	GEMM	11	35	4	11.4%	8
4	Attention	26	289	9	3.1%	11
5	Conv2D (NHWC)	26	59,503	682	1.1%	25
6	Conv2D + ReLU (NHWC)	56	440,428	1,428	0.3%	33
7	Capsule Routing	127	1,023,516	12	0.001%	32

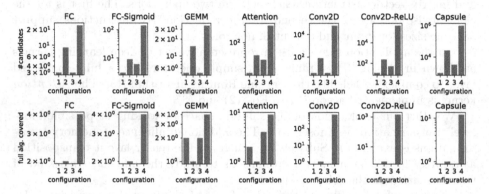

Fig. 2. Impact of four different transformation configurations on finding a kernel with full algebraic coverage. The configurations are detailed in Table 3. The top row shows the number of generated candidates, the bottom row the number of candidates with full algebraic coverage.

our ISA is two, every higher dimension is masked out by default, reducing the number of masking combinations.

The independent nature of the transformations can lead to the creation of the same kernel multiple times. We track the performed transformations, set of involved nodes and point in time to ensure uniqueness.

5.2   Solution Space

Table 2 shows the evaluated kernels, together with characteristics of the search and solution space. The number of generated candidates varies immensely, especially between kernels 4 (*Attention*) and 5 (*Con2vD*) of Table 2. Although they have exactly the same number of nodes, the number of resulting candidates differs by two orders of magnitude. This is rooted in the structural differences of the graphs. *Conv2D* generates a 4-dimensional tensor, using four algebraic operations. The first step in our search space creates a subgraph for each algebraic operation in the kernel. This leads to four subgraphs, each with at least four *tensor* nodes, which increases the number of possible combination of fusions. In the *Attention* kernel, the fission only creates three subgraphs with a maximum of three *tensor* nodes. The same explanation holds for kernels 1 (*FC + Bias*) and 2 (*FC + Bias + Sigmoid*), as they are a sequence on vector operations, instead of complex, high-dimensional computations.

The fifth column shows the number of solutions, which are candidates that have 100% algebraic coverage. Algebraic coverage is the coverage of *compute* and *reduction* nodes. In other words, we ignore the parts of the graph that represents loops and focus on the computational part. If a kernel can be computed by a sequence of available instructions and possibly outer loops to cover tiling and outer dimensions of the tensor, it has 100% algebraic coverage. Only a fraction of the generated candidates can actually be fully mapped onto the hardware. While the total number of solutions mostly increases with the search space, the sixth column shows that the relative number of solutions shrinks with an increased number of candidates. An exception to this is kernel 7 (*CapsuleRouting*). Compared to the other workloads, the number of possible combinations in the masking operation explodes due to the higher number of sequential computations, and resulting higher number of *input* nodes consuming the result of previous computations. At the same time, the possible number of *fusions* is lower, due to the lower dimension count and less regular output layout.

The median number of transformations required to achieve full algebraic coverage shows only a modest growth compared to the absolute number of generated candidates, which can grow exponentially. This suggests that the combination of transformations is more important than their total amount. One possible consequence is the need for careful pruning of the search space. Cutting a branch too early could potentially discard a whole class of candidates.

5.3   Transformation Impact

To study the impact of transformations on the search space and the resulting candidates, we used different configurations of transformations. The configurations are described in Table 3. *Swap* and *Mask* (Config. No. 1) are always included

Table 3. Configurations in the transformation study

Config. No	Swap	Mask	Fission	Fusion + Inline
1	✓	✓	x	x
2	✓	✓	✓	x
3	✓	✓	x	✓
4	✓	✓	✓	✓

because they are necessary to generate any match. The data in the top row of Fig. 2 shows that the configuration with the most transformations creates the most kernels. The relative differences between the configurations remain similar across kernels, regardless of the absolute number of candidates. Except for the *GEMM* and *Attention* kernels, no kernel can produce a solution with full algebraic coverage only relying on configuration 1.

Adding fission (Config. No. 2) creates solutions for all kernels with a convolution as part of the workload, because the standard convolution can be separated into a sequence of vector and reduction operations. This transformation also increases the number of inputs nodes in the kernel. Thus, more candidates are generated because each input leads to a higher number of masking options.

The number of candidates by Config. No. 3 depends on the number of compute statements in the original kernel. *Conv2D* and *GEMM* kernels create the same number of candidates as the first configuration. They have only one subgraph in the original kernel and therefore no option for fusion.

Config. No. 4 uses the full search space design as proposed in Sect. 5.1, leading with fission, then subsequent fusion. The high number of candidates of Config. No. 4 across all workloads is explained by the dynamic between these two transformations. Each fission creates additional computation subgraphs, which in turn creates opportunity for fusion. More interesting is the fact that for all original kernels, most candidates with full algebraic coverage are found by this configuration. This suggests that finding the right granularity of computation is important to generate valid solutions. From the original formulation, the workload has to be transformed, such that the granularity of the individual computations matches operations available in the ISA. Generating a set of transformation that creates the required granularity is an important goal during search space design. While our exhaustive approach eventually reaches a solution, it does not scale well with additional transformations.

5.4   Memory Transformations

In addition to changing the structure of a computation, the memory layout is also a crucial part of the search space. For example, TVM and TCG try to match innermost tensor to the instructions. Therefore, not only the loop structure, but also the memory layout is relevant for an embedding. While ISAMIR can infer transpositions from a found mapping, more advanced memory transformations, like folding or broadcasting tensor dimensions, are not mentioned as part of its capabilities. This section studies the effects of memory layout transposition on search space and solutions using *Conv2D* and *GEMM* kernels as examples.

The *Conv2D* kernel has one output and two input tensors, with four dimensions each. We extend our search space from Sect. 5.1 by preceding the fission step with a transpose of the input and output dimensions. This way, no transposition of intermediate results is necessary. In the case of *Conv2D*, many deep learning frameworks offer predesigned tensor layouts, mostly image major (NCHW) and channel major (NHWC), for all tensors in the operator. However, to explore the more general case of matching any workload to an arbitrary instruction set we cannot assume knowledge about the semantics of tensor dimensions. This means we have to explore all possible layout permutations of the four dimensions. We will transpose all inputs and outputs in the same way, since there are 24 different permutations of four dimensions. Transposing them individually would create 13824 base cases for the rest of the search space evaluation, which is computationally intractable.

Table 4 shows the number of candidates in the extended search space, the found solutions, and the percentage of solutions creating full coverage. The number of candidates increased roughly linear with the number of possible tensor permutations, with a factor of 23.06 for $Conv2D$ and 2.08 for $GEMM$. The rightmost column shows the factor of how the absolute number of solutions changes compared to Table 2. This adds to the observation that for an increase in the complexity of kernels, the number of viable solutions to the embedding problem increases in absolute numbers, but shrinks in relative terms.

Table 4. Effect of tensor transpose operations on the search space. Hit rate is the ratio of solutions to candidates.

Kernel	#candidates	#solutions	Hit rate	Solutions rel. to Table 2
GEMM	73	5	6.8%	1.25
Conv2D	1,372,653	3,810	0.27%	5.5

6 Conclusion

We have presented a graph-based IR for deep learning workloads and methods to automatically map these to an available accelerator ISA. Through graph rewrites and pattern matching we can find a valid solution for a set of common kernels.

The evaluation showed that a relatively small number of transformations is enough find a candidate that can be mapped fully. Selecting the right combination of transformations however is crucial. As the transformation space analysis showed, this combination has to create the right granularity of computations. However, the search space is vast and only a small number of candidates fully implement the kernel with the target ISA.

The exploration shows two major challenges in the search space design. First, even the limited set of transformations presented in this paper can blow up the search space to intractable sizes. This goes hand-in-hand with a shrinking relative number of solutions. Kernels with sequential computations, like $Con2D + ReLU$ or $CapsuleRouting$, are especially affected by this. Additionally, transformations like fission introduce such sequences even in simpler kernels. This hints towards a solution that limits the complexity by attempting to find an embedding locally, and only gradually widens the scope when necessary. This is especially important when operator fusion is performed on the network level, which has shown promising results for performance improvements [7].

The second difficulty we see is that the decision making in this loop-based matching is top-down and made without knowledge about how this will affect the search space and found solutions. This difficulty is increased even more, when operations like zero padding or broadcasts are necessary to create a mapping. A more extensive search using more transformations will ultimately not help to solve the embedding problem. The results of the transformation impact study and the low number of transformations that are actually necessary suggest an approach where the search is guided by properties of the target ISA. Properties like tensor layout, number and type of operations or access functions could act as guidelines for an algorithm that only follows branches in the search that go towards these desired structures.

A   Tensor Compute Graphs

Figure 3 contains the construction rules for the Tensor Compute Graphs.

A.1   Access Functions

Array access functions are described in terms of its consumers, meaning that *tensor* and *reduction* nodes define iterators to compute the access pattern for each dimension of an *input*. Every *tensor* and *reduction* node defines an iteration domain as an integer interval $I = [l, n)$ with l and n being the lower and upper bounds. The iteration domain can have a regular stride $s > 1$. To express the access function computation, we build an arithmetic expression for each input tensor dimension. Each element is either an iterator, a constant value or an arithmetic operation. This expression is then represented as tree for pattern matching.

A.2   Data Dependencies

Transformations of kernels with more than one computation need to maintain correctness and one aspect of this is not to violate the original data dependencies. Because tensor values cannot be modified in place, tracking read-after-write dependencies is sufficient.

Instead of just looking at complete tensors, we can analyze data dependencies between two computations by calculating the produced and consumed intervals of the tensor dimension of interest. Since we have a linear interval for each tensor dimensions, the analysis of multiple dimensions results in a rectangular space. This is used in the generation of the search space in Sect. 4 in order to verify transformations. For example, it is possible to make sure that the new computation only consumes data from an interval which has already been computed. While this rectangular approach can conservatively overestimate such an interval, TVM and Halide have shown that this method is still viable in practice.

```
node = tensor
       | reduction
       | compute
       | input
       | access

iterator = reference to: tensor | reduction
operator = Arith/Logic op
           interval = {
           upper : <integer>,
           lower : <integer>
}

tensor = { parent : tensor | NULL
           left child : tensor | NULL
           right child : tensor | reduction | compute | input
           data-user : input | NULL
           size: interval
}

reduction = {
           parent : tensor | reduction | compute
           left child : compute | reduction | input
           right child : input
           size : interval
           stride: <integer>
}

compute = {
           parent = tensor | reduction | compute
           left child = compute | reduction | input
           right child = compute | reduction | input
           op = operator
}

input = {
           parent = tensor | reduction | compute
           dependency = tensor   | NULL
           children = [access]
}

access ={
           parent = input | access
           val = iterator | operation | scalar constant
           children = [access] | NULL
}
```

Fig. 3. Tensor Compute Graph construction rules

B   Instruction Selection

B.1   Instruction Representation

Instructions are represented as TCGs. We differentiate between variable sized and fixed size instructions. Fixed size instructions are designed with static input and output array dimensions. Since an ISA can have instructions that perform the same computation, but with different input and output dimensions, we allow multiple iteration intervals for *tensor* and *reduction* nodes in the TCGs of instructions. For variable size instructions, the dimensions of input and output tensors are part of the instruction's arguments. For this type of instructions, we only need to know the upper and lower bound of each argument. Instruction are always rooted in a *tensor* node and the computed results are always continuous in memory.

B.2   Preprocessing

The preprocessing transforms a graph described in the presented TCG IR into a graph with strict tree property, meaning there exists only one path connecting any two nodes in the graph. The parent and child connections already have this property. However, edges formed by data dependencies and iterators introduce additional paths in the TCG. We expand the iterator edges to their respective paths along the parent or child edges. A path is a list of directions taken from source to target node. Since a node defining an iterator always dominates the node using an iterator, every element of the path points to its parent. Therefore, we can represent the path simply by its length. This path length replaces the index in the *Access* node. Data dependencies are also expanded to their respective paths. After we found a match, we compare the data dependency paths.

B.3   Selection Algorithm

Pattern matching can produce multiple, conflicting ways of covering a kernel with instructions. A conflict exists if two matched instructions share one or more nodes in the tree. The selection is driven by a global cost optimization. Each instruction has an associated cost function that contributes to the global cost. For this paper we use coverage as a heuristic metric. Coverage is defined as:

$$C_{nodes} = \frac{sum\ of\ nodes\ covered}{total\ nodes\ in\ tree} \tag{4}$$

Maximizing coverage globally maps the highest number of nodes in the kernel to an instruction. The selection algorithm is agnostic to the exact cost function and can be used with other metrics. Algorithm 1 is used to find the best combination of instructions recursively. Branches are bound if they offer no improvement over the best local selection. The bounding decision is made by analyzing the next possible match in the tree. For every instruction matched at the local node

Algorithm 1. Selection Algorithm

```
function SELECTION(matches[], index)
    if index == matches.size then
        return MAXINSTR(matches[index])
    end if
    for instr : matches[index] do
        node,nId = NEXT(instr, matches, index)
        maxCont = MAXINSTR(continuation[nId], instr)
        continuation[nId] = maxCont
    end for
    if continuation[index+1].empty then
        continuation[index+1] = Nullpattern
    end if
    for (nId,node) : continuation do
        candidate = SELECTION(matches, nId)
        candidate = candidate ∪ node
        candidateList.insert(candidate)
    end for
    return BEST(candidateList);
end function
```

we search for the next instructions not overlapping with the local selection. This next node is called continuation. Only the local selection with the best cost properties for each continuation is stored. The function returns the best candidate, which is a combination of the local selection and continuation. The algorithm locally selects the best instruction for the current node using the *MaxInstr* function, *Next* calculates the continuation. *Best* selects the candidate with the best global cost function property. If the next node in the match list is not a possible continuation, a null pattern is used to allow exploration of search paths not selecting any match at this location.

References

1. Abadi, M., et al.: Tensorflow: a system for large-scale machine learning. In: OSDI (2016)
2. Aho, A.V., Ganapathi, M., Tjiang, S.W.K.: Code generation using tree matching and dynamic programming. ACM Trans. Program. Lang. Syst. **11**(4), 491–516 (1989). https://doi.org/10.1145/69558.75700
3. Chen, T., et al.: TVM: end-to-end optimization stack for deep learning. arXiv:1802.04799 (2018)
4. Chetlur, S.: cuDNN: efficient primitives for deep learning. arXiv:1410.0759 (2014)
5. Hoffmann, C.M., O'Donnell, M.J.: Pattern matching in trees. J. ACM **29**(1), 68–95 (1982). https://doi.org/10.1145/322290.322295. ISSN 0004-5411
6. Hurkat, S., Martínez, J.F.: Vip: A versatile inference processor. In: 2019 IEEE International Symposium on High Performance Computer Architecture (HPCA), pp. 345–358 (2019). https://doi.org/10.1109/HPCA.2019.00049

7. Jia, Z., Padon, O., Thomas, J., Warszawski, T., Zaharia, M., Aiken, A.: TASO: optimizing deep learning computation with automatic generation of graph substitutions. In: Proceedings of the 27th ACM Symposium on Operating Systems Principles (2019). https://doi.org/10.1145/3341301.3359630

8. Lattner, C., et al.: MLIR: a compiler infrastructure for the end of Moore's law. arXiv:2002.11054 (2020)

9. Liu, S., et al.: Cambricon: an instruction set architecture for neural networks. In: 2016 ACM/IEEE 43rd Annual International Symposium on Computer Architecture (ISCA) (2016). https://doi.org/10.1109/ISCA.2016.42

10. Mogers, N., Steuwer, M., Dubache, C.: Towards mapping lift to deep neural network accelerators. In: EDLA@HiPEAC, Valencia, Spain (2019)

11. Paszke, A., et al.: Pytorch: an imperative style, high-performance deep learning library. In: Advances in Neural Information Processing Systems, vol. 32. Curran Associates Inc. (2019)

12. Ragan-Kelley, J., et al.: Decoupling algorithms from schedules for high-performance image processing. Commun. ACM **61**(1), 106–115 (2017). https://doi.org/10.1145/3150211. ISSN 0001-0782

13. Roesch, J., et al: Relay: a new IR for machine learning frameworks. In: MAPL@PLDI (2018)

14. Roth, W., et al.: Resource-efficient neural networks for embedded systems. arXiv:2001.03048 (2020)

15. Sabour, S., Frosst, N., Hinton, G.E.: Dynamic routing between capsules. arXiv:1710.09829 (2017)

16. Sotoudeh, M., Venkat, A., Anderson, M., Georganas, E., Heinecke, A., Knight, J.: ISA mapper: a compute and hardware agnostic deep learning compiler. In: Proceedings of the 16th ACM International Conference on Computing Frontiers (2019). https://doi.org/10.1145/3310273.3321559

17. Steuwer, M., Remmelg, T., Dubach, C.: Lift: a functional data-parallel IR for high-performance GPU code generation. In: Proceedings of the 2017 International Symposium on Code Generation and Optimization (2017). ISBN 978-1-5090-4931-8

18. Vaswani, A., et al.: Attention is all you need. arXiv:1706.03762 (2017)

On the Difficulty of Designing Processor Arrays for Deep Neural Networks

Kevin Stehle[✉], Günther Schindler, and Holger Fröning

Computing Systems Group, Institute of Computer Engineering,
Heidelberg University, Heidelberg, Germany
stehle@stud.uni-heidelberg.de

Abstract. Systolic arrays are a promising computing concept which is in particular inline with CMOS technology trends and linear algebra operations found in the processing of artificial neural networks. The recent success of such deep learning methods in a wide set of applications has led to a variety of models, which albeit conceptual similar as based on convolutions and fully-connected layers, in detail show a huge diversity in operations due to a large design space: An operand's dimension varies substantially since it depends on design principles such as receptive field size, number of features, striding, dilating and grouping of features. Last, recent networks extent previously plain feedforward models by various connectivity, such as in ResNet or DenseNet. The problem of choosing an optimal systolic array configuration cannot be solved analytically, thus instead methods and tools are required that facilitate a fast and accurate reasoning about optimality in terms of total cycles, utilization, and amount of data movements. In this work we introduce CAMUY, a lightweight model of a weight-stationary systolic array for linear algebra operations that allows quick explorations of different configurations, such as systolic array dimensions and input/output bitwidths. CAMUY aids accelerator designers in either finding optimal configurations for a particular network architecture or for robust performance across a variety of network architectures. It offers simple integration into existing machine learning tool stacks (e.g TensorFlow) through custom operators. We present an analysis of popular DNN models to illustrate how it can estimate required cycles, data movement costs, as well as systolic array utilization, and show how the progress in network architecture design impacts the efficiency of inference on accelerators based on systolic arrays.

1 Introduction

Deep learning techniques are continuously being applied to more and more applications, with different tasks such as image, signal or speech processing, and deployments including resource-constrained environments such as edge or mobile computing. As a result, one can observe an increase in diversity in network architectures, which addresses application-specific requirements as well as

© Springer Nature Switzerland AG 2020
J. Gama et al. (Eds.): ITEM 2020/IoT Streams 2020, CCIS 1325, pp. 229–240, 2020.
https://doi.org/10.1007/978-3-030-66770-2_17

operational constraints. This diversity is substantially different to commonly known plain feedforward convolutional networks, including in particular specialized convolutions, such as dilated, grouped or separable ones, extended by various connectivity (ResNet, DenseNet), and vectorized operators (Capsule Networks). While such network architectures continue to demand for more processing performance, due to technical constraints CMOS scaling is staggering in terms of feature size and absolute performance, among others. A direct result of this trend is massive parallelization, with systolic arrays being a promising candidate. A systolic arrays is a regular linear or planar array of processing elements (PE), where each PE may only exchange data and instructions with neighboring PEs. Contrary to a pipeline stage in common processors, a PE has more autonomy including local storage and possibly some limited independent control flow. Systolic arrays are in particular promising as they are a simple abstraction of a massive amount of parallelism, minimizing orchestration overhead in spite of thousands of instructions executing in parallel.

Still, an optimal match between application and processor architecture requires specialization, with particular attention on array size and memory provisioning. As the reasoning about such architectural parameters is neither intuitive nor trivial, there is a demand for methods and tools to assist designers in finding good or even optimal configurations.

Principally, such predictive modeling can be separated into different concepts [15]. Analytical models, including rather informal back-of-the-envelope calculations but also methodologically sound methods, are fast, easy to use, flexible and scalable but usually inaccurate. Contrary, simulations are much more accurate but result in slow down of about 5–6 orders of magnitude. Furthermore, they are limited in scaling, flexibility, and ease of use (considering massive architectural changes as often required in design space explorations). Simulations can be further distinguished into functional ones [4], and cycle-accurate ones [12], which mainly differ in speed and accuracy. An emulation are often considered as another option, which differs from simulation with regard to how behavior is replicated. In simulation, software is being employed for an exact replication of the original system, while in emulation a different system, not necessarily based on software, is used to replicate internal functions and their relations. A good example for emulation is the acceleration of simulations by relying on reconfigurable hardware to mimic the behavior of the original system, as often being done by implementing a processor architecture on an FPGA (e.g., [4]). Last, there also exist various hybrid concepts, for instance Aladdin [13] which combines architecture-level core and memory hierarchy simulations with RTL models and even optimization passes. Still, Aladdin is closer to simulation in terms of flexibility and speed than analytical models or emulation.

In particular for quick explorations of fundamental design parameters, such as array size and/or memory provisioning, one can observe a lack of tools. As for such a setting we assume speed being of higher importance than accuracy, we consider emulation as a promising concept. However, to avoid the implications of FPGA prototyping, we rely on standard CPUs as emulation platform, and instead leverage an identical platform to directly connect the emulator to TensorFlow as a representative for a pervasively used machine learning framework.

We introduce an emulation framework called CAMUY - *Configurable Accelerator Modeling for (workload) Understanding and AnalYsis* , which implements computations using (fast) CPU instructions and focuses on reporting abstract performance metrics such as total cycle count, utilization, and data movements. Thereby, CAMUY allows for a quick and sufficiently accurate exploration of design alternatives, and in particular can assess the suitability of a given architecture (network or processor) to its counterpart. The main contributions of this work are as follows:

1. Design of technology-agnostic emulation concept and TF integration, reporting abstract metrics such as cycle count, data movements, utilization, and others.
2. To demonstrate the effectiveness of CAMUY, we detail about the implications of various network architectures for different arrays configurations.
3. Furthermore, we provide recommendations on configurations which are robust across a variety of network architectures.

While neglecting many architectural details, such as implementation of floating-point units, on-chip network contention, bank conflicts when accessing on-chip memory, CAMUY is focused on fast explorations which are later being refined using other tools. CAMUY is publicly available[1].

2   Related Work

Systolic arrays were introduced in the early 1980s [10] and have recently gained increasing interest for deep learning. There exist a large variety of systolic implementations, ranging from commercial (TPU [8]) to research variants (Eyeriss [1], Gemmini [4]). CAMUY is inspired and modeled following the TPU design, however, it is also extendable to other systolic concepts.

A few exploration tools for systolic arrays have been proposed in the context of deep learning: SCALE-SIM [12] is a configurable, systolic-array-based, cycle-accurate simulator for design space exploration, which is based on a never-stalling array for which traces of read and write addresses are generated, which are then parsed to derive execution time. Gemmini [4] is a systolic array generator that generates a custom ASIC design based on RISC-V and user-defined parameterization, such as bit width and array dimensions. Evaluation is performed using a cycle-accurate FPGA-accelerated simulation platform. Further exploration tools, but not centric to systolic arrays, include for instance Aladdin [13], which is a power-performance accelerator modeling framework for system-on-chip (SoC) simulations. Similarly, Cash [16] is a hardware-software co-design framework for rapid SoC prototyping.

---

[1] https://github.com/UniHD-CEG/Camuy.

CAMUY differs from previous efforts as it focuses on quick and easy explorations of legacy or emerging neural architectures through a simple Tensorflow extension without the need for specialized hardware or software. The tool aims to assist deep learning experts to develop neural architectures that fit well onto a certain processor array and hardware experts to design processor arrays based on certain neural architectures. Consequently, CAMUY adds an important link between high-productivity machine learning frameworks, such as TensorFlow, and hardware evaluation, for instance based on Gemmini or a TPU.

3   Emulator Design

This work is primarily concerned with design space explorations, in order to quickly assess the suitability of a given architecture configuration for a particular DNN or DNN mix. For such an exploration it is sufficient to assess this suitability based on a set of abstract metrics, thus emulation is chosen as underlying method, which is in particular fast in comparison to simulations.

We furthermore focus this work on systolic arrays, which are a variant of massively parallel processor arrays, very suitable for regular problems such as linear algebra operations, and a promising candidate to address the increasing costs of data movements. Systolic arrays minimize instruction fetch costs, which can otherwise be prohibitive given the vast amount of PEs, and the constrained data flow also avoids network contention effects, which otherwise can be substantial given the non-scalable bisection bandwidth of n-dimensional meshes. However, data movements can only be reduced if locality effects are sufficiently exploited, and the data flow constraints of a systolic array can result in under-utilization and latency increase. In this regard, metrics of primary interest include latency in cycles, number of data transfers in between PEs and in and out of the systolic array, resulting bandwidth requirements for a stall-free execution, and utilization as a result of operator size, array dimensions and sparsity.

In more detail, in this work we use a weight-stationary dataflow concept, similar to Google's TPUv1 [8]. While this is controversially discussed [1,18], principally CAMUY can also support other concepts. In this regard, while this work is mainly concerned with exploring the implications of different array dimensions, further architecture configuration parameters of interest include other dataflow concepts, PE SIMDification (multiple multiply-accumulate units per PE), local PE memory (varying with dataflow concept), and the sizing of memory structures such as FIFOs, accumulator array, and global memory.

The basic architecture of CAMUY is modeled after the TPUv1 [8] and summarized in Fig. 1. Notably some alterations were made to better suit the intended use case in resource-constrained environments, such as including only on-chip memory (*Unified Buffer*) for weights, input and output activations. In the TPUv1, on-chip memory was only used for input and output activations. The core is a weight-stationary *Systolic Array* of parameterized width n and height m. Note that control flow within the array is not shown for readability reasons. Its PEs perform MAC operations using partial sums, weights, and activations

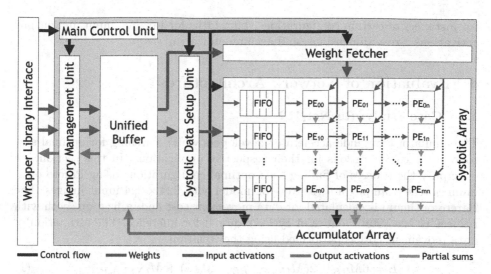

Fig. 1. Overview of the CAMUY processor, with systolic array, memory modules, and auxiliary units.

loaded from neighboring PEs respectively input FIFOs for the boundary PEs. Thus, each PE only requires 4 data registers: two weight registers to support double buffering, one activation register, and output register for the partial sum. This register arrangement is a variant of the arrangement proposed by Kung et al. [11]. As for the TPUv1, activations and partial sums flow horizontally respectively vertically through the PE array. Similar applies to the dataflow from memory to the array, with a *Weight Fetcher* moving weight matrix tiles. Note hat for a stall-free execution, multiple concurrent weight updates might be necessary, thus multiple such weight updates might be necessary at the same time to ensure stall-free execution, thus our model allows an arbitrary amount of simultaneous updates and reports this concurrency in terms of bandwidth requirements. The flow of activations from memory to the PEs is managed by the *Systolic Data Setup Unit*, which fetches one activation row to the FIFOs in a way that waveform requirements are ensured. Again following the TPUv1 design, the partial sums produced by the array are accumulated before writing them back to memory (*Accumulator Array*). While not principally required as neither pipelined activation nor pooling/normalization stages are implemented, it substantially reduces the associate bandwidth requirements. The *Main Control Unit* orchestrates the different units, in particular for a pipelined and overlapped execution of fetching weight matrix tiles and input activations, performing the systolic operation, and writing back output activations. Additionally, it controls the *Memory Management Unit*, which transfers data in and out of this processor.

To simplify the integration of the emulator into existing machine learning frameworks, we implemented a wrapper library that dynamically creates emulator instances of certain configurations (bit widths for weights, input and output activations, array dimensions, and accumulator array size).

4   Evaluation of Network Architectures

4.1   Case Study: ResNet-152

The emulator can guide accelerator developers while searching for optimal systolic array configurations for their respective applications. In this section, we exemplify the process of finding such optimal configurations using Pareto optimum on the example of a ResNet-152 model with 224×224 input images. The Pareto optimum is calculated for data movement cost and utilization, both with respect to the total number of cycles required for inference. The estimation of data movement cost is performed using the equation

$$E = 6M_{UB} + 2(M_{INTER\_PE} + M_{AA}) + M_{INTRA\_PE} \qquad (1)$$

derived from the estimations performed by Chen et al. [1]. M_{UB} is the total amount of read and write accesses to the unified buffer. The amount of read accesses of PE to registers of neighboring PEs is given by M_{INTER_PE}. M_{INTRA_PE} is the amount of register read and write accesses inside a PE and M_{AA} is the amount of data movements from the systolic array to the accumulator array. The dimensionless normalized total energy movement cost E can be used to compare the energy cost resulting from data movements between CAMUY configurations.

The explored space of systolic array sizes are all possible width and height combinations from 16 to 256 in increments of 8, for a total of 961 possible dimensions.

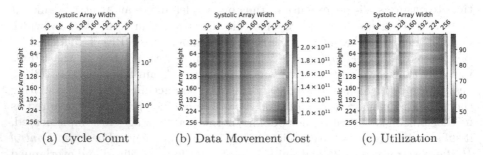

(a) Cycle Count   (b) Data Movement Cost   (c) Utilization

Fig. 2. Data movement cost and utilization for inference of ResNet-152 using different systolic array dimensions.

Figure 2 shows an overview of the measured data movement cost and utilization of the analyzed dimensions in the form of heatmaps in order to give insights on the affects in performance when scaling the two array dimensions. As can be

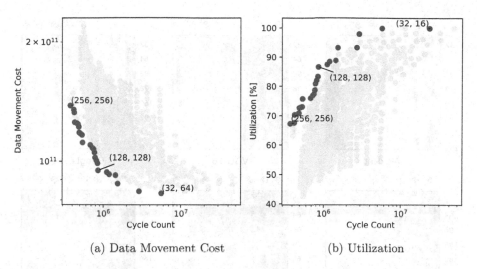

(a) Data Movement Cost   (b) Utilization

Fig. 3. Blue dots: Pareto set for data movement cost to cycle count and utilization to cycle count for ResNet-152. Gray dots: Non-optimal dimensions. (Color figure online)

seen, data movement cost is more sensitive to scaling the array's height than width while the utilization is highly sensitive to the scaling of both. Furthermore, systolic configurations which are powers of two show a particularly good utilization.

Next, we calculate the Pareto set using NSGA-II [3], a multi-objective optimization algorithm, in order to find configurations that are optimal for data movement cost and utilization with respect to the amount of cycle. Figure 3 shows the set of all dimensions, with the Pareto frontier highlighted in blue, and the array sizes as annotations in the format *(height, width)*. Based on the Pareto sets of the analyzed model, the user is able to choose configurations that best fit their particular use case, be it lowest energy consumption, fastest execution, or a trade-off.

4.2 Impact of DNN Architecture Development on Systolic Array Performance

We conduct further performance analyses (as described in Subsect. 4.1) for a wide range of CNN models to show the impact of evolving neural architectures on parameter optimality of systolic array configurations. We focus on the most popular CNN models as well as their implications on the operand's dimensions for the required matrix multiplication, and show the difficulty of choosing an optimal systolic array configuration.

AlexNet [9] and VGG-16 [14] are classic CNN architectures where the operand's dimension for the required matrix multiplication only depends on the amount of filters and receptive field size. GoogLeNet and Inception-v2 improved these straight-forward models by applying different receptive fields (1×1, 3×3

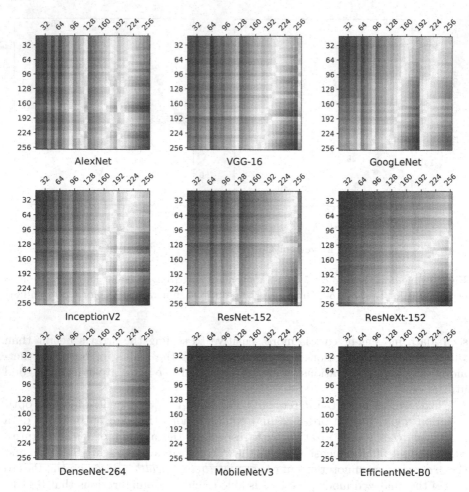

Fig. 4. Comparison of data movement heatmaps for different CNN models, with varying dimensions (height on y axis, width on x axis) of the systolic array. Data movement costs are visualized using the spectrum from green (low data movement cost) over yellow (medium data movement cost) to red (high data movement cost). (Color figure online)

and 5 × 5) on the same features, thereby increasing variance in the operand's dimension.

A major breakthrough in neural architectures is the introduction of advanced connectivity between layers which leads to significant improvements in parameter and computation efficiency. The connectivity through residual connections (such as in ResNets [5]) enables much deeper models with thinner layers by reducing the vanishing gradient problem, but also results in a reduced operand's dimension for the matrix multiplication. Dense connectivity (such as in DenseNet [7]) allows even deeper models, where the amount of filters per layer is increased linearly with the model's depth, causing high diversity in the operand's dimensions.

All state-of-the-art CNN models heavily use group convolutions in order to increase parameter and computation efficiency. This grouping, however, leads to a serialization of matrix multiplications (one per group), where the operand's dimensions vary with group size g. We use ResNeXt-152 [17] with $g = 32$ as well as MobileNetV3 and EfficientNet-B0 with $g = 1$ (depthwise convolution) as representative for models with group convolution.

We report results from these various CNN models for systolic array configurations of varying height and width, and focus in this work on data movement costs. This choice is based on the importance of energy efficiency, that data movements are orders of magnitude more energy consuming than arithmetic operations [1,6], and that systolic arrays are in particular suitable to minimize data movements.

As can be seen in Fig. 4, all models are more sensitive to increasing the systolic array's width than the height, indicating that an optimal array configuration is not quadratic. Comparing residual with dense connections, one can observe that residual ones favor larger array sizes while dense connections benefit from smaller arrays. Furthermore, dense connections seems to be rather unaffected by varying height, while width matters much more. Contrary, residual connections are equally sensitive to height and width.

Similar applies to models with group convolutions, where smaller arrays are clearly more beneficial. Last, all but models with group convolution show an advantage if the width is a power of two (at least), while for group convolutions no such effect is visible. For models such as AlexNet, GoogLeNet, BN-Inception, VGG-16, and ResNet-152, a similar effect on the height is apparent.

The overall observation is that the inference of almost all analyzed CNN models is significantly more efficient for small systolic arrays and especially for arrays with a low width-to-height ratio. This finding is in contrast to the commercially available TPU, whose systolic array is quadratic with an edge length of 256, and furthermore conflictive with the need for parallelization as main technique to further reduce processing time.

5   Robust/Optimal Processor Architecture Configuration

In Sect. 4.2, we analyzed tendencies of several popular CNN models using data movement costs for varying systolic array configurations. Next, we aim to find configurations that delivers robust performance in terms of data movement costs and required cycles across the variety of models.

To find such configurations, multi-variate optimization is performed using the averaged normalized results of all analyzed models. Figure 5 shows the result of this analysis, with the Pareto frontier highlighted in blue and the array sizes as annotations in the format *(height, width)*.

A surprising result of this analysis is that the configurations with lowest average cycle count are configurations with a width that is larger than the height which goes against the previously observed trend of lower data movement cost for variants with larger height than width. On the other hand, the configurations with larger height than width achieve much lower data movement costs, while only increasing the cycle count relatively moderately. While the configuration with a systolic array width and height of 16 incurs the least data movement cost, it also requires a significantly increased average cycle count relative to the entry with second lowest data movement cost in the Pareto frontier.

Regarding robustness, the configurations in the lower left corner of Fig. 5 should be considered, which are all based on a non-square configuration with height larger than width. Deviations from such configurations lead to significant increases in either data movement cost or cycle count, with only minor improvements in the other dimension.

While this suggests non-square configurations with height larger than width as best solution, we note that this is based on the data transfer model of Eq. 1 and the underlying relation of different types of data movements. If this relation changes, for instance due to technology scaling, the result optimality of this analysis will also change. Future work can for instance evaluate the energy data for 14 nm, as reported by Dally et al. [2].

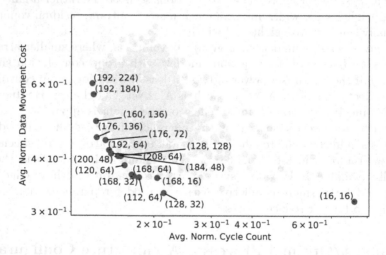

Fig. 5. Pareto optimal systolic array dimensions *(height, width)* with regards to average normalized data movement cost relative to latency (Blue Dots). Gray Dots: Dominated dimensions. (Color figure online)

The last point of interest is the performance for extreme height to width ratios, in order to evaluate the potential of such configurations. For this purpose, the same configuration space is analyzed as done by Samajdar et al. [12] in their investigation of weight-stationary systolic array configuration. The result of this analysis is illustrated in Fig. 6 for the average normalized data movement cost. We find that extreme height to width ratios generally result in low performance, which is inline with similar findings of Samajdar et al.

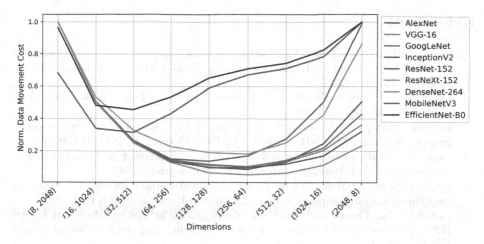

Fig. 6. Normalized data movement cost for inference of analyzed models using systolic array dimensions with equal PE counts.

6   Conclusion

We have presented CAMUY, a lightweight model of a weight-stationary systolic array for quick explorations of neural architectures. The presented tool offers fast and accurate reasoning about optimality in terms of total cycles, utilization, and amount of data movements, in order to reason about the implications of different systolic array configurations, such as optimality or robustness. For that, we analyzed a large variety of popular CNN models, such as straight-forward, complicated-connected, and grouped architectures. Our findings suggest that energy and cycle efficiency is optimal for small systolic arrays with a low width-to-height ratio, which is in contrast to recently proposed systolic processors.

Our primary goal for this work is to show the performance gap of modern neural architectures on available systolic hardware, and to further motivate the intersection between hardware design and machine learning. On that note, we hope that CAMUY can assist hardware experts to design processors arrays based on emerging neural designs, and machine learning experts to design neural architectures that fit well onto a certain processor.

In future work, we will extent CAMUY to different systolic concepts, such as output stationary variants and multi-array concepts, in order to improve parallelism for modern CNN models. Furthermore, we plan to study the impact of emerging and heterogeneous neural architectures, such as transformers and capsule networks, on systolic arrays.

Acknowledgments. We gratefully acknowledge funding by the German Research Foundation (DFG) under the project number FR3273/1-1.

References

1. Chen, Y.H., Emer, J., Sze, V.: Eyeriss: a spatial architecture for energy-efficient dataflow for convolutional neural networks. ACM SIGARCH Comput. Archit. News **44**, 367–379 (2016)
2. Dally, W.J., Turakhia, Y., Han, S.: Domain-specific hardware accelerators. Commun. ACM **63**, 48–57 (2020)
3. Deb, K., Pratap, A., Agarwal, S., Meyarivan, T.: A fast and elitist multiobjective genetic algorithm: NSGA-II. IEEE Trans. Evol. Comput. **6**, 182–197 (2002)
4. Genc, H., et al.: Gemmini: an agile systolic array generator enabling systematic evaluations of deep-learning architectures. arXiv e-prints (2019)
5. He, K., Zhang, X., Ren, S., Sun, J.: Deep residual learning for image recognition. In: Conference on Computer Vision and Pattern Recognition (CVPR) (2016)
6. Horowitz, M.: Computing's energy problem (and what we can do about it). In: IEEE International Solid-State Circuits Conference Digest of Technical Papers (ISSCC) (2014)
7. Huang, G., Liu, Z., Weinberger, K.Q.: Densely connected convolutional networks. In: Conference on Computer Vision and Pattern Recognition (CVPR) (2017)
8. Jouppi, N.P., et al.: In-datacenter performance analysis of a tensor processing unit. In: ACM/IEEE 44th Annual International Symposium on Computer Architecture (ISCA) (2017)
9. Krizhevsky, A., Sutskever, I., Hinton, G.E.: ImageNet classification with deep convolutional neural networks. In: Advances in Neural Information Processing Systems (NIPS) (2012)
10. Kung, H.T.: Why systolic architectures? Computer **15**, 37–46 (1982)
11. Mead, C., Conway, L.: Introduction to VLSI Systems. Addison-Wesley, Boston (1980)
12. Samajdar, A., Zhu, Y., Whatmough, P., Mattina, M., Krishna, T.: Scale-sim: systolic CNN accelerator. arXiv preprint (2018)
13. Shao, Y.S., Reagen, B., Wei, G.Y., Brooks, D.: Aladdin: a pre-RTL, power-performance accelerator simulator enabling large design space exploration of customized architectures. In: ACM SIGARCH Computer Architecture News (2014)
14. Simonyan, K., Zisserman, A.: Very deep convolutional networks for large-scale image recognition (2015)
15. Spafford, K.L., Vetter, J.S.: Aspen: a domain specific language for performance modeling. In: Proceedings of the International Conference on High Performance Computing, Networking, Storage and Analysis (SC) (2012)
16. Tine, B., Elsabbagh, F., Seyong, L., Vetter, J., Kim, H.: Cash: a single-source hardware-software codesign framework for rapid prototyping. In: ACM/SIGDA International Symposium on Field-Programmable Gate Arrays (2020)
17. Xie, S., Girshick, R., Dollár, P., Tu, Z., He, K.: Aggregated residual transformations for deep neural networks. In: Conference on Computer Vision and Pattern Recognition (CVPR) (2017)
18. Yang, X., et al.: Interstellar: using Halide's scheduling language to analyze DNN accelerators (2020)

ITEM 2020: Methods

When Size Matters: Markov Blanket with Limited Bit Depth Conditional Mutual Information

Laura Morán-Fernández[1]([ID]), Eva Blanco-Mallo[1][ID], Konstantinos Sechidis[2][ID], Amparo Alonso-Betanzos[1][ID], and Verónica Bolón-Canedo[1][ID]

[1] CITIC, Universidade da Coruña, A Coruña, Spain
{laura.moranf,eva.blanco,ciamparo,vbolon}@udc.es
[2] School of Computer Science, University of Manchester, Manchester, UK
konstantinos.sechidis@manchester.ac.uk

Abstract. Due to the proliferation of mobile computing and Internet of Things devices, there is an urgent need to push the machine learning frontiers to the network edge so as to fully unleash the potential of the edge big data. Since feature selection becomes a fundamental step in the data analysis process, the need to perform this preprocessing task in a reduced precision environment arises as well. To achieve this, limited bit depth conditioned mutual information is proposed within a Markov Blanket procedure. This work also shows the process of generating approximate tables and obtaining the values required to test the independence of the variables involved in the algorithm. Finally, it compares the results obtained during the whole process, from preprocessing to classification, using different numbers of bits.

Keywords: Conditional mutual information · Markov blanket · Feature selection · Data analysis · Internet of Things · Edge computing

1 Introduction

Internet of things (IoT) devices continuously generate zettabytes of data, which must be fed to a machine learning system to analyze information and make decisions. However, limitations in the computational capabilities of portable embedded systems—small memories and limited computing power—inhibit the

This research has been financially supported in part by the Spanish Ministerio de Economía y Competitividad (research project TIN2015-65069-C2-1-R), by European Union FEDER funds and by the Consellería de Industria of the Xunta de Galicia (research project GRC2014 /035). CITIC as a Research Centre of the Galician University System is financed by the Conselleria de Education, Universidades e Formación Profesinal (Xunta de Galicia) through the ERDF (80%), Operational Programme ERDF Galicia 2014–2020 and the remaining 20% by the Secretaria Xeral de Universidades (Ref. ED431G 2019/01). Project supported by a 2018 Leonardo Grant for Researchers and Cultural Creators, BBVA Foundation.

© Springer Nature Switzerland AG 2020
J. Gama et al. (Eds.): ITEM 2020/IoT Streams 2020, CCIS 1325, pp. 243–255, 2020.
https://doi.org/10.1007/978-3-030-66770-2_18

implementation of most of the current machine learning algorithms on them. To meet this demand, a new computing paradigm, Edge Computing [16], has emerged. Until recently, these millions of devices that conform the IoT just recorded data, and send them to the cloud or a computer center where there were processed to obtain information and knowledge from that data. Edge computing aims at changing this passive situation and improving efficiency by allowing the nodes of the network or the very own devices to analyze the generated data. In this way, besides avoiding unnecessary network traffic, this paradigm allows to obtain real-time process knowledge. There are also factors that will make this type of paradigm even easier in the future: the increasingly reduced cost of devices and sensors joins the increasing power of even modest devices. There are also industrial needs that contribute to betting on Edge Computing: in certain environments the only way to further optimize processes is to try to avoid communication with the cloud as much as possible. This allows to reduce latencies, consume less bandwidths—it is not necessary to send all the data to the cloud at all the times—and immediately access analysis and evaluation of the state of all those sensors and devices. Besides, there is another interesting advantage: security. The less data is in a cloud environment, the less vulnerable is this environment if it is compromised. Of course, the security in those "micro data centers" should be taken care of properly. However, this does not mean at all that Cloud Computing environments disappear: both trends might contribute providing more computing options to the organizations, identifying needs and costs, and adopting the best solution. For example, Edge computing is more appropriate when speed and low latency are required while if remarkable computing power is needed Cloud computing will be preferred.

Recent research trends show that much effort is being put into accelerating and compressing neural networks, focusing on both inference and training [14]. Several papers have attempted this approach through quantization, the process of reducing arithmetic complexity by decreasing the number of bits required to represent each weight. In relation to inference accuracy, many studies have shown that we can achieve the same results with reduced precision of weights and activations [6,7,10]. Regarding learning, Hubara et al. [8] introduced a method to train Quantized Neural Networks using extremely low precision and runtime activations, reaching an accuracy comparable to networks trained using 32 bits. The research of Yu et al. [20] presents a method of quantification with mixed data structure and proposes a hardware accelerator. This allows them to reduce the number of bits needed to represent neural networks from 32 to 5, also without affecting their accuracy. Finally, the work of Gupta et al. [6] shows that it is possible to train deep networks using a 16-bit fixed-point representation and stochastic rounding. With regard to feature selection—most of the times a mandatory preprocessing step in machine learning , we presented in [12] a limited bit depth mutual information that can be applicable to any feature selection method that uses internally the mutual information measure. Thus, with the aim of extending this approach to other feature selection methods, in this work we consider the information theoretic measure of conditional mutual information with reduced precision parameters. Therefore, we are able to provide a limited bit depth conditional mutual information, and—through Markov

Blanket—experimentally achieve classification performances close, and even better, to those of 64-bit representations for several real and synthetic datasets.

The remainder of this paper is organized as follows. Section 2 provides the background of conditional mutual information and Markov Blanket. Section 3 presents our limited bit depth conditional mutual information approach. Section 4 provides and discusses an experimental study over several real and synthetic datasets. Finally, Sect. 5 contains our concluding remarks and proposals for future research.

2   Background

There are strong links between structure learning algorithms and feature selection algorithms. This is due to the properties of Markov Blankets. As a Markov Blanket is the set of nodes which make the target node independent from the rest of the graph, it is also the set of features required for optimal prediction of that target node. Thus, a structure learning algorithm can be thought of as a global feature selection algorithm, which learns the features required to predict each node in turn. The first work about the optimality of the Markov blanket in the context of feature selection was published by Koller and Sahami [9].

2.1   Conditional Mutual Information

There is one commonly used concept in Information Theory, the Conditional Mutual Information (CMI) between two variables, conditioned on a third. The conditional mutual information measures the dependency between two variables when the state of a third is known, and is defined in terms of an expected KL-Divergence as follows,

$$I(X;Y|Z) = H(X|Z) - H(X|YZ)$$

$$= \sum_{z \in Z} p(z) \sum_{x \in X} \sum_{y \in Y} p(xy|z) log \frac{p(xy|z)}{p(x|z)p(y|z)} \quad (1)$$

Unlike the conditional entropy, the conditional mutual information can be larger than the unconditioned mutual information. This is due to a *positive interaction* between the variables, where the dependency between two variables is increased by the knowledge of the state of a third. The conditional mutual information is zero when the two variables are independent, conditioned on the presence of the third variable. The maximal value of the conditional mutual information is the minimum of the two conditional entropies $H(X|Z)$ and $H(Y|Z)$, again achieved when the knowledge of one variable (and the conditioning variable) allows perfect prediction of the state of the other.

In order to estimate CMI we need the estimated distributions $\hat{p}(xy|z)$, $\hat{p}(x|z)$ and $\hat{p}(y|z)$. The probability of any particular event $p(X = x)$ is estimated by maximum likelihood, the frequency of occurrence of an event $X = x$ divided by the total number of events.

2.2   Markov Blanket Discovery Algorithm

The Markov Blanket (MB) of the target Y is a set of features X_{MB} with the property $Y \perp\!\!\!\perp Z | X_{MB}$ for every $Z \subseteq X \setminus X_{MB}$ [15]. A set is called Markov boundary if it is a minimal Markov Blanket, i.e. none of its subsets is a Markov Blanket. In probabilistic graphical models terminology, the target variable Y becomes conditionally independent from the rest of the graph $X \setminus X_{MB}$ given its MB X_{MB}.

2.2.1. Incremental Association Markov Blanket (IAMB)

The first theoretically sound algorithm for Markov blanket discovery was the Grow-Shrink (GS) [11]. This adopted the two stage structure which is common to many local learning algorithms, first growing the candidate Markov Blanket by adding new features until all remaining unselected are conditionally independent of the target, then shrinking the candidate Markov Blanket to remove any false positives which may have been selected. The IAMB algorithm [17], which can be seen in Algorithm 1, is a refinement of the GS algorithm. Many measures of association have been used to decide which feature will be added to the candidate Markov Blanket during the growing phase (lines 1–4 in Algorithm 1), the main one being the conditional mutual information. But in [19], the use of the *significance of the conditional test of independence* was suggested, since it is more appropriate in statistical terms than the raw conditional mutual information value. This conditional test of independence (lines 1–5 and 9 in Algorithm 1) plays a crucial role. Besides, to choose the most strongly related feature in Line 4, the p-values for the conditional tests are evaluated and the feature with the smaller one is selected.

Algorithm 1: IAMB

Input: Target Y, features $X = X_1, ..., X_d$, significance level α
Output: Markov Blanket: X_{MB}
1 Phase I: forward - growing
2 $X_{CMB} = \emptyset$
3 **while** X_{CMB} *has changed* **do**
4   Find $X \in X \setminus X_{CMB}$ most strongly related with Y given X_{CMB}
5   **if** $X \not\perp\!\!\!\perp Y | X_{CMB}$ *using significance level* α **then**
6   Add X to X_{CMB}

7 Phase II: backward - shrinkage
8 **foreach** $X \in X_{CMB}$ **do**
9   **if** $X \perp\!\!\!\perp Y | X_{CMB} \setminus X$ *using significance level* α **then**
10   Remove X from X_{CMB}

2.2.2. Testing Conditional Independence in Categorical Data

IAMB needs to test the conditional independence of X and Y given a subset of features Z, where in Line 5 $Z = X_{CMB}$ while in Line 9 $Z = X_{CMB} \setminus X$. In fully observed categorical data we can use the G-test, a generalised likelihood ratio test, where the test statistic can be calculated from sample data counts arranged in a contingency table.

G-statistic: We denote by $O_{x,y,z}$ the observed count of the number of times the random variable X takes on the value x from its alphabet $\mathcal{X}$, Y takes on $y \in \mathcal{Y}$ and Z takes on $z \in \mathcal{Z}$, where z is a vector of values when we condition on more than one variable. Besides, we denote by $O_{x,...z}, O_{.,y,z}$ and $O_{.,.,z}$ the marginal counts. The estimated expected frequency of (x, y, z) assuming X, Y are conditional independent given Z, is given by $E_{x,y,z} = \frac{O_{x,.,z}O_{.,y,z}}{O_{.,.,z}} = \hat{p}(x|z)\hat{p}(y|z)O_{.,.,z}$. To calculate the G-statistic we use the following formula:

$$\hat{G} - statistic = 2 \sum_{x,y,z} O_{x,y,x} ln \frac{O_{x,y,z}}{E_{x,y,z}} = 2 \sum_{x,y,z} ln \frac{O_{.,.,z}O_{x,y,z}}{O_{x,.,z}O_{.,y,z}}$$

$$= 2N \sum_{x,y,z} \hat{p}(x,y,z) ln \frac{x,\hat{y}|z}{\hat{p}(x|z)\hat{p}(y|z)} = 2N\hat{I}(X;Y|Z) \quad (2)$$

where $\hat{I}(X;Y|Z)$ is the maximum likelihood estimator of the conditional mutual information between X and Y given Z [5].

Hypothesis Testing Procedure: Under the null hypothesis that X and Y are statistically independent given Z, the G-statistic is known to be asymptotically $\mathcal{X}^2$-distributed, with $v = (|X| - 1)(|Y| - 1)|Z|$ degrees of freedom [1]. Knowing that and using Eq. 2 we can calculate the $p_{X,Y|Y}$ value as $1 - F(\hat{G})$, where F is the CDF of the $\mathcal{X}^2$-distribution and $\hat{G}$ the observed value of the G-statistic. The p-value represents the probability of obtaining a test statistic equal or more extreme than the observed one, given that the null hypothesis holds. After calculating this value, we check to see whether it exceeds a significance level α. If $p_{x,y,z} \leq \alpha$, we reject the null hypothesis, otherwise we fail to reject it. This is the procedure followed to take the decision in Lines 5 and 9 of the IAMB Algorithm 1. Besides, to select the most strongly related feature in Line 4, we evaluate p-values and the feature with the smaller one is chosen.

3 Limited Bit Depth Conditional Mutual Information

The main goal of feature selection is to select a small subset of features that carries as much information as possible. One of the most common measures to catch dependencies between features in machine learning is the conditional mutual information. As said above, to calculate conditional mutual information we need to estimate the probability distributions. Internally, it counts the occurrences of values within a particular group (i.e. its frequency). Thus, based on previous works for approximately computing probabilities [13,18], we investigate CMI with limited number of bits by considering this measure with reduced precision counters. To perform the limited bit depth approach, we followed a fixed-point representation instead of the 64-bit resolution used typically by the standard hardware platforms. Fixed-point numbers are characterized by the number of integer bits bi and the number of fractional bits bf. The motivation to move to fixed-point arithmetic is two-fold: (i) these bit representation compute units are typically faster and consume far less hardware resources and power than the conventional floating-point computations and (ii) low-precision data representation reduces the memory footprint, enabling larger models to fit within the given memory capacity and lowering the bandwidth requirements.

CMI parameters are typically represented in the logarithm domain. For the reduced precision parameters, we computed the number of occurrences of an event and use a lookup table to determine the logarithm of the probability of a particular event. The lookup table is indexed in terms of number of occurrences of an event (individual counters) and the total number of events (total counter) and stores values for the logarithms in the desired reduced precision representation. To limit the maximum size of the lookup table and the bit-width required for the counters, we assumed some maximum integer number M. The lookup table L is pre-computed such that:

$$L(i,j) = \left[\frac{ln(i/j)}{q}\right]_R \cdot q \tag{3}$$

where $[\cdot]_R$ denotes rounding to the closest integer, q is the quantization interval of the desired fixed-point representation (2^{-bf}), $ln(\cdot)$ denotes the natural logarithm, and where the counters i and j are in the range $\{0, ..., M-1\}$. To ensure that the counters stay in range, the algorithm identifies counters that reach their maximum value M, and halfs these counters.

Finally, in order to use this reduced approach on the conditional mutual information measure, we apply the product and quotient rules for logarithms on Eq. (1), resulting in:

$$I(X;Y|Z) = \sum_{z \in Z} p(z) \sum_{x \in X} \sum_{y \in Y} p(xy|z)(log(p(xy|z))$$

$$- (log(p(x|z)) + log(p(y|z)))) \tag{4}$$

3.1   Empirical Study

To evaluate the performance of the reduced precision conditional mutual information against the full version using a 64-bit representation, we generated synthetic data. In order to test independence, we apply the G-test with a significance level of $\alpha = 0.05$ to test the assertion $X \perp\!\!\!\perp Y|Z$. To sample data under this conditional independence, we used a fork model $X < -Z- > Y$. Firstly, we randomly sampled random variable Z, and then we generated X and Y. Since the null hypothesis ($X \perp\!\!\!\perp Y|Z$) is true, we expect a false positive rate (FPR) of 5% [15]. Let's say we would like $|X| = 2$, $|Y| = 2$ and $|Z| = 10$ and generate 10,000 samples.

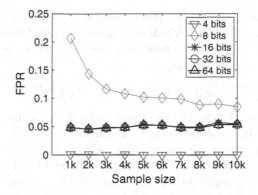

Fig. 1. Type-I error changing as a function of number of samples, for fixed $\alpha = 0.05$.

As can be seen in Fig. 1 for different sample sizes, this is verified (over 5,000 repeats) for the reduced precision approaches using 32 and 16 bits and the 64-bit full version. The slight fluctuation comes from the limited sample size. Besides, we can see that the 8-bit approach does not achieve the desired Type-I error (5%), but it is consistent since it converges to the desired value as the sample size increases. Otherwise, the 4-bit approach shows very low false negative rates as it obtains underestimated values of the conditional mutual information. This bit representation takes negatives values in 36% of the iterations, which could not be possible since, due to the non-negativity property of the conditional mutual information, it is always true that $I(X; Y|Z) \geq 0$.

In light of the results obtained, we proceed to use our limited bit depth conditional mutual information approach within a more sophisticated method. In this work, we have chosen to apply it into a Markov Blanket procedure. Despite the poor results using 4 bits, we have kept this approach in order to see how it affects the accuracy of the IAMB algorithm.

3.2 IAMB with Limited Bit Depth CMI: Approximation of the P-Value

As detailed above, the IAMB algorithm needs to test the conditional independence of X and Y given a subset of features Z, and for that we can use the G-test. The hypothesis testing procedure needs a $\hat{p} - value$ that can be calculated as $1 - F(\hat{G})$, where F is the CDF of the $\mathcal{X}^2$-distribution with $v = (|X|-1)(|Y|-1)|Z|$ degrees of freedom and $\hat{G}$ the observed value of the G-statistic. By using a small number of bits, a lot of accuracy is lost in obtaining this result as computations are made. Therefore, instead of calculating the $\hat{p} - value$ each time is required, a table is used to approximate it, which once generated is stored in reduced precision. The table architecture is composed of a T matrix and two value vectors as indexes, G and V. Basically, it is necessary to have a set of values of $\hat{G}$ and v stored in the index vectors. Then the $F(G)$ of each V is obtained and stored in T, which will be used to approximate future samples. Therefore, the spectrum covered by these sets should be as representative as possible and their choice becomes a fundamental issue, which is explained in depth below. For a value of $\hat{G}$ observed with v degrees of freedom, the resulting $\hat{p} - value$ is obtained from the approximate table as follows:

$$\hat{p} - value(\hat{G}, v) = 1 - T(i, j)$$

where i is the index of the value of V whose distance is minimum at v and j is the index of the value of G whose distance is minimum at $\hat{G}$. As mentioned above, this is the value checked with a significance level α to carry out the conditional independence test required in lines 5 and 9 of the IAMB algorithm. All the procedures performed around this algorithm, both to generate the tables and to obtain the final results presented in this paper, were carried out using $\alpha = 0.05$. However, note that this approach could be adapted to any specific alpha value, as well as to any set of datasets and function f determined to solve any ad-hoc problem.

To get the subsets of $\hat{G}$ and v from which to build the approximate table, 60 real datasets with very different dimensional feature vectors were used, 70% to generate the table and 30% to test it. All the data involved in this research are freely available online, accessible through public databases [3]. Both the number of instances and the number of features of the datasets used have a broad range, in particular in the intervals [21, 67557] and [8, 12533] respectively, facing from binary to multi-class classification problems with 15 possible outputs. Therefore, a wide variety of data is involved, both in depth and in quantity. The first step

---

Algorithm 2: Algorithm to get the most relevant values

Input: List of values X and a maximum result size m
Output: Set of target values $edges$

1   $U, C = unique(X)$;
2   **if** $|U| < m$ **then**
3 | $edges \leftarrow U$;
4   **else**
5      $s = \sum(C)/m$;
6   **while** $U \neq []$ **do**
7   **if** $\sum(C) \geq s$ **then**
8              $U', C' = U_i C_i | \sum C_i \leq s$;
9   **if** $U' \neq []$ **then**
10                  $edges \leftarrow u'_j | c'_j = max(C')$;
11                  $U, C = U_i C_i | \sum C_i > s$;
12   **else**
13                  $edges \leftarrow u'_j | j = 1$;
14                  $U, C = U_i C_i | \sum i > 1$;
15   **else**
16              $U = []$;

17 **return** $edges$

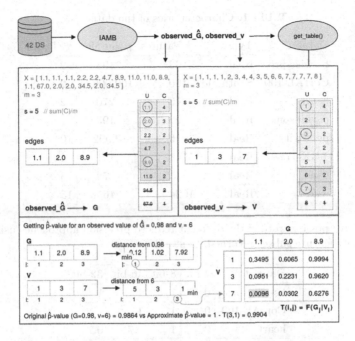

Fig. 2. Example of value selection, generation and use of approximate table to obtain the $\hat{p} - value$.

was to extract all the observed values of $\hat{G}$ and degrees of freedom v needed to obtain the required $\hat{p} - values$ when processing each of the selected datasets with the IAMB algorithm. Then, the most representative values of each subset are selected following Algorithm 2, exemplified in Fig. 2. This process receives a list of values, $X = \{x_1, ..., x_x\}$ and a maximum size of output elements, m. First, the unique set of X values, $U = \{u_1, ..., u_n\}$, and its associated frequency, $C = \{c_1, ..., c_n\}$, are computed. If the total number of unique elements is less than or equal to m, the final output will be U. Otherwise, an approximate size is calculated to group the U elements according to their frequency, specifically by dividing the total of X elements by m. Then, the U elements are iteratively extracted as long as their accumulated sum is less than or equal to the approximate size, and the one with the highest frequency of each extraction is selected as part of the output. When the accumulated sum of the final U elements is less than the approximate size or there are no more elements left, the process ends.

4   Experimental Results: Application in Markov Blanket

Our limited bit depth conditional mutual information can be applicable to any feature selection method that uses internally the CMI measure. In this work, we have chosen to do so within a Markov Blanket procedure. We have considered several synthetic [2,4]—which relevant features are already known—and real

Table 1. Characteristics of the datasets.

Dataset	Type	#features	#samples	#classes
bs-wisc-prog	Real	33	198	2
CorrAL-100	Synthetic	100	100,000	2
heart	Real	13	270	2
parkinsons	Real	22	195	2
pendigits	Real	16	10,992	10
TOX-171	Real	5748	171	4
wine	Real	13	178	3
yale	Real	1024	165	15

Table 2. True positive rate of the different reduced precision approaches using IAMB. For an empty feature subset returned, '-' stands.

Dataset	4-bit	8-bit	16-bit	32-bit
bs-wisc-prog	0	1	1	1
CorrAL-100	0	1	1	1
heart	0	1	0.7	0.7
parkinsons	0	0.5	1	1
pendigits	-	1	1	1
TOX-171	-	0.5	1	1
wine	-	1	1	1
yale	-	0	1	1

datasets [3]. Table 1 details the main characteristics of the chosen datasets. Experiments were executed in the Matlab2018a and Weka environments.

4.1   Quality of the Selected Features

To evaluate the similarity between the selected features obtained by the reduced precision versions and the 64-bit IAMB algorithm, we show the true positive rate (TPR) for each dataset. The true positive rate measures the proportion of features that are correctly identified as such, using the full IAMB (64 bits) as the ideal feature subset. As can be seen in Table 2, in general, the reduced precision approaches using 16 and 32 bits selected the same features that the 64-bit version. Contrarily, and as expected by the results obtained in the empirical study (Sect. 3.1), the 4-bit approach was not able to select any of the features obtained by the 64-bit version. In fact, in 4 of the 8 datasets used in the experiments—marked on the table with a hyphen—, this reduced precision approach returned an empty feature set. For this reason, we eliminated this reduced precision size approach for the following experiments.

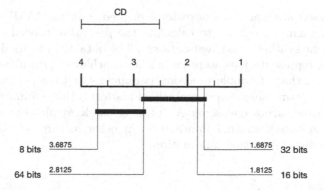

Fig. 3. Critical difference diagram showing the average ranks after applying IAMB on the three reduced precision approaches (8, 16 and 32 bits) and the full version (64 bits).

4.2 Classification Accuracy

After the feature selection process—through IAMB algorithm—, and in order to estimate whether the reduced precision might affect classification, a study using classifiers was carried out. At this point, it is necessary to clarify that including classifiers in our experiments is likely to obscure the experimental observations related to feature selection performance using a limited number of bits, since classification methods include their own assumptions and particularities. Therefore, in these experiments, we used a simple nearest neighbor algorithm (with number of neighbors $k = 3$) as classifier since it makes few assumptions about the data, and we also avoid the need for parameter tuning. To estimate the error rate we computed a 3×5-fold cross validation, including both feature selection and classification steps in a single cross-validation loop.

To explore the statistical significance of our classification results, we analyzed the ranks of the reduced precision approaches by using a Friedman test with the Nemenyi post-hoc test. Figure 3 presents the critical difference diagrams where groups of methods that are not significantly different (at $\alpha = 0.10$) are connected. As can be seen, 32 and 16 bits perform better but with no statistical significance over the 64-bit approach. This could be happening because, in addition to the features selected by the 64-bit IAMB algorithm, both 16- and 32-bit IAMB approaches add features to the final set that can lead to a better performance. However, it is important to notice that deriving the Markov Blanket does not guarantee optimality in terms of classification accuracy and this is an issue that needs further study.

5 Conclusions

In this work we have proposed conditional mutual information using reduced precision parameters within a Markov Blanket procedure. To test the adequacy of the proposed approach, we have implemented it in the IAMB algorithm—using an approximate scheme to calculate the $\hat{p} - value$ needed—, applied to a suite of eight synthetic and real datasets. The obtained results demonstrated that low bit representations were sufficient to achieve performances close, or even better, to that of double precision parameters and thus opening the door for the use of feature selection in embedded platforms that minimize the energy consumption and carbon emissions. As future research, we plan to use our limited bit depth conditional mutual information in other feature selection methods based on conditional mutual information.

References

1. Agresti, A., Kateri, M.: Categorical Data Analysis. Springer, Heidelberg (2011). https://doi.org/10.1007/978-3-642-04898-2_161
2. Arizona State University: Feature selection datasets. http://featureselection.asu.edu/datasets.php. Accessed March 2020
3. Bache, K., Linchman, M.: UCI machine learning repository. University of California, Irvine, School of Information and Computer Sciences. http://archive.ics.uci.edu/ml/. Accessed March 2020
4. Bolón-Canedo, V., Sánchez-Maroño, N., Alonso-Betanzos, A.: A review of feature selection methods on synthetic data. Knowl. Inf. Syst. **34**(3), 483–519 (2013)
5. Cover, T.M., Thomas, J.A.: Elements of Information Theory. John Wiley, Hoboken (2012)
6. Gupta, S., Agrawal, A., Gopalakrishnan, K., Narayanan, P.: Deep learning with limited numerical precision. In: Proceedings of the 32nd International Conference on Machine Learning (ICML-15), pp. 1737–1746 (2015)
7. Gysel, P., Motamedi, M., Ghiasi, S.: Hardware-oriented approximation of convolutional neural networks. arXiv preprint arXiv:1604.03168 (2016)
8. Hubara, I., Courbariaux, M., Soudry, D., El-Yaniv, R., Bengio, Y.: Quantized neural networks: training neural networks with low precision weights and activations. J. Mach. Learn. Res. **18**(1), 6869–6898 (2017)
9. Koller, D., Sahami, M.: Toward optimal feature selection. Technical report Stanford InfoLab (1996)
10. Lin, D., Talathi, S., Annapureddy, S.: Fixed point quantization of deep convolutional networks. In: International Conference on Machine Learning, pp. 2849–2858 (2016)
11. Margaritis, D., Thrun, S.: Bayesian network induction via local neighborhoods. In: Advances in Neural Information Processing Systems, pp. 505–511 (2000)
12. Morán-Fernández, L., Bolón-Canedo, V., Alonso-Betanzos, A.: Feature selection with limited bit depth mutual information for embedded systems. Multi. Digit. Publishing Inst. Proc. **2**(18), 1187 (2018)
13. Morán-Fernández, L., Sechidis, K., Bolón-Canedo, V., Alonso-Betanzos, A., Brown, G.: Feature selection with limited bit depth mutual information for portable embedded systems. Knowl. Based Syst. **197**, 105885 (2020)
14. Murshed, M., Murphy, C., Hou, D., Khan, N., Ananthanarayanan, G., Hussain, F.: Machine learning at the network edge: A survey. arxiv 2019. arXiv preprint arXiv:1908.00080

15. Sechidis, K., Brown, G.: Markov blanket discovery in positive-unlabelled and semi-supervised data. In: Appice, A., Rodrigues, P.P., Santos Costa, V., Soares, C., Gama, J., Jorge, A. (eds.) ECML PKDD 2015. LNCS (LNAI), vol. 9284, pp. 351–366. Springer, Cham (2015). https://doi.org/10.1007/978-3-319-23528-8_22

16. Shi, W., Cao, J., Zhang, Q., Li, Y., Xu, L.: Edge computing: vision and challenges. IEEE Internet Things J. **3**(5), 637–646 (2016)

17. Tsamardinos, I., Aliferis, C.F.: Towards principled feature selection: relevancy, filters and wrappers. In: AISTATS (2003)

18. Tschiatschek, S., Pernkopf, F.: Parameter learning of Bayesian network classifiers under computational constraints. In: Appice, A., Rodrigues, P.P., Santos Costa, V., Soares, C., Gama, J., Jorge, A. (eds.) ECML PKDD 2015. LNCS (LNAI), vol. 9284, pp. 86–101. Springer, Cham (2015). https://doi.org/10.1007/978-3-319-23528-8_6

19. Yaramakala, S., Margaritis, D.: Speculative Markov blanket discovery for optimal feature selection. In: Fifth IEEE International Conference on Data Mining (ICDM 2005), p. 4 IEEE (2005)

20. Yu, Y., Zhi, T., Zhou, X., Liu, S., Chen, Y., Cheng, S.: Bshift: a low cost deep neural networks accelerator. Int. J. Parallel Programm. **47**(3), 360–372 (2019)

Time to Learn: Temporal Accelerators as an Embedded Deep Neural Network Platform

Christopher Cichiwskyj[✉], Chao Qian, and Gregor Schiele

University of Duisburg-Essen, Bismarckstr. 90, 47057 Duisburg, Germany
{christopher.cichiwskyj,chao.qian,gregor.schiele}@uni-due.de

Abstract. Embedded Field-Programmable Gate Arrays (FPGAs) provide an efficient and flexible hardware platform to deploy highly optimised Deep Neural Network (DNN) accelerators. However, the limited area of embedded FPGAs restricts the degree of complexity of a DNN accelerator that can be deployed on them. Commonly an accelerator's complexity is reduced to fit smaller FPGAs, often at the cost of significant redesign overhead. In this paper we present an alternative to this, which we call *Temporal Accelerators*. The main idea is to split an accelerator into smaller components, which are then executed by an FPGA sequentially. To do so, the FPGA is reconfigured multiple times during the execution of the accelerator. With this idea, we increase the available area of the FPGA 'over time'. We show that modern FPGAs can reconfigure efficiently enough to achieve equally fast and energy efficient accelerators while using more cost efficient FPGAs. We develop and evaluate a Temporal Accelerator implementing an 1D Convolution Neural Network for detecting anomalies in ECG heart data. Our accelerator is deployed on a Xilinx Spartan 7 XC7S15. We compare it to a conventional implementation on the larger Xilinx Spartan 7 XC7S25. Our solution requires 9.06% less time to execute and uses 12.81% less energy while using an FPGA that is 35% cheaper.

Keywords: DNN · CNN · FPGA · Embedded · Temporal accelerator · IoT

1 Introduction

Field Programmable Gate Arrays (FPGAs) have emerged as a promising hardware platform for application specific, highly optimised accelerators on embedded devices [1]. However, cheap low-power FPGAs only contain a limited amount of resources, typically referred to as available area, to instantiate accelerator circuitry. If the accelerator is too complex, then it needs a bigger, more costly and energy hungry FPGA.

The authors acknowledge the financial support by the Federal Ministry of Education and Research of Germany in the KI-Sprung LUTNet project (project number 16ES1125) as well as the KI-LiveS project (project number 895 01IS19068A).

© Springer Nature Switzerland AG 2020
J. Gama et al. (Eds.): ITEM 2020/IoT Streams 2020, CCIS 1325, pp. 256–267, 2020.
https://doi.org/10.1007/978-3-030-66770-2_19

This is often the case for Deep Neural Network (DNN) accelerators. Therefore, a common approach to deploy such solutions on smaller FPGAs is to reduce the complexity of the accelerator, e.g. through binarisation or pruning [2]. This reduces the required area on an FPGA and potentially allows the developer to use a smaller FPGA.

In this paper, we present an alternative approach to supporting DNNs on small, embedded FPGAs by "increasing" the available area over time. We call this concept *Temporal Accelerators*. By making use of modern SRAM-based FPGAs' low overhead reconfiguration capabilities, we split a given DNN accelerator into smaller components, that each fit on a smaller FPGA, and execute each component sequentially. By deploying this split design, Temporal Accelerators can execute equally powerful and accurate accelerators on more energy-efficient and cheaper FPGAs, without the need to modify the DNN architecture.

Intuition dictates that the continuous reconfiguration of an FPGA should produce an overhead significant enough for this concept to not be viable. We show in this work, that this is no longer true with modern FPGAs. Instead, the shorter reconfiguration time of smaller FPGAs allows for multiple reconfigurations before their energy consumption becomes as high as that of larger counterparts. We demonstrate the potential of Temporal Accelerators by extending our previous work on a 1D Convolution Neural Network (CNN) that detects anomalies in ECG heart data in real time [1]. We compare the performance of a single configuration 1D-CNN designed for the Xilinx Spartan 7 XC7S25 with a Temporal Accelerator implementation of the same CNN designed for a Spartan 7 XC7S15.

The remainder of this paper is structured as follows: In Sect. 2 we present an overview of current related work. We then present in Sect. 3 the concept of Temporal Accelerators. Section 4 describes how the Temporal Accelerator concept is applied to the original CNN design. We evaluate both CNN implementations in Sect. 5 and conclude our work in Sect. 6.

2   Related Work

Embedded FPGAs only have a limited available area. Thus, many optimisation techniques aim to minimise the required area to instantiate DNN accelerators on them. A common approach for optimisation is to reduce the complexity of a DNN by quantising or even binarising it partially or fully [2–4], thus reducing memory and computational demands. Additionally, the underlying mathematical model of a DNN can be simplified, e.g. by using an XNOR-network to reduce the complexity of computations in the convolutional layers of a CNN [5] or by using the FPGA's native lookup-tables as inference operators [6].

Pruning is another, often used optimisation technique [2,7]. The idea is to remove unnecessary neuron inputs. Optimal brain damage (OBD) tries to take into account the effect of this on the learning process [8]. Energy aware pruning [9] takes the resulting energy consumption into account when making pruning decisions and can reduce the energy consumption of a CNN by 3.7× with less than 1% top-5 accuracy loss. While reducing the required area for implementing DNNs, they all come at the risk of losing inference accuracy and require a significant redesign of underlying neural network structures. In contrast to that, our approach aims to *increase* the available FPGA area, allowing to deploy DNNs without reduced accuracy.

Instead of using FPGAs, specialised neural processing units (NPUs) like Google's tensor processor unit [10] aim to speed up matrix multiplication of internal DNN computations. CONV-SRAM [11] integrates dot product calculations into an SRAM-component. This reduces data transfers and achieves similar or better energy efficiency compared to conventional full-digital implementations with small bit widths. Although extremly performant, NPUs require an additional hardware component to be included into embedded devices and are less flexible than FPGAs to take over other tasks.

While the flexibility of FPGAs to implement different circuits through reconfiguration is often cited as a major advantage, it is often reduced to firmware-like updating. To the best of our knowledge, we are the first to propose using multiple runtime reconfigurations that enables DNNs *on smaller, embedded FPGAs*. A similar idea is used in fpgaConvNet [12], incorporating reconfigurations into the system design. However, as it aims to improve the performance of each CNN component the introduced overhead is only amortised when processing large enough data sets. It does not consider deployment on FPGAs of different size.

3   Temporal Accelerators

As we target embedded applications with our work, we assume for the remainder of this paper that the FPGA operates within a duty cycle-like application behaviour. The FPGA is put regularly into a deep sleep mode or turned off completely to conserve energy. As such it always has to reconfigure at least once when waking up to perform a task. Even though this introduces additional reconfiguration overhead, the lower sleep mode power consumption combined with a faster accelerator execution on the FPGA leads to a more energy efficient system than performing the same tasks on the MCU alone [13].

Commonly, when designing accelerators, all components of that circuit are included into a single FPGA configuration (described by a bit file), limiting the maximum size of the design to $1\times$ the available area of a targeted FPGA. While not applicable to all designs, many components within such an accelerator are either executed sequentially e.g. due to data dependencies, or in parallel to each other to increase the performance. However, in both cases these components are comparatively isolated and communicate by exchanging data. By modelling accelerators in such a way that they can be split across multiple FPGA bit files, we can increase the amount of available area "over time". This enables very resource constrained FPGAs to execute much more complex accelerators. We refer to this concept as *Temporal Accelerators*.

3.1 Splitting an Accelerator

Given a set of subcomponents of an accelerator, where each can fit into a bit file for a target FPGA, we can execute each of these components sequentially on the FPGA by reconfiguring it several times, passing intermediate data between these components. We model the structure in a Temporal Accelerator as a Directed Acyclic Graph similar to [12], often also referred to as a Task Graph [14,15]. An example of such a Task Graph can be seen in Fig. 1.

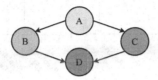

Fig. 1. A Temporal Accelerator modelled as a Task Graph.

Each subcomponent is a single node within the Task Graph. Edges define data dependencies between the different components. As an example, the subcomponents B and C require for their execution the intermediate result from subcomponent A. While the Task Graph can be arbitrarily complex in its structure, due to our device only containing a single FPGA, the execution of subcomponents happens sequentially, as long as they satisfy all data dependencies. For simplicity we assume that the structure of the Task Graph remains static during its execution. Therefore finding an optimal execution sequence can be done at design time.

As the Temporal Accelerator is meant as an alternative way to support DNNs on small FPGAs, the split up of an accelerator is the only applied change to the internal structure. This means that all internal circuitry of an accelerator remains unchanged to reduce redevelopment overhead.

3.2 Execution and Intermediate Results

Another important aspect of executing a Temporal Accelerator stems from the general internal structure of FPGAs. These cannot retain any intermediate data within registers, flip-flops or BRAM between reconfigurations. Intermediate results, that need to be passed between subcomponents, have to be transmitted off the FPGA before reconfiguration and transmitted back onto the FPGA after reconfiguration.

With an external memory component the FPGA can manage the offloading as part of each subcomponent configuration. The necessary management logic, however, increases the required FPGA area for each subcomponent, thus reducing the available area for the actual accelerator parts [16].

By interconnecting an MCU with the FPGA, the MCU is able to perform the necessary management and buffer intermediate results more efficiently. At the same time it frees resources on the FPGA for the accelerator [13,16,17]. Additionally, certain tasks within an accelerator are potentially executed more efficiently on a classical MCU. This can further reduce the overall energy consumption of accelerators. While not limited to such a device architecture, for the remainder of this paper we will assume this system architecture.

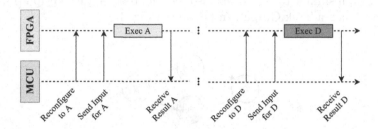

Fig. 2. Example execution of a Temporal Accelerator on the Elastic Node

Including the data offloading, an example execution of the Task Graph from Fig. 1 can be seen in the sequence diagram in Fig. 2. The execution is strictly sequential due to all components of the Task Graph being executed on a single FPGA. After reconfiguring to a subcomponent, the FPGA receives the initial or intermediate data from an MCU, executes the subcomponent and sends the intermediate result back to the MCU before the next reconfiguration begins. This process is repeated until all subcomponents have been executed. Finding an optimal split in the general case is a research question in itself and outside the scope of this paper.

3.3 Overhead of Executing a Temporal Accelerator

As mentioned in Sect. 1, intuition would dictate that using a Temporal Accelerator introduces significant overhead. This overhead manifests in two regards. Firstly, due to splitting up the circuit design into multiple subcomponents we require to reconfigure the FPGA each time we switch between subcomponents. Secondly, due to the FPGA's inability to store intermediate results between reconfigurations, we get additional overhead for transferring intermediate results between subcomponents. Together, these overheads could increase the execution time and energy consumption of a Temporal Accelerator so much, that it would be much better to execute the same logic on a larger FPGA.

This statement, however, does not take into account that the more resources are available on an FPGA the bigger its bit files are. A bit file is loaded by the FPGA and used to describe how it should configure itself to instantiate a specific circuit design. As the hardware interface used to load the bit file to an FPGA is generally identical within a chip family such as the Xilinx Spartan 7 Series [18], larger FPGAs, using the same clock speed and bus width for their reconfiguration hardware interface, take longer to reconfigure. This in return means that the fewer resources are available on an FPGA, the shorter the reconfiguration time [18] and the lower the FPGA's energy consumption per reconfiguration. We see this as the largest impact factor in making Temporal Accelerators a viable alternative for energy efficient and cheap embedded DNNs. We analyse and evaluate this in Sect. 5.

The overhead for offloading intermediate data is hard to estimate, because the data size is highly application dependent. Our initial results (see Sect. 5.2) however indicate that it is less significant than the reconfiguration overhead. Although it may become a bottleneck for applications with many intermediate results, in practice we expect other limitations becoming an issue earlier, such as the available internal memory of the MCU. We are currently investigating alternative system architectures, that include an additional dual-port SRAM component between MCU and FPGA to increase the system performance and mitigate the MCU's memory limitation. This is however still ongoing research.

4   CNN as a Temporal Accelerator

We previously developed a 1-dimensional CNN to detect anomalies in ECG heart monitoring data [1]. The CNN's architecture is shown in Fig. 3 and consists of four core components: Two convolutional layers, each including an activation and pooling layer, a global average layer and a fully connected layer. All CNN information, such as the network weights are stored in the same bit file and loaded during reconfiguration. These four layers are decoupled by buffering any intermediate data between them in the FPGA's DRAM. This data decoupling allows us to easily split the original accelerator design to implement it as a Temporal Accelerator. We used this CNN as a starting point for our work in this paper. To be able to cope with more complex problems, we increased the fixed-point precision to 40 bits with 24 fractional bits. The resulting CNN easily fits on the Xilinx Spartan 7 XC7S25.

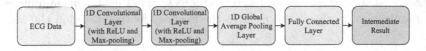

Fig. 3. A 1D CNN on FPGA for ECG analysis

Our goal is to develop a Temporal Accelerator for this CNN. As a first step we must select an appropriate FPGA as target platform. Its available area defines how much of an accelerator can be included in a single FPGA configuration. This also defines how many reconfigurations are required for the execution. Using an analytical model to estimate the energy cost per reconfiguration (see Sect. 5.1), we selected the XC7S15 with about 50% of the logic cells and 25% of the DSP slices of the XC7S25. Initial considerations on selecting the XC7S6, with a potentially lower energy cost per reconfiguration, were discarded as both the XC7S6 and XC7S15 use bit files of identical size [18] and initial experiments with both chips showed that the energy consumption during reconfiguration were near identical. In such a scenario the XC7S15 provides more resources for a very similar energy cost per reconfiguration (and nearly the same monetary cost) and is therefore preferable to use.

We then analysed the CNN's synthesis report, which stated, that this design would require 125% more DSP slices than available on the XC7S15. With this information we can determine the amount of required reconfigurations. By reconfiguring two times we can use twice as many DSP slices "over time". This allows us to fit all subcomponents of the CNN and necessary communication logic to load and offload the intermediate results on the XC7S15.

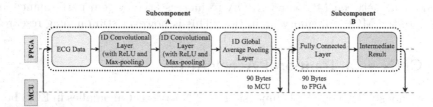

Fig. 4. CNN Split between Average Pooling Layer and the Fully Connected Layer

The next step is to define how to split the CNN. It is possible to split the original architecture between any of the layers in Fig. 3 due to the decoupled design. Yet, the amount of data that is passed between layers differs significantly. That determines how much data has to be transmitted between the MCU and the FPGA. The potential options are between the 1st and 2nd convolutional layer requiring 5580 bytes, between the 2nd convolutional layer and the average pooling layer requiring 2016 bytes or between the average pooling layer and fully connected layer requiring 90 bytes. We chose the third option and implemented that split as a Temporal Accelerator as seen in Fig. 4. This minimises the communication overhead and reduces the memory footprint within the MCU.

5   Evaluation

To demonstrate the potential of using Temporal Accelerators, we first evaluate how the reconfiguration energy cost differs across FPGAs from the Xilinx Spartan 7 chip family using an analytical model. We compare and verify it with experimental results on a Spartan 7 XC7S50. Afterwards, we evaluate the execution performance and energy efficiency of our Temporal Accelerator variant of a 1D-CNN for a Spartan XC7S15, as presented in Sect. 4, and compare it to the original single configuration CNN for the XC7S25.

5.1   Reconfiguration Overhead

Following our description in Sect. 3.3 the viability of Temporal Accelerators lies in the difference in energy cost per reconfiguration across differently sized FPGAs. This is dependent on the chip's power consumption and the time required to reconfigure. Differently sized FPGAs however show significant differences in their reconfiguration times. This is due to the differences in bit file size. To visualise this the bit file sizes for FPGAs of the Spartan 7 chip family can be seen in Table 1. As the hardware interface for reconfiguration is identical across all Spartan 7 chips [18], the bit file sizes are the main defining factor for the reconfiguration time.

Table 1. Bit file size (bits) comparison for FPGA from the Xilinx Spartan 7 chip family [18].

	XC7S15	XC7S25	XC7S50	XC7S75	XC7S100
Size (bits)	4310752	9934432	17536096	29494496	29494496

Based on this we created an analytical model following Xilinx's official documentation [18–22] to estimate the energy cost per reconfiguration for the Spartan 7 family. With the Spartan 7 chips we are limited to serial SPI-Flash based reconfiguration interfaces [23]. The results can be seen in Fig. 5(a). For readability's sake we restricted the figure to reconfigurations using 2-SPI running at 50 MHz. Other reconfiguration configurations behave accordingly across all chips.

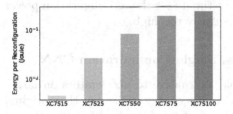

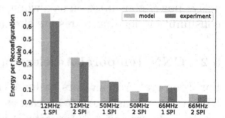

(a) Estimated energy cost per reconfiguration for different Xilinx Spartan 7 chips using a 2-SPI at 50 MHz (log scale)

(b) Comparison of analytical model estimations vs. experimental results on a Spartan 7 XC7S50

Fig. 5. Reconfiguration cost estimated by our analytical model and comparison to experimental results

Figure 5(a) shows significant differences in energy consumption between FPGAs. While XC7S75 and XC7S100 use the same bit file size the slight difference between them stem from the difference in chip power consumption [21] instead of reconfiguration time. Based on the reconfiguration cost alone, a smaller chip can reconfigure two or more times before it consumes as much energy as the next larger FPGA doing a single reconfiguration, with the exception of the XC7S75 to the XC7S100. The larger the gap between the FPGAs, the more reconfigurations the smaller chip can perform.

As these values are estimations based on manufacturer information, we tried to verify the analytical model by running experiments on our Elastic Node platform [13,16,17]. The Elastic Node platform includes an MCU interconnected with an embedded FPGA, following the system architecture described in Sect. 3.2. The current version of the Elastic Node supports various Spartan 7 chips.

We executed a number of reconfigurations of the XC7S50 and measured the power consumption and the required time. We compared different reconfiguration interface settings supported by the Elastic Node, namely a 1-SPI and 2-SPI hardware interface for reading in the XC7S50's bit file at various clock frequencies, and mirrored these in our analytical model. We then mirrored these settings and calculated the corresponding results using our analytical model. The results can be seen in Fig. 5(b).

Across all configurations we can see a slightly lower (approx. 5–16%) energy consumption than predicted by the model. While we were able to confirm that the reconfiguration timings match the documentation, the power consumption values of the analytical model differ from the experimental results. This is to be expected as we could not find accurate information on the power consumption during reconfiguration. Therefore, we had to estimate this power consumption. According to the Power Methodology Guide [22], an FPGA's power consumption during reconfiguration is "always lower then active power", referring with active power to the static and dynamic power consumption of the whole FPGA once it is fully configured and actively working. For this reason we used the higher active power consumption as a worst-case estimate for the reconfiguration power consumption, leading to results that are slightly too high.

5.2   CNN Temporal Accelerator vs. Single Configuration CNN

For Temporal Accelerators to be a viable alternative to accelerators on larger FPGAs, they must execute at least as fast and as energy efficient as their original single configuration counterparts. It is important to remember that the internal architecture of the CNN is identical in both designs. The only applied change lies in the split up of the original accelerator. We therefore evaluate the difference in execution overhead.

To evaluate this, we executed the Temporal Accelerator CNN (see Sect. 4) on an Elastic Node with a XC7S15. We compared its timings for the different execution steps with the execution of the original CNN design on an Elastic Node with a XC7S25. Both devices use identical reconfiguration settings of a 2-SPI interface running 50 MHz and both CNN variants are executed at 32 MHz. As stated in Sect. 3 we assume that in both setups the FPGA operates within a duty cycle like application, i.e. is regularly set into a deep sleep mode. Therefore, it has to reconfigure at least once on wake up. The result can be seen in Fig. 6(a). While the standard CNN only requires to perform one reconfiguration, one sending of input data, one execution and one receiving of result data, the Temporal Accelerator CNN performs all of these steps twice. The receiving and sending of intermediate results are counted as receiving of result and sending of input data. For readability, the multiple steps are summed together in the timing breakdown.

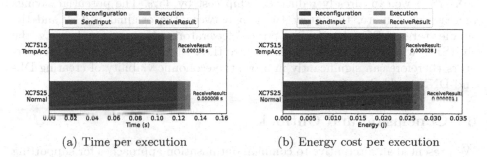

(a) Time per execution   (b) Energy cost per execution

Fig. 6. Comparing execution time and energy overhead for Temporal Accelerator CNN on a XC7S15 and a single configuration CNN on a XC7S25

We can see that overall the Temporal Accelerator outperforms the original CNN implementation, even though the XC7S15 has to reconfigure twice. It is 9.06% faster than the original CNN. The predominant factor in this is the difference in the reconfiguration time. While having to offload data between reconfigurations increases the time overhead for sending and receiving, its impact on the execution is negligible, as the amount of additional data transmissions is only increased by 90 bytes (see Fig. 4). The same applies for the reception of intermediate result data being increased by the same 90 bytes. Next, we evaluated the energy consumption for both implementations. We collected the power measurements using the monitoring circuitry on our Elastic Node platform [16]. The results can be seen in Fig. 6(b). These results are summed up the same way as in Fig. 6(a). Unsurprisingly, due to the shorter reconfiguration time of the XC7S15, it can execute the Temporal Accelerator CNN using 12.81% less energy than the normal CNN on the XC7S25. This confirms that Temporal Accelerators can enable developers to create equally efficient or even more efficient accelerators by using a smaller FPGA.

5.3 Device Price Reduction

We see the true benefit of Temporal Accelerators in deploying an identically structured accelerator design to achieve the same accelerator performance while using cheaper FPGAs. To illustrate this we present the price in Euro for different chips of the Xilinx Spartan 7 chip family in Table 2. These values are the result of a web search [24] and as such may vary.

As we can see, larger FPGAs become more and more expensive. When switching from the original accelerator on the XC7S25 to a Temporal Accelerator on

Table 2. Pricing comparison for FPGAs of the Spartan 7 chip family

	XC7S15	XC7S25	XC7S50	XC7S75	XC7S100
Price (€)	18.58	28.59	47.81	80.32	107.53

a XC7S15 we can already reduce the chip cost by 35%. The potential savings increase even more, the larger the gap between the original FPGA and the smaller target FPGA for the Temporal Accelerator is. If we can replace e.g. the XC7S100 with the XC7S50 we can reduce the cost by 55%. Temporal Accelerators therefore can significantly improve the economic viability of creating DL- and DNN-enabled devices.

6   Conclusion and Outlook

We presented an alternative to common optimisation approaches for supporting DNNs on embedded FPGAs with limited available area, called *Temporal Accelerators*. We showed the applicability of this approach by implementing a 1D-CNN for anomaly detection in ECG data and evaluated its viability by comparing it to a single configuration CNN that only fits a larger FPGA. We showed that our Temporal Accelerator solution requires 9.06% less time to execute while using 12.81% less energy and reduces the device cost 35% by using a smaller FPGA, i.e. an XC7S15 instead of an XC7S25.

In future work we would like to investigate the scalability of our approach with regards to resource consumption and execution time of different accelerators. Additionally, we want to investigate under what conditions Temporal Accelerators can outperform larger chips. A focus here will be how to process multiple data inputs on the same accelerators e.g. via batch processing, as well as different input data sizes.

References

1. Burger, A., Qian, C., Schiele, G., Helms, D.: An embedded CNN implementation for on-device ECG analysis. In: 2020 IEEE International Conference on Pervasive Computing and Communications Workshops (PerCom Workshops) (2020)
2. Han, S., Mao, H., Dally, W.J.: Deep compression: compressing deep neural networks with pruning, trained quantization and Huffman coding. arXiv preprint arXiv:1510.00149 (2015)
3. Iandola, F.N., Han, S., Moskewicz, M.W., Ashraf, K., Dally, W.J., Keutzer, K.: Squeezenet: Alexnet-level accuracy with 50× fewer parameters and <0.5 MB model size. arXiv preprint arXiv:1602.07360 (2016)
4. McDanel, B., Teerapittayanon, S., Kung, H.T.: Embedded binarized neural networks. arXiv preprint arXiv:1709.02260 (2017)
5. Rastegari, M., Ordonez, V., Redmon, J., Farhadi, A.: XNOR-Net: ImageNet classification using binary convolutional neural networks. In: Leibe, B., Matas, J., Sebe, N., Welling, M. (eds.) ECCV 2016. LNCS, vol. 9908, pp. 525–542. Springer, Cham (2016). https://doi.org/10.1007/978-3-319-46493-0_32

6. Wang, E., Davis, J.J., Cheung, P.Y., Constantinides, G.A.: Lutnet: rethinking inference in FPGA soft logic. In: 2019 IEEE 27th Annual International Symposium on Field-Programmable Custom Computing Machines (FCCM). IEEE (2019)
7. Roth,W., et al.: Resource-efficient neural networks for embedded systems. arXiv preprint arXiv:2001.03048 (2020)
8. Hassibi, B., Stork, D.: Second order derivatives for network pruning: optimal brain surgeon. In: Advances in Neural Information Processing System (1993)
9. Yang, T.J., Chen, Y.H., Sze, V.: Designing energy-efficient convolutional neural networks using energy-aware pruning. In: Proceedings of the IEEE Conference on Computer Vision and Pattern Recognition (2017)
10. Jouppi, N., Young, C., Patil, N., Patterson, D.: Motivation for and evaluation of the first tensor processing unit. IEEE Micro **38**(3), 10–19 (2018)
11. Biswas, A., Chandrakasan, A.P.: CONV-SRAM: an energy-efficient SRAM with in-memory dot-product computation for low-power convolutional neural networks. IEEE J. Solid-State Circ. **54**(1), 217–230 (2018)
12. Venieris, S.I., ouganis, C.S.: fpgaConvNet: a framework for mapping convolutional neural networks on FPGAs. In: 2016 IEEE 24th Annual International Symposium on Field-Programmable Custom Computing Machines (FCCM) (2016)
13. Burger, A., Cichiwskyj, C., Schiele, G.: Elastic nodes for the Internet of Things: a middleware-based approach. In: Proceedings - 2017 IEEE International Conference on Autonomic Computing, ICAC 2017 (2017)
14. Cordone, R., Redaelli, F., Redaclli, M.A., Santambrogio, M.D., Sciuto, D.: Partitioning and scheduling of task graphs on partially dynamically reconfigurable FPGAs. IEEE Trans. Comput.-Aided Des. Integr. Circ. Syst. **28**(5), 662–675 (2009)
15. Knocke, P., Gorgen, R., Walter, J., Helms, D., Nebel, W.: Using early power and timing estimations of massively heterogeneous computation platforms to create optimized HPC applications. In: Proceedings - 2014 International Conference on Embedded and Ubiquitous Computing, EUC 2014, 609757 (2014)
16. Schiele, G., Burger, A., Cichiwskyj, C.: The elastic node: an experimentation platform for hardware accelerator research in the Internet of Things. In: 2019 IEEE International Conference on Autonomic Computing (ICAC) (2019)
17. Burger, A., Schiele, G.: Demo abstract: deep learning on an elastic node for the Internet of Things. In: 2018 IEEE International Conference on Pervasive Computing and Communications Workshops (PerCom Workshops) (2018)
18. Xilinx. 7 Series FPGAs Configuration User Guide - UG470 (2018)
19. Xilinx. 7 Series FPGAs Data Sheet: Overview (2018)
20. Xilinx. Spartan-7 FPGAs Data Sheet: DC and AC Switching Characteristics (2019)
21. Xilinx. Xilinx Power Estimator (XPE) (2020)
22. Xilinx. Power Methodology Guide - UG786 (v14.5) (2018)
23. Inc. Micron Technology. Micron Flash Memory Support for Xilinx Platforms (2019)
24. Mouser. Electronic Components Distributor - Mouser Electronics Germany (2020)

ML Training on a Tiny Microcontroller for a Self-adaptive Neural Network-Based DC Motor Speed Controller

Frederik Funk[1], Thorsten Bucksch[2], and Daniel Mueller-Gritschneder[1]($\boxtimes$) (iD)

[1] Chair of Electronic Design Automation, Technical University of Munich,
Arcisstr. 21, 80333 Munich, Germany
daniel.mueller@tum.de
[2] Infineon Technology AG,
Am Campeon 1-15, 85579 Neubiberg, Germany
thorsten.bucksch@infineon.com,
https://www.infineon.com/, https://www.ei.tum.de/eda/startseite/

Abstract. Neural-Network (NN)-based controllers have the potential to achieve better control performance than classical PID controllers. Yet NN deployment on tiny microcontrollers, which are used in DC motor control due to strict cost requirements, is challenging as NNs are computationally intensive and memory demanding. We propose a lightweight direct inverse NN-based control approach for controlling the angular speed of a permanent magnet DC motor, which runs on a tiny Arm Cortex-M0 microcontroller with only 4 kB of RAM. Moreover, the NN-based controller can self-adapt to the DC motor characteristics without the need of any external machine learning frameworks such as TensorFlow. For this, we are not deploying a pre-trained network for inference but implement a fully automated training process on the microcontroller, which also includes the dataset collection.

The result is a self-adaptive control algorithm that is able to drive the motor at the desired speed after it learned the motor characteristics in an initial training phase. Furthermore, the approach is extended such that it enables the controller to constantly self-adapt to later changes in the motor characteristics caused by heating or wear-out while it is operating in standard control mode.

Keywords: Neural network-based control algorithms ·
Self-adaptation · Microcontroller · Extreme edge AI · TinyML ·
On-device training

1 Introduction

Using neural networks (NNs) for control applications has been studied for a long time. Due to the ability of representing non-linear functions, the strength of NN-based controllers lies especially in the control of non-linear systems [12].

© Springer Nature Switzerland AG 2020
J. Gama et al. (Eds.): ITEM 2020/IoT Streams 2020, CCIS 1325, pp. 268–279, 2020.
https://doi.org/10.1007/978-3-030-66770-2_20

Yet, PI and PID controllers are still the standard in industrial applications such as the control of Direct Current (DC) motors because they are lightweight and can be executed on low-cost, tiny microcontrollers with, e.g., only few kByte of SRAM memory. In contrast, the deployment of NN-based control applications on tiny microcontrollers is challenging as NNs - and their training in particular - are computationally intensive and memory demanding. The usual approach for running NN controllers on a microcontroller is to use a static pre-trained model for inference only. This requires to collect training data from an experimental setup, to move the data to an external PC, and to train the controller offline using frameworks such as TensorFlow [2]. In case of a DC motor, the developer of the NN-based motor control needs to built up the experimental setup and needs machine learning knowledge for training NNs.

In this paper, we propose a lightweight direct inverse NN-based control app-roach for controlling the angular speed of a permanent magnet DC motor, which is able to run on a tiny microcontroller. For this, we not only implement the inference on the microcontroller but also the data collection and the complete training process. This results in a fully automated setup, where the NN-based controller self-adapts to a specific DC motor's characteristics without requiring any external training on a PC. The training data is extracted by connecting the microcontroller to the motor in the same way it is later used when operating on the motor. Hence, the developer would just connect the microcontroller to the motor and let it run in certain training modes, in which the controller learns the motor characteristics, without requiring any knowledge about the internals of the NN-based control scheme. After this initial training phase, the NN-based controller has learned how drive this specific DC motor at the desired speed. Additionally, the controller can be further enhanced to continue the training in the background during normal operation. This extension allows the controller to self-adapt to later changes in the motor characteristics, e.g., caused by heat or wear-out. The scientific contributions of the paper are the following: (1) A direct inverse NN-based DC motor controller and a port for ML training on tiny micro-controllers to achieve a self-adapting control scheme. (2) A new strategy for ML training on tiny microcontrollers: The training is conducted in phases similar to mini-batch training such that only a small batch of the training data needs to be collected directly from the motor or control plant in general. After it is used for training, it is overwritten by the next mini-batch. The necessary memory size for storing the training data is thus minimal. (3) An extension of the training strategy that runs during operation and enables a self-adaptive control that can learn later changes in motor characteristics.

The approach is verified on a full experimental setup with an industrial DC motor and the control scheme implemented on a tiny Arm Cortex-M0 micro-controller with only 4 kB of RAM. The result shows that the controller indeed learns the motor characteristics and drives the motor at a desired speed with high control performance as well as is capable to adapt to changes in the char-acteristics.

Finally, due to the constrained resources on the microcontroller the approach has limits that needs to be taken into account. We used a lightweight direct inverse control scheme, which requires a very small NN. Additionally, we avoided network quantization since it is a process that is hard to port and automatize on a microcontroller and instead compute the NN in floating point.

2   Related Work

Several approaches (including the usage of an NN-based inverse model) were described by Psaltis et al. in 1988 [13]. Weerasooriya and El-Sharkawi used NNs to effectively control the rotor speed of a DC motor in 1991 [15]. A variety of NN approaches have been used to solve different problems such as aircraft landing [14] and temperature control [9] where Khalid and Omatu also show that their controller is able to outperform a PID controller. While the common approach was to use NNs to learn the system behaviour and use this information to design a controller, in recent years the idea of designing a controller directly without modeling the system became more and more popular. Hafner and Riedmiller achieved a data-efficient, reinforcement learning motor controller, which works over a wide speed range [5].

In contrast to Weerasooriya and El-Sharkawi [15] who used the backpropagation and gradient descent method for training their DC motor controller, we are using the newer Adam optimizer [10], which is most commonly used in the area of deep learning. Moving AI and neural networks to the edge is subject to many ongoing research (e.g. [3,4,16]) works. But to the best of our knowledge, we are presenting one of the first working self-training neural network controllers that is trained and executed on a tiny microcontroller.

3   Background on Direct Current (DC) Motors

DC motor is an umbrella term for different types of motors which are operated with direct current. In the course of this work, a permanent magnet DC (PMDC) motor is used. The equivalent circuit of a PMDC motor is shown in Fig. 1a. The behaviour of the motor is described by the equations

$$v_a(t) = R_a\, i_a(t) + L_a \frac{di_a(t)}{dt} + e_b(t) \tag{1}$$

$$e_b(t) = K_F\, \omega(t) \tag{2}$$

$$K_T\, i_a(t) = J \frac{d\omega(t)}{dt} + B\,\omega(t) + T_L(t) \tag{3}$$

with the input voltage v_a, the armature resistance R_a, the armature current i_a, the armature inductance L_a, the motor back emf K_F, the rotor speed ω, the torque constant K_T, the rotor inertia J, the viscous friction B and the load torque T_L. By transforming the equations into the Laplace domain, one obtains

$$i_a(s) = \frac{v_a(s) - K_F\,\omega(s)}{L_a\, s + R_a}; \quad \omega(s) = \frac{-T_L(s) - K_T\, i_a(s)}{J\, s + B}. \tag{4}$$

A Simulink model that is derived from these equations (see Fig. 1b) is used for the simulation in Sect. 5.1. As can be seen in Eq. 2, the back emf (BEMF) voltage e_b is proportional to the rotational speed. To avoid an additional sensor, the motor speed is determined by measuring the BEMF voltage in this work.

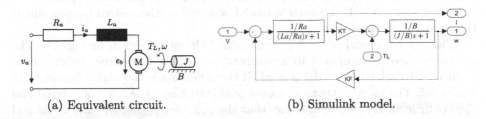

(a) Equivalent circuit.   (b) Simulink model.

Fig. 1. Permanent magnet direct current motor.

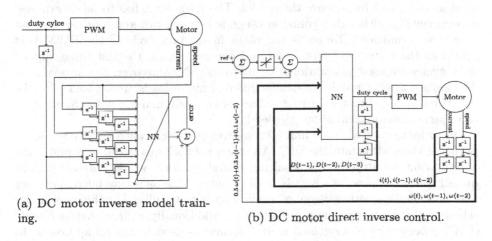

(a) DC motor inverse model train-   (b) DC motor direct inverse control.
ing.

Fig. 2. DC motor direct inverse control approach.

4   Self-adaptive DC Motor Control Scheme

The goal of our new approach is to use ML training on the tiny microcontroller to realize a self-adaptive NN-based controller. The idea is that during an initial learning phase, the direct inverse controller learns the characteristics in the form of the inverse behavior of a specific motor. Afterwards, the controller can be used to control the motor effectively.

4.1 NN-based Direct Inverse Control (DIC)

The idea of the direct inverse control (DIC) approach is to use a NN to learn an inverse model of the plant, in this case the motor, and to use this model directly in the control application. Prerequisite is that a stable inverse of the plant exists. The inverse model cancels the poles of the plant and essentially produces a deadbeat controller. If the inverse model is accurate, the system output equals the desired reference input.

The inverse model is used in the control circuit as shown in Fig. 2b. The reference speed is compared to a weighted sum of the last three speeds, hence a third order reference model is used. If the difference is too high, the reference is limited. This ensures that the motor is able to follow the reference signal and the coefficients are chosen in a way that the poles are within the unit cycle and the reference model is asymptotically stable [15].

The training configuration for a DC motor inverse model is shown in Fig. 2a. Additional to the motor speed $\omega(t)$, the last plant outputs $\omega(t-1) \dots \omega(t-k)$ are used as NN input to improve the model. The value for k has to be determined experimentally, although a common range is between two and four. In our case $k = 2$ was sufficient. Target is the plant input duty cycle of the PWM that produces the system outputs speed and current. Again, the last three applied duty cycles are used as additional input to the NN. Moreover, as our goal is to develop a controller which can handle different motor loads, we are also using the last three sampled motor current values as an additional input to the network as it carries information about the load.

In order to cope with the limited resources of a microcontroller, we are incorporating these ideas into the DIC: Although network quantization would bring a significant speedup for the resulting neural network, we do without it. The quantization is a process which is hard to automatize on a tiny microcontroller and thus conflicts with our goal of a self-adapting controller. For this reason, our scheme only uses floating point calculations. Additionally, a direct inverse control (DIC) scheme with a very small neural network is used as control approach. To find the best architecture of the NN, a simulation-based Network Architecture Search (NAS) was conducted. The results are listed in Sect. 5.1. The small size of the identified NN compensates for the slow execution caused by the floating point calculations and the NN is small enough to fit into a tiny microcontroller.

4.2 Training Strategy for Tiny Microcontrollers

As the necessary amount of training samples for training the inverse model exceeds the usual amount of RAM on tiny microcontrollers, we are proposing a cycle-based training strategy where only a small part of the dataset is stored at the same time. Additionally, we target a fully automated training process needing no developer interaction. For this, the motor is connected in the same way to the microcontroller during the training phase as it is done for normal operation. Training samples are collected from the plant and are directly used on the microcontroller for learning the motor characteristics. For the ML training on

---

Algorithm 1. The self-learning control scheme which is designed for an application on a small microcontroller.

Require: Functions random, collect, train, and run_control
Require: Threshold θ ▷ Threshold when the training should be stopped
 1: $S \leftarrow \emptyset$ ▷ Initialize dataset
 2: $NN \leftarrow$ random()   ▷ Randomly initialize NN
 3: $t \leftarrow \infty$ ▷ Initialize MSE
 4: **repeat**
 5:     $S \leftarrow$ collect()   ▷ Collect new training samples from the plant
 6:     $NN \leftarrow$ train(NN, S)   ▷ Train inverse model with the new samples
 7:     $t \leftarrow$ mse(NN, S)   ▷ Compute MSE for the current dataset
 8: **until** $t \leq \theta$ ▷ Stop training when MSE threshold is reached
 9: run_control(NN)   ▷ Run direct inverse control

---

the microcontroller all necessary NN functions (activation functions and derivatives, feedforward, backpropagation, batch-gradient calculation and Adam) were ported onto the microcontroller.

The training strategy used for the proposed self-adaptive control scheme is given in Algorithm 1. It requires functions to randomly initialize the NN, to collect the training data from the plant, to train the NN and to finally run the control. The threshold value θ for the mean squared error (MSE) determines when the training procedure is over and the control can be activated.

After initializing the dataset S, the neural network NN and the current MSE t, the cycle-based training starts in line 4. At the beginning of each training cycle, a small number of training samples are collected from the plant while it is run with random input signals. This idea originates from the classical mini-batch gradient descent where small mini-batches are sampled randomly from a larger dataset. In our case, we are sampling directly from the plant instead of a larger dataset, which means that only the mini-batch currently in use needs to be stored. The number of training samples that are collected per cycle must be found by experimenting and is limited by the available RAM.

Afterwards, the neural network inverse model is trained with the collected training samples. In theory, any neural network training algorithm can be used (as long as the microcontroller's resources are sufficient) but we are using Adam [10] in our experiments.

In the last step, the mean squared error t is computed for the current dataset and is then compared to the threshold θ. If it is equal or smaller, the training is over and we can run our direct inverse controller with the trained inverse model. If not, the dataset is overwritten with a new dataset and a new training cycle starts. The value for θ depends on the plant and needs to be found by experimenting. More sophisticated methods for finding the point when to stop the training are conceivable (test and validation datasets), but the described method worked for our setup and is – as it is the easiest solution possible – the most well-suited for a tiny microcontroller application.

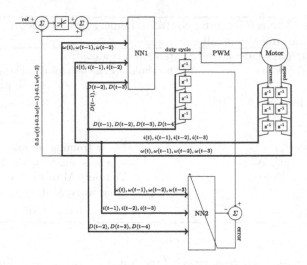

Fig. 3. DIC adaptive extension.

4.3   Self-adaptation During Operation

The approach so far includes an inverse model training and its application in a direct inverse control circuit. Once the network has been trained, it is kept as a static model which is not further adjusted. If the system changes, e.g. due to mechanical wear-out or heating, the inverse model is not longer optimal. We extend the control scheme by the feature to adapt the inverse model to system changes *while* the control is running.

When the NN-based DIC is executed in normal operation it does not require the full operational power of the microcontroller. The remaining computational budget can be exploited to update the inverse model. To achieve this, the data that occurs during the operation is used as training data as it reflects any system changes. After each control cycle, the neural network is trained with the measured values (in case of a DC motor speed and current) and the last plant inputs in the same way as in the initial training phase (Fig. 2a). In contrast to the initial training, the changes to the network are smaller. Therefore, less samples and a smaller learning rate can be used. To make sure that the neural network training does not interfere with the control, the training is applied to a copy of the neural network as shown in Fig. 3. NN1 is the standard NN that is used for control while NN2 is used for learning changes in the motor characteristics. NN1 and NN2 have the same structure. When a full update on NN2 is done, for which the interval can be decided by the developer, the weights and biases are copied from NN2 to NN1. If there were major changes in the plant characteristics, they will be captured by NN2. By overwriting NN1 with NN2, the control self-adapts to these changes.

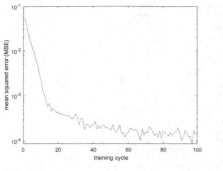 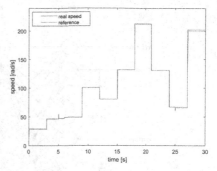

(a) DC motor inverse model training.　　(b) DC motor direct inverse control.

Fig. 4. DC motor direct inverse control approach.

5 Experiments

5.1 Simulation-Based NN Architecture Search and Training Setup

In a first step, we use the DC motor Simulink model from Fig. 1b to search a good network architecture and determine a good training setup . The motor model has the following specifications: $L_a = 350\,\mu H$, $R_a = 0.6\,\Omega$, $J = 1.554 \cdot 10^{-5}\,kgm^2$, $B = 10^{-3}\,Nms$ and $K_F = K_T = 0.0191\,Nm\,A^{-1}$. The load is varied between $0\,Nm$ and $30\,mNm$, the sample time while collecting the training data and running the DIC is $45\,ms$ and the maximum allowed PWM change per control cycle is 40%.

To explore a good training setup, the input-target samples for the training are collected by applying random PWM duty cycles and random loads to the DC motor Simulink model from Fig. 1b. The Adam optimizer [10] with standard parameters $\alpha = 0.001$, $\beta_1 = 0.9$, $\beta_2 = 0.999$ and $\epsilon = 10^{-8}$ is used as training algorithm. In order to keep the implementation as simple as possible and to allow an easy transferring to C code, all the functions (activation functions and their derivatives, feedforward, backpropagation, batch-gradient calculation and Adam) were implemented from scratch with only using basic Matlab functions. No machine learning toolbox is used. We found that a total of 300 input-target samples per cycle which are used for 10 epochs each with a batch size of 150 lead to good results with respect to controller performance.

The network architecture search resulted in a fully connected NN with a single hidden layer consisting of seven neurons (see Fig. 5). Thus, the network architecture is 10 - 7 - 1: 10 input neurons, 7 neurons in the hidden layer and a single output neuron. The activation function of the hidden layer is rectified linear unit (ReLU) and pure linear for the output neuron. Other activation functions such as sigmoid or tangens hyperbolicus have been tested but were not better and are more computationally intensive. The training results for this NN are given in Fig. 4. In the course of the inverse model training, the MSE decreases and finds its lower limit at around 10^{-4}. The DIC simulation is given

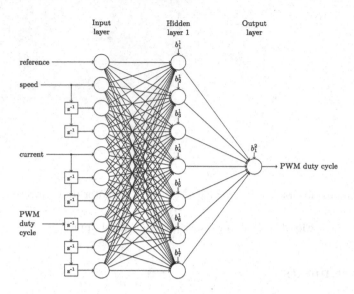

Fig. 5. Used neural network structure.

in Fig. 4b. It can be seen that the controller is able to drive the motor at the desired reference speed. Nevertheless, small offset errors are visible where the inverse model is not precise enough. Load changes were applied at 5s, 10s and 25s and it can be seen that the motor quickly is driven back to the desired speed. Hence, the found NN-based DIC has good control performance.

5.2 Implementation on a Cortex-M0 Microcontroller

Experimental Setup. The motor whose speed is to be controlled is 12 V 60W permanent magnet DC motor without any nearer specifications available. To simulate different loads, a 12 V 36.88 W permanent magnet DC motor is coupled to the first one.

For running the training and the DIC, an Infineon TLE9855QX microcontroller [7] mounted on an TLE985X evaluation board [8] is used. The chip comes with 4 kB of RAM, 64 kB of flash and runs with 40 MHz clock. No floating point unit is available, all floating point calculations are done in soft float. The evaluation board features an H-bridge to drive the motor and includes a 5 mΩ resistor in the current path to measure the current. For measuring the BEMF voltage and the voltage across the shunt resistor, the 10 bit ADC1 is used. The data for creating the plots in Fig. 6 is sent out to a host computer via UART1.

Software Setup of the NN-based DIC and ML Training. Existing NN frameworks for microcontrollers such as CMSIS-NN [11] or the experimental Tensorflow Lite for microcontrollers [1] only support the execution of pre-trained models. As our goal is to run also the training on the microcontroller, all necessary neural network functions (activation functions and derivatives, feedforward, backpropagation, batch-gradient calculation and Adam) were implemented from scratch in embedded C. For the mathematical operations, the CMSIS-DSP library [6] is used whenever possible since it brings a significant speedup. Unfortunately, there is no random numer generator available on the microcontroller. Therefore, for all the operations that depend on the use of random numbers (network initialization and random application of PWM duty cycles during the generation of training data) the random numbers are generated in advance and stored in the flash.

The control runs in an interrupt service routine which is executed every 15 ms. In the routine, only the BEMF voltage and the voltage across the shunt resistor are measured during the first two executions. During the third execution, the values are measured again and the average of all three measurements is used for control. Hence, the actual control action takes place every 45 ms. The training samples that are used during the training cycles are also taken every 45 ms (average over three measurements every 15 ms).

Results. The NN configuration is the same as for the simulation as well as Adam configuration. However, a smaller batch size of 15 is used which leads to more NN parameter updates per epoch and hence a faster training. The training is stopped after 310 epochs which equals a total of 31 training cycles, while the training took 100 cycles in the simulation (Fig. 4a). The total training time for all the cycles (including the data generation) is around 15 min. The adaptive training is carried out with plain gradient descent and a learning rate $\alpha = 0.001$.

The results for the described setup are shown in Fig. 6. The DIC is able to keep the speed at the desired speed (setpoint) (Fig. 6a) and is able to react on sudden load changes (Fig. 6c). The setpoint deviation which belongs to Fig. 6a is shown in Fig. 6b. When leaving out the spikes that belong to the setpoint changes, the average deviation from the BEMF voltage setpoint is 38.4 mV. The corresponding speed error can be calculated using Eq. 2 when the BEMF constant K_F is known. The constant for our motor has been determined experimentally to 2.873 mV/rpm, which gives 13.36 rpm for the average speed error. However, a part of this error is due to measurement inaccuracies as the resolution of the ADC is limited to 30.25 mV.

The prove that the adaptation during operation is working is shown in Fig. 6d. It can be seen that the there is a small offset error after the load changes, which is caused by an imprecise inverse model. The information about the offset error is part of the training data, which is used to update the inverse model during operation and pushes the speed to move towards the desired setpoint by updating the NN. Hence, the in-operation adaption to changing motor characteristics is working.

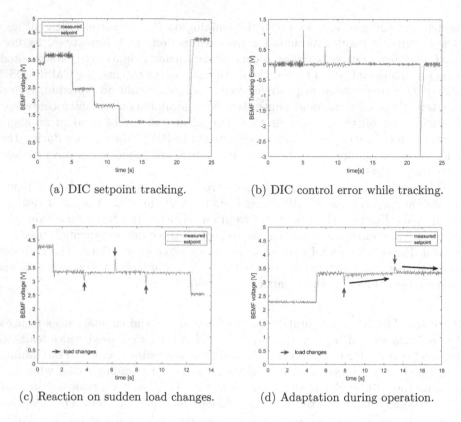

(a) DIC setpoint tracking.   (b) DIC control error while tracking.

(c) Reaction on sudden load changes.   (d) Adaptation during operation.

Fig. 6. Results of the microcontroller implementation.

6   Conclusion

In this work, we proposed a working NN-based direct inverse speed controller for a permanent magnet DC motor, which can be trained and executed on a tiny ARM Cortex-M0 microcontroller. This proved the general feasibility of training a NN controller on a microcontroller and thus is a major step towards the application of these controllers in commerical applications.

While the objective of this work was to verify the feasibility, the next step is to further improve the control performance. This can be done by changing the control cycle time and implement special acceleration features into the microcontroller.

References

1. TensorFlow lite for microcontrollers (2020). https://www.tensorflow.org/lite/microcontrollers
2. Abadi, M., et. al.: TensorFlow: Large-scale machine learning on heterogeneous systems (2015). http://tensorflow.org/, software available from tensorflow.org

3. Cotton, N.J., Wilamowski, B.M., Dundar, G.: A neural network implementation on an inexpensive eight bit microcontroller. In: 2008 International Conference on Intelligent Engineering Systems, pp. 109–114 (2008)
4. Fedorov, I., Adams, R.P., Mattina, M., Whatmough, P.: Sparse: sparse architecture search for CNNs on resource-constrained microcontrollers. In: Wallach, H., Larochelle, H., Beygelzimer, A., d'Alché-Buc, F., Fox, E., Garnett, R. (eds.) Advances in Neural Information Processing Systems, vol. 32, pp. 4977–4989. Curran Associates, Inc. (2019)
5. Hafner, R., Riedmiller, M.: Neural reinforcement learning controllers for a real robot application. In: Proceedings 2007 IEEE International Conference on Robotics and Automation, pp. 2098–2103 (2007)
6. ARM Inc.: CMSIS DSP software library (2020). http://www.keil.com/pack/doc/CMSIS/DSP/html/index.html
7. Infineon Technologies AG: Infineon TLE9855QX microcontroller (2020). https://www.infineon.com/cms/en/product/microcontroller/embedded-power-ics-system-on-chip-/h-bridge-driver-ic-integrated-arm-cortex-m0/tle9855qx/
8. Infineon Technologies AG: Infineon TLE985X evaluation board (2020). https://www.infineon.com/cms/en/product/evaluation-boards/tle985x-evalboard/
9. Khalid, M., Omatu, S.: A neural network controller for a temperature control system. IEEE Control Syst. Mag. **12**(3), 58–64 (1992)
10. Kingma, D.P., Ba, J.: Adam: a method for stochastic optimization. In: Bengio, Y., LeCun, Y. (eds.) 3rd International Conference on Learning Representations, ICLR 2015, San Diego, CA, USA, 7–9 May 2015, Conference Track Proceedings (2015)
11. Lai, L., Suda, N., Chandra, V.: CMSIS-NN: efficient neural network kernels for Arm Cortex-M CPUs. arXiv e-prints, January 2018. http://arxiv.org/abs/1801.06601
12. Liu, K., Tokai, R.L., McVey, B.D.: An integrated architecture of adaptive neural network control for dynamic systems. In: Tesauro, G., Touretzky, D.S., Leen, T.K. (eds.) Advances in Neural Information Processing Systems, vol. 7, pp. 1031–1038. MIT Press (1995)
13. Psaltis, D., Sideris, A., Yamamura, A.A.: A multilayered neural network controller. IEEE Control Syst. Mag. **8**(2), 17–21 (1988)
14. Schley, C., Chauvin, Y., Henkle, V., Golden, R.: Neural networks structured for control application to aircraft landing. In: Lippmann, R.P., Moody, J.E., Touretzky, D.S. (eds.) Advances in Neural Information Processing Systems 3, pp. 415–421. Morgan-Kaufmann (1991)
15. Weerasooriya, S., El-Sharkawi, M.A.: Identification and control of a dc motor using back-propagation neural networks. IEEE Trans. Energy Convers. **6**(4), 663–669 (1991)
16. Zhang, Y., Suda, N., Lai, L., Chandra, V.: Hello edge: keyword spotting on microcontrollers. CoRR abs/1711.07128 (2017). http://arxiv.org/abs/1711.07128

ITEM 2020: Quantization

Dynamic Complexity Tuning for Hardware-Aware Probabilistic Circuits

Laura I. Galindez Olascoaga[1]([✉]), Wannes Meert[2], Nimish Shah[1], and Marian Verhelst[1]

[1] Electrical Engineering Department, KU Leuven, Leuven, Belgium
{laura.galindez,nimish.shah,marian.verhelst}@esat.kuleuven.be
[2] Computer Science Department, KU Leuven, Leuven, Belgium
wannes.meert@cs.kuleuven.be

Abstract. Probabilistic inference is a well suited approach to address the challenges of resource constrained embedded application scenarios. In particular, probabilistic models learned generatively are robust to missing data and are capable of encoding domain knowledge seamlessly. These traits have been leveraged to propose hardware-aware probabilistic learning and inference strategies that induce Pareto optimal accuracy versus resource consumption trade-offs. This paper proposes a model-complexity tuning strategy that relies on ensembles of probabilistic classifiers to identify the difficulty of the classification task on a given instance. It then dynamically switches to a higher or lower complexity setting accordingly. The strategy is evaluated on an embedded human activity recognition scenario and demonstrates a superior performance when compared to the Pareto-optimal trade-off obtained when the ensembles are deployed statically, especially in low cost regions of the trade-off space. This makes the strategy amenable to embedded computing scenarios, where one of the main constraints towards always-on functionality are the device's strict resource constraints.

Keywords: Hardware-aware probabilistic models · Probabilistic circuits · Resource constrained embedded applications

1 Introduction

Embedded machine learning strategies have shown great promise in meeting the real-time performance demands of many smart portable applications, such as speech recognition, autonomous navigation and medical monitoring. When coupled with edge computing paradigms, these strategies can further mitigate some of the shortcomings of cloud computing, such as communication bandwidth restrictions, and privacy and latency concerns [24].

However, machine learning algorithms often come with demanding workloads that impose further challenges on heavily resource-constrained embedded devices. Hardware-algorithm co-optimization has recently taken a central role in addressing the fundamental trade-off between accuracy and resource scarcity.

J. Gama et al. (Eds.): ITEM 2020/IoT Streams 2020, CCIS 1325, pp. 283–295, 2020.
https://doi.org/10.1007/978-3-030-66770-2_21

In particular, efficient implementations of embedded neural networks have been incessantly studied, and have been increasingly adopted by mainstream portable applications as a consequence [22]. At the same time, the hardware design community has been steadily contributing dedicated platforms that successfully handle increasingly complex neural network workloads [24].

With all their success in advancing the state-of-the-art in terms of accuracy for many fundamental AI tasks, neural networks can be ill equipped to handle some of the challenges of always-on portable applications: they are often not robust to missing and noisy data, they can not seamlessly encode domain knowledge, and their training often relies on a vast amount of data. Probabilistic models, in contrast, are capable of encoding joint distributions and can be learned generatively, which can make them robust to missing data; they rely on smaller data and can encode expert knowledge. Finally state-of-the-art probabilistic models have been able to successfully balance expressiveness with inference efficiency [3].

This last goal has driven the field of Tractable Probabilistic Modeling. Perhaps one of its most promising contributions is the probabilistic circuit (PC) [3], a deep architecture that encodes a joint probability distribution over a set of random variables. PCs possess a variety of desirable properties that can support tractable inference for many complex probabilistic queries. The properties of PCs such as sum product networks (SPNs) [19], arithmetic circuits (ACs) [4] and probabilistic sentential decision diagrams (PSDDs) [15], have been recently exploited by several works located at the intersection between algorithm and hardware optimization, with contributions that range from energy-efficient low-precision computation [20,21,26] to hardware-aware learning [8]. Yet, their widespread adoption by the field of edge computing can only be enabled by addressing the relevant application driven challenges.

This paper proposes a run-time strategy that dynamically switches between models with varying complexity. This results in an improved cost versus accuracy trade-off when compared to that attained by using a fixed-a-priori model, as evaluated on a human activity recognition use case. The switching strategy can select among a collection of PSDD pairs of different complexity, each model in the pair encoding a different joint probability distribution but expected to attain similar cost versus accuracy performance. The divergence between the two models is taken into consideration to switch to a pair of more complex—and more reliable—models when their classification confidence is low, and to move to a cheaper model when their confidence is high.

2   Background

Notation. Variables are denoted by upper case letters X and their instantiations by lower case letters x. Sets of variables are denoted in bold upper case $\mathbf{X}$ and their joint instantiations in bold lower case $\mathbf{x}$.

2.1 Probabilistic Sentential Decision Diagrams

Probabilistic sentential decision diagrams (PSDDs) are logical-circuit representations of joint probability distributions over binary random variables [15]. The inner nodes of PSDDs alternate between AND and OR gates (equivalent to multiplication and addition, respectively) and each leaf node encodes a distribution over a variable X. The root (or output) of a PSDD must be an OR gate. Furthermore, the input edges of OR gates are annotated with a normalized probability distribution $\phi_1, ..., \phi_n$ (see Fig. 1).

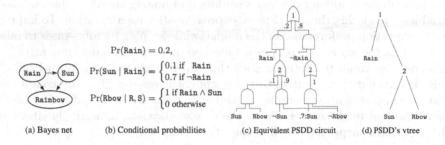

(a) Bayes net   (b) Conditional probabilities   (c) Equivalent PSDD circuit   (d) PSDD's vtree

Fig. 1. A Bayesian network and its equivalent PSDD (taken from [16]).

The output (or root) node of a PSDD encodes the following joint probability distribution, given in terms of independent distribution over variables $\mathbf{X}$ and $\mathbf{Y}$:

$$Pr_q(\mathbf{XY}) = \sum_i \phi_i Pr_{p_i}(\mathbf{X}) Pr_{s_i}(\mathbf{Y}). \tag{1}$$

Here, the *prime* sub-circuit is defined over variables $\mathbf{X}$, and the *sub* sub-circuit over variables $\mathbf{Y}$. For example, in Fig. 1, the prime variable of the PSDD's root node is Rain, whereas the sub variables are {Sun,Rbow}. This splitting into primes and sub variable sets is determined by the *vtree* in sub-figure (d). Note that each inner node of this vtree corresponds to an AND node in the PSDD in sub-figure (c).

In Eq. 1, the notation Pr_{β_i} signals that the distributions over prime or sub variables are defined recursively. At the root node in our example, the distributions over the sub Pr_{s_i}(Sun, Rbow) take on the same form of Eq. 1: they decompose into independent distributions over prime variable Sun and sub variable Rbow.

PSDDs possess a number of syntactic restrictions [15] that can guarantee tractable marginal probabilistic queries on them. This is useful for the classification tasks we pursue in this paper, defined by Bayes rule as:

$$Pr(C|\mathbf{F}) = \frac{Pr(C, \mathbf{F})}{Pr(\mathbf{F})} \sim Pr(\mathbf{F}|C) \cdot Pr(C), \tag{2}$$

where C is the class variable and $\mathbf{F}$ is the set of feature variables. PSDDs can be used to efficiently compute the marginal probabilities (such as $\Pr(\mathbf{F})$). This allows the models to remain robust when features are not available due to, for example, sensor malfunction, as the unobserved features can be marginalized. These two factors motivate the use of PSDDs for the strategy proposed in this work, in addition to the fact that they can be learned incrementally and in a hardware-aware fashion as described below.

The work in [16] proposed a data-driven PSDDs learner that iteratively increases the model's structural complexity by attempting to maximizing log-likelihood given data. The induced structural changes can, for example, establish new dependencies among random variables and among specific values of those variables[1], rendering the model more expressive after each iteration. To improve the classification performance of the model, while keeping its robustness to missing features, the work in [7] proposes a method that encodes a discriminative bias enforcing the circuit to contain a node that directly expresses the term $\Pr(\mathbf{F}|C)$. This discriminative-generative learning approach ensures that the conditional relation between feature and class variable relevant to the classification task is always present in the model, like in the case of Bayesian network classifiers [6], which perform surprisingly well despite their simplicity.

2.2   Cost Versus Accuracy Pareto Trade-Off Extraction

Learning PSDDs from data with the strategies above entails a trade-off between the model's complexity and its fitness in terms of log-likelihood. The work in [8] introduced a hardware-aware strategy that leverages this fact, in addition to the previously discussed PSDD properties, to extract the Pareto-optimal set of models and system configurations (in terms of e.g. number of features and sensors used) in the accuracy versus hardware-aware cost space. The hardware-aware cost can be given in terms of a measurable resource of interest such as energy consumption, in which case it is defined as:

$$C_{HA}(\alpha, \mathbf{S}, \mathbf{F}) = C_{AC}(\alpha) + \sum_{S \in \mathbf{S}} C_{SI}(S, \mathbf{F}_S), \tag{3}$$

where C_{SI} is the cost of interfacing with the sensors (S) and extracting features from them ($\mathbf{F}_S$) and C_{AC} is the cost of inference (or the cost of evaluating the PSDD) and can be determined by factors like the number of arithmetic opreations to perform, the number of bits used, and the number of parameters to fetch from memory.

The strategy proposed in [8] learns the PSDDs iteratively from data with the learner proposed in [16], as described in Sect. 2.1 It then goes on to apply a local search strategy that iteratively prunes features (and the corresponding unobserved nodes in the PSDD) by minimizing an objective function given in terms of accuracy and hardware-aware cost (given in terms of relative energy

---

[1] This is known as context specific independence [27].

consumption). The final step consists on extracting the set of Pareto optimal models, described by their configurations $\sigma^* = \{\{\alpha_i^*, \mathbf{F}^*{}_i\}_{i=1:p}\}$, where α_i^* are the set of (pruned) PSDDs to be used and $\mathbf{F}^*{}_i$ indicate the feature subsets that are observable in each model. The strategy can also consider other available sources of hardware-driven quality scaling, such as turning sensors off or reducing the number of bits used for representation and arithmetic.

3 Model-Complexity Switching Strategy

We propose a model complexity switching strategy that dynamically adjusts the complexity of the model by evaluating the discrepancy between two PSDDs, one learned generatively with [16] and the other one learned with the discriminative bias proposed in [7]. If the classifiers disagree in their prediction of the current instance, the classification task on this instance is deemed challenging, and is therefore delegated to a pair of models with higher complexity, which can better handle the task. The motivation behind using the two types of classifier within an ensemble is that they can achieve similar performance in terms of accuracy and hardware-cost, but they encode different joint probability distributions, and may therefore disagree in their predictions of instances that tend to be more difficult to classify (due to e.g. ambiguity of class membership).

The available set of model ensembles is described by $\pi^{(SW)} = \{(\alpha_1^{(G)}, \alpha_1^{(DG)})$, $\ldots, (\alpha_n^{(G)}, \alpha_n^{(DG)})\}$, where $\alpha_j^{(G)}$ and $\alpha_j^{(DG)}$ denote the generative and the discriminative-generative classifiers, respectively; and ensemble 1 is the lowest complexity/cost ensemble, and n the most complex one. The models used for the construction of these ensembles are Pareto optimal in the hardware-cost versus accuracy trade-off space, and are extracted by the hardware-aware strategy described in the previous section. Moreover, each ensemble is generated by grouping classifiers with similar hardware-cost.[2]

The strategy relies on an objective function that measures the discrepancy between the two classifiers in ensemble number j and is given by:

$$ \mathrm{OF}_j = \left| \sum_{i=1}^{2} \max_C \Pr(C|\mathbf{F}, \alpha^{(\mathrm{type},i)}) \cdot w_i \cdot \gamma_i \right|, \tag{4} $$

where $\max \Pr(C|\mathbf{F}, \alpha^{(\mathrm{type},i)})$ is the maximum class posterior probability for each type of classifier (generative or discriminative-generative), w_i is the confidence of the correspondent classifier and is proportional to it's train-set accuracy:

$$ w_i = (\mathrm{Accuracy}_{\alpha^{(\mathrm{type},i)}}) / \sum_{i=1}^{2} \mathrm{Accuracy}_{\alpha^{(\mathrm{type},i)}}, \tag{5} $$

---

[2] The models learned with the discriminative bias tend to have a higher classification accuracy than those learned generatively, so the ensembles are constructed on the basis of cost similarity.

and γ_i is 1 for both classifiers when the class that maximizes their posterior probability is the same; and -1 for one and 1 for the other otherwise.

This objective function is the basis of the policy that decides, at every T^{th} sample, and based on two user-defined confidence levels θ_1 and θ_2, whether a more complex classifier ensemble is called for or whether a less complex classifier can be switched to. Specifically, the policy consists of the following three actions:

1. *High level of difficulty in the prediction.* If $\text{OF}_j \leq \theta_1$: $j = j+1$, unless $j == n$, in that case, go to action 2.
2. *Medium level of difficulty in the prediction.* If $\theta_1 < \text{OF}_j < \theta_2$: accept the prediction of the classifier with $\text{argmax}_\alpha(Pr(C|\mathbf{F}, \alpha) \cdot w)$.
3. *Low level of difficulty in the prediction.* If $\text{OF}_j \geq \theta_2$: accept prediction of classifier $\text{argmax}_\alpha(Pr(C|\mathbf{F}, \alpha) \cdot w)$ and do $j = j - 1$, unless $j == 1$.

The confidence hyperparameters θ_1 and θ_2 can be tuned to prioritize cost reduction or accuracy maximization. Lower values for θ_1 and θ_2 prioritize cost savings, while higher values prioritize higher accuracy. The parameter T, which determines the rate at which the policy will be applied, can be defined according to the desired trade-off between overhead costs and preciseness of the application of the policy. For example, if the policy is seldom applied, then the overhead cost is very low but there might be several missed opportunities to go to a more complex ensemble when the current one lacks confidence.

Note that we assume that the time it takes to move from the simplest to the most complex classifier in the evaluation of the policy is lower than the rate at which predictions must be made (according to application requirements). In other words, one must make sure that the policy implementation does not increase prediction latency. This is easy to guarantee for the tractable models considered in this paper, as they readily encode the formula to compute marginal probabilities. Their time complexity can therefore be calculated precisely.

This policy takes into consideration an important aspect of many embedded applications, as illustrated in the experimental section. Each of the possible classes, or activities in our case, takes place over a period of time. For example, in activity recognition, every activity will last a few seconds, while there is a new incoming sensor sample to be classified every few miliseconds. Thus, every time a new model ensemble is selected, the following few samples are likely to also benefit from this new model setting. For example, action 3 of our policy accepts the prediction, but sets a less complex ensemble setting for the following test-sample, assuming that this new test-sample belongs to the same activity group as the current one. This is also the case for action 1 of our policy, which changes to a more complex ensemble in preparation for dealing with a sequence of high difficulty classifications.

Finally, note that, even though both classifiers within an ensemble are generative, each encodes a different probability distribution because it has learned different conditional relations among the available features; and it considers different feature sets due to the hardware-aware strategies applied on them. This means that there is a significant divergence between them—even if they train-set accuracy and cost are close to each other—which we exploit to evaluate whether the current classification attempt is difficult.

4   Experiments

We empirically evaluate the proposed technique on a human activity recognition benchmark [1] consisting of smartphone inertial data and 6 classes: *standing, sitting, laying down, walking, walking downstairs and upstairs.*

Dataset Pre-processing and Cost Calculation. We discretized numerical features using the method in [5] and binarized them using a one-hot encoding. We then subjected them to a 75%-train, 10%-validation and 15%-test split. We re-organized the test data such that each activity takes place for at least 10 time instances and at most 30 instances, following a random activity sequence, in order to evaluate the strategy under different activity durations. To avoid overfitting, we performed feature selection following the method in [10]. This results in a dataset consisting of 55 binary features extracted from accelerometer and gyroscope measurements. We consider only the computational cost C_{AC}, given in terms of the memory energy-cost used to fetch parameters (as this is the most significant contribution towards the overall cost) [8]. In all experiments, we normalize the costs in accordance to the most expensive (most complex) model.

Model Learning. We learned the models on the train and validation sets with the LearnPSDD algorithm [16] for the generative case and with the D-LearnPSDD algorithm [7] for the discriminative-generartive case. Specifically, we retained a model every $N/10$ iterations, where N is the number of iterations needed for convergence. We then ran the feature selection and model pruning strategy described in [8] on the validation set and extracted the Pareto optimal configuration.

4.1   Ensemble Set Construction

Figure 2(a) shows the validation set accuracy and normalized cost after running the feature selection and model pruning steps in [8] on each learned PSDD. In particular, the black lines show the results on the discriminative-generative model set and the gray ones on the generative ones. Each line shows the cost versus accuracy trade-off sets achieved during the different stages of feature/model pruning. The sections of the lines with the lowest cost correspond to smaller models with small feature subsets available (the models have also been pruned accordingly), whereas the more expensive ones represent more complex models with larger feature subsets available. The blue and red curves show their Pareto optimal fronts extracted from the set of all available pruned models. As discussed before, the models learned with a discriminative bias tend to achieve

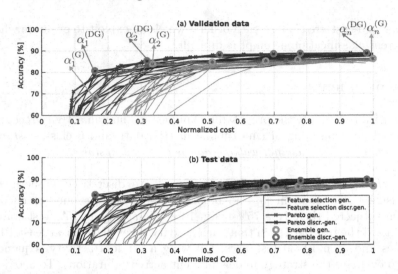

Fig. 2. Cost versus accuracy trade-off of the set of Pareto-optimal PSDDs and models user for the ensembles evaluated on validation data (a) and test data (b). (Color figure online)

higher accuracy than the purely generative ones while remaining equally or less costly. Figure 2(b) shows how this maps to accuracy versus cost on the test set.

For the ensemble-set construction, we set accuracy $\geq 50\%$ on the validation set and set the number of ensembles equal to 6. Figure 2 also shows the validation-set and test-set evaluation of the six selected classifiers in green for the generative case and in magenta for the discriminative-generative case.

4.2   Comparison of Static Ensembles and Switching Strategy

Figure 3 shows an example of how our strategy switches among the six possible ensembles (in blue) throughout a period of 100 policy iterations. The red lines mark those time instances at which the current prediction is accepted. Thus, the instances that are not marked in red are part of the switching strategy: the predictions made in those instances serve the evaluation of the policy but are not yet accepted as predictions. For example, at iteration 44, the objective function is lower than θ_1 so we move to a more complex ensemble at iteration 45. The objective function continues to be too low, so we move to ensemble number 4 for iteration 46, at which the prediction of the current test instance is finally accepted. Thus, the classification of this particular instance requires in total three iterations of the policy, thus incurring in some cost overhead.[3] This figure also shows an example of action 3: at iteration 66 the objective function value is low and therefore the prediction is accepted, but the policy decides to move to a lower complexity ensemble for iteration 67 to save cost.

---

[3] The overhead is in terms of the additional cost from evaluating classifier ensembles multiple times. It is assumed that there is no time overhead or latency increase.

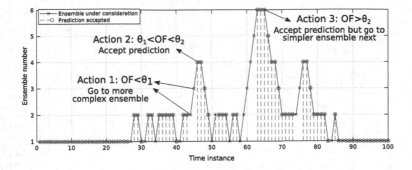

Fig. 3. First 100 iterations of the strategy and examples of the policy's actions.

The main experiment in this section evaluates the performance of the switching strategy when compared to a static policy, as shown in Fig. 4. The blue line with star markers shows the average test-set cost versus accuracy of each of the ensembles selected in the previous section. Specifically, each point shows the trade-off achieved by accepting the prediction of the classifier α_i that maximizes the weighted posterior probability ($\mathrm{argmax}_\alpha Pr(C|\mathbf{F}, \alpha)$). This would be equivalent to applying step number two of our policy on the same ensemble without the need to evaluate the objective function OF or move to a different ensemble. The cost axis here surpasses 1 since we consider the overhead of evaluating the two available classifiers per ensemble at each test instance (it is therefore almost equal to 2). The colored markers show the trade-off attained by implementing the policy with different values of θ_1 and θ_2 and policy implementation period $T = 1$. That is, the policy is evaluated every time there is a new sample to classify.

The switching policy clearly yields operating points that are beyond the static Pareto ensemble. In particular, the policy is good at improving accuracy of the classifier ensembles at low cost regions. Low cost regions of the trade-off space are reachable by setting a low value of θ_1 and a relatively low value of θ_2 (≤ 0.95). With these settings the policy is rather intolerant of classification samples with low ensemble confidence (low OF values) but is also capable of switching to a simpler model equally easily. Experiments with larger θ_2 achieve higher accuracy in general (see triangle markers), but at a higher cost. The fact that our policy is more effective at low cost region is relevant to the application scenario of interest: we may want to rely on dynamic tuning strategies in situations where the battery is low and we want to save energy as much as possible while preserving accuracy.

5   Related Work

Several works have focused on addressing the run-time challenges of implementing machine learning algorithms in resource constrained embedded applications. A body of work catered to the efficient implementation of neural networks has considered selective execution strategies at different levels of abstraction of the system. For example, [17] proposed a feed-forward neural network that augments

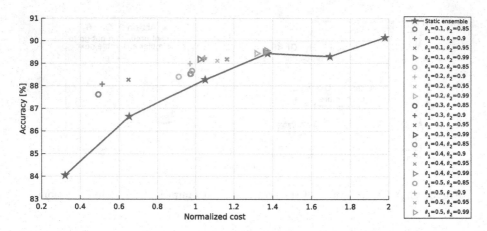

Fig. 4. Static Pareto ensembles versus switching strategy for different hyperparameters.

a traditional architecture with controller modules that activate or deactivate subsets of the network. The work in [9] considers a keyword spotting application that exploits such selective execution in a cascaded fashion and optimizes the models in accordance to the input class distributions. Closer to our work, [11] proposes a prediction strategy that dynamically determines whether to ensemble more predictions based on confidence levels on their output probability.

In the realm of resource-efficient run-time probabilistic inference, [25] proposes a layered computational model that selectively activates the use of state-of-the-art classifiers and uses a probabilistic model to reason about their outputs, taking into account information from the past to determine the present state. The work in [23] proposes to augment naive Bayes classifiers with "stopping points", which are capable of dynamically determining, for each individual query instance, whether more features should be observed before making a decision.

6 Discussion

This paper introduces a dynamic model-complexity tuning strategy that aims to improve the accuracy versus cost trade-off of resource constrained embedded classification scenarios. The technique relies on ensembles of probabilistic models to measure the difficulty of the classification task on a given instance and dynamically switches to a higher or lower complexity setting accordingly. The strategy was evaluated on a human activity recognition scenario, demonstrating superior performance when compared to using a fixed classifier ensemble. The strategy proves to be particularly effective in low cost regions of the trade-off front, making it amenable to embedded application scenarios where resource limitations are very strict and small accuracy losses are acceptable.

Future work should further study the impact of the policy implementation frequency T. A lower policy implementation frequency can result in lower overhead cost, but may risk not identifying difficult-to-classify instances, leading to reduced accuracy. The effect of value T is also highly dependent on the average duration of the activities considered. The longer the average duration of activities, the more confidently we can set T to a smaller value.

The experiments in this paper consider only the computational costs associated with evaluating the PSDDs for inference. However, we expect our strategy to be more effective in model ensembles that consider the cost of the full system (e.g. the cost of sensors and the cost of different resolutions), since they make available additional operating points with more varied resource saving opportunities. This should take into consideration system level costs based on measurements from the targeted hardware, as proposed in [8,12].

There is a vast body of work that looks at how to reason about the performance of classifiers under missing data, and also their reliability under such circumstances [2,13,14,18,23]. Some of these works also rely on PCs and Bayesian classifiers, or exploit discriminative-generative relations between models to compute the expected performance of a classifier under missing data. Several of the theoretical notions in these works could be incorporated to propose alternative objective functions and policies that complement the strategy proposed here.

Acknowledgements. This work was partially supported by the EU-ERC Project Re-SENSE grant ERC-2016-STG-71503, the "Onderzoeksprogramma Artificiële Intelligentie Vlaanderen" programme from the Flemish Government, and a gift from Intel.

References

1. Anguita, D., Ghio, A., Oneto, L., Parra, X., Reyes-Ortiz, J.L.: A public domain dataset for human activity recognition using smartphones. In: 21th European Symposium on Artificial Neural Networks, Computational Intelligence and Machine Learning (ESANN) (2013)
2. Choi, Y., Van den Broeck, G.: On robust trimming of Bayesian network classifiers. In: Proceedings of the 27th International Joint Conference on Artificial Intelligence (IJCAI) (2018)
3. Choi, Y., Vergari, A., Van den Broeck, G.: Lecture notes: Probabilistic circuits: Representation and inference (2020). http://starai.cs.ucla.edu/papers/LecNoAAAI20.pdf
4. Darwiche, A.: A differential approach to inference in Bayesian networks. J. ACM (JACM) **50**(3), 280–305 (2003)
5. Fayyad, U., Irani, K.: Multi-interval discretization of continuous-valued attributes for classification learning. In: Proceedings of the 13th International Joint Conference on Artificial Intelligence (IJCAI) (1993)
6. Friedman, N., Geiger, D., Goldszmidt, M.: Bayesian network classifiers. J. Mach. Learn. **29**(2), 131–163 (1997)
7. Galindez Olascoaga, L.I., Meert, W., Shah, N., Van den Broeck, G., Verhelst, M.: Discriminative bias for learning probabilistic sentential decision diagrams. In: Proceedings of the Symposium on Intelligent Data Analysis (IDA) (2020)
8. Galindez Olascoaga, L.I., Meert, W., Shah, N., Verhelst, M., Van den Broeck, G.: Towards hardware-aware tractable learning of probabilistic models. In: Advances in Neural Information Processing Systems (NeurIPS), pp. 13726–13736 (2019)

9. Giraldo, J., O'Connor, C., Verhelst, M.: Efficient keyword spotting through hardware-aware conditional execution of deep neural networks. In: 2019 IEEE/ACS 16th International Conference on Computer Systems and Applications (AICCSA), pp. 1–8. IEEE (2019)

10. Hall, M.A.: Correlation-based Feature Subset Selection for Machine Learning. Ph.D. thesis, University of Waikato, Hamilton, New Zealand (1998)

11. Inoue, H.: Adaptive ensemble prediction for deep neural networks based on confidence level. In: The 22nd International Conference on Artificial Intelligence and Statistics (AISTATS), pp. 1284–1293. PMLR (2019)

12. Karbachevsky, A., et al.: Hcm: hardware-aware complexity metric for neural network architectures. arXiv preprint arXiv:2004.08906 (2020)

13. Khosravi, P., Choi, Y., Liang, Y., Vergari, A., Van den Broeck, G.: On tractable computation of expected predictions. In: Advances in Neural Information Processing Systems (NeurIPS), pp. 11169–11180 (2019)

14. Khosravi, P., Vergari, A., Choi, Y., Liang, Y., Van den Broeck, G.: Handling missing data in decision trees: a probabilistic approach. In: The Art of Learning with Missing Values Workshop at ICML (Artemiss) (2020)

15. Kisa, D., Van den Broeck, G., Choi, A., Darwiche, A.: Probabilistic sentential decision diagrams. In: International Conference on the Principles of Knowledge Representation and Reasoning (2014)

16. Liang, Y., Bekker, J., Van den Broeck, G.: Learning the structure of probabilistic sentential decision diagrams. In: Proceedings of the Conference on Uncertainty in Artificial Intelligence (UAI) (2017)

17. Liu, L., Deng, J.: Dynamic deep neural networks: optimizing accuracy-efficiency trade-offs by selective execution. In: Thirty-Second AAAI Conference on Artificial Intelligence (2018)

18. Perello-Nieto, M., Telmo De Menezes Filho, E.S., Kull, M., Flach, P.: Background check: a general technique to build more reliable and versatile classifiers. In: 2016 IEEE 16th International Conference on Data Mining (ICDM), pp. 1143–1148. IEEE (2016)

19. Poon, H., Domingos, P.: Sum-product networks: a new deep architecture. In: 2011 IEEE International Conference on Computer Vision Workshops (ICCV Workshops), pp. 689–690. IEEE (2011)

20. Shah, N., Galindez Olascoaga, L.I., Meert, W., Verhelst, M.: Problp: A framework for low-precision probabilistic inference. In: Proceedings of the 56th Annual Design Automation Conference (DAC) 2019, pp. 1–6 (2019)

21. Shah, N.A., Galindez Olascoaga, L.I., Meert, W., Verhelst, M.: Acceleration of probabilistic reasoning through custom processor architecture. In: 2020 Design, Automation and Test in Europe Conference and Exhibition (DATE), pp. 322–325 (2020)

22. Sze, V., Chen, Y.H., Yang, T.J., Emer, J.S.: Efficient processing of deep neural networks: a tutorial and survey. Proc. IEEE 105(12), 2295–2329 (2017)

23. Verachtert, A., Blockeel, H., Davis, J.: Dynamic early stopping for naive Bayes. In: Proceedings of the Twenty-Fifth International Joint Conference on Artificial Intelligence (IJCAI), vol. 2016, pp. 2082–2088. AAAI Press (2016)

24. Verhelst, M., Murmann, B.: Machine learning at the edge. In: NANO-CHIPS 2030, pp. 293–322. Springer (2020)

25. Vlasselaer, J., Meert, W., Verhelst, M.: Towards resource-efficient classifiers for always-on monitoring. In: Brefeld, U., et al. (eds.) ECML PKDD 2018. LNCS (LNAI), vol. 11053, pp. 305–321. Springer, Cham (2019). https://doi.org/10.1007/978-3-030-10997-4_19

26. Weber, L., Sommer, L., Oppermann, J., Molina, A., Kersting, K., Koch, A.: Resource-efficient logarithmic number scale arithmetic for SPN inference on FPGAs. In: 2019 International Conference on Field-Programmable Technology (ICFPT), pp. 251–254. IEEE (2019)
27. Zhang, N.L., Poole, D.: On the role of context-specific independence in probabilistic inference. In: 16th International Joint Conference on Artificial Intelligence, IJCAI 1999, Stockholm, Sweden, vol. 2, p. 1288 (1999)

Leveraging Automated Mixed-Low-Precision Quantization for Tiny Edge Microcontrollers

Manuele Rusci[1,2]([⊠]), Marco Fariselli[2], Alessandro Capotondi[3], and Luca Benini[1,4]

[1] Università di Bologna, Bologna, Italy
manuele.rusci@unibo.it
[2] Greenwaves Technologies, Bologna, Italy
[3] Universitá di Modena e Reggio Emilia, Modena, Italy
[4] IIS ETH Zurich, Zurich, Switzerland

Abstract. The severe on-chip memory limitations are currently preventing the deployment of the most accurate Deep Neural Network (DNN) models on tiny MicroController Units (MCUs), even if leveraging an effective 8-bit quantization scheme. To tackle this issue, in this paper we present an automated mixed-precision quantization flow based on the HAQ framework but tailored for the memory and computational characteristics of MCU devices. Specifically, a Reinforcement Learning agent searches for the best uniform quantization levels, among 2, 4, 8 bits, of individual weight and activation tensors, under the tight constraints on RAM and FLASH embedded memory sizes. We conduct an experimental analysis on MobileNetV1, MobileNetV2 and MNasNet models for Imagenet classification. Concerning the quantization policy search, the RL agent selects quantization policies that maximize the memory utilization. Given an MCU-class memory bound of 2 MB for weight-only quantization, the compressed models produced by the mixed-precision engine result as accurate as the state-of-the-art solutions quantized with a non-uniform function, which is not tailored for CPUs featuring integer-only arithmetic. This denotes the viability of uniform quantization, required for MCU deployments, for deep weights compression. When also limiting the activation memory budget to 512 kB, the best MobileNetV1 model scores up to 68.4% on Imagenet thanks to the found quantization policy, resulting to be 4% more accurate than the other 8-bit networks fitting the same memory constraints.

Keywords: Mixed-precision · Automated quantization · Microcontrollers · TinyML

1 Introduction

Tiny smart devices feature low-end processing units to interpret sensor data and extract meaningful and compressed information. Among the digital processing solutions, Micro-Controller Units (MCUs) are highly desirable because

© Springer Nature Switzerland AG 2020
J. Gama et al. (Eds.): ITEM 2020/IoT Streams 2020, CCIS 1325, pp. 296–308, 2020.
https://doi.org/10.1007/978-3-030-66770-2_22

of high flexibility, due to the software programmability, low-cost and ultra-low power consumption, which can be as low few mW, hence compatible with the requirements of battery-operated edge sensor systems. However, MCUs feature a tightly bound on-chip memory budget (mostly for cost reasons), i.e. typically not more than a few MB of internal flash storage and 1 MB of RAM. Such a *memory bottleneck* stands as the major limitation for bringing the state-of-the-art inference Deep Learning (DL) models on these devices [1]. For instance, the MobileNetV1 [11] model features up to 4.24 M parameters, resulting in a 16 MB of weight storage (32-bit floating point, i.e. FP32, format), which is much higher than the typical size of on-chip memories.

Figure 1 plots the required compression ratio to be applied to several Imagenet classification models [3] for fitting into a memory budget of 2 MB. To reach the goal, a >100× compression factor is required for highly accurate models, e.g. InceptionV4 and ResNet-152, while optimized topologies, e.g. Mobilenets, demand a ~10× compression. Typically, quantization is used to shrink a DL model at the cost of an accuracy penalty with respect to the full-precision counterpart. Recent works demonstrated that 8-bit quantization applies almost losslessly but leads only to a 4× compression over full-precision models (FP32). Therefore, to meet such requirement, a sub-byte quantization, i.e. using less than 8-bit, must be applied at the cost of a (potential) non-negligible accuracy loss [5,7]. To reduce the accuracy degradation when applying aggressive quantization, Mixed-Low-Precision quantization techniques have been introduced [18,21]. Differently from homogeneous quantization, which relies on a network-wise Q-bit compression, a mixed-precision scheme defines an individual bitwidth for every weights and activation tensors of a deep model [18], namely the *quantization policy*. Hence, an effective mixed-precision quantization framework aims at finding the best quantization policy that leads to the highest accuracy under given memory and computational constraints. While Rusci et. al. [18] proposed a rule-based, but accuracy-agnostic, mechanism to determine the quantization policy based on the memory characteristics of the target MCU device, Wang et al. proposed HAQ [21], which automates the search phase by means of a Reinforcement Learning (RL) agent to effectively explore the accuracy vs quantization policy space. Unfortunately, the HAQ study relied on a clustering-based, hence non-linear, quantization scheme when optimizing for memory compression, which cannot be effectively mapped on the integer-only arithmetic of low-end micro processors.

In this work, we improved the automated mixed-precision framework [21] for targeting the tight computational and memory constraints of a tiny MCU device. Besides the on-chip memory limitations, we constrained the quantization policy search to ensure a solution that efficiently maps on the software backends *PULP-NN* [2] or *CMix-NN* [4], the leading solutions for mixed-low-precision deployment on RISCV and ARM-Cortex M devices, respectively. Specifically: (a) the search is conducted under the memory constraints dictated by both FLASH and RAM memory sizes, which impact respectively, the weights and activation feature maps compression, (b) instead of non-linear quantization, the

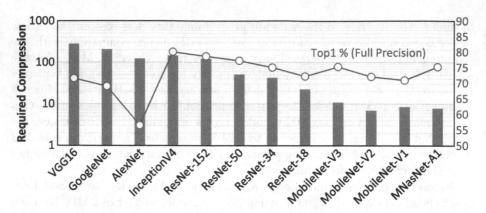

Fig. 1. The histogram (left axis) shows the required model compression of popular state-of-the-art CNNs for fitting in 2 MB. The red line (right axis) displays the Top1% on Imagenet task for the same models [3]. (Color figure online)

RL agent enforces an *Uniform* quantization optimized for tiny MCU devices and (c) the tensor bit precision is restricted to the set of *power-of-2* formats (2-, 4-, 8-bit), the formats supported by the target software libraries.

The main contributions of this paper are:

- We present an automated mixed-precision quantization flow constrained by the HW/SW characteristics of the target tiny MCU device.
- We quantify the impact of Uniform Linear quantization within the HAQ framework given the memory and computational constraints.
- We apply the automated mixed-precision on the more efficient models for Imagenet classification, i.e. MobileNetV1 [11], MobileNetV2 [19] and MNas-Net [20], under the typical MCU memory budget.

When experimenting DL models for Imagenet classification optimized for mobile deployments, such as MobileNetV1, MobileNetV2, and MNasNet, we show that a Uniform weight-only quantization strategy, also combined with a restricted bitwidth selection, results to be lossless if compared to the optimal non-Uniform quantization featured by the HAQ framework. For both cases, we observed the RL agent converging towards quantization policy solutions that fill the target memory budget. When introducing the quantization of activations, the highest accuracy has been measured on MobileNetV1 with a Top1 of 68.4% on ImageNet under a memory constraint of 512 kB of RAM and 2 MB of FLASH, which is 4% higher than the best 8-bit uniform quantized network that fits the same memory budget (MNasNet 224_0.35).

2 Related Work

Recent hand-crafted model design for image classification task has been driven from efficiency rather than accuracy metrics only. MobileNetV1 [11],

MobileNetV2 [19] or ShuffleNet [22] are relevant examples of deep networks that trade-off classification errors with respect to model size and execution latency. More recent Neural Architecture Search (NAS) methodologies automate the model design process, employing Reinforcement Learning (RL) [20] or backpropagation, i.e. Diffentiable NAS [16]. This work is complementary to this class of studies: besides model compression, low-bitwidth quantization reduces the computational and memory bandwidth requirements concerning the full-precision model, e.g. up to 4× smaller and faster in case of 8-bit quantization. Efficient models, such as MobileNetV1, have been turned into an 8-bit integer-only representation with an almost negligible accuracy loss through a quantization-aware retraining process [13], which is currently state-of-the-art for resource-constrained devices. However, 8-bit quantization is not sufficient to fit the tiny memory budgets of MCUs. On the other side, going below 8 bits on both weights and activation values demonstrated to be challenging [23]. Krishnamoorthi et al. [14] employed per-channel quantization rather than per-tensor to recover accuracy degradation when lowering the precision to 4 bits. In the case of extreme single-bit quantization, the accuracy gap concerning full-precision networks is still high, preventing their usage on complex decision problems [12,17]. All these works feature homogeneous quantization, which is sub-optimal if targeting the compression for resource-constrained devices.

Motivated by the low on-chip memory budgets of low-cost MCUs systems, the SpArSe framework [9] exploits pruning to fit the RAM and ROM memory budgets for, respectively, intermediate activations values and weights parameters. Rusci et al. [18] addressed the same deployment problem on more complex Imagenet classification models using low-bitwidth mixed-precision quantization. In this approach, the selection of the quantization bitwidth is driven by a heuristic rule-based process aiming at fitting the memory constraints. This process resulted effective by showing a 68% MobileNetV1 model fitting the 2 MB FLASH and 512 kB RAM constraints of an MCUs. However, the optimality of this quantization approach is limited by being accuracy-agnostic. On the other side, HAWQ-V2 [8] individuates the bit precision of weights and activations based on a layer-wise hessian metric, which quantifies the sensitivity of any parameter to low-bitwidth quantization concerning the loss. More interestingly, the HAQ framework [21] exploits an RL actor to explore the mixed-precision quantization space given a memory constraint. The framework reported state-of-the-art accuracy metric for quantized MobileNetV1 and MobileNetV2 models under memory constraints of less than 2 MB. However, the framework makes use of optimal non-uniform quantization when optimizing for memory, which makes the solution not suitable for integer-only inference required for MCU's deployment. Moreover, HAQ exploits arbitrary quantization formats (in the range between 2- to 8-bit), which are not effectively supported by most of the MCU backend library for CNNs. In this work, we extend HAQ for deployment on MCU, hence introducing uniform quantization for both weights and activation values for mixed-precision quantization policy search under the MCU's memory constraints.

3 Automated Mixed-Precision Quantization for MCU

Given a pretrained full-precision model, the presented mixed-precision flow produces a tensor-wise quantization policy that 1) leads to the lowest accuracy drop with respect to the full-precision model and 2) matches the computational and memory constraints of the target MCU architecture. In this section, after formulating the optimization objectives and briefly describing the state-of-the-art HAQ framework [21], we describe the improvements applied to HAQ to quantize a DL model for deployment into a tiny MCU device.

3.1 MCU-Aware Optimization Objectives

An automated mixed-precision quantization framework for MCUs operates with a double scope. On one side, (i) the memory requirements of the quantized model must fit the on-chip memory resources of the target MCU and, at the same time, (ii) the quantized model must be linearly quantized to low-bitwidth to be efficiently processed on a general-purpose CPU featuring integer-only arithmetic.

Memory Requirement. MCU's on-chip memory distinguishes between RAM and ROM memories. In this context, embedded FLASH memories are classified as ROM memories, because writing operations does not typically occur at runtime. As a design choice, we store the weight parameters in the ROM memory, while intermediate activations values are stored in RAM [6,9,18]. Hence, we derive the following constraints:

M1 The memory requirement due to weight parameters, including bias or other stationary values, must fit the system's ROM memory (M_{ROM}).
M2 The RAM memory must store any intermediate activation tensors at runtime. In addition to the input and output tensors of any network layer, tensors of optional parallel branches (e.g. skip connections) must be also kept in memory (M_{RAM}).

Computational Requirement. Low-bitwidth fixed-point inference tasks typically operate on 8- or 16-bit data [15]. The leading software backends *PULP-NN* [2] (RISCV) and *CMix-NN* [15] (ARM Cortex M) for mixed-precision inference supports 2- and 4-bit datatypes in addition to the widely used 8-bit compression. Operations on sub-bytes datatypes are software-emulated using 8-bit or 16-bit instructions with low overhead. On the other hand, efficient software implementations for other quantization levels, i.e. 3-, 5-, 6-, 7-bits, have not been presented. Hence, we restrict the quantization bitwidth selection to *power-of-2* format (2-, 4- and 8-bit) and exploit *Uniform* linear quantization rules to enable the usage of integer-only arithmetic for computation. This latter implies that quantization levels are uniformly spaced across the quantization range [13].

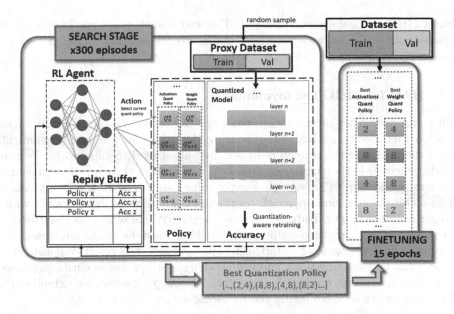

Fig. 2. Overview of the search and fine-tuning steps in the HAQ framework [21].

3.2 Automated Precision Tuning

The framework HAQ [21] is the leading automated methodology to optimally select the quantization bitwidth of individual weight and activation tensors given memory and computational constraints. HAQ works as a two-stage process: (i) a first *Search* stage, driven by a Reinforcement Learning agent to find the best quantization policy followed by a (ii) *Fine-Tuning* stage, where the model parameters are updated by a quantization-aware training process. Figure 2 illustrates the main modules of the HAQ engine. The *Search* stage occurs over a fixed number of episodes. At any episode, a NN-based RL agent selects a quantization policy for the target DL model and triggers a quantization-aware training process on a proxy dataset for few epochs (1 epoch in our setting). The proxy dataset is a subset of the original dataset, composed by randomly sampled points. The scored accuracy is returned to the RL agent as the reward function and stored within a replay buffer. Based on these collected data, the RL agent try to learn the relation among the quantization policy and the accuracy over the proxy-dataset. So doing, the RL agent adapts over the episodes and improves its ability to select the best quantization policy, i.e. the one that maximizes the network accuracy while matching the memory or performance requirements. To guarantee a sufficient action-reward diversity, the RL generates a random policy during an initial batch of episodes, i.e. the warm-up period. After this, the RL agent starts to produce policies based on historical data (the internal model predictions). After a fixed number of episodes (300 in our setting), the search engine outputs the quantization policy that leads to the highest score on a proxy dataset (the *best quantization policy*). This latter feeds the *Fine-Tuning* stage, which applies a quantization-aware training over a longer training period (15 epochs in our setting).

3.3   HAQ for MCU Deployments

When optimizing for memory size, the work [21] exploits a non-Uniform quantization rule based on a KMeans clustering algorithm. Such a quantization rule maps the real weight parameters in a finite subset of $\mathbb{R}$, composed by 2^Q centroids, where Q is the number of bits. Hence, if storing the centroid values into a per-tensor lookup table, any parameter value can be coded as a Q-bit integer index. This quantization approach results not compatible with the low-bitwidth integer-only arithmetic featured by our target SW backends: as described in Sect. 3.1, either activation values, and weights must be uniformly quantized to exploit instruction-level parallelism. Additionally, the resource-constrained devices can lack floating-point support, making a full-precision clustering-based compression not deployable [10]. Therefore, to bridge this gap, we extended the HAQ framework by introducing the following major improvements.

Uniform Weight and Activation Quantization. Weights parameters are uniformly quantized using a linear Per-Channel mapping [18]. Activations values are also quantized tensor-wise by means of a linear rule. To this aim, fake-quantization layers are inserted at the input of any convolutional layer [13] to learn the dynamic range through backpropagation [5] during training. Only *power-of-2* bit precision levels (2-, 4-, 8-bit) are considered by the engine.

Weight and Activation Bitwidth Selection. During the *Search stage*, the RL agent can operate according to two strategies: (a) a *Concurrent search*, where the activation and weight bitwidths are selected concurrently at every episode, or (b) a *Independent search*, where the weight quantization-policy is firstly found by keeping the activation at full-precision and then a second search finds the best quantization policy for the activation tensors, under this weight quantization setting. In addition, for more complex network structures like MobileNetV2 and MNasNet, we found the compression of the residual activation layers as the main culprits of the model accuracy degradation. Due to their importance in the system and the limited memory footprint (<15% of RAM occupancy for the biggest network configurations, i.e. 224×224 input dimension and width multiplier of 1), we set them up with fixed 8-bit quantization.

Memory Constraints. Given the targeted memory model, the RL agent can independently check the memory constraints *M1* and *M2* against, respectively, the weight and activation bitwidth that are selected at any episode. Concerning the weight parameters, if the total memory requirement of the selected policy exceeds the available M_{ROM} memory, the bit precision of the largest weights tensor is reduced (i.e. from 8 to 4-bit or from 4 to 2-bit). Such a process is repeated until the *M1* constraint is satisfied. On the other side, any computational node satisfies the *M2* constraint if the occupation of its input and output tensors fits

Table 1. Accuracy after the *Fine-Tuning* of Weight-Only Quantized Models under a memory constraint of 2 MB

Model	# params	No Quant FP32	Kmeans INT-$\{2,..8\}$	Kmeans INT-$\{2, 4, 8\}$	Uniform PC INT-$\{2, 4, 8\}$
MobileNetV1	4.24M	70.6%	69.0%	69.6%	70.1%
MobileNetV2	3.47M	72.0%	71.4%	71.3%	70.6%
MNasNet-A1	3.9M	75.2%	69.8%	72.2%	67.1%

the RAM memory budget. Note that parallel skip connections present in residual layers, increase the memory requirements as they have to be preserved in memory during the computation of the parallel branch of the graph.

4   Experimental Results

The conducted experiments evaluate the impact of the proposed automated quantization methodology on the precision of state-of-the-art topologies for image classification when compressed to fit the typical MCU memory budget constraints. To identify and quantify these effects we divide the experiments in two steps. First, we focus on the evaluation of the uniform quantization process on the weight parameters with a restricted bit choice (*power-of-2* formats 2-, 4-, 8-bit) instead of an optimal non-uniform rule. Second, we evaluate the accuracy achieved on a state-of-the-art edge MCU device when we apply the automated mixed-precision methodology on both activation and weight values with a uniform linear rule.

4.1   Experimental Setup

The mixed-precision framework is evaluated over efficient state-of-the-art models for Imaganet classification, such as MobileNetV1 [11], MobileNetV2 [19] and MNasNet [20]. In our experiments, the quantization policy search is constrained by the memory targets $M_{ROM} = 2MB$ and $M_{RAM} = 512\,kB$, corresponding to the memory footprint of a typical high-performance MCU SoC, such as an STM32H7. The proxy-dataset used for the *Search stage* is composed of 20k ImageNet random samples for the training and 10k samples for validation. The training procedure of both the quantization policy search and the quantization-aware fine-tuning makes use of an ADAM optimizer with a learning rate of 1×10^{-4}. During the search phase, the RL agent selects a random policy for the initial 60 episodes, also denoted as the warm-up period. At any episode, the target model is initialized with pre-trained full-precision parameters and trained by means of a quantization-aware process on the proxy Imagenet.

4.2   Automated Search for Weight-Only Quantization Policies

In this section, we analyze the impact on the classification accuracy when running the mixed-precision search of the weight parameters bitwidth with an uniform

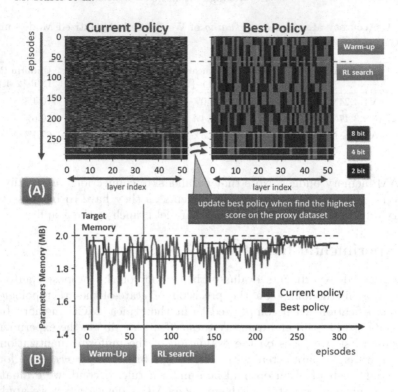

Fig. 3. RL-based search of the quantization policy for MobileNetV2 given a memory constraint of 2 MB. The plots shows (A) the bit-precision and (B) the memory occupation of the current and best policies selected by the RL agent at every episode.

quantization rule, under the memory constraint $M_{ROM} = 2$ MB (activations are kept in full-precision). Specifically, we compare our uniform weight quantization settings featuring a limited choice of bit precision levels (2, 4, 8 bits) with respect to a non-uniform optimal compression scheme (based on Kmeans clustering), either with constrained and unconstrained bitwidth selection. This last setting corresponds to the baseline HAQ [21] framework.

Figure 3A graphically shows the quantization space explored by the agent when searching the best policy for MobileNetV2 with an Uniform quantization scheme. The left plot depicts the evolution over the episodes (y-axis) of the weight quantization bit precision at any layer (x-axis), i.e. the current policy, as selected by the RL agent. In the plot, bit-precision levels are represented by different colours. The plot on the right shows the evolution of the best policies over the episodes: the best policy value is updated when the current policy scores the best Top1 accuracy on the proxy-dataset. Figure 3B plots the memory occupation over the episodes of the target model when featuring the current policy or the best quantization policy. We find the memory footprint of best and current policies to converge towards the memory target (2 MB). This behaviour is observed for all the considered models, demonstrating either that (i) higher Top1 scores are achieved with higher available memory resources and (ii) the RL agent learns to explore more densely the solutions close to the target. Overall, the memory footprint of the best policies found during the search phase fits the 97th percentile of the memory objective.

Table 1 reports the Top1 accuracy scores on Imagenet after the *Fine-Tuning* stage under multiple quantization settings. When restricting the number of bits to *power-of-2* format, the search space is smaller (3^l vs 7^l possible combinations with a *l*-layers network) and the RL problem gets simpler, therefore the agent can find better quantization policies with higher accuracy scores (MobileNetV1 +0.6% and MNasNet +2.3%) within the same number of episodes. When combining the bitwidth restrictions to a Uniform quantization rule, MobileNetV1 shows the same performance level with respect to an unrestricted Kmeans quantized model. On MobileNetV2 and MNasNet, the accuracy drop is, respectively, limited to −0.8% and −2.1%.

4.3 Automated Search for Weight and Activation Quantization Policies

We evaluate either the *Concurrent* or the *Independent* search approaches to determine the optimal bit precision of both weights and activations under the memory constraints $M_{ROM} = 2MB$ and $M_{RAM} = 512\,kB$. We experimentally observed that both the *Concurrent search* and the *Independent search* outputs the same quantization policies for both MobileNetV2 and MNasNet. However, to make the *Concurrent search* converge on the proxy-dataset we found effective to double the number of warm-up and total episodes, from 300 to 600 episodes, with a warm-up period lasting 120 episodes. Also for the activation policy search, we observed the RL agent selects activation bitwidths that maximize the available memory. Table 2 reports the Top1 accuracies of the fully-quantized models after *Fine-tuning* using the mixed-precision flow together with the achieved compression factors, either for weights and activations, against the full precision model. A uniform quantization scheme is used either for the search and fine-tuning stages. We run experiments by varying the input resolution $\rho = \{224, 192, 160\}$ and width multiplier $\alpha = \{0.75, 1.0\}$ of the target models (indicated by ρ_α in the following). The MobileNetV1 224_1.0 shows the best accuracy, reaching up to 68.4% on Imagenet. On the contrary, MobileNetV2 and MNasNet 224_1.0 demand a high compression ratio on the initial layers due to the memory overhead to store the residual values. This leads to a non-negligible accuracy drop, respectively of 17% and 13% with respect to the full-precision models. For model configurations with smaller input dimensions, the memory constraint on the activation can be met with less aggressive quantization strategies. This results in a smaller accuracy drop with respect to the full-precision model. For this reason, MobileNetV2 160_1.0 reaches an overall accuracy of 67.5% after fine-tuning, only −1.3% lower with respect to the full-precision model. Overall, our solutions show up to +4% Top1 on Imagenet with respect to an 8-bit MNasNet-A1 224_0.35 model that fits the same memory constraints, even assuming a lossless compression if compared to the full-precision model.

Table 2. Top1 accuracy scores of mixed-precision quantized models with M_{ROM} = 2 MB and M_{RAM} = 512 kB

Model	#Params (M)	FP32 Top1 Accuracy	Mixed Prec. Top1 Accuracy	Mixed Prec. Weight Compression	Mixed Prec. Activ. (average) Compression
MobileNetV1 (224_1.0)	4.2	70.6%	**68.4%**	9x	5.1x
MobileNetV1 (224_0.75)	2.6	68.4%	68.0%	5.4x	4.6x
MobileNetV2 (224_1.0)	3.4	72.04%	55.1%	7.6x	5.1x
MobileNetV2 (192_1.0)	3.4	70.7%	58.0%	7.4x	5.2x
MobileNetV2 (160_1.0)	3.4	68.8%	67.5%	7.4x	4.4x
MNasNet-A1 (224_1.0)	3.9	**75.2%**	62.6%	9.4x	4.7x
MNasNet-A1 (224_0_35)	1.7	64.1%	64.1%*	4x (8-bit)	4x (8-bit)

* optimistic score: we assume a lossless 8-bit compression w.r.t. FP32

5 Conclusion

This work presented a framework that automates the mixed-precision quantization policy search for MCU-constrained targets. The solutions found by our engine tends towards the maximization of the memory objective. If applied to state-of-the-art DL models, we demonstrated that uniform mixed-precision weight quantization with restricted *power-of-2* bitwidth does not degrade the accuracy with respect to a non-uniform compression and can be deployed on low-end MCU. Moreover, we reported a fully-quantized mixed-precision network, scoring up to 68.4% with the best mixed-precision quantization policy found, resulting to be up to +4% than the best 8-bit network fitting the same memory constraints.

Acknowledgments. Authors thank the Italian Supercomputing Center CINECA for the access to their HPC facilities.

References

1. Banbury, C.R., et al.: Benchmarking tinyml systems: challenges and direction. arXiv preprint arXiv:2003.04821 (2020)
2. Bruschi, N., Garofalo, A., Conti, F., Tagliavini, G., Rossi, D.: Enabling mixed-precision quantized neural networks in extreme-edge devices. In: Proceedings of the 17th ACM International Conference on Computing Frontiers, pp. 217–220 (2020)
3. Canziani, A., Paszke, A., Culurciello, E.: An analysis of deep neural network models for practical applications. arXiv preprint arXiv:1605.07678 (2016)
4. Capotondi, A., Rusci, M., Fariselli, M., Benini, L.: CMix-NN: mixed low-precision CNN library for memory-constrained edge devices. IEEE Trans. Circ. Syst. II: Express Briefs **67**(5), 871–875 (2020)
5. Choi, J., Wang, Z., Venkataramani, S., Chuang, P.I.J., Srinivasan, V., Gopalakrishnan, K.: Pact: parameterized clipping activation for quantized neural networks. arXiv preprint arXiv:1805.06085 (2018)
6. Chowdhery, A., Warden, P., Shlens, J., Howard, A., Rhodes, R.: Visual wake words dataset. arXiv preprint arXiv:1906.05721 (2019)
7. Courbariaux, M., Hubara, I., Soudry, D., El-Yaniv, R., Bengio, Y.: Binarized neural networks: training deep neural networks with weights and activations constrained to +1 or −1. arXiv preprint arXiv:1602.02830 (2016)
8. Dong, Z., Yao, Z., Cai, Y., Arfeen, D., Gholami, A., Mahoney, M.W., Keutzer, K.: Hawq-v2: Hessian aware trace-weighted quantization of neural networks. arXiv preprint arXiv:1911.03852 (2019)
9. Fedorov, I., Adams, R.P., Mattina, M., Whatmough, P.N.: Sparse: sparse architecture search for cnns on resource-constrained microcontrollers. arXiv preprint arXiv:1905.12107 (2019)
10. Flamand, E., et al.: Gap-8: a RISC-v SoC for AI at the edge of the IoT. In: 2018 IEEE 29th International Conference on Application-Specific Systems, Architectures and Processors (ASAP), pp. 1–4. IEEE (2018)
11. Howard, A.G., et al.: Mobilenets: efficient convolutional neural networks for mobile vision applications. arXiv preprint arXiv:1704.04861 (2017)
12. Hubara, I., Courbariaux, M., Soudry, D., El-Yaniv, R., Bengio, Y.: Binarized neural networks. In: Advances in Neural Information Processing Systems, pp. 4107–4115 (2016)
13. Jacob, B., et al.: Quantization and training of neural networks for efficient integer-arithmetic-only inference. In: Proceedings of the IEEE Conference on Computer Vision and Pattern Recognition, pp. 2704–2713 (2018)
14. Krishnamoorthi, R.: Quantizing deep convolutional networks for efficient inference: a whitepaper. arXiv preprint arXiv:1806.08342 (2018)
15. Lai, L., Suda, N., Chandra, V.: CMSIS-NN: Efficient neural network kernels for arm cortex-m CPUs. arXiv preprint arXiv:1801.06601 (2018)
16. Liu, H., Simonyan, K., Yang, Y.: Darts: differentiable architecture search. arXiv preprint arXiv:1806.09055 (2018)
17. Rastegari, M., Ordonez, V., Redmon, J., Farhadi, A.: XNOR-Net: ImageNet classification using binary convolutional neural networks. In: Leibe, B., Matas, J., Sebe, N., Welling, M. (eds.) ECCV 2016. LNCS, vol. 9908, pp. 525–542. Springer, Cham (2016). https://doi.org/10.1007/978-3-319-46493-0_32
18. Rusci, M., Capotondi, A., Benini, L.: Memory-driven mixed low precision quantization for enabling deep network inference on microcontrollers. arXiv preprint arXiv:1905.13082 (2019)

19. Sandler, M., Howard, A., Zhu, M., Zhmoginov, A., Chen, L.C.: Mobilenetv 2: Inverted residuals and linear bottlenecks. In: Proceedings of the IEEE Conference on Computer Vision and Pattern Recognition, pp. 4510–4520 (2018)
20. Tan, M., et al.: Mnasnet: platform-aware neural architecture search for mobile. In: Proceedings of the IEEE Conference on Computer Vision and Pattern Recognition, pp. 2820–2828 (2019)
21. Wang, K., Liu, Z., Lin, Y., Lin, J., Han, S.: Haq: hardware-aware automated quantization with mixed precision. In: IEEE Conference on Computer Vision and Pattern Recognition (CVPR) (2019)
22. Zhang, X., Zhou, X., Lin, M., Sun, J.: Shufflenet: an extremely efficient convolutional neural network for mobile devices. In: Proceedings of the IEEE Conference on Computer Vision and Pattern Recognition, pp. 6848–6856 (2018)
23. Zhou, S., Wu, Y., Ni, Z., Zhou, X., Wen, H., Zou, Y.: Dorefa-net: training low bitwidth convolutional neural networks with low bitwidth gradients. arXiv preprint arXiv:1606.06160 (2016)

Author Index

Printed in the United States
By Bookmasters